Frederic R. Blachford

Letters

Frederic R. Blachford

Letters

ISBN/EAN: 9783337818401

Printed in Europe, USA, Canada, Australia, Japan

Cover: Foto ©ninafisch / pixelio.de

More available books at **www.hansebooks.com**

LETTERS

OF

FREDERIC LORD BLACHFORD

UNDER-SECRETARY OF STATE FOR THE COLONIES
1860–1871

EDITED BY

GEORGE EDEN MARINDIN

LONDON
JOHN MURRAY, ALBEMARLE STREET
1896

PREFACE

IN putting together the following collection of letters one object has been that the book should contain as little as possible besides the letters themselves; in other words, that it should be Lord Blachford's letters and not a biography, while at the same time it should be quite possible to trace the whole life and character of the writer from his own letters, with the aid of the few words of introduction which have been placed at the beginning of each chapter. Some such connecting thread, with notes here and there, seemed necessary to explain the circumstances under which the letters at various periods were written and the events to which they allude.

Lord Blachford left some notes of autobiography, written for his family, regarding which he expressed a wish that they should not be published, disliking (as he wrote) 'the rage for printing at the present day;' but he gave a discretionary power to extract any part, not of a private nature, if it should seem desirable for any purpose to do so. Some extracts from these reminiscences have accordingly been inserted in the introductions to the chapters. He had a remarkable gift for sketching character in a few telling words, and some of these sketches, taken from his reminiscences, have been included. With regard to some others, describing public men whom he thought blameworthy, the conclusion has been reached, not, it must be confessed, without reluctance, that he would not have wished them to appear in a printed book. His own feeling as regards the publication of letters is expressed in a letter to Sir Henry Taylor which appears on page 345.

His most constant correspondent, outside his own family,

in his earlier life—and, with the exception of Dean Church and Sir Henry Taylor, the most constant also at a much later period—was Cardinal Newman. It is much to be regretted that a box containing, with other papers, about forty letters to Cardinal Newman, as well as a few of those to Dean Church, was lost last year by the South Western Railway, when it was being sent to the editor from Devonshire. There is little hope of its recovery—indeed there can hardly be any doubt that the letters were long ago burnt by a disappointed thief. Some months afterwards, however, when this book was partly in type, the kind search of Cardinal Newman's literary executor, the Rev. Father Neville, discovered seventy letters written to Newman before he joined the Church of Rome. After that time there had been a cessation of the correspondence for several years, and the lost letters, which were, it is understood, chiefly on public matters of the day and on books, all belonged to the last twenty years of Lord Blachford's life.

The seventy letters, so kindly placed at the editor's disposal, belong to the period between 1832 and 1842, during part of which Rogers and Newman appear to have written to one another once or twice a week, whenever either was absent from Oxford. The very closeness of the intimacy in this interchange of thought makes a large number of these letters unsuitable for publication. They are mere scraps of answer or comment, which, taken by themselves, throw no light on the matters under discussion, and would be as difficult for the reader to follow as a dialogue in which the words of one of the speakers are omitted. Of the thirty-two letters which have been selected, several bear to some extent on discussions, or proposals, or persons connected with the Oxford Movement, and will be both clear and interesting to those who still follow out that history; and some have a separate value besides, as explaining letters of Newman already published, which answer them or are answered by them.

G. E. MARINDIN.

BROOMFIELDS: *September* 1896.

CONTENTS

CHAPTER		PAGE
I.	School Life and Undergraduate Life at Oxford	1
II.	Residence at Oxford as a Fellow of Oriel	14
III.	Winter at Rome. Relinquishment of Oxford Life	63
IV.	In London, reading law and writing for the 'Times,' and early official life (1842–1850)	112
V.	Continuation of Work as Commissioner of Emigration	139
VI.	Mission to Paris on the Coolie Question	170
VII.	Under-secretary for the Colonies	225
VIII.	Last Years of Official Life (1866–1870)	263
IX.	Eighteen Years (1871–1889); Partly Parliamentary Life; but chiefly Life at Blachford	306

PORTRAITS

Lord Blachford (*from a crayon by George Richmond*) . . *Frontispiece*

Lord Blachford (*from a photograph by W. Heath & Co. Plymouth*) . . . . *to face p.* 306

Errata

Page 131, line 15, *for* Elliott *read* Elliot.
,, 224, note, *for* Loundon *read* Lowder.
,, 258, line 23, *for* Foster *read* Forster.
,, 276, line 18, *for* Stanfield *read* Stansfeld.

LETTERS

OF

FREDERIC LORD BLACHFORD

CHAPTER I

School Life and Undergraduate Life at Oxford

FREDERIC ROGERS, afterwards Lord BLACHFORD, was born in 1811. His father, Frederick Leman Rogers, at that time in the Audit Office, was a younger brother and eventually the successor of Sir John Rogers of Blachford, near Ivybridge in South Devon; his mother was a daughter of Colonel Deare, of the Bengal Artillery. The Blachford property and the baronetcy passed in succession to Frederic Rogers himself, to his next brother John, and to his youngest surviving brother Edward, who died in 1895 as tenth and last baronet.

In the first half of the century school life began early, and Frederic Rogers went when he was seven years old to Mr. Polehampton's school at Worplesdon. Among his schoolfellows there, and subsequently at Eton, was James Colvile (the late Sir James Colvile), whose sister he afterwards married. A holiday visit which Frederic Rogers paid to the home of his school friend is alluded to in a letter written by Mrs. Colvile.

'Rogers is so happy that he stays till Tuesday, instead of going to-morrow. When I asked him if he thought he might stay two nights more, he said : " My mother, ma'am, said if you liked me to stay she had not the least objection, but at the same time she thought it very unlikely you would ask me." Mr. Polehampton would have been quite flattered if he had heard James and Rogers settling quite gravely at dinner that their sons should certainly go to " Poley's," for Rogers said " he was quite convinced there was not so good a school in England of the kind." He is a clever boy of his age, up to so much conversation of all kinds. He asked James whether he thought John Napper (a schoolfellow) a good arguer. Jem said he supposed he was, " for he always got him into a puzzle in five minutes." " Ah ! but that is because he takes unfair advantage. If one makes a real mistake, a palpable one, he takes hold of that, and, whatever one says after, throws that mistake in one's teeth. I hold that not to be close arguing." Certainly the world is more forward than it was, when boys of eleven and twelve argue about arguing.'

The directness of reply and the turn for analysing are both characteristic. From Worplesdon he went in 1821 to Eton, to Miss Angelo's house. His tutor for the first year was Mr. Drury, on whose retirement from Eton he became the pupil of Mr. Chapman, afterwards Bishop of Colombo. Those who know the Eton history of that time will understand why this change of pupil-rooms was not unwelcome to him. Of Chapman he always spoke with gratitude—' not a clever man,' he says in some notes of autobiography, ' and inordinately given to long words, but enough of a scholar to teach scholarship, with the steady influence for good, moral and intellectual, of a man who made me feel that I was his friend and that he was anxious for my good.'

In his six years at Eton he won several distinctions, especially for Greek and Latin verses, and reached the position of ' Captain of the Oppidans.' In his leisure time he was fond of cricket, in which he became proficient enough to be in the ' Second Eleven ; ' but his favourite amusement was swimming, and among his anecdotes of Eton life, he tells how he once jumped off Windsor bridge in company with Arthur Hallam, at that time his most intimate friend. 'What induced him to propose it, I do not know, unless it was the example set by Selwyn [1] or some such *philolute*. As far as I was concerned, water was by this time my element. The "Angelo water rats" (Shadwells, Snows, Denisons, &c.) was a proverbial phrase. The feat was performed to our own satisfaction. I remember a quick sensation as I was making my way through the air to the black water below—" Shall I go back? No, I can't." It was a simple proceeding if you could only keep yourself perpendicular, otherwise you might sprain your back or get a tremendous slap from the water when you reached it.' Another Eton story, which seems to carry us still further away from the customs of the present time, gives one of his experiences, as a sixth-form boy, of Dr. Keate's remarkable fancy for working himself up into a passion and fulminating a threat which he could not well put into execution. Keate, because some boys had been inattentive, chose to keep his division long after the usual time of dismissal. 'I ejaculated (too distinctly), "Well, if this is not a shame, never was one." He turned on me red as a turkey-cock, howled out his reprobation, and told me to stay and speak to him afterwards—not privately, but in the presence of several boys. He asked me fiercely whether I still thought it a shame. I replied, I was very sorry for what I had said. "But do you still think it a shame, sir?" ("Sir" having always in his mouth the effect of "sirrah"). I said, "I spoke hastily." "But, sir, do you still think it a shame? because, if you do, say so at once, and I will expel you on the spot." I ought to add that he afterwards had me up privately and talked to me in a tone of remonstrance, which from its kindness and reasonableness brought the tears into my eyes.'

[1] Afterwards Bishop of New Zealand.

In his last year at Eton, Frederic Rogers took a leading part in a literary periodical, 'The Eton Miscellany,' which had been first set on foot by Arthur Hallam and Doyle (afterwards Sir Francis Doyle), in the hope that it might have the same success and length of life as 'The Microcosm' and 'The Etonian.' He has left the following record of it : 'Gladstone [2] became at once the backbone, editor and responsible for filling up the pages. After July 1827, Gladstone, Doyle, and I were the committee of management. Gladstone's most effective production was, I think, a humorous poem in twelve-syllable lines on a deserting member of the corps—afterwards Lord Hanmer. Hallam was always straining after something above his powers. Doyle was a spirited writer of verses, but rather too plagiaristic. I was successful in one or two papers containing translations of nursery rhymes into Greek, and in a mock heroic Spenserian composition. But the affair was a failure, and most of my doings contemptible. The book contains characters of all the contributors under *noms de plume*. Bishop Selwyn figures as Anthony Heaviside, Gladstone as Bartholomew Bouverie. I appear as Philip Montagu, Hanmer was David ap Rice ; Doyle was Francis Jermyn.'

The 'Eton Miscellany,' of which copies still exist, ranks higher in merit among kindred publications than Lord Blachford's words would imply. It has, indeed, fewer papers which escape dulness than the 'Etonian,' and it certainly did not approach the reputation which that magazine enjoys—a reputation, it must be confessed, not perfectly easy for an unprejudiced reader at this distance of time to understand—but it has more real merit than most school periodicals. Among the causes for a lesser measure of success than the talents of its promoters might lead us to expect, it may be noted that all its contributors were schoolboys, whereas some of the writers in the 'Etonian' had passed on to the University ; and also that in 1827 the educational mills were already beginning

---

[2] Right Hon. W. E. Gladstone.

(rightly enough) to grind smaller, and there was not quite as much liberty for particular genius to go its own way in literature, outside the school course, as there had been even ten years earlier.

In 1827 he went from Eton to Oxford, and entered at Oriel. His Eton reputation for ability and scholarship had preceded him. The younger Fellows of Oriel were at this time eagerly exerting themselves to raise the standard of their College, and it was said that Newman had lately written to a friend among the Eton masters asking him to recommend some good Eton men for admission to Oriel. Newman was the tutor who could make most of any brilliant man who passed through his hands, and to him Frederic Rogers was allotted as a pupil. But he speaks also of obligations to two other tutors of Oriel—to Hurrell Froude and to Robert Wilberforce,[3] ' whose solid knowledge and industry were valuable in the group of tutors, furnishing a kind of complement to Newman and Froude. In particular he had a method of laying out history so that facts hung on to each other in a way which made you recollect the time, place, and conditions of each, as part of a chronological whole.' Of Hurrell Froude he says : ' He was anything but learned. In lecture he gave you the idea of not being, in knowledge, so very much in advance of those whom he taught ; but he had a fine taste, a quick and piercing precision of thought, a fertility and depth of reasoning, which stimulated a mind which had any quickness and activity. He had an interest in everything ; he would draw with you, sail on the river with you, talk philosophy or politics with you, ride over fences with you, skate with you—all with a kind of joyous enjoyment. Mischief seems to have been his snare as a boy, and a controlled delight in what was on the edge of mischief gave a kind of *verve* to his character as a man. This made him charming to those whom he liked. But then he did not choose to like

[3] Son of William Wilberforce and elder brother of the Bishop.

any whom he did not respect; and he could be as hard and sharp as you please on what he thought bad—profane, vicious, or coxcombical.' These three men—the more inspiring among the tutors of Oriel at that day—had some difference of opinion with the dons of the old school, as to whether the tutor was to be (as they thought right) *in loco parentis* to his pupils, charged with the responsibility of their moral and intellectual development, and having some discretionary power to carry it out, or whether he was to be little more than a lecturer under the supervision of the Provost and Dean. As a result Newman gave up all his pupils except Frederic Rogers, who was marked out by high character and by ability—he had already in 1829 won the Craven scholarship—as an undergraduate of special promise. He was thus, in his fourth year at Oxford, Newman's only pupil, working very hard under his guidance. The intimacy between tutor and pupil became still closer, when, in the long vacation of 1831, he took lodgings at Iffley near Newman's house, and not only read with Newman, but spent most of his evenings with him and his mother and sisters. Among the ties of sympathy was a common love of music.

To his Sister.

Oxford (Iffley): August 12, 1831.

My dear Marian,—Many thanks for the housekeeping advice, which I doubt not I shall find most useful. I am beginning to get into the way of reading, and of not being very miserable, which at first I was rather, for I find that the two miles divide me completely from Gladstone, Denison,[4] &c., and though I like Newman very much, and more as I know more of him, yet in the first place his leisure hours are spent much with his family, and secondly, we are

---

[4] Henry Denison, a friend at Eton, at Oxford, and in later life. He gained a double first class in 1831. He was brother of the Speaker and of the Bishop of Salisbury.

not quite of the same age. However, now I begin to feel very comfortable and independent, and really it would be quite ridiculous if one were to feel unhappy whenever left by oneself for a month or two. However, as aforesaid, I am beginning now to feel very comfortable. My day is spent pretty much as follows: I get up; walk out with a book for about half an hour; breakfast; read about four or five hours; go out, generally row up to Oxford, which, with whatever I may have to do there, takes me nearly three hours; dine; stroll for about half an hour, and then return and read till I go to bed. On the whole I am exceedingly glad I came here, for I am sure it is almost the only thing which would have made me read *hard*, and I think I shall do that now. By-the-by, I have something to mention which perhaps will be an agreeable surprise to my father, viz. that the other morning as I was leaving Newman's room he informed me, in a very embarrassed kind of way, that he hoped I understood that I was reading with him as *a college pupil and friend*, an intimation which certainly to me was as unexpected as anything could be. I said what occurred to me on the subject, and the matter is now settled, only as that is the case I must take care not to pester him. However, I really think I shall get as much good from him by merely being under his superintendence as from any regular drudging, for he is a person who does me more good, I think, in his remarks on my essays and such like than in regular cram, and really he seems disposed to give a very great deal of time to me if I could with a good conscience exact it. However, at any rate, it will be a serious diminution of one's yearly expenditure.

Your affectionate brother,
F. ROGERS.

In the early part of 1832 his eyes began to fail, and he was obliged to give up reading and go home for a time. Though this necessarily reduced the number of books which he took up, he came back in the summer with greater vigour for the final schools, and perhaps did not lose by the enforced idleness; at any rate, he secured a double first, in classics and mathematics—the only double first of that year.

To Mrs. Rogers.

Oriel: May 27, 1832.

My dear Mother,—I am sorry to say our suspense must be rather more protracted than I at first supposed. I fear I shall not be able to give you news of the classes being settled for near a fortnight; we are now in for paper work, and our *viva voce* will not, I hear, begin till that is finished, which will hardly be before next Thursday or Friday. The *viva voce* must take a week at least, and I suppose till it is literally all over there will be little chance of knowing how matters stand. We have had already three days of it. The first day I managed very ill; however, Newman says he is not dissatisfied with what I did, in itself, but that I ought to have done much better. It was a moral essay, 'Examine the sentiment "Vice loses half its evil by losing all its grossness," and show how far principles of taste were allowed by the ancient moralists as principles of ethics.' I liked the subject exceedingly, but spent so much time in thinking on it and trying to lay out a plan that I had not time to do more than the first part of the subject, and the latter part of that in a very hurried way. I was annoyed with myself, as I should have liked particularly to have written on the last part. But it is impossible (at least I find it so) to start at once and write a complete moral essay in one sitting; and I trust others found it so too. Every one was dissatisfied with what they had accomplished; I most dreadfully so; but I hope I have done pretty well what I have done. I filled about four and a half foolscap pages.

The next day we had *Logic*, which I think I did fairly, and three pieces of English to turn into Latin. I finished one and a half, which I fancy must have been what the generality did. Newman said I had done well with the piece I had finished which was in Livy's style, but had not very well hit off the half piece which was in Cicero's. I do not and never did pique myself on my Latin prose writing, but at the same time I do think nothing could be less calculated to be turned into Latin than that piece, so that I hope others have failed too. But I could not hope to do it well, as I had read so very little Cicero, and that not lately. The third day, Saturday, we had eight hours given us in order to draw up an accusation or defence of a person accused of murder (the story being given us) on the principles laid down in Aristotle's 'Rhetoric.' Now, as I had not read the said 'Rhetoric' and did not take it up, I could not be expected to do this; so I just mentioned on my paper that I did not *take it up*, and therefore did a Greek oration in the manner (as far as I could) of the Greek Orators, upon the little I knew of Aristotle's principles. This Greek oration occupied rather more than three sides of foolscap, and Newman said it was a very good imitation of their style, and that he thought I should get a good deal of credit for it. To-morrow we set to again. What we shall have I know not. Hitherto I am pretty well satisfied with what I have done. But the *viva voce* will be the trying part, and that will not come on for some days. My eyes have stood it capitally. They only felt a very little uneasy yesterday, and I hope I shall be able to get through the whole without having any one to write for me, which will be an amazing advantage. Poor ——, you will be extremely grieved to hear, has actually by keeping his mind constantly fixed on one subject (even after he had put off his degree) nearly driven himself out of his mind. The night before last, about six o'clock, he disappeared, and did not appear again till a tutor of Balliol the next day met him wandering about Oxford about five o'clock, quite unable to give any account of himself. He had been wandering about on the London road all night, and then came in exhausted and ill. He was immediately put to bed, and under Dr. Wootton's care, and is now very much better. But you may judge what low spirits he had been in lately, when I tell you that one of his friends said what a relief it would be to him to find that he had been *only drowned bathing*, and that they were on the point of dragging a little stream which was round a university walk which he had walked in a good deal the two evenings before. Of course the anxiety of every one till he reappeared was extreme; but I cannot say I ever apprehended anything like what some seem to have feared. However, I will now finish and not work my eyes any more, as I wish to rest them a little to-day. So with love to all, believe me

Your affectionate son,
FREDERIC ROGERS.

To Mrs. Rogers.

Oriel, June 9, 1832.

Hurrah! I have not yet seen the class list, but the first class contains:

1. Something or other Brewer,[5] Queen's.
2. Francis Hastings Doyle,[6] Christchurch.
3. Frederic Rogers, Oriel.

I shall write to-morrow and tell you all about it.

Your affectionate son,
FREDERIC ROGERS.

To Mrs. Rogers.

Oxford, June 10, 1832.

My dear Mother,—I suppose you have received the three lines which I sent off by coach last night in order to take you out of your anxiety. In case you should not I repeat that there are only *three* first classes, *myself, Brewer* of Queen's, and *Doyle*. Brewer, I fancy, must be the best; the list of books which he took up seems to have been something more enormous than anything which has ever been heard of, and he really knew them, and had profited by them. His essays (on history in particular) were excellent, and his *viva voce*, too, capital. Doyle and myself I should think were pretty much on a par. My papers, I think, were better than his, and his *viva voce* was very decidedly far better than mine. In fact, as I told you before, mine was a failure. I never expected it would have been otherwise.

Borrett, an Ireland scholar, has got only a second. I think what has done well for me is that Greek oration of which I spoke to you. I do not think anything else of mine could

---

[5] J. S. Brewer, the historian.
[6] The late Sir Francis Doyle, afterwards Professor of Poetry at Oxford.

have been very shining: on that I do pique myself. W.'s failure was owing to *very bad* divinity. He told them that Jeroboam was the son of Rehoboam, and that the son of Saul who was a friend of David's was named *Absalom*. On which they asked him whether he had ever read the Old Testament, and he answered, in a kind of jaunty way, 'Yes, yes, that he had read most of it, he had got a good way in it.'

As to mathematics, I am not very sanguine; I find that what I have forgotten is *immense*, and my eyes are certainly not strong enough to bear more than about six hours a day even of the kind of writing which mathematics requires, so that I almost despair of making up my lost ground on that point. Johnson,[7] too, I hear, expresses doubts. However I hope that now I have got the principal one you will not let the secondary matter trouble you at all. A double first is a very nice thing certainly, and one would rather have a double than not; but at the same time a first and second is a most excellent thing to sit down on, and a thing that one has no manner of right to fidget oneself about.

To Mrs. Rogers.

Oriel, June , 1832.

I write in a very great hurry just to say that I have got my first [in mathematics] in spite of a little bad luck in the examination. On the whole, the examination was easy and tolerably favourable, but an unlucky accident happened. I had taken up Hydrostatics at a shot, knowing that there was hardly anything in them, and intending to get up a few formulae the night before the Hydrostatic paper was given, and then try my chance. I heard the Hydrostatic paper was to be on Thursday, and went in on Wednesday evening, not having ever in the course of my life opened a book on the subject, and knowing consequently practically nothing about the subject. Conceive of my astonishment and consternation on seeing before me the very Hydrostatic paper. I did, by good luck, one question, a *tolerably* difficult one luckily, which did not

---

[7] His mathematical 'coach,' afterwards Dean of Wells.

imply much knowledge of fluids, and half of another, and then my knowledge failed me. Since then I rather (as I thought) failed in Optics and Mechanics, and have been rather queer these two last days. However, I fancy I did the first papers very well—well enough, at least, to make up beforehand all the ground I since lost—and here I am in the first class. Johnson is profuse in praises; he says he considers it as even more creditable to me than my classical first, from the very great disadvantage I laboured under, &c. He is a man who had no idea of a man's getting a first in mathematics by any other method than by knowing by heart every formula that ever was invented, which of course with my eyes was impossible, and I have now and then rather astonished him by my ignorance of these formulae, and sometimes by showing him that it was possible to answer a question without them. However, I must finish, as it is candle-light, and I am in a great hurry.

Your affectionate son,
FREDERIC ROGERS.

To Frederick Leman Rogers, Esq.

Oriel : July 1, 1832.

My dear Father,—I send you, as you see, a class list, not that I suppose there will be anything particularly interesting in it to you (though perhaps Mamma may like to see my name actually *in print*); but as you must pay postage you may as well have the classes as well as the letter. We are actually employed here in getting up a subscription to found a prize or something of that kind in honour of the Duke of Wellington. I do not know what you think of his conduct lately, but here we are all in the highest admiration of him.[8] Bruce showed me three letters (at least copies of them), one from Lord Harrowby to Lord Wharncliffe, one from Lord Wharncliffe to the Duke, and the Duke's answer immediately

---

[8] This refers to the Duke of Wellington's action in regard to the Reform Bill; to his advice to the King that he should recall Lord Grey to power, and to his withdrawal from active opposition to the Bill in deference to the King's wish.

previous to the second reading of the Bill in the House of Lords, which were extremely characteristic and which certainly gave me an entirely high opinion of the Duke's character. I hardly know what to do with my books, whether to leave them here or at least the greater part of them till I stand at Oriel, as I should probably want them in case I got in, or to bring them all home at once and have done with the matter.

Your affectionate son,
FREDERIC ROGERS.

CHAPTER II

Residence at Oxford as a Fellow of Oriel

IN 1833 Mr. Rogers was elected to a Fellowship at Oriel, and in the following year he gained the Vinerian Scholarship.[1] From this time till 1841 he was regularly in residence at Oriel, taking pupils, and pursuing his own reading as far as the weakness of eyes at that time permitted. Some of his letters show how much pains he took to encourage and direct the private reading of his youngest brother Edward, who was then an Eton boy, and some years later a Student of Christ Church.

As a Fellow of Oriel he was drawn into even closer friendship with Newman, of whose power of sympathy with congenial minds he writes strongly : 'Newman seemed to have an intuitive perception of all that you thought and felt, so that he caught at once all that you meant or were driving at in a sentiment, a philosophical reflection, or a joke—within a certain circle, no doubt, but within a circle which comprehended all your common sympathies. And so there was in talking with him that combination of liveliness and repose which constitutes ease ; you seemed to be speaking with a better kind of self, which was drawing you upwards. Newman's general characteristics—his genius, depth of purpose ; his hatred of pomp and affectation ; his piercing insight into the workings of the human mind—at least that part of it which is best worth knowing—his strong and tenacious, if

---

[1] A scholarship in Law.

somewhat fastidious, affection (not, it must be confessed, without a certain tenacity of aversion also)—are all matters of history. I should add that he always seemed to me to have a kind of repugnance to the highly finished manners of the man of the world. Nothing covers what is behind it so completely as moral or physical polish. It reveals nothing but what it reflects. And this Newman did not like. It baffled him and kept him at a distance. He did not know what matter of interest he could touch with confidence; and this to a man, who is keenly alive to sympathy or the want of it, means an atmosphere of artificial constraint. As the [Oxford] movement gathered power in his hands he became somewhat more disinclined to men who affected an independent position, and was quick in detecting a growing divergence, though sometimes curiously over-confident in his power of counteracting an adverse prepossession . . . . . In Newman's Sermons and Hurrell Froude's conversation I found an uncompromising devotion to religion with a discouragement of anything like gushing profession, which I had been brought up to dislike and distrust—also a religion which was fervent and reforming in essentials with a due reverence for existing authorities and habits and traditions, all which I had been brought up to respect—also a religion which did not reject, but aspired to embody in itself, any form of art and literature, poetry, philosophy, and even science which could be pressed into the service of Christianity. And this met my own desires and tastes—not to say my own conception of what man was made for. And lastly I was greatly captivated by the idea that it was possible for a Church not only to teach the truth, but by its discipline to clear itself from impurities and enforce to a certain extent holiness of life among those who belonged to it. Like the rest of our small circle, I fully believed that Newman was to do something indefinitely great in the direction of Christian Church revival—revival in holiness, discipline, and authority.'

Newman was even more anxious to have Frederic Rogers as a confidant, with whom he could talk over all difficulties, after the death of Hurrell Froude in 1836; and for the next year or two they were together a great part of most days during the Oxford term. Dean Church has made clear the history of what followed this period in a narrative [2] which for style has hardly been surpassed in the English language. On this history it would be out of place to dwell here: all necessary explanation can best be given by quoting a few words from an article which Dean Church wrote upon Lord Blachford's death. 'From Mr. Newman his pupil caught that earnest devotion to the cause of the Church which was supreme with him through life. He entered heartily into Mr. Newman's purpose to lift the level of the English Church and its clergy. While Mr. Newman at Oxford was fighting the battle of the English Church, there was no one who was a closer friend than Rogers, no one in whom Mr. Newman had such trust, none whose judgment he so valued, no one in whose companionship he so delighted; and the master's friendship was returned by the disciple with a noble and tender and yet manly honesty. There came, as we know, times which strained even that friendship; when the disciple, just at the moment when the master most needed and longed for sympathy and counsel, had to choose between his duty to his Church and the claims and ties of friendship. He could not follow in the course which his master and friend had found inevitable; and that deepest and most delightful friendship had to be given up. But it was given up, not indeed without great suffering on both sides, but without bitterness or unworthy thoughts. The friend had seen too closely the greatness and purity of his master's character to fail in tenderness and loyalty, even when he thought his master going most wrong. He recognised that the error, deplorable as he thought it, was the mistake of a lofty and

[2] *The Oxford Movement.*

unselfish soul; and in the height of the popular outcry he came forward, with a distant and touching reverence, to take his old friend's part and rebuke the clamour. And at length the time came when disagreements were long left behind and each person had finally taken his recognised place; and then the old ties were built up again. It could not be the former friendship of every day and of absolute and unreserved confidence. But it was the old friendship of affection and respect renewed, and pleasure in the interchange of thoughts. It was a friendship of the antique type, more common, perhaps, even in the last century than it is with us, but enriched with Christian hopes and Christian convictions.' [3]

To Rev. J. H. Newman.

Eliot Place: December 21, 1832.

My dear Newman,—I hope you received before you started two letters of introduction for Malta. . . . I suppose you saw the classical class list before you started: in the Mathematics, Froude of course has his first; Maule (if you know the man) is the only double; Marriott has got a second. Does not the present system appear from the class list to be abominable? As far as my own acquaintances go, their places seem to have been regulated by their powers of using philosophical talk (or rather the talk seems a *sine qua non*), without reference to whether they understood it or not. (I do not mean any disrespect to several men who I know deserved well what they got.)

The Elections, as I suppose you will see by the papers, are dreadful—the Tories beaten everywhere—*e.g.* Hampshire returns four Whigs—Pusey is thrown out for Berkshire—Sadler for Leeds, Wetherall for Oxford, &c., &c. (though, on the other hand, Manners Sutton is returned for Cambridge University, and Sir R. Vyvyan for Bristol, and Gladstone turns out Wilde for Newark). Cobbett and Gully are likewise among our legislators. The only consolation is that the

---

[1] Reprinted, by permission, from the *Guardian*.

Parliament cannot be worse than it was. However, their system of dividing the polling places, Registry, &c., certainly does seem to have answered; there have been few riots, and the elections seem each fairly finished in two days. . . .

With kindest remembrances to Froude,

Believe me yours affectionately,

FREDERIC ROGERS.

To Rev. J. H. Newman.

Oriel : April 12, 1833.

My dear Newman,—In the first place *I am in*.[4] Wilson, I am truly sorry to say, is not; Marriott being the other winner. I suppose your having leave till September (which I hope you have by this time heard of) will not keep you out till then. If it will, pray tell me, and also tell me your plans; for I shall feel strongly tempted in that case to make a start myself towards you. However, this will of course depend on my health and eyes. I shall give up everything to these last. They have stood the examination most splendidly, though I suppose I shall feel it now that the excitement is gone off.

All this time I have not thanked you for your letter, which I was truly delighted to receive, and for the permission to see your verses, for which I was equally thankful.[5] I have only been able to see some of them, as I have had one opportunity only since your letter to me arrived. I need hardly say how much I was pleased with what I did see.

II. Wilberforce is here, well, and intending to be ordained the next opportunity; he is to take Mr. Sargent's curacy as you, I suppose, know. *You* (or rather *We !!*) really should make him some college officer whose duty would be connected with the elections. He would perform it so well. Even at present he clearly thinks he ought to come up to all the

---

[4] *I.e.* have gained an Oriel Fellowship.

[5] This refers to a long letter from Mr. Newman, dated Rome, March 5, 1833, which is printed in ' Letters and Correspondence of J. H. Newman,' vol. i. p. 361. The 'verses' were a series of poems which Newman wrote during his travels and sent home. Many of them were published eventually in the 'Lyra Apostolica;' among them 'Lead, Kindly Light,' which he wrote on the voyage from Palermo to Marseilles (Newman's 'Apologia,' p. 35).

Elections. He is going now to finish this letter, as my eyes are, after all my boasts, not quite up to the work, without at least delaying the letter.

Keble wishes me to suggest to you that you might make something useful (for the 'British Critic,' I suppose) out of the state of the clergy abroad as you have observed it, to show people what it is to have a depraved sort of clergy. An amplification, in short, of what you have written home to me and others.

Yours most affectionately,
F. ROGERS.

To Edward Rogers.[6]

Oriel : November 15, 1833.

Dear Edward,—I have not had time to answer your letter before, else I should have done so. You know that what I want you to do is to get as much of a taste for poetry as you can, and the ability to see what is and what is not poetical. Now I think there are some papers in the 'Spectator,' and there certainly are some in the 'Rambler,' which criticise Milton. I should like you to look out these and read them attentively over, and when you have looked them over, and think you well understand what are the chief points which they notice—*e.g.* whether they praise or blame his choice of expressions, his harmony, or his thoughts—whether they think he is too bombastical, or only just artistic enough for his subject, &c., &c.—when, I say, you have seen what is said on points such as these, begin to read the first, and if you like, the second book of Milton's 'Paradise Lost' carefully, two or three times over, and try to make up your mind for yourself whether what is said in praise or blame of him is just and true, or not. I do not know how long you will be about this, but when you have done it, write to me, and tell me some of the passages which you like, and (if you can) why you like them, and tell me any expressions which you think describe well what they want to describe, and whether you think the lines are more or less harmonious than other blank verse which you have

[6] Then a boy at Eton.

read—*e.g.* Southey's 'Roderick,' which you can look at again for the purpose; this you must find out by spouting them both to yourself—and anything else which occurs to you like this, and do not be afraid of making mistakes, but say everything which suggests itself to you. If you like Milton you can go on: if you do not, then write to me and I will tell you something else. And if I do not answer you immediately, it will always do you good to go over those poems of Southey's or Scott's which you have liked, trying to look not merely for the story but for poetical passages, and spirited or beautiful descriptions, good similes, &c., and when you get to anything which strikes you, read it over and over again, and do not be satisfied till you know it pretty well. However, this is enough on the subject of reading. I shall be glad to hear from you how you are getting on with your tutor and your school work; recollect always that that is the *first* point. I was much amused, too, at your account of the row at the Fair, which I had not heard of before. I am going home for a day or two to-morrow to keep term at Lincoln's Inn; and then shall come home a second time, I suppose, soon after you will.

Remember me to both the Wilders and my tutor if you have an opportunity. I am *extremely glad indeed* that you are more comfortable in Long Chamber.[7]

Your very affectionate brother,
FREDERIC ROGERS.

To Miss Rogers.

Oriel: November 13, 1834.

My dear Katherine,—I am now safely lodged in the Vinerian Scholarship, without opposition, and it was only by the most providential chance that I missed having the Vice-Chancellor, both the Proctors, and divers other functionaries as registrars, &c., with their noses in the air for an hour or two waiting to admit me. I concluded that, like other

---

[7] Edward Rogers was a 'Colleger' at Eton; and the 'Long Chamber' of College in those days (before the new buildings were erected under Provost Hodgson and Dr. Hawtrey) was the reverse of comfortable.

concerns of that kind, it would take its course without any trouble on my part, and accordingly, about the time when the election was going on, quietly took my hat and stick and set out with a friend to walk. However, that kind of instinctive sense of where my interest lay—common to all classes of animals—insensibly led me towards the schools where I knew they were employed upon me ; and I had not gone far before I met a functionary called the Marshal hurrying down to tell me that I should be wanted almost directly to be admitted with cap, gown, bands, white neckcloth, and all the et ceteras of academical habit. If they had been a quarter of an hour longer about the election, I should have been a mile off. As it was, I instantly borrowed a white cravat from one friend, bands from another, swore allegiance to His Majesty, and specified all that was damnable, heretical, and so on in excommunications of princes, abjured the authority of the Pope of Rome, and became Vinerian Scholar, or, as the Vice-Chancellor words it, 'was admitted to all the privileges, honours, and emoluments of the Vinerian Scholarship,' to the great credit of the University and my own no small profit.

The Duke of Wellington and our 'Parliamentary friends' have written down to the Heads of Houses to say that they find great difficulty in defending our present position with regard to our imposition of the Articles at Entrance. True enough for them. I should think they would be about as much at home in defending the doctrine of Justification, or the Articles themselves. However, our Heads have been persuaded, and are to bring forward a form of declaration which they intend substituting for it. I suppose the question will soon come on in Convocation, and there will be, I presume, a great fight.[8] However, I do not know whether you

[8] Undergraduates at Oxford (though not at Cambridge) were at that time required on their matriculation to subscribe to the Thirty-nine Articles. Dr. Hampden had published a pamphlet advocating the abolition of this rule, with a view to the admission of Nonconformists. He was opposed not only by the extreme Tractarian party, but (strange as it may seem now) by a great many others as well. On November 10, 1834, the Heads of Colleges, by a majority of one, decided to bring before Convocation a measure for freeing undergraduates from subscription. In May 1835, the measure was rejected in Convocation by a very large majority (see Church's *Oxford Movement*, pp. 125-138).

take enough interest in these University details to know what I am talking about.

Your affectionate brother,
FREDERIC ROGERS.

To Rev. J. H. Newman.

Eliot Place : December 28, 1834.

My dear Newman,—Many thanks for your note which I was most extremely glad to receive. Of course we shall be delighted to see you at Blackheath ; tell me somewhat beforehand when you can come, and I will take care to have some Oxford friends to meet you.

Gladstone, I hear, is to be a Lord of the Treasury, which I suppose is a very good start for a young man, *if true.* He is in town, and, I suppose, has not come up for nothing. By the way, do not the Ministerials seem to guard their expressions of opposition to the admission of Dissenters with us? I see always '*as a claim of right*' scrupulously inserted in such declarations. What do you say of the Ministry? I was rather struck at the description of Dissenters they have at Bradfield, where, if anywhere, I should have hoped to find they had not penetrated.[9] They seem to be quite in the old Charles I. style, believing almost in their own inspiration, and practising such very audacious dishonesty without detriment to their religion. One man professing particular piety justifies keeping his beershop open on Sunday by its being *in the way of business.* Another will not vote for Pusey,[1] because he will give his vote to no man who has not the fear of God in his heart. Meantime he has been detected in gross cheating in horse-dealing. I got rather into a scrape there for advocating amusements for the poor on Sunday—Keble is in bad odour for having done it before me.

I have nothing to tell you that you will not see in the

---

[9] Bradfield in Berkshire. Mr. Stevens, the founder of Bradfield College, at that time held the living.

[1] Mr. Philip Pusey, elder brother of Dr. E B. Pusey, was standing for Berkshire against Mr. John Walter (the elder), by whom he had been defeated in 1832. He was elected in 1834 and held the seat for many years.

papers. The City meeting to address the King conservatively seems to have succeeded in spite of the interruption of all speaking by some Radicals.

To Miss Rogers.

Oriel : May 2, 1835.

All the Convocation affair [2] went off most triumphantly for the party who wished no change, the numbers being 459 to 57 ; rather more than eight to one [3] against the Declaration. The only unpleasant part is that the beaten party are excessively angry, and it must be confessed that what happened to them was a trial of temper. The division was in the Theatre (N.B. not the play-house), and undergraduates were admitted to the gallery, who took the liberty of expressing their opinion by shouts &c. pretty freely. The voters (the M.A.s) were in the area (which would be in a play-house the pit, but without benches), and just as they were beginning to give their votes, which they usually do by going up one by one to the Proctor and whispering in his ear, one of the anti-reformers cried out 'Non placet' (the form of negativing) and walked to one side of the Theatre. It seemed from the gallery, where I was, as if the whole crowd were following him. You just saw a few spots here and there stationary, in the midst of the great current, and rather struggling not to be carried away in it, as little bits of dirt do when you are pouring water out of a basin ; and after a short settling we saw about forty gentlemen left 'alone with their glory' in the middle of the room, looking very foolish, and hardly knowing whether to stand boldly forth or not, to bear as best they might the shoutings of the opposite party and the undergraduates. However, the others soon took compassion on them and spread themselves again over the whole area, and their only penance after that was to listen to the expression of the undergraduate feelings, till the Proctor had done counting the votes. It is rather curious that these very young gentlemen whom people are so anxious to liberate

---

[2] On the question of releasing candidates for matriculation from subscription to the Thirty-nine Articles (see note on page 21).

[3] The figures here are consistent. In Church's *Oxford Movement* the majority is said to have been *five* to one.

from the yoke of subscription are the most vehement and noisy opponents of any 'relief bill' that are to be found. I only wish they had confined themselves to applause, whereas they took the liberty of hissing our respectable Provost, who is the great patron of change. Of course we have been inundated with pamphlets, with and without names. . . .

In the meantime I certainly had a very pleasant two days. Wilson, Ryder, Wilberforce, Harding, spent several days here, with a quantity of other contemporaries, and Hurrell Froude arrived just in time from Barbadoes to cut into the middle of it. It quite surprises me how little people change. All these gentry, married and single, were so exactly what they always had been, that I could hardly believe I was not a freshman again. The only painful thing was that I fear Barbadoes has not done much for Froude. I was quite shocked to see him, but I suppose I had been too sanguine; his wretched thinness struck me more than it had ever done. They say, however, that no one ever gains flesh in the West Indies, but that it tells when they come back. I most earnestly trust it may be so. He talks of spending the winter at Rome again, going straight there and coming straight back. He certainly cannot spend it in England. I cannot describe the kind of sickness I felt in looking at him when just the first meeting was over. I suppose it is a hopeful sign that his spirits are just as high as they always were; at least were so when he first came here, for I am afraid we must look for a change in that, as Newman tells me he has heard to-day that his sister who was so ill is given over; I have not seen him since his hearing the news. However, I am getting mopish.

Yours most affectionately,
FREDERIC ROGERS.

To Miss Rogers.

Oriel : October 25, 1835.

My dear Katherine,—Many thanks for your letter. I *did* for some time delay writing till the Queen was gone, and since that employments and engagements and calls came one on another so as to put my writing off two or three days longer. The results of the audit were, as I expected, not very satisfactory, the Fellowships making rather a poor show in consequence of all the low prices &c. that farmers complain of.

So much for the Fellowship. The Queen [4] has been well received, and seems to have made a very favourable impression. The precise amount of illuminations, dinners, &c., you will find in the papers far better than I can tell you. Everybody went to a drawing-room, which she held at the Angel, to show their loyalty, and I among the rest. The poor Dean of Christ Church [5] has got into more general odium than ever by mismanaging his part of the matter so as not to have the Queen at Christ Church. There are various versions of the story, most people putting it down to some incivility or brusquerie in his way of offering his house, which is likely enough, as he is a man who speaks and writes rather too shortly for court etiquettes. The most unfavourable account is that he wrote to Lord Howe that there was such and such a number of rooms unoccupied in his house which Her Majesty might have; the most favourable, and, I believe, the true one, that he wrote to say that his own house and two of the Canons' houses were at Her Majesty's service, but that they would require some putting in order and consequently some time. However, the Queen could not wait, and in consequence went to the Angel Inn; probably he did it clumsily. Be that as it may, he bears the whole blame, and, I fancy, is extremely vexed and annoyed. The Duke of Wellington lionised her, and seemed in great force.

Newman is, of course, come back bringing as good an account of Froude [6] as could be expected. He seems quite stationary; the lungs certainly are not affected, and he has strength enough to have thrown off quite the attack he had in August. His father says that his being with him has done him good, by keeping up his spirits, and he seems very much to long after his Oxford friends. Newman has pledged himself to Froude that somebody shall go down to him at Christmas;

---

[4] Queen Adelaide.
[5] Dean Gaisford.
[6] Hurrell Froude was at his father's house, the rectory at Dartington, in South Devon.

and wants me to do it, which I should very much like, and half think of doing; however, we can talk of that when I come home in November.

Miss P.'s admiration, Samuel Wilberforce, with his wife, has passed through here, and hopes to see me in the Isle of Wight if I go that way. Also I have just been hearing her great friend Moberly preach two admirable University sermons, in the anti-Evangelical line. He and Wordsworth will be a great gain to them at Winchester. I am only sorry we lose him here. Keble is married, but I cannot hear of any further chance of ——'s success, so that we shall, I suppose, only have two vacant Fellowships next Easter. The elder Mozley [7] is here to reside, and I think I shall get on with him better than I expected. I had fancied him less of a sociable animal than he is; he talks, I see, a great deal, and cleverly, though in a peculiar line which would not be generally interesting. Doyle is here to stand for All Souls, and Vaughan and Harrison and Liddell to stay the term. By the way, it was, I believe, attempted to get up a town and gown row in honour of the Queen's visit, but there was a difficulty about it from their being at that moment both on the same side, and the thing dropped rather dead; nothing but the breaking of one 'snob's' head for frightening horses with crackers. As for us, we set our tower on fire in Her Majesty's honour, but, as she left Oxford just as the fire (which was in the chimney) began to burn up, we thought we might as well put it out again, which we did at our leisure. The chimney which the porter chose for lighting, besides affording singular facilities for such a manœuvre from being (in parts) never swept, belonged to the room in which all our deeds, leases, account books, &c., are kept, which would have placed our illumination far beyond any one's else, at any rate in expensiveness.

To Rev. J. H. Newman.

Bridehead: January 16, 1836.

My dear Newman,—I have just left Froude, who professes to remain much as he has been, rather weaker than

[7] Mr. Thomas Mozley, whose 'Reminiscences' were published in 1882 and 1885. He married a sister of Newman.

when you were with him, from never being in the open air, but not worse than he has been from the beginning of his confinement. I am afraid, too, he is not quite in so good spirits as he used to be. Perhaps that was so when you were down. You ought to send Harrison down to him to take lessons on the subject of the Reformers, for certainly he has a way of speaking which carries conviction in a most extraordinary manner, over and above the arguments he uses.'

Coming through Exeter and being too late for a coach, I had the very good luck to meet Dornford,[9] who has by this time written to the College to resign his Fellowship, not that he was bound by the letter of the Statute, but he felt convinced that Adam de Brome [1] did not intend his benefaction for persons situated like him. (1) Dornford (on that occasion) meeting Wilson's brother-in-law, Major Blanshard, did in the course of conversation say that he considered himself now as a married man. Major B. thereupon congratulated, asked when the day was. D. responded that 'he was married to his church; his church was and would be his only wife.' B. hoped he did not entertain Roman Catholic views. 'Oh! no, no, it is from the *high opinion* I entertain of the ladies that I shall remain a bachelor. I consider a wife as a luxury, not a necessary. If I thought it a necessary, I should get one.'

He then walked about Exeter with me for about an hour and a half, talking of the Peninsular War, upon which he said his mind fell back much more than on his Oriel life, or than it used to do while he was at Oriel. And this leads me to (2). Dornford being engaged in puffing the military profession and his own military life to Major B., the said Major B. pointed out that he at any rate was now in a line more satisfactory in the highest respects. 'Ah! no, no, I am not so sure of that; it is very gratifying and remarkable to observe

---

' It should be observed that there are expressions in this letter and others of about the same date, implying a disapproval of many of the principles of the Reformers which was not endorsed by Lord Blachford's later judgment.

[9] A Fellow of Oriel who had in earlier life served in the Peninsular War.

[1] The original founder of Oriel College (in 1324) was Adam de Brome, Almoner of Edward II. and Rector of St. Mary's, Oxford (Rashdall's *Universities of Europe*, ii. 492).

the satisfactory way in which the military profession is spoken of in Scripture whenever it occurs, "the centurion who," &c. It is a very remarkable contrast with the lawyers, who, you will observe, are never introduced without a sentence of reprobation.'

Did Froude tell you that some good lady, who has read you, wonders how it is that you and Arnold should have any difference between you (as seems to be the case from a note on one of your sermons), 'your sentiments and general tone so perfectly agreeing, as your respective sermons show them to do'?

I hear of a certain Mr. Glover, who is a very high Churchman—too much so, and too political for the people here. He has been dunning Williams to propose a repeal of the *Præmunire*, talking about the glory of the English Senator who should make the first step in freeing the Church. Do you know who, or what, he is? I shall try to find out. Williams is to give him a volume of Oxford Tracts.

Ever yours affectionately,
FREDERIC ROGERS.

I heard the other day that you were sure to be a bishop.

To Miss M. Rogers.

Oriel : March 30, 1836.

I did not give you much of an account of Hampden's Convocation,[2] and there was not much to say, as it was

---

[2] Dr. Hampden was supposed to have used words in his *Bampton Lectures* which allowed no authority to anything that depended upon decrees of the Church and not directly upon the words of Scripture—no authority therefore *per se* to Creeds or Articles. This at least was held to be the logical conclusion of his teaching. On this account his appointment by the Crown to the post of Regius Professor of Divinity was strongly disapproved of, not only by the 'Tractarians' at Oxford, but also by Evangelicals ; and side attacks, which few, if any, would now defend, were made upon his authority. Among them was a proposal, submitted by heads of houses to Convocation, that Dr. Hampden should not be allowed a voice in the appointment of Select Preacher to the University. This proposal was defeated by the veto of the Proctors in March 1836, but in May of the same year it was brought forward again and was passed by 474 to 94 (see *Oxford Movement*, pp. 139-151).

almost the same as the affair of the Articles. We had a good many friends up, and were very comfortable and glad to meet; most of them stayed a day or two, which made it almost worth while for them to come for pleasure, and we bedded them all in College. To many, of course, the Proctors' veto must have been most provoking. But really (barring the inconvenience to non-residents) I should not myself be very sorry. The more the matter is thought of, the more I hope people will see the absurdity of allowing all the King's Church Patronage to be distributed by a premier, who may be himself infidel, heretic, or anything else. The Proctors did not give out their intentions at all till *Saturday* afternoon, and then not in a way which seemed to be against their retracting, and not putting on their veto in case they should find themselves in a majority. I do not think they meant it unfairly, but they did not *pledge* themselves to act certainly one way or the other, and of course nothing less than a distinct pledge would have made it safe for us to countermand the voters on our side. And indeed we could not possibly have countermanded those *beyond* London, for on Saturday there was no post through London, and consequently no letter could reach people beyond town that way till *Tuesday morning*, long before which time they would have left home, as on Tuesday at 2 o'clock the Convocation met. The requisition to the Vice-Chancellor which I sent you received about 380 signatures, which are, I believe, to appear in print. Some left by mistake before signing, and very many indeed were prevented from coming up by the rumours about the Proctor's intentions, so that it is sure to come on again next term. At the last moment, when it was quite clear that we should be vetoed, a rather important question arose, whether the Proctors' veto *stopped* proceedings, or only *nullified* them (as the King's refusing assent to a bill in Parliament), or, in other words, whether the veto was interposed *before* the 'division' or *after*, and, to the surprise of all persons present, a Mr. Vaughan Thomas, a very grandiloquent and pompous gentleman, chairman of our meeting, as the question was about to be put, started off at score with a long Latin speech to show that they could not prevent us from dividing, which, could he have got his point, would have

almost made the veto a dead letter, as the division would have
been in itself a declaration of the opinion of the University.
However, the Latin produced not the smallest effect. When the
question was put and the Proctors gave their 'non placet,'
the V.C. got up, dissolved Convocation, and was halfway out
before any one knew what was going on. There was a due
proportion of noise, especially from the undergraduates, who
I hope will not be let in again on a similar occasion. All
hands then adjourned to Brasenose Common Room, where
some very bad speeches were made by one or two people who
came from town, Lord Encombe and a Mr. Trevor; elec-
tioneering kind of claptrap speeches, quite out of place, and
the requisitions, which had been prepared before by sensible
people, proposed, carried, and signed. The names, I fancy,
are to appear in the 'Standard.' And there the matter has
ended for the present. I hear the 'Morning Chronicle' has
had an attack on Newman and Pusey by name, for being at
the bottom of it. . . . . .

To Rev. J. H. Newman.

Eliot Place : July 2, 1836.

My dear Newman,—Wood is most sanguine, and eager to
know every one who holds out prospect of being bettered. He
nods his head and says, 'Do you know, Rogers, I do not see
why we should not absorb *all* young Evangelicals.' This
à propos of ——, on whom we are to call together, εὖ γένοιτο.
Wood is eager for controversy with people, and his *sine qua
non* for thinking them promising is an anxiety to discuss and
argue the questions: which he will find in Palmer. He is
most warm in his expressions of affection for Bowden. What
a hit you have made there! He hardly ever sees him, he
says, without finding out something fresh to like in him.

. . . I have set to work fairly this week at attending Courts.
One great gain will be that it will bring me very much across
Wood ; he lets me sit in his room when I am tired of hearing
arguments in Court, and tells me what to read, and lectures
me. How long this will please him I do not know. I hope
and trust I shall not bore him, and it is consoling to think

that he will probably tell me when I do. In the meantime this does not agree very well with [the review of] Bentham, I confess; but I hope that if the 'British Critic' does not come out till near the end of the month I may have got through something or other by that time.

... What do you think of doing about the *Lyra*? If I could be of any use I should be very glad and should like it much, *i.e.* in case you have not time, and can find no better person.[3] I hardly know it all at present, and so should start at a disadvantage compared with many men. And I know, too, that I am not up to half your meanings in different places, but still I might save you trouble, and you might talk to me about a general arrangement when you come here, and polish it up afterwards. If you have any one in your eye (Mozley, *e.g.*) who will answer the purpose better, and will do it, so much the better. Tell me when you are likely to come, or if you are likely to be prevented.

Ever yours affectionately,
F. R.

To Miss M. Rogers.

Hursley: August 14, 1836.

My dear Marian,—I have had a variety of good and bad luck since I have been here. In the first place my journey was very prosperous. It was, as you know, a fine day, and I was not dreadfully crowded in the coach, though very nearly so. We had one very fat man sitting outside, on the same bench with me; fortunately we were not full at starting, so that we were able to allow him two places to his own proper share, without any inconvenience to ourselves. But, as we went on, it was only the obvious physical impossibility of the case, as pointed out calmly and impressively by the fat man,

---

[3] Arranging and editing the *Lyra Apostolica*. In Newman's answer to this letter on July 5 (Correspondence, ii. 199), he says: 'Thanks for your offer about the *Lyra*; your assistance will be everything. I have told Rivington you will call for any loose sheets he has from the *British* [Magazine] with Lyras in them. What I should like you to do (unless my proposal goes beyond your offer) would be to get a blank quarto book and paste them in. ... I should wish the series to begin with Scripture subjects.'

which prevented the coachman from intruding a fourth person (for whom the coach was in any ordinary state of things calculated) on our bench. The fat man's mode of argument was truly irresistible. Just as the coach stopped, we all saw what was coming, and exclaimed with one voice to the fat man, 'You must fight our battle, sir.' He accordingly composed himself into the attitude of a candid man, aware that his specific gravity defies all attempts to turn him out, ready to do anything that can in reason be expected of him, but with no thoughts of making room for a fourth passenger. As the coachman with the expectant came up, he began looking to one and the other side of him as if to see where it was that the coachman would expect to put him; and answered his 'Now, sir, if you please,' with 'Quite impossible—you see, my friend, it's *quite* impossible. Do what you will, you *can not* get me into less than this'—and then he put his two hands at the distance of about a yard and a half asunder, to those points in the bench where his body terminated on each side; and all with the innocent tone of a man who was trying to stretch (or rather contract) a point for the coachman, if in any way possible. And the perplexing thing was that what he said was so undeniably true. It was perfectly vain to talk of its being 'a very unbusinesslike way of doing things, to lose a passenger because one gentleman happened to be a little stouter (a singular understatement of our argument) than the rest,' while the solid and unyielding fact was what it was. And coachee was obliged to carry off the passenger to sit third on the box; leaving our friend grumbling on 'quite impossible' with the complaining air of a goodnatured man whom people have attempted to put upon. We had previously ascertained that he only paid for one place.

Keble is at Freshwater for his wife's health, and proposed my going there with him on Monday, which I did. Thursday and bits of Wednesday and Friday I spent with S. Wilberforce at Brighstone, and found R. Wilberforce staying for some time there, and H. Wilberforce with his wife came over for a day, so that all this was most lucky. Now I am back here, just beginning again my visit to Wilson.[1] So far, so good, now per

---

[1] Mr. Wilson was Mr. Keble's curate at Hursley.

contra : Keble and I, going to Cowes, in our way down seem to have lost, he, his bag and great coat, I, my cloak, and a small valise of Wilson's with sundry of my own clothes in it. Whether these unhappy things have gone to Havre by a packet which started for that place when we started for Cowes, or whether a porter is now wearing my nice nankeens and new silk waistcoat, the fates have not yet suffered to transpire. I trust the former. Either alternative is melancholy, and one, I fear, inevitable. I must say that I was so far only blameable in that I put a blind confidence in Keble, which I never will do again in any man that writes verses, and that I put no direction on my package, for which I the less reproach myself, as his having done so seems in no degree to have alleviated his fate. However, it is not, I hope, quite impossible that we may see them again, and in the meantime I console myself with thinking that it was not my very best coat that was in it. I met Mrs. Sargent at the Wilberforces', who is a nice kind of person, I should think, but I did not see much of her She seemed much scandalised at R. Wilberforce for using disparaging expressions of the Reformation ; which considered, she seems to have managed ill in marrying three (at least) out of her four daughters to people who would hold the same objectionable language. Newman, I hear, the great oracle of all four of them, she votes 'a confirmed old papist.'

To Rev. J. H. Newman.

Bransgore [5] : August 18, 1836.

My dear Newman,—Keble seems very little inclined to send his Parochial Sermons up to you : he says ' Newman has been troubled enough with reading things that won't do.' However, he says, 'some time' he will select some for publication himself. I have attacked him several times, and will again when I go back to Hursley : which will be next Thursday. I cannot get him to say anything about the Church Commission article ; he says he is sure that if you are not up to it, he is not, and that he supposes it wants know-

[5] Mr. Henry Wilberforce at that time held the living of Bransgore, in Hampshire.

ledge of law, but does not speak like a person who decidedly will not do it. You are of course welcome to all the poetry in the 'British Magazine.' He says he has two more Lyras for you, but cannot lay his hand on them, and I cannot get anything satisfactory out of him. Your letter only reached me on Saturday evening, and H. Wilberforce took me off unexpectedly to Bransgore on Wednesday, so that I have not pressed for answers as I should have done. I can only say I will. I talked to him about monasteries, and he asked whether you had any details ready about them, and whether it would not be worth while putting some people (Sir W. Heathcote, *e.g.*, he said) upon saving a little money for them in case of necessity. He said he thought he would not take a Bishopric, but should not feel decided enough to advise a friend: and so encouraged I talked rather about the Provostship, which he seemed to think quite another thing, but did not pronounce (when I put the τόπος before him) whether it might not be embarrassing oneself with the system. My own view certainly is against your declining it, unless you feel that any oaths, pledges, &c., which you would have to take, would be entangling. The *prima facie* advantages are so great that I cannot think you would have the opportunity put before you (if it is put) for nothing; and, as to the stall at Rochester, having a share of a cathedral in your hands *might* turn out a great thing. I am sure New College service is, even at present, one of the most powerful instruments that we have at Oxford. . . .

To Rev. J. H. Newman.

August 29, 1836.

My dear Newman,—Keble certainly is the most impracticable of men. I have bullied him with questions till I am afraid of affronting him about the 'British Critic' article, and all I can get out of him is, that he will look at Collier: and an injunction not to give you any hopes of his writing, because he had disappointed you often enough already. He has been at a Visitation Sermon, which he has just finished, on *Tradition*, to be preached at a visitation of Dealtry's. He talks of sending it up to you soon to look at, and at the same time a bundle of 'Village Sermons.' And this has taken up most of his time lately. Indeed, since I spent some days with him at Freshwater, I have hardly ever seen him for more than a few minutes at a time, and that generally when he has been talking with Wilson about parish business, excepting one or two evenings when all his family have been with him. He tells me that he hears that G. Denison goes about the country puffing you and your views of things.

If there is any chance of a new edition of your 'Arians,' I do wish you could make the Economy[6] a little more palatable; so many people seem to me to find it hard of digestion. I think I told you long ago that it was the point on which Twisleton fastened, and I hear that Sir W. Heathcote, who people say is a clever man, and I suppose a well-principled, has need of all his respect for you and apostolicity to help him to stomach it at all.

To Miss S. Rogers.

August 1836.

I suppose people at home have told you all the news that was to be told before I left home. In the first place I had a very prosperous and amusing journey to Winchester. The amusing feature of it was an inordinately fat man who occupied the place next to me; but having already given an account of the same in a letter home I will not serve you up the same dish, but will only say that this morning, looking at the paper, I perceived that on Lablache and some other singers presenting themselves to get places in the Southampton (the same) coach, the book-keeper declined taking Lablache

---

[6] 'The principle of the Economy is this: that out of various courses, in religious conduct or statement, all and each *allowable antecedently and in themselves*, that ought to be taken which is most expedient and most suitable at the time for the object in hand. Instances of its application and exercise in Scripture are such as the following: (1) Divine Providence did but gradually impart to the world in general, and to the Jews in particular, the knowledge of His Will.... It may be said that this principle, true in itself, yet is dangerous, because it admits of an easy abuse, and carries men away into what becomes insincerity and cunning. This is undeniable; to do evil that good may come, to consider that the means, whatever they are, justify the end, to sacrifice truth to expedience, unscrupulousness, recklessness, are grave offences. These are the abuses of Economy' (*Apologia*, p. 343).

unless he would pay for two places. It seems the omission of that precaution in the case of our fat friend had made them wiser.

I never saw so much of Keble before, and am delighted to have done so now. I spent the whole days from Monday to Saturday with his family (except two which I spent with Samuel Wilberforce), and came home to Hursley with them, and most delightful people they all are most certainly. I never could have conceived a person keeping as Keble does his boyish spirits, till I had seen him pelting his young nephew in to his lessons in the most reckless way. At the same time *I* am very much afraid of him, I confess, from not being able quite to understand him always, or to make myself always understood by him, and in talking of serious subjects he has a disconcerting way of keeping silence sometimes, which may mean either that he thinks you have been over forward and are talking sillily, or that what you say is new to him and he has no answer to make. I sometimes wonder how two men so very unlike as Newman and he could have got to understand one another so perfectly as they do. I suppose they hardly could have done so unless they had had Froude as an interpreter at first. Mrs. Keble I have been more taken with than any one I have met for a very long time indeed. She is so weak and ill that she rests (in walking) every thirty or forty yards, but never takes any one little privilege of an invalid, and is constantly exerting herself to keep all round her cheerful and in good spirits, and that with so little of the manner of a weak person that it is not for some time that you see that it is an exertion. There is something certainly inexpressibly taking in seeing a person who has a right to be lying idle on a sofa, paying the sharpest attention to the little comforts of every one present; at the same time it is most painful to see how *very* ill she is. One evening in particular, after I had just heard of the death of Mrs. —— (which you have probably seen in the papers), I felt it quite sickening to look at her talking pleasantly and looking after every one's cups of tea, and seeming all the time so pale and weak that one felt that almost every word she spoke livelily was an imprudent exertion.

To Mrs. Rogers.

Bransgore: September 18, 1836.

My dear Mother,—I left Keble's finally on Thursday, which is the place I certainly have left with most regret of any, the whole party, besides their other likeable qualities, being so kind and glad to see you, and intimate. Mrs. Keble hopes much to see any of my sisters who may happen to be in this part of the world; this she volunteered, and repeated several times that I must understand her to be in earnest, and not take the invitation as a matter of compliment, which I said I should do.

Tell Marian I have been unhappy enough to recommend the 'Stabat Mater' to Mrs. Wilberforce, the consequence of which has been that there has come from the Southampton music shop the music indeed, but set to regular Evangelical English words, the *pertransivit gladius* stanza being put to the following words (by way of a specimen):

> Mercy's streams I here am viewing
> Precious drops my soul bedewing
> Plead and claim my peace with God. ! ! !

I have tried what I could do, by supplying most of the right words, to give the poor music a fair chance, but against such ludicrous mangling I am afraid I can scarcely hope to succeed. And tell her likewise that some choruses (gipsy chiefly) in the 'Preciosa' are perfectly beautiful, and it will be worth her while trying it. Mrs. Keble played it to me from a P.F. setting of some nobody's.

I think I told you that I half expected Acland to join us in our Normandy expedition. He will be a great acquisition, both for other reasons and as a sketcher, one of which article it is highly desirable to have in a party. I hope too that Wilson will pass through Boulogne while I am there, on his way home from Switzerland.

To Miss E. Rogers.

St. Helier's, Jersey: September 24, 1836.

My dear Emily,—When last I wrote to you I think it was from H. Wilberforce's. While there I received intimation that Newman's consecration [7] was on the 22nd, the day after we had intended to start. H. W., my host, and Mrs. H. W., had promised to be there, and there was altogether to be a party. Accordingly Mr. and Mrs. H. W. and myself started from Bransgore on Tuesday, slept at Hursley (I at Wilson's in his absence), and had a pleasant journey to Oxford and a very pleasant party there. Newman's church, now finished, is certainly one of the most perfect things for its size I ever saw. The altar is beautiful, and the rest is so well kept under that when you come in you seem to see nothing but the altar; never certainly was anything so unlike modern churches. The builders &c. are extremely puzzled at the capricious and unseemly (as to them appears) way in which his ornament is spent; no cushions in the armchairs by the side of the altar, mere rush hassocks for the priest to kneel on there; no cushion to support the prayer-book on the altar; no cushions *or hangings* on the pulpit *at all*, and instead of a reading-desk, the kind of stand that a person plays the violin before, with a bran hassock to kneel on when necessary; while the altar itself was carved stone, with seven very pretty Early English arches behind it, surmounted by a three-lighted window in the style of those of Christ Church Chapter-house; all very expensive.

We were all in fear as to what the Bishop would say; in the first place, stone altar, and in the second crosses over: these are papistical, and Newman we thought was a person who could not look over a hedge &c.; moreover, so was the ceremony of priests turning to the east to say the prayers, which was to be essayed nevertheless; moreover, there was no vestry for the Bishop to robe in, and the pulpit was even *illegally* destitute of appurtenances. However, his Lordship was highly pleased and complimentary, and everything went

---

[7] The consecration of Newman's church at Littlemore, near Oxford.

off in the greatest style. Williams,[a] whom my sisters know of, is the curate.

After a very jolly day and a half at Oxford I started at 8 o'clock by the Southampton coach, extremely disgusted to find, with the fear of the equinox before our eyes, that the wind was getting up and that we should be wet through by the time we reached Southampton, and be miserable all our passage. However, we stopped (again) at Keble's and made him give us victuals and dry our wet things, and lodged ourselves in tolerable comfort on the Jersey steamer at 7 o'clock P.M. on Friday, September 23, 1836, with a good sharp S.W. wind blowing, and with the swell consequent on what had blown through the day. Till we got to the Needles, as a look at the map will point out to you, everything was delightful, except that everybody knew what they had to look forward to; and I have seldom seen anything more beautiful than the Needles were by moonlight with clouds flying about the tops of the cliffs. And indeed the whole passage by the north of the Isle of Wight was beautiful in the same way from the quantity of white clouds, the skirts of which seemed to be hanging over the hills with breaks here and there and a full moon every now and then. At the Needles the sharp pitching sent everybody down to bed like a shot. *I* myself walked about deck for some time longer, and never felt less unwell, or more like a god in my life; walking down a ship as it is descending a wave seems to me (next to skating) the nearest approach to flying that is given to man.

To Rev. J. H. Newman.

Boulogne-sur-Mer: October 10, 1836.

My dear Newman,—I write just to say that I certainly intend to be at Oxford on Saturday night, or rather Sunday morning, by the mail. My plans are to come to London by a packet which leaves this at twelve on Friday night and professes to cross in about twelve hours. So that I shall have just an hour or two, I hope, at home, and then pass on to you

---

[a] Mr. Isaac Williams (see below, p. 107).

people at Oxford. Our tour has been very successful, in spite of some small impediments to our perfect happiness in the shape of bad weather and unwholesome French living. I certainly seem to have attained to some few fresh ideas on the subject of Gothic architecture—how wonderfully beautiful some of the cathedrals are! I confess I do not attain to a distinct view about their services, music, &c.; in fact, *generally* speaking, I was not much struck. However, not understanding what is going on, and being occupied in a search through one's Missal to find the place during the greater part of the service, interfere somewhat, as well with your perception of beauties and proprieties, as with other things.

The priests seem not to be much respected by the class of people one meets in *diligences*, and to have lost entirely their hold on the national education. I travelled with a boy who is at one of the Government Colleges, and I should fancy that the French system had as great capabilities of becoming a magnificent, flourishing, anti-Christian system as can well be conceived. Are we to come to this? Or will the two universities save us? Like Acland, I think you ought to put forth something positive, and don't know what.

However, I shall see you within a week, so I need not have any compunction at sending you a short note like this— merely to tell you to have rooms ready for me—particularly as it is at your command that I make my appearance. Kind remembrances to all at Oriel.

Ever yours affectionately,
FREDERIC ROGERS.

To Rev. J. H. Newman.

Eliot Place: February 1837.

My dear Newman,—I was, as you seemed to forebode, knocked up with the influenza the day but one after I received your letter. I suppose you have forgotten what you wrote to me about; however, I shall assume that you remember. I cannot really judge about a title for your book; I have not the book enough in my head; probably have not heard enough of it to know what title would be *appropriate*. I should, *e.g.*, not have thought that the *Pastoral Office*, &c., was the subject of your book.[9]

S. Wilberforce, I believe, was not attacked at Islington; on the contrary, he wanted to get an opportunity of speaking at Bramston's special desire, but could not. Archdeacon Hoare gave you all up but Keble, and could not consent to call 'the great Keble a heretic.' I hear generally they find now that the 'Christian Year' contains all evil hidden in it. Archdeacon H. considers that Keble and himself are the two most sympathetic souls in the diocese of Winton. Do you know him? By the way, I dined with Sir R. Inglis to meet Thornton the other day, and met Rose, Southey, and one of the Coleridges, which last talked of Arnold, who, he said, stated to friends that his fingers itched to review Keble's 'Hooker,' but that he did not do it on account of their old friendship. He said Arnold considered Keble as quite the leader and representative of Church views. Rose, I thought, seemed very much down in the mouth—perhaps it was only that he expected Southey to exhibit—which he did not. He hardly said anything, except that he abused Arnold for imputing to people (old friends of his own) what he must have known to be false motives. . . .

Townshend of Durham told somebody that, dining with Rose, he had for a long time had great difficulty in containing himself, and at last Rose said that he thought it very doubtful whether we had got more good or evil from the Reformation. —'Then,' he said, 'I could stand it no more, so I rose and gave it him, hip and thigh.'

Can I be of any use in translating for the Fathers?[1] I have been thinking over it, and if I could be of use shall be glad to be so.

Ever yours affectionately,
FREDERIC ROGERS.

---

[9] *Romanism and Popular Protestantism*, published in 1837.

[1] The *Library of the Fathers, translated by Members of the English Church*, edited by Newman, Keble, and Pusey.

To Rev. J. H. Newman.

University Club : April 27, 1837.

My dear Newman,—I never thought very much of my tract suggestion, but Wood brought some objections to a pamphlet which did not apply to them, so I suggested them. The said Wood states first, that he does not remember, and does not believe, that you ever commissioned him to write to Manning about the Optatus.[2] Secondly, that he did say to S. Wilberforce that it was idle of H. W. to have thrown up the Confessions : and will never again say a word to one Wilberforce about another—but that he was led astray by your having written to him to ask him to suggest some translator for the Confessions—H. W. having taken the Letters.[3] That, therefore, as he has only done you one disservice, and since you count his letter as a service, he considers himself quits with you.

I see Hope twice a week, and really he seems both a very nice fellow, and very well inclined to go thoroughly with us. Jeremy Taylor, as far as I can see, seems his great man. It is rather absurd to see how many people take *Sewell's* ground —quite believing your people to be *the* right set—but thinking that they individually are more likely to be useful to right views by not being party men.

Vaughan, I hear, is gone to Hampstead to think out principles, and has joined to himself Twisleton. The account I heard from one of the Denisons was that he said he had taken his views for some time on authority, and wanted to satisfy himself for himself.

You do not tell me how I am to get an Ambrose to translate from. I told Acland you liked his article, and had a long talk with him about Maurice. I was amused at your respective ways of putting the same fact. You complained of Pusey's being sacrificed to a theory. Acland said that it was Maurice's very admiration for Pusey which made him select him as the best and most living specimen he could get of the English High Church view of the Sacraments.

[2] *I.e.* a proposal that he should translate the writings of Optatus of Milevi against the Donatists.

[3] The translation of St. Augustine's Confessions and of St. Cyprian's Letters.

To Rev. J. H. Newman.

May 31, 1837.

Carissime N.,—I am afraid it is vain to hope that my sister will recover. The physicians say just what they used to do about Froude. . . .

Wood has just spoken to me about Froude's 'Remains.' As far as I have an opinion I should say with him, publish them as soon as they are ready: unless, of course, there is anything which, on consideration, he as a clergyman of the Church of England had no right to publish. I cannot help feeling as if his death was a kind of call to publish them now. Perhaps (or I may say certainly) I should have thought it bad policy to publish them so soon, if circumstances had not pointed that way; for I am not so ready as Wood to throw away your character for judgment and moderation; I hope it may serve you and Oxford many a good turn yet. But, as it is, I should go *quo fata vocant.*

How far does Froude's view of the Eucharist go beyond what Knox's implies, where he speaks of the consecrated elements being to us 'all and more than all' that the Shechinah was to the Jews? If not much, will it be so very startling to people at large?

Our clergyman here (Legge of All Souls[4]) seems edging forwards towards daily service: last year he had it on Saints' days—then in Lent on Wednesdays and Fridays, and now every week on *Tuesdays, Wednesdays,* and *Fridays,* and Saints' days. Wood tells me Dodsworth is to have his church always open, really for the benefit of poor people who live two or three families in one room.

Ever yours affectionately,

F. R.

To Rev. J. H. Newman.[5]

Eliot Place: July 3, 1837.

I confess myself a good deal at a loss and rather anxious to know accurately what is the state of things; which, con-

---

[4] Hon. and Rev. Henry Legge, Vicar of Blackheath. He married a sister of Frederic Rogers in 1842.

[5] Newman's answer to this (dated July 5) is printed in *Letters and Correspondence,* ii. 237.

sidering my oath to obey, I certainly have not been diligent in informing myself of. If I were to come up at the Audit a few days before the rest, should I be able to get hold of the Statute Book and make up something of one's mind quietly beforehand? I really should like to hear a little what your view of things is, if it is not troubling you. Is this heretical? The statutes about Prayer for the Founder, *quâ* statutes, are repealed by the Act of Parliament and Convocation which made it wrong to obey them; we do not swear to them; they *are not* statutes; but they should be kept in the Book, (1) as monuments of our benefactors' intention, binding as such on all of us, as far as we *can* rightly observe them (or [*qu.*] substitute something for them), a guide to such as wish to do so, and possibly a still more literal and exact guide to future and better times: (2) (if there is nothing really *per se* wrong in them, which you know best) as existing still *in posse* and liable to be called into life at any moment, if Convocation (*qu.* and Parliament?) repealed those of their laws which make it wrong to obey them literally at present. Then as to the 'eloquio fruantur Latino' and such like which *are* part of our present statutes, I should be glad to see them got rid of, for Lord Radnor's reasons.

Have pity on me and tell me how much of this is absurd. For, in spite of all you may say to the contrary, it is pleasant for a weak conscience to be able to refer one's actions to a rational principle. Don't treat me Wilsonicè for this.

I met and talked with Ward of Balliol the other day at the Club, and was rather pleased with his way of talking, not that we talked at all on Catholic subjects; but he talked (as Marriott says) like a man in earnest, who wished to see how he ought to act. The Balliol people in their petition to Parliament have asserted that they can alter their statutes; but they have since found that they cannot, which discovery seems to have perplexed him in many ways.

Ever yours affectionately,
FREDERIC ROGERS.

To Rev. J. H. Newman.

Eliot Place : August 30, 1837.

I have been setting to work (on Dr. Doyle's recommendation partly) to read Isaiah, which I mention in order to acknowledge the benefit conferred on all such readers by your sermons on the Kingdom of the Saints, and your view of Prophecy as a record of God's (partly frustrated) intentions. I cannot say how your notions seem to make everything fall into order to me, and what a meaning they give to what otherwise would have been *to me* only poetry. They seem to me to grow into a key to every fresh prophecy.

How kind the 'Dublin Review' is to you, 'amiable young man,' and what a 'floor' its defence of Dr. Wiseman from your charge of unfairness is ! Wood seems rather penetrated by its (and his own) arguments against Keble's Rule of Faith. He complains that you and Keble tax his faith too hardly, not merely requiring him to believe *generally that the Fathers assert the subordination of Tradition*, which he would readily do (though his own knowledge went the other way) till he knew as much about them as you do ; but also that *this opinion of theirs is proved by certain passages which you adduce ;* from which passages his own reason tells him no such inference can be drawn.⁶

Rev. J. H. Newman.

Eliot Place : November 27, 1837.

By the bye, you know Froude used to say that neither Laud nor the Reformers could be acquitted of coarseness (on the 'spirit of the age' τόπος). He said to me of Laud that

---

⁶ Newman in his reply (August 31) says : 'Your judgment about *The Kingdom of the Saints* is most valuable : first, because it is the first I have had on the subject, certainly the first deliberate one after a perusal of Scripture ; next, because it is a very essential theory in the Anglican system, indeed it is the heart of it. . . . I wish Wood would put down on paper *where* and *how* he disagrees with me. I see no more than the man in the moon. All I have said is, that the Fathers do appeal in all the controversies to Scripture as a final authority' (*Letters and Correspondence*, ii. 243).

all he saw in him was that he was a *brave* man, with some good views, adding that all our divines since the Reformation had been very dark about Church Independence. I don't know whether this is desirable to preserve in Froude's 'Remains.'

I saw Manning the other day—very stout about Church Commission, and generally, in fact, very respectably revolutionist. What do you think, as a sign of the times, of his introducing me to Archdeacon Hoare as a gentleman who would go all lengths with him (the Archdeacon), 'a thoroughly good *Catholic*'? This was taken as a full title to confidence, and I was flooded with the contents of the Archdeacon's heart accordingly.

And now for something which will rather amuse you. I have been broaching my law-school scheme at home, which seems to be well received. But what potion do you think I have used to make their 'absinthia tetra' palatable? I really have hardly the face to write it. The *possibility of its leading to the university membership!!* I really do think that, looking at things simply as they are at this present moment, such a thing is quite enough on the cards to make it not hypocrisy to use it as I do, and much more likely than any *equal* distinction in any other line. Hope suggested it for this particular purpose. And as far as I have talked yet, the whole scheme seems to have been *quite caught at*.

To me it certainly will be an exceeding comfort to think that I am reading and living here with a definite view of making myself useful, ultimately at Oxford (as lecturer, not as member).

To Rev. J. H. Newman.

Eliot Place : February 24, 1838.

Antiquissime,[7]—I cannot help writing to say how much I have been struck with your joint Preface to Froude's book.

---

[7] Two or three letters of this date begin with this *sobriquet*, and one with ὦ ψυχὴ ἀποστολική. See Newman's *Apologia*, p. 106) : 'The Anglican disputant took his stand upon Antiquity or Apostolicity, the Roman upon Catholicity. The Anglican said to the Roman "There is but one faith, the Ancient, and you have not kept to it ; " the Roman retorted " There is but one Church, the Catholic, and you are out of it " '

It really seems to me the noblest thing I have seen for a very long time, and exactly to hit the right points. There is a bold frank tone about it that to me seems very taking. I suppose pointing out that the 'oppressor' view applied to the Articles (according to Maurice's theory) you considered a degree of audacity too great even 'perditissimis hominibus.'

I was a good deal amused at your American project for me, which Wood told me of. Apostolical bagman would certainly be an amusing trade. I mean this, really; but that must be put off till I can do it on my own account, which I am afraid will approach the Greek Kalends. Paris is more feasible, as I think I could manage that, without finding a balance on the wrong side, in October. If I went there, I think I should go after the Oriel election, and should stay a month or two.

Hallam (whom I have been beginning to read) says that when conciliation was the object it was held out by our Church that *the Liturgy* was essentially the same as the *Mass Book*, referring to Strype and Holinshed (Const. Hist. i. 117, note). I do not know whether you know him, but I have been rather struck to see how much he agrees with Froude in *the facts* he states, or grants. He calls Collier the fairest historian of the Reformation. He performs the part of 'advocatus diaboli' very respectably, especially in the matter of Cranmer and Edward VI.

Acland took me the other evening to hear a debate on the ballot, and really I wonder the Radicals do not carry things before them more than they do. They seem to me so obviously the straightforward side. I never saw anything more absurd than Peel's shuffling retreat on finding that he had hastily avowed his real reason for opposing it; unwillingness, viz., to trust the unbiassed votes of the constituency.

So, in spite of Sir Robert, Sodor and Man survives:[8] who is to have it? I hear that Denison came up from Salisbury on purpose to vote for it, on some late occasion.

---

[8] In a letter to Keble (October 26, 1837) Newman writes: 'Sir Robert Inglis [M.P. for Oxford University] has been to the Isle of Man, and tells me the clergy there have signed a petition *for*, instead of *against*, the suppression of their see. . . . The laity are getting up a petition against.'

To Rev. J. H. Newman.

Eliot Place : March 20, 1838.

I was most exceedingly pleased the day before yesterday to receive a copy of dear Froude's book 'from the editors,' and you are hereby desired to conceive yourself thanked 'pro rei suavitate ;' and not 'pro facultate nostra.' It seems like having you all three bound up together and put in one's bookshelves bodily, and I hope will give ὅσιόν τι καὶ ἐνεργὲς to the reading of it, as well as to the sight of the blue backs.

I have only to complain that editors and authors do not have a set of title-pages sent down to them to indite with their own hand the words of gift, instead of leaving it to Mr. Rivington. You see you can never satisfy people.

I heard from Wilson that Judge Coleridge had protested, and went to see whether I could hear anything about it from J. Froude. He said his father had written to him to say that Coleridge had sent him a very kind letter, but 'strongly animadverting' on the publication of some passages—what, he did not say. I was glad to find from what he said that the Archdeacon and his family had made up their minds well to that, and a great deal more of such remonstrances.

I met Utterton in an omnibus the other day, who told me it was the prevailing subject of conversation at Oxford, and that *reasonable* (!) people generally acquiesced in your reasons for publication.

To Miss Rogers.

Oriel : May 12, 1838.

I have committed the extravagance of hiring a pianoforte for a month, to the infinite annoyance, I have no doubt, of Daman who is over my head ; but such is my infirmity of purpose that I know if I had it not I should be always drawing by candlelight or some such trick.

Newman wants me to write a review of a couple of small volumes of poems by two Cambridge men called Trench [9] and Milnes [1] for the 'British Critic,' but as it is to be done in the

---

[9] Archbishop Trench.   [1] Monckton Milnes (the late Lord Houghton).

course of the next fortnight or three weeks I do not feel very hopeful. I shall give up all notion of translating Ambrose. Wood, when I was in town, offered to take it off my hands, and I shall accept his offer. I am pretty regular in my two hours' law; I generally get an hour of Hume, irregularly one with Edward [2] (who is, besides reading, doing some Latin composition with me), and I scarce know how I get rid of the rest of the day. To-morrow I am going to make a holiday, a thing I have by no means earned, and make an expedition about 8 miles on the London road with Courtney and another friend, to a curious and pretty church at Dorchester, which we all want to lionise.

Your affectionate brother,
FREDERIC ROGERS.

To Rev. J. H. Newman.

Temple : July 30, 1838.

My dear Newman,—Wood and I feel honoured by being selected as pursebearers for the movement. Wood only suggests that the managers ought to be resident at Oxford, which is at least uncertain in both our cases. Young Mozley seems likely hereafter to be in the right position for administering it. Certainly we ought, as you say, to be clerics. Of course, if from any circumstances I should think myself an unfit person to manage the money, I should not be breaking trust in transferring it to such persons as our friends might think best fitted to take my place. I understand myself bound either to administer the fund for the ends which you have in view, or to take care that it is put into the hands of those who will so act.

I was somewhat amused at a view of you people I heard the other day *à propos* of Mr. Davenport. A coxcombical diner-out, whose name I don't know, was talking of the extreme difficulty of pronouncing where religious enthusiasm ended and madness began, and observed that Mr. D. brought different bishops to vouch for his sanity, and 'again Pusey

---

[2] His brother, then at Christ Church.

and those Oxford men, who, by the way, are themselves just on those confines where it is so puzzling to pronounce.' Really you had better look sharp or you will all find yourselves under Dr. Warburton's care some of these days. In mere prudence Pusey ought to set up a britzcha.

To Rev. J. H. Newman.

Eliot Place : August 1, 1838.

My dear Newman,—I went yesterday with my sister to see Westmacott's drawing, and it seems to me as if it would be quite beautiful, and not in the least ostentatious. It and Littlemore Chapel will be quite worthy of one another. My sister, to whom I had read your account of it, went not quite prepared to find fault, but certainly with considerable misgivings, and was quite converted by the sight of it to unqualified admiration. However, all I had to say I said to Westmacott. He was uncommonly good-natured in showing all the beautiful things in his studio, and talked very warmly about you, and hesitatingly about his possible 'British Critic' article. So the acquaintance began very flourishingly, and I am to call on him when we are in town together again. Really he may be a most valuable aid if he will take in good earnest to reviving the old $\mathring{\eta}\theta o \varsigma$ in sculpture, which seems quite his notion.

What do you think of Gladstone's exculpation of you? And what of the face Froude would have made at being quoted in the House of Commons as 'an accomplished gentleman' by Lord Morpeth?[3] And what of Sir R. H. Inglis's pledging himself that the University was not 'becoming day by day a less loyal child of the Reformation'? Overhasty Sir Robert !

Gladstone, by the bye, is engaged on a book on 'Church and State,' or rather, Wood says, 'the Duties of the State to the Church.' I do not know whether to be glad or not ; he

---

[3] See a letter from Newman to James Mozley (*Letters and Correspondence*, ii. 255): 'You see Lord Morpeth has been upon me in the House, as editor of the *Remains* [of Hurrell Froude]. Gladstone has defended me, Sir R. Inglis the University.'

certainly must pledge himself to principles far above those held by any modern statesman, and from the way in which he talks of Erastianism and Church grievances, and Hook, I hope he won't tether himself the wrong way.

To Rev. J. H. Newman.

Eliot Place : October 4, 1838.

My dear Newman,—I cannot say I got anything beyond amusement from my trip : the size of our family party made it even more than usually difficult to pick up information, and I am never much of a hand at it. The priests seem to have identified themselves with the Revolution very much—so every one says. In the cathedral is a monument to a certain Count Mérode who was killed, they write, 'Catholicae fidei patriaeque jura tuendo,' but the civil authorities, and the one or two laics to whom I could talk, seemed to put it on the mere 'liberty' ground. I suppose that is partly from Leopold's being a Protestant. Do you see that Lacordaire (of 'Avenir' memory) is putting himself at the head of a re-establishment of the Dominicans in France? Also do you observe in Blackwood an attack on a book of Guizot's for being Roman Catholic? He seems from the little I saw to be doing wonderfully good service to the Middle Ages.

I was sorry to hear that your friend, Mr. Stephen of the Colonial Office, was the author of the article on Froude ; though it is better than if it had been a younger man. Doyle talked of it, and spoke of the 'Remains' as having produced the impression of an *unamiable* character.

To Rev. J. H. Newman.

Eliot Place : January 21, 1839.

My dear Newman,—I am very glad to hear what you say generally about the going on of things ; certainly one cannot go anywhere without hearing of the 'Oxford Tract party,' &c. I could scarcely write a letter in the club-room the other day, so much was my attention distracted by two men who were discussing you—and you seem by degrees to be taking possession even of the public streets; at least the last time I crossed St. Paul's Churchyard I heard the words 'Newmanite' and 'Puseyite' (a new and sonorous compound) from two passers-by, who were talking very intently. I hear people talk of the desirableness of some systematic, or at least compendious, statement of what you really do teach. What regard is due to the complainants I scarce do know. They were *elderly* people, and more or less Establishmentarians, and certainly within my own experience hereabouts I should say—what one has seen elsewhere—that the rising generation are our hope: elderly people believe newspapers and periodicals; which is a great disadvantage. Wood seems sanguine, as does the redoubtable Nathaniel Goldsmid, and one or two other *youngers*—contrariwise certainly the elders.

I am sorry to hear the bishops join the Cranmer business,[1] and, I must say, sorry also that they make it a church not a monument, as the farther they went in identifying it with Cranmer, the more intelligible was the ground that one could take against them.

If you want to see a fresh crime of Cranmer's, look at the comment with which he accompanies his signature to certain answers to certain questions on doctrinal points, submitted by Henry VIII. to the bishops and learned men of the Church. Also look at the Bishop of London's (I believe Bonner's) answer to the first question, on the definition of a sacrament (Burnet, vol. i. part 2, pp. 314 and 367). I am *exceedingly* glad you speak so highly of Gladstone. What do you think of the following glee (which I have just fallen foul of) as a compendium of the 1688 $\mathring{\eta}\theta os$?

> Let's live good honest lives,
> And make much of our wives,
> And since all flesh is grass
> Let's merrily drink our glass.
> God bless our noble King, what need we fear the Pope,
> the Jesuits, Jews and Turks?
> For we defy the Devil and all his works.

---

[1] The Martyrs' Memorial at Oxford. (This letter is in answer to one from Newman of January 14, which is printed in *Letters and Correspondence*, ii. 279).

To Rev. J. H. Newman.

Eliot Place: September 13, 1839.

My dear Newman,—Edward tells me that you purposed writing to me soon, so I take the initiative in order to bring your good intentions to a point. I have not much satisfactory to say concerning myself, having spent my time in a very pleasant idleness at H. Wilberforce's and up the Seine with my sister.

At Rouen, which was our farthest point, I was a good deal pleased and amused with a French priest, almoner of a hospital, to whom H. W. introduced me. H. W. had told me that he was a simple, unlearned, amiable kind of man who confined himself to his duties, but from his intercourse with him (H. W.) and Shadwell (a friend of ours) he has obviously conceived a hope that he may be in his little way instrumental in the great work which he considers going on in England. And accordingly I found him with the end of his tongue thoroughly furnished with all the quips and quirks, and sly questions, which could be launched against an Anglican, and obviously unable to resist any opportunity of bringing them out. He evidently liked H. W. very much; confessed, as he said, a 'faible pour M. Wilberforce,' but could not resist cuts at him as a family man; wanted to know whether we had not a kind of hereditary priesthood in England; observed in showing us his vestments that Madame W. must have regretted much the disuse of them, 'she would have been very well pleased to see her husband in these fine dresses;' was constantly observing, ' *We*, who are *not* reformed, who are *behind* the rest of the world, have preserved this custom,' or 'take a good deal of care about these little things,' as he was showing off vestments, chapels, and everything else that he thought by any possibility could captivate us. He kept Wilberforce's and Shadwell's cards with great care, because they would be valuable when the said W. and S.

turned Catholic; was anxious I should do so, urging the authority of Marshal Turenne, who was converted by Bossuet's Exposition, which he accordingly gave me; asked whether there were no Catholic priests in England whom I could consult; cross-examined me to elicit the uncertainty of the Church of England teaching; argued in (I must say) rather a light, controversial, skin-deep way about the Eucharist, and floored me most uncommonly by asking me whether I could in my conscience say that I had no doubts in my heart about my own Church being right; my sister said *she* had none, but he did not seem inclined to accept that as an answer, and the consequence was that a certain uncomfortable silence, which I kept, must have considerably strengthened an impression (much to be deplored, but which certainly existed in his mind) that the English Church had not the strongest conceivable hold on the mind of her children. I should like much to send him Hope; he is particularly anxious that all of us should send him 'beaucoup de vos amis.' He tells me I am not far from the kingdom of Heaven, as, I hear, he told Shadwell; but obviously his sympathies are entirely, at present, with individuals, not with our Church. And I take discredit to myself for not having properly stuck up for my Mother. One thing is, it is so difficult to get beyond commonplaces, unless you understand a language much better than I do French.

I (who like my friends' wives, though 'presbyterae') passed a very pleasant time with H. W., who seems to me flourishing. He really keeps his edge very sharp, in spite of the country tendencies that you complain of.

Did you talk over with Wilson, when at Hursley, his notion of being a candidate for the Mastership of Acland's London Normal School, and the opposition to him *as curate of Keble's*, raised by him of London, and Wood's gentlemanly and quiet request (at the Board) that, for the convenience of all proscribed parties, a definite line of exclusion might be drawn, to which the authorities declined acceding?

Has your long vacation produced anything besides Dionysius? However, you will tell me all about that; I shall *expect* to hear great things, for I think one's notions of other people's capabilities are much increased by one's own idleness.[5]

Ever yours affectionately,
FREDERIC ROGERS.

To Rev. J. H. Newman.

Eliot Place : September 16, 1839.

My dearest N.,—I did not calculate on eliciting such a pathetic apology as the exordium of your letter by my P.S. Another time I will write at the bottom 'this is a joke,' as I see you do, though I must say such exceeding caution seems to me more considerate than complimentary.

As you make an attack on me, let me tell you that your well-wishers here are all in the act of being extremely scandalised at reports which reach them (not through me) of your making yourself conspicuous by short trousers, worsted stockings, and bad gloves.—a kind of notoriety more befitting a Methodist preacher than an 'Anglo-Catholic' priest, and which those who have the onus upon them of defending or explaining all that you think yourself justified in doing have much right to complain of. If you can't mend in any other way, you must be compelled to wear wellingtons and straps.

I wish you would come here for a day or two, though I do not know that I have much to attract you : my playing sister is away, so you would not have any Beethoven, and I suspect everybody is out of town. Church has promised me a day or two before the vacation is over, and I would try and bring him up at the same time. Do try to pare an end off somebody's visit, and let me have it. I only limit myself to a day or two because I suppose it is hopeless to ask for more ; I hope you do not want to be told that nothing would give us greater pleasure than to have you with us for the rest of the vacation.

---

[5] Newman's answer, dated September 15, is printed in his *Letters and Correspondence*, ii. 285. In the course of it he says : ' You see, if things were to come to the worst, I should turn Brother of Charity in London—an object which, quite independently of any such perplexities, is growing on me.'

I don't wonder at what you say about 'brother of Charity.' It is a kind of thought that causes even me sometimes a certain unsubstantial fidgety aspiration, such as people have after those acts of self-denial from which circumstances seem most effectually to protect them. But what do you mean by 'things coming to the worst'? Ejectment from Oriel and St. Mary's, or the Triple Crown? Oibò! That you should be contemplating such contingencies! As to our ill-treatment of them, I do think they should remember that if we hanged, they burnt, and if we have married Bishops, they have had profligate Popes.

I must finish, as I am going to town to wish Henry Denison of All Souls' good-bye. He is going off with a younger brother to settle in New South Wales. Of all the birds in the air![6]

To Miss M. Rogers.

Oriel : October 30, 1839.

My dear Marian,—My occupations since I left home have been principally confined to accounts (which do not suggest any interesting topics) and certain necessary letters (which are much in the same predicament). The only thing which has happened to me lately which has not happened to me twenty times before, is that I have taken a lesson or two of Johnson in the art of *observing* (stars, that is), which I can fancy very interesting. It certainly is remarkable to see a star waddle across the field of a telescope, set to the right place half an hour before, exactly where and when you expected it ; and there is something exceedingly satisfactory in the wonderful accuracy with which you note down its proceedings. Johnson's two first observations told the same story within $\frac{1}{100}$ *of a second.* And my own first observation (on which I pride myself) I think verified itself to about $\frac{1}{10}$ of a second. Then there is a kind of tranquil punctuality about the observer's way of going on which is highly edifying. You get to appreciate such infinitely small fractions of time as a

---

[6] It was in answer to this letter that Newman wrote the letter, dated September 22 (*Letters and Correspondence*, ii. 286) about the article by Dr. Wiseman, containing the quotation from St. Augustine, 'Securus judicat orbis terrarum,' which, he says in the *Apologia*, so strongly affected him.

matter of course, you consider yourself as having 'plenty of time' to get yourself in order for an event which is to happen in 15 seconds, and this when being too late even by one second is irretrievable. Two things are absolutely necessary, never to be too late, and never to be in a hurry, and it is a decided object not to be many seconds too soon. I can't fancy any more magnificent practice for a fidgety person who wanted to be unfidgeted.

Oxford is very full of our friends, Johnson, Mozley, Hope, and Church being the principal, besides Newman.

. . . .

I hear Wilson will probably be settled in London, being likely to be nominated master of one of the National Society (Acland's) Training Schools for masters. It is a great act of self-devotion on his part going from Hursley to be a schoolmaster in London, and so I think he feels it, but I should think he would be uncommonly useful. I shall like to see him now and then. The Bishop of London objected to him as Keble's curate, and was only won over by the very high character Sir H. Oakeley gave of Wilson. It seems amusing that Sir H. Oakeley's good opinion should compensate for the guilt of a connexion with Keble.

I have been not a little amused since writing all the above at a regular pitched battle between a Roman Catholic priest, who has been picked up here by a good-natured friend of mine named Hamilton [7] (chaplain to Bishop Denison), and Palmer,[8] of whom you have heard from the Winters. Hamilton asked me to meet the Roman Catholic, and Palmer was of the party! After dinner the Roman Catholic set to, and Palmer in like manner. Strange to say, I seldom remember having laughed more, the two men were so unlike, and their modes of attack so very amusing. The Roman Catholic was as unfair as he could be, but he certainly gave Palmer one or two sharp shakings. He was a clever man, up with the particular points in question, and prepared to lie when he

---

[7] Walter Hamilton, who was in the remove above Frederic Rogers at Eton. At this time he was a Fellow of Merton and examining chaplain to Bishop Denison, whom he succeeded in 1854 as Bishop of Salisbury.

[8] William Palmer, brother of the late Lord Selborne. He afterwards joined the Church of Rome.

thought he would not be found out (as he was once), and every now and then coming a bit of eloquence, very much reminding me of Malan in his way of putting awkward questions, and sneering by implication at our deficiencies; Palmer, on the contrary, prosing away in a dry humorous way, with answers for *almost* everything sometimes grievously far-fetched, and when he had no answer simply resuming the thread of his discourse as if nothing had happened and flowing on again with equanimity. I am somewhat amused at *Hamilton's* having been the man to pick up the Papist, and that by a kind of accident.

You have probably not heard what you will be very sorry to hear, that Henry[9] goes after all to the West Indies. He starts on the 15th of November. I have just heard it from home.

Ever yours affectionately,
FREDERIC ROGERS.

To Miss S. Rogers.

Oriel : November 12, 1839.

My dear Sophy,—I duly sent off the music to Mrs. Keble, but forgot that your note was not in the parcel with the music, but elsewhere; your note therefore I sent by itself afterwards, crossing a note from Keble to acknowledge what *had* come, and to state that your note (which I had alluded to in a letter to him) had not. I will copy his sentence not because there is anything in it, but because I know people (and I suppose you) like particular acknowledgments. 'Let me now thank you and your sister most kindly in Charlotte's name and my own for the letter, music, and buckle, all of which were most acceptable in their kind; but there was no letter from Miss Rogers in the parcel which I think you gave us reason to expect; there was a slip of paper with a pattern for painted glass which we conjectured might have slipped in by mistake for the note. Shall I return it, and will your sister send her letter in exchange?'

---

[9] His brother, then in the Artillery.

I have set going here a little singing meeting with one of the young Aclands[1] and Anderdon (who is just up for his degree now) under the auspices of a certain Mr. Elvey[2] which I hope will get on into something. Two hours in the evening once a week to practise a little old sacred music. There has been some bad luck about our start, engagements interfering, &c., which (as Elvey is rather an odd-tempered gentleman, whom I particularly want to talk over) I somewhat regret. But we shall see what we shall see.

Oxford is full of friends. Acland[3] is up, though not at this moment, else I should get him to frank this. Two of our friends (Pattison and Christie by name) have just got Fellowships at different colleges, and altogether things are very pleasant; only perhaps rather *too many* engagements. We have all sorts of queer people coming here now, having got rid of the Papist; we have had a Syrian Christian from Beyrout, interpreter to the Persian princes, dining about here. He dined with Newman one day in his fez &c., very much indeed to the amusement of the undergraduates. Unluckily, just as he was coming we heard reports of his being a great scamp, which materially lessened our satisfaction at his presence, particularly by making us anxious about our silver spoons. If it had not been for this report, which I really believe was only the malice of some missionary, he would have been a great lion. He talked English as grammatically and far more fluently than I can, and was only too happy to hold forth about the Syrian Church, which certainly from his account is terribly bullied. Whenever any Christian power displeases the Grand Turk he bastinadoes all the bishops, priests, and deacons in his dominions.

I must finish, as I have to go to one of Newman's soirées and am late. Love to all.

Your affectionate brother,
FREDERIC ROGERS.

[1] The present Sir Henry Acland and a younger brother.
[2] The well-known composer, Sir George Elvey.
[3] The present Sir Thomas Acland, at that time M.P. for West Somerset.

To Rev. J. H. Newman.
January 21, 1840.

My dear Newman,—It seems almost absurd to write to you now, as I shall see you on Saturday, but I do not like to come back without having thanked you for your letter, which was a most exceeding relief to me.

I have just seen Wood for the first time, after many ineffectual attempts: he is contemplating a little account of *Endowments* (Monasteries, Colleges, Tithes, Hospitals) for the Christian Knowledge Society, to be one of a set of books which Hope is busying himself about, in favour of which he has given up Churton's 'Englishman's Library.'

I see a popular way of speaking is beginning to be that 'without agreeing with the Oxford people, it must be allowed they have done good hitherto.' A young clergyman was saying that, in the country, people who talked in that way were altering their practice in a way that 'we town people' had no notion of, and he spoke of a *fox-hunting* style of clergyman, who, 'without any agreement with the Oxford Tracts,' had been setting up services on Saints' days and other days. He himself, he said, was on the point of taking a curacy under a friend of his, but found to his amazement that he would involve himself in *three* daily services, one at 6 o'clock in the morning, and, not liking either to go on with this or to leave it off, receded.

I met Blakesley the other day. I see the *intellectual* thing at Cambridge is to despise exceedingly the 'vulgar outcry' about Froude, and to admire him as a phenomenon with more or fewer reservations (professing to be more refined than those of the populace) according to the individual. As if they and Froude were clever enough to understand one another, and to have a kind of communion on the basis of intellect, however they might differ. James Spedding, Froude's cousin, seems an exception to this liberal way of viewing things, which Blakesley exceedingly wonders at, because 'Spedding is a man of so remarkably *catholic* a mind, a man who can understand and be intimate with men from whom he differs in every single article of opinion.' I suggested that Froude could make himself disagreeable on occasions, but could not make Blakesley view it as a reality, that though most fascinating in general, he might have chosen to be otherwise to Spedding. I myself should scarcely have expected it, for Spedding is, I should think, anything but a random talker, indeed (whether for good or for bad) a remarkably calm-sighted, thoughtful, observant kind of man—I mean I should have expected F. to have been rather *distant* than severe or hostile to him.

The House of Commons seems with Sir R. Peel at their head to have got into a most uncommon scrape with the Judges; among lawyers I fancy there can scarce be said to be two opinions, and Follett, who *was* the great authority on the Commons' side, has changed his opinion on looking at the cases.[4] I see very few people, but can scarce make out how so little excitement is felt about this, or about the Chartists. The prospect of being without tea seems to me what principally affects people of all the various political subjects going.

To Rev. J. H. Newman.

Eliot Place: June 14, 1840.

My dear Newman,—I don't know that I have much reason for writing except to inform you of the fact that I am come back to England, and hope to set to work in earnest on Bentham No. 2. I suppose you do not expect it for this next number.[5]

I consider myself to have had a very successful fortnight abroad, almost entirely occupied however in looking at scenery, Cologne and Mayence Cathedrals being the only ecclesiastical things which we saw.

I came across one Roman Catholic priest with whom I

---

[4] A Mr. Stockdale had prosecuted Messrs. Hansard for publishing a libel in the Parliamentary Debates and had obtained damages in the Court of Queen's Bench. Sir R. Peel joined with Lord John Russell in treating it as a matter of Privilege, and passed a motion committing the sheriffs who had levied damages upon Hansard. [See *Greville Memoirs*, 2nd part, i. 257.]

[5] Of the *British Critic*, which Newman edited from 1838 to 1841.

had some conversation on a railroad. We got as far as a little skirmishing just in the old style; he repeated Malais's jeers against Henry VIII.'s spoliations, and I the natural retort of the desecrated churches in France. He had told me that he was travelling for amusement, and I had told him to come to England; he said he travelled in *Catholic* countries, I said *we* called ourselves Catholic; he asked how it was then that we had not decorations in our churches, which led to Henry VIII., &c. I told him I would show him some churches *bien soignées* in Oxford if he would come there, on which he asked if there were not some professors there who ' se rapprochent à la religion Catholique ;' I replied rather quickly ' Ils la tiennent, Monsieur,' on which he closed the conversation with an impatient ' Augh,' as if it really were too bad that a person of education should persevere in talking such nonsense.

The Archbishop of Cologne's business people consider as likely to be settled, the Archbishop not returning to his diocese, and Rome winking at the mixed marriages. A Frenchman (who seemed to me a raff) told me that the plan in France was for the marrying parties (or party) to give the promise required by the Church (that children of *both* sexes should be brought up as Catholics) *verbally*, with which the clergy were satisfied; then, when children made their appearance, the promise was broken without redress, as the law (if appealed to) will enforce its own general rule, unless a *written* promise can be produced to the contrary : that rule being that males follow the father, and females the mother. The clergy, he said, did not much like this, but 'faisaient bonne mine à un mauvais jeu,' or some such phrase.

CHAPTER III

Winter at Rome.   Relinquishment of Oxford Life.

In the autumn of 1840 he went to Italy with James Hope (afterward Hope-Scott). They remained there—principally at Rome—through the winter, and returned to England in May 1841. Both the friends had desired, among other objects of travel, to make themselves in some degree acquainted with the organisation and management of the Roman Church. Whatever the result to Mr. Hope (who joined the Roman Church some years later), the effect on Frederic Rogers was to strengthen his anti-Roman convictions. On his return to Oxford he found the storm raging which had been raised by Tract 90. He was now divided by pronounced differences of opinion, not only from the more advanced men, such as Ward and Oakeley, but also from Newman himself, and did not in all points agree with the attitude adopted by the leaders of the more moderate and steadfast party in the movement, such as Keble, Pusey, and Sir G. Prevost. Those of whose opinions and actions in Oxford he now most approved were Church, who from this time to the end of his life was his closest and most intimate friend, and James Mozley. The result of this breaking of old ties was that, after two terms spent at Oxford, he settled to give up the University life, and to read law in London, taking advantage at the same time of a proposal that he should write leading articles for the ' Times.'

To Miss Rogers.
Oriel : July 2, 1840.

My dear Kate,—I have had young Walter with me again pressing me to write for his father even if I cannot edit, and suggesting the Opium Question for a few articles. This unattached way of doing things seems to me very feasible. . . . I almost think I shall try my hand. No one will know anything about the matter except my own private friends, and I can do just as much and as little as I please. Hope[1] wants me very much to go with him to Italy this winter. He goes for his health, and Newman will have it I ought to go for mine. It is tempting, as I cannot hope to have such a pleasant companion often (perhaps ever) again. And he would have capital introductions and all my own tastes. I doubt about leaving the Treasurership [at Oriel], about having quite money enough, and whether after all my health would be sufficiently benefited to give me an honest excuse for going. Perhaps by these articles I might turn a penny or two which would help me. I should like to hear what all you think of it.

Yours very affectionately,

FREDERIC ROGERS.

To Edward Rogers, Esq.

Lyons, Hôtel du Nord : November 3, 1840.

My dear Edward,—I told you I should give you a line from Lyons, where I am shut in by rain. I have been somewhat unlucky in my journey here, as I was rather in my crossing from Southampton. Paris was prosperous enough, as I have duly written home. I found the Châlons diligence started 12 hours later than I wished, and so had to take the Nevers and Moulins road to Lyons, travelling 36 hours to Moulins, there sleeping, passing Sunday, and on Sunday evening at 9 o'clock starting again, intending to get to Lyons in about 20 odd hours. I hear, however, somewhat startling accounts of the floods consequent upon the last few days of heavy rain in all the hilly country between Moulins and Lyons (part of which is very pretty, or more). As we got on, these reports began to increase in vigour ; people 'did not recollect the water so high since 1812 ;' 'at a place called Pont Charlan the water was 4 or 5 feet deep over the road,' &c. &c. ; however, we

---

[1] James Hope, afterwards Hope Scott of Abbotsford.

passed the '4 foot' boldly and found it not much over the axles, and we hoped that all would be equally manageable (we were to arrive at Lyons after 24 hours' travelling at 11 o'clock and there sleep); however, the reports which met us became more and more threatening, the faubourg between us and Lyons was 'impassable, under water, houses going, 34 bodies picked up of people drowned by the inundation.' At the *relais* before we got to Lyons we heard pretty much the state of the case. First, the Rhone had risen tremendously and carried away all sorts of things that are too near it or too low, manufactories and houses, stopping up all straight communication with Lyons on the Italian side (as some English travellers told us at the *relais* who had been stopped for some time), then the Rhone subsided and people began to think themselves quit, but in the night the Saône rose twice as high and did most tremendous havoc; the houses are of mud, so that the river had nothing to do but eat away for a short time at the foundations and down the whole came, and, as it was unexpected, I fear very many lives were lost. The woman of the house was in a great state of fright about a son of hers who had a manufactory near the banks of the Saône. However, we went on as close to Lyons as we could, and about 12 o'clock arrived within a mile or two with nothing between us and it but this suburb (Vaize), which was under water and quite impassable, and no way but a roundabout one, which I walked when it became light. It would have been madness for a diligence to attempt it at night. So we stopped (according to orders which had met the *conducteur*) at a little auberge for the night. Beds, of course, there were none, and every one was rushing from their houses down below in terror and filling up everything; one woman came in who had been confined not 24 hours; what they did with her I don't know; I proposed making a kind of couch on a billiard table which was in the room, and as that was not done I suppose something better was. A man gave us an account, which I only half understood, of his having been let down through a window and got off, but having heard others who could not be carried off crying out 'Oh! ça coule, ça coule' (meaning the house was falling). One man had seen 26 houses go at once another 18. This went on, people coming in and out for most of the night (perhaps all) till I went to sleep (*taliter qualiter*) in the diligence, and the next morning as I walked in with two Frenchmen by the roundabout way I saw what had been a house (the flooring and the stairs or rather steps being all that betrayed much of its origin) washed through the bridge under my feet. All the steamboats had of course been discontinued; it is all that the water can do by itself to get under some of the bridges, and besides people say steamers would be washed clear away into the country, and if they could get down safe, getting up again would be quite out of the question. And now (at least three hours ago) they told me the water was still rising, and, as the rain goes on hard, one does not see what chance there is of its ceasing to rise.

I have had a letter from Hope, who will be at Milan till the 10th. I shall start hence over Mount Cenis to Turin by *malle-poste* to-morrow morning at 5 o'clock, and they profess that forty-two hours (I suppose really about forty-eight or fifty) will take us to Turin. Then I shall stop a day and night to rest and look about me, spend the Sunday probably at Vercelli, Novara, or some such place, and on Monday on to Milan, where you had better direct to me until further orders at Reichman's Hotel.

I have just been to the *table d'hôte* and out to do divers things and look about me. I never saw such an uncomfortable affair. The streets are narrow and very high; I counted nine stories once in a new house, very dirty and smoky-looking. Then there is a drizzle, occasionally increasing into hard rain, and with all this all the streets leading to the Saône are crowded with people walking about in a vague kind of way, with dripping umbrellas; then at the end of each street is an actual crowd watching the advance of the water up the street. I stood in one crowd for some little time in a street which did not lead direct to the Saône, but into another parallel to the river. How many streets there were between me and the Saône I don't know, but I expect more than one; and yet the water was advancing up the street where I stood in pulses at about half a minute's distance (I should guess), each pulse advancing perhaps a foot and a half farther than the one before it. It was very hopeless wandering about, as really I never knew when I should or should not be intercepted by a flooded street. Once or twice I was obliged to turn back when I thought I had got into the middle of the town and fairly turned the flank of the water. At a church door I saw a crowd of people reading a Proclamation, or at least a letter to his Curés from the Archbishop, telling them to use, till November 15, a form of Mass before commanded, adding the prayer 'ad compescendam aquarum inundationem,' to come to an understanding with the Mayor about subscriptions and covering for those who were out of their houses, offering his own 'salles de l'Archevêché' for the effects of those who wanted to bestow them somewhere, and telling them to bid their parishioners implore the succour of her whom the Church called the 'Consolatrice des affligés,' and who had so often benefited the city of Lyons. The people, I thought, seemed pleased with it. Since I began my letter a bridge has gone, but I could not get near it, nor indeed near the Saône, without more trouble and paddling than I liked. It is really a frightful thing to think of the *thousands* that are thrown clean out into the streets, unless so far as their neighbours house them, for fear their houses should fall on their heads. I have written as fast as I can write and cannot read over (candle-light), so I dare say there are mistakes. You may as well send it to Church with my compliments. He is a gossiping fellow who will be edified by it; as for Newman, he would say I was practising for reporter to a newspaper.

Ever yours affectionately,
FREDERIC ROGERS.

Extract from a fragment of journal written at Milan in November 1840:

Friday, November 13.—We went to Manzoni's[2] at half-past ten; found Vitali[3] who says he sees him every morning. He

---

[2] Manzoni was living close to Milan. He had written *I Promessi Sposi* about thirteen years before. Lord Blachford writes elsewhere: 'A gentle, refined, sensitive purity and earnestness is what remains in my memory of him.'

[3] Ambrogio Vitali, Secretary to the Archbishop of Milan. His brother Giuseppe was a Professor at Monza.

made us seat ourselves, and observed, laughing, 'You see, I order about here as if it were in my own house.' He went in to tell Manzoni, who came out and almost immediately began controversy, as we had expected. His breakfast came in, coffee and bread, which he took at a table a little removed from us, going on with the conversation, with one or two interruptions which were despatched pretty summarily. Part of his argument was: The Gospel is not only for men of leisure and acquirement, but for the poor. Now, a peasant, whose allegiance the English and Roman Church each claim, can say to the English, 'You confess there was a time (previous to the Reformation), when you held what you now contradict. You say you were wrong. How then can you ask me to follow your teaching implicitly? God commands me to have an assurance, a full undoubting faith in what I hold. I cannot have this, except as based on an infallible guide.'

He said he felt a kind of 'effroi' at reading some account of the Queen of England's coronation oath, that the doctrine of Transubstantiation was abominable, &c. 'On what ground could a young girl pretend to anathematise with such certainty the whole Catholic Church? Was it on the strength of her own individual judgment, or on the authority of a Church which did not pretend to be unerring?'

Hope said that if Roman Catholics were to convince us they must first study us. Manzoni said he himself was certainly ignorant on these points, but it must be remembered that Roman Catholic controversialists would often appear less learned than they were, from avoiding details purposely, as knowing that the question was one of principles and therefore declining any challenge to descend from them.

He spoke of the appointment of French bishops as wonderfully ordered for good, though in the hands of an infidel government.

He said: 'If you have to do with an atheist, you cannot make him see proof of God in all that you regard as such; he has an answer for all your positive arguments. So it is with the Church. She cannot be proved by argument; she proves herself by her appearance; and then, when objections are brought against her, seeing they are intrinsically false and unreasonable, they can be answered by reason. This perception of the Church and all truth God gives; but'—in answer to an objection of Hope's—'discussion is still useful to excite interest and remove prejudice.'

Hope observed that Manzoni might have this faith in the Roman Catholic Church's infallibility from early education; but, for us, we wanted positive evidence. Manzoni interrupted him seriously: 'Stop: let me speak for myself. I was for many years of my life (I pray God to pardon me for it) in utter infidelity, nay, anxious to make proselytes. I hated the Church, and had some liking for Protestantism, as its enemy.' He then told how he began reading Protestant controversies with Rome, and was convinced 'by her majestic attitude' of her truth. Hope said, to speak frankly, that fact explained to him the stress which Manzoni laid on the necessity of an infallible authority, as the expression of an unnatural craving and the consequence of a disordered state of mind; and that he had another Roman Catholic friend whose history was the same, and who argued in the same way. Manzoni replied: 'There is then a living man in this case, whose name I know not, besides myself. Let me add another—St. Augustine.' As we took our leave he said: 'I trust it is God that is working in you. You are not like Protestants who deny that they have a Mother. You are only bewildered and do not know who your Mother is.'

On Sunday we went to Manzoni again. I only remember disjointed things which he said, partly because people came in—among others Grossi, the author of 'Visconti.' Manzoni talked of priests as often not well instructed because they cease reading when they are employed in their parishes; but a priest is regarded as a gentleman whatever his father may be; hence the poorer classes are anxious to have a son a priest, to raise the family; but for the very poor the education is too expensive. The Church, he thought, wanted a fresh Order; the old Orders had lost their force; even in the Jesuits he did not see any elements of great power.

He spoke of reform in the Italian language, a hobby of his, and observed that we 'had paramount authority in

London'! which ruled pronunciation, whereas in Italy no state would concede the supremacy to another; the superiority of Tuscan pronunciation was now contested. He spoke of Rosmini (whom he was anxious we should meet) as a 'forte tête.' 'His philosophy has too much pretension, but his demolition of other philosophies is good.' This Manzoni seemed to think was all that philosophy could do—demolish falsehood.

He recurred to doctrinal questions and said that what the Pope pronounced he accepted, because he believed it *true*, the Pope being infallible, but, as I understood, he would not on a point of doctrine shrink from writing against or submit to be silenced by his Bishop, any more than by any other man, or suspend his judgment out of respect for him. 'Our duty is to promulgate what we believe to be truth, and nothing is to stop us but evidence against it. The Pope's voice, however, is conclusive.'

To Miss S. Rogers.

Genoa : November 26, 1840.

Here I am at Genoa—beginning to recover my temper after a most offensive journey from Milan in M. Bonafous's diligence, said diligence having performed the journey (about 100 miles) in 40 hours, stopping at a dirty frontier village (25 miles from Milan) 9 hours, to wait for its corresponding diligence to come up, we all this time being $1\frac{1}{2}$ miles from Pavia and about seven from a most beautiful Chartreuse which I could easily have seen if I had grasped that we were to wait half the time which we did. And this after having made us start at 4 o'clock in the morning, and arriving at the said frontier at 10 o'clock in the morning. I started by diligence, leaving Hope to follow with a sick friend (I am afraid consumptive) in his carriage, so as to see Genoa before he comes up and be ready to start with him forthwith for Leghorn. I expect him to-morrow evening

I don't think much happened at Milan after my last letter. We called again on the Vitalis, of whom the sick one is particularly anxious we should turn Romanists. He was confined to his bed and I should be afraid was not likely to get better. He took our hands one after another and begged us quite pathetically to make ' un pas en avance '—' je mourrais content.' We called in the evening and found his brother sitting with a couple of clerical friends and Grossi the author of ' Visconti,' who left as we came in ; and a very comfortable talk we had with these same black-frocked people concerning matters in general, most of them plain, good, straightforward people. I am much surprised to find they all read Byron. I gave one of them (who has given me Manzoni's hymns) Keble's ' Christian Year,' to improve his notions. We are going to send them Newman's ' Romanism ' and the ' Tracts for the Times ' to crack their teeth upon. Most of them are Ultramontanes, *i.e.* hold the strongest views of the Pope's own private authority, except one jolly comfortable Professor of Dogmatical Theology at the Seminary, who wanted Hope to send him Paley's and all other Evidences he could lay his hands on, and who settled Ultramontanism in a most summary way ; little to the edification of the Vitalis who were present ; finally asserting that they only held these opinions as a theory, did not realise them, and if a case were to arise when the Pope decided, and the body of the Church hesitated to accept his decision, they (the Ultramontanes) would not act up to their own principles, but would suspend their own judgment too. The professors of the Seminary have a billiard table, at which he was engaged when we called ; and N.B., he is the only Italian who has offered us anything to eat or drink, *videlicet* ' un café.'

We saw Manzoni once again, and while we were there Grossi dropped in, whose manner I liked much. If I had stayed at Milan I should have tried to get really acquainted with him. I have never felt my bad French such an impediment as since I have been in Italy. It is all very well *tête à tête* to speak bad French and boggle, but in a company of clever men who all speak with ease and fluency one must speak readily or not at all. They so decidedly think we are going to become Papists that I half feel as if I was sailing under false colours. However, if people will draw conclusions for themselves they must take the consequences.

I am beginning to fire off Italian in conversation (*tête à tête*) and comprehend tolerably when people speak to me slowly, but my own sentences are sadly apt to miss fire. Hope makes wonderful progress. I have not managed to make the most of my time here; have seen the three principal collections, mounted the heights and gone a little way out to sea, and the principal churches, but none thoroughly—the days are sadly short and I don't get up early enough.

We start to-morrow evening for Città Vecchia, staying the greater part of the Sunday at Leghorn but starting again in the evening. Watson, Hope's sick friend, is a former ward of his father's, without father or mother, and it is plainly a great object with him to get to the warm part of Italy (which this is not) immediately, which makes us press to Rome rather faster than we should otherwise. As far as my own personal liking goes, I am glad of this, as I want to get settled.

I am astonished to find how many Americans are to be met. I met a third, a sculptor, yesterday morning. All that travel seem 'Whigs,' which is in fact the kind of mercantile aristocracy which is growing up, and is the American Conservative. . . . Hope and I take some credit to ourselves for having spent some days (at least the greater part of them) in the Ambrosian library collating for Pusey a MS. of a treatise of Tertullian, which we have satisfactorily finished, creating, I hope, in the Italians a creditable notion of Oxford industry, seeing we flatter ourselves we knocked it off in businesslike style. Dreadfully dull work, amounting principally to noting down all the errors of a stupid copyist. However, I rejoice to have done *one* useful thing here.

To Mrs. Rogers.

Rome, 60 Piazza Barberini: December 16, 1840.

To-day I have had a pleasant day, in spite of the weather. I went with Richmond [4] to a Convent of St. Onofrio where Tasso died, and of which I believe he was *almost* a

[4] Mr. George Richmond, R.A.

member, which seems to me an uncommonly interesting place, though I can scarce tell why. There are some beautiful frescoes by a painter whose name I never heard till I came here, but who seems to me (for devotional subjects) as beautiful as almost anything I ever saw, by name Pinturicchio, a fellow pupil with Raffaelle of Perugino. Almost all his pictures that I have seen are of the Virgin, and much alike and of the old stiff style, but all of them sweetness and purity itself. Then I went with Richmond and his brother, and a Christ Church man, by name Ruskin, again to the Vatican, and really enjoyed it; we did not attempt to look at more than two or three of Raphael's frescoes, 'Heliodorus,' 'The School of Athens,' 'The Dispute of the Sacrament' (which perhaps you don't know), and scarce anything else. Richmond was a very great help to understanding the merit of what I saw, and about these particular frescoes I do think I begin to feel as I ought; the tapestry (cartoons) and the loggia I still feel wonderfully unable to appreciate. Soon after I got back, a certain Dr. Baines, a great man about Bath, of whom you may have heard, came to call on Hope, and finding me only, came in, and I had a pleasant talk with him for a short time. I hear he has given offence to the Propaganda by what he has done in England, and is kept here by them, much to his own inconvenience. He calls himself on his card Vescovo di Siga, but really is coming, or rather has been, with episcopal authority to England, claiming jurisdiction (among other places) over part of what the Pope calls *his* diocese, Salisbury. He is smooth, as many of the English Roman Catholics seem to be. He said the Pope had told him of a variety of fine things that Mehmet Ali was sending him, some mummies and some 15 or 20 alabaster columns for St. Paul's, a new church being built about 1½ miles from Rome, and for which the Emperor of Russia (though labouring under the Pope's indignation for taking some thousands of his subjects slap over from him to the Russian Church) is going to send an altar of malachite or at least malachite for an altar.

December 17.

I found my letter getting so very dull last night, that I left off till I had something more to say. To-day I went at half-past nine o'clock to see two Cardinals instituted, and I cannot say much for the process. It certainly did not impress one with much sense of the *majesty* of Roman Catholicism. We first walked into the Consistory, where there was a large assortment of priests, Englishmen and women, and Swiss guard, and then took as good a place as we could get, and waited till the Cardinals dropped in, which they did one by one, each with his Chaplain, who sat himself down at the Cardinal's feet, and an usher, who arranged for him his great violet-coloured silk train. Some of them were striking-looking men, but scarce any, perhaps not more than two or three of those whose faces I saw, men who gave one the notion of being what a cardinal ought to be. Presently we heard some hymn being (well) sung outside, and in came the two new Cardinals, who had (I should say) been half admitted on Monday, and only had now to receive the hat. The Pope[5] had just come and sat himself down in his throne, in a great gold tissue mitre (not triple crown) and wrapped up in a rich crimson and gold mantle. All the Cardinals kissed hands, and bowed themselves back to their places, their chaplains performing genuflexions to the Pope, just as they do to the altar. Then, as aforesaid, the new Cardinals came, kissed first, the Pope's foot, then his hand, then his cheek. Then they went round kissing all their brother Cardinals on each side of their faces, or at least making as if they did; an operation which seemed very much to amuse all parties. I was standing close behind the Cardinals' seats, like a footman at dinner, within arm's length of their red caps, so that I had a good sight of this process. The new Cardinals generally seemed to have something pleasant to say to their senior friends; I could have fancied they took that opportunity of thanking their friends for their good offices. However that may have been, there was generally a laugh about the matter. Then they went out, and a set of gentlemen in dresses I did not understand presented a petition in Latin for the canonisation of somebody, which occupied the time till they came back. Then (we are informed by a Monsignore Baggs[6] to whom we

[5] Pope Gregory XVI.
[6] Monsignore Baggs was head of the English College at Rome.

were introduced) it was referred to the Committee of Rites to investigate the evidence for the miracles alleged to have been performed, which are always a necessary preliminary to canonisation. Then they came back with singing (I think) again, and the Pope placed the hat on each of their heads successively, with a form not unlike our form of conferring degrees. And then all parties dispersed with singing again. Hope was excessively disgusted at the whole affair. I not much, because I did not expect much, but he had been struck by a conversation he had with Overbeck the painter, an able, excellent man and enthusiastic Romanist (converted from Protestantism), who had put before him a grand pictorial view of His Holiness's acts, contrasting his power with the divided helpless state of Protestant Churches. 'An old man sitting in the Vatican writes ten lines upon a piece of parchment, and sends it forth, and all Christendom is moved' (meaning, I suppose, his allocution against the Emperor of Russia); and then all this pompous external parade of Swiss guard and purple gowns, with so very little appearance of seriousness or solemnity, was rather an unexpected commentary on Overbeck's little romance—particularly to Hope, who has an especial objection of his own to the mixture of temporal and spiritual.

We have got hold of an uncommonly nice Italian master named Armellini, full of fun. It is amusing to see how obviously he has been used to work up lazy people; his whole system of teaching presupposes a state of the most excessive indisposition to do anything in his pupil, and his great aim accordingly to hammer the rules of grammar into us in a way by 'which we shall not be *annojati.*' He is full of attacks on our countrymen and us (at a venture) for thinking nothing good but what is English, and is in fine a very nice clever merry little man. Hope, who *picks up* the language from all quarters very quickly, had used the word *arrangiato* in his exercise, a word perfectly understood hereabouts, with which A. found fault (as I had done before), and on Hope's asking whether it was not Italian told us, 'Si dica—si dica—ma non è Italiano, è lingua di Piazza di Spagna' (the place where the hotels and shops and English residents are).

I am going to engage the captain of the Swiss guard, simply to talk to me for an hour a day at the price of 3 pauls (about 1s. 6d.) an hour, by which I expect to do wonders. I should like to be able to talk Italian for the last month that I spend here. I have been to-day to look at a very magnificent church, *St. John Lateran*, and saw a list of relics which certainly petrified me. The list was in mosaic and very old, possibly 1,000 years; probably the church does not profess to possess them now. Not satisfied with St. John Baptist's camel's hair girdle, fragments of five barley loaves, and the table on which the last supper was eaten, they actually possess, in gold and olive mosaic, two phials of the blood and water that came from our Saviour's side; also the ark of the covenant, two tables of the Law, manna, and shewbread. The boy who showed the curiosities showed me a large piece of porphyry in the wall of the cloisters as the stone on which the soldiers cast lots for our Lord's vesture, and there was an inscription showing that it professed to be so; also a column of the Jewish temple split at the time of our Saviour's crucifixion and some columns with a slab on them professing to be exactly of His height.

On Saturday, in the evening, I go to Lady Davy's, a very good-natured person but not very wise, and fond of paying herself compliments, which thing always embarrasses me to such an extent that I can't get on with people who do it.

To Miss Rogers.

Rome, 60 Piazza Barberini : December 20, 1840.

Lady Davy, Hope's friend, is lively (or rather perhaps talks incessantly), very good-natured, clever in her way, and has lived among distinguished people, and, being established as a lady patroness of long standing at Rome, one meets pleasant people at her house, but, unfortunately, in the particular article of *sense* she is uncommonly lacking, at least as far as one sees by mere company talk. I fancy she is to introduce me to. Madame Potemkin, the Russian Ambassadress, who ' receives ' every Wednesday, and Hope tells me is a nice person.

I am getting to work pretty fairly at Italian, besides

Armellini twice a week; every morning I have a man to talk for an hour named Pfyffer, attached to the Pope's Swiss guard and a regular gossip. His family have been in the Papal guard for 200 years, and are descended from 'the great Ludovic' Pfyffer, who was general of the forces of Lucerne in the battle of something.[7] He gives a most miserable account of the parish clergy, even more in the country than in the city, as drunken &c., but praises much the Dominicans and *Capuchins* (mendicants), and only abuses the Jesuits (which he does handsomely) for being intriguing and ambitious and successful. He abuses also the Cardinals, but praises much a certain Cardinal Micara, a Capuchin, Bishop of Frascati, who continues all the rigour of a monastic life still, and has got his bishopric into very good order, but has so set against him the other Cardinals by his measures of reform that he now never appears at Rome, but confines himself to his own see, dining with the pupils in the seminary, performing his visitations on his mule, sleeping on a straw mattress, and castigating his clergy. We project a visit to him to look what manner of man he is. Hope does not get much out of his Jesuits, though he much likes the Father General, and has gone the length of asking him (1) how it is that the Jesuits have managed to bring down upon themselves such universal suspicion, and (2) whether it is not bad policy to give them all that bland manner and downcast look which is peculiar to them. The Father General answers: (1) 'Blessed are ye when men speak evil of you,' and (2) that courtesy and modesty are Christian virtues, and of the latter modesty of the eyes is a great part. They seem to be considered as the movers of almost all that goes on here. I think I mentioned that at the time of the cholera, when the other priests held back, they came forward and exposed themselves most brilliantly, being everywhere and doing everything.

We have seen several ceremonies, (1) conferring the hat

---

[7] This seems to refer to Colonel Pfiffer, Pfyffer, or Pfeiffer, surnamed 'Roi des Suisses,' born at Lucerne in 1530. He took service with the French and fought both in Piedmont and in France. He commanded, it is said, 6,000 Swiss in 1567, when he rescued Charles IX. and the Queen Mother at Meaux and convoyed them to Paris; and he fought at Jarnac and at Moncontour. Afterwards he went home to Lucerne and held various offices in the Confederation.

on two Cardinals, (2) consecrating of a Bishop (or at least part), (3) ordination of about one or two hundred men to the six other orders (Priest, Deacon, Sub-deacon, Acolyte, Reader, Door-keeper), and tonsure by the Bishop, (4) High Mass before the Pope at the Sistine Chapel, (5) a mass for the Princess Borghese, and English sermon in her honour by Dr. Baggs, head of the English College here, whom we know. I cannot say that their ceremonies impress me: they strike me as mere scenery. The music in the Sistine Chapel and the 'Dies Iræ' &c. in the Mass for the Princess Borghese were certainly very beautiful, but the whole affair was so decidedly by way of being a sight that it altogether left a very unsatisfactory impression on my mind. And so much are the Roman Catholic services intended to be looked at, not literally joined in, that a portable Latin [service book?] is a thing which is *not to be got in Rome.* The careless way in which Protestants crowd to see the sight is bad, and perhaps it is that in a great measure which prevents one from feeling the solemnity of what is going on, but I cannot help thinking that Roman Catholics do very much the same, and are practically (though not of course in theory) expected to do so; this, however, may be uncharitable. Certainly Rome strikes me as the least devotional of any Roman Catholic city I have been in. I do think if I wanted to stop my own self from turning Romanist, Rome is the place I should fix myself in.

I was a good deal amused the other day by going over a Carthusian Church (Santa Maria degli Angeli, constructed by Michel Angelo out of the old baths of Domitian) with one of the monks, a Frenchman named Father Bruno, evidently most proud, first of his order, which he said was the only one which had never had to be reformed, secondly of his convent, its pictures and relics (which were, for the most part, more unpretending, and had more appearance of genuineness than those at St. John Lateran), and thirdly of his own countrymen in the convent. It seems their rule is only to leave the walls of the convent once a week. This the Italian monks complained of as impracticable, and begged for dispensation accordingly; however, Father Bruno and five other French monks were sent for, who have kept the rules rigorously, to the no small triumph of the said Bruno. They have each three rooms, a small garden, and a fine airy cloister to walk in, with plenty of orange trees. I asked Father Bruno a question of Church's, whether private friendships were discouraged, an idea which he rather contemptuously repelled, telling me that his order did not perform any 'capuchinades,' and that all their penances and exercises were such as were plainly improving. But it turned out that their opportunities for private friendship are not very great, as they only meet (for purposes of conversation &c.) on Sundays (at least, so I understood) unless there was some peculiar reason, when they asked leave of the prior to see each other: their spiritual director, however, they might always see. They eat no meat, and often, as *e.g.* for the whole of Advent and Lent, have only one meal a day, and get up for two or three hours for service at midnight. Once there was a notion that the *maigre* diet was unwholesome, and the Pope thought of relaxing this rule, but they sent up a deputation of men between 80 and 120, the very sight of whom convinced him that no reform was necessary. Father Bruno says there are not to be found in the world such a set of healthy, long-lived men as the Carthusians. He himself is certainly a good portly specimen.

I wish you could see the servant we are condemned to, Maria by name, commonly called about the house 'Mariuccia.' Our padrona tells us she is given to drink, and certainly she never recollects any one thing we tell her by any chance, and then all we get on remonstrance is 'Ah, oggi abbi pazienza,' an expression which was supplicatory at first, but which is fast becoming admonitory, a piece of impertinence which moves my wrath; for though I know that patience is a great virtue, and an incapable servant is a capital exercise for it, still that is hardly the particular view of the case which one expects to have enforced on one by the criminal herself. I am to go to bed, so goodbye to you all. I hope you had a merry Christmas and will have a happy New Year. Love to all.

Ever your affectionate brother,
FREDERIC ROGERS.

P.S. I told you in my last that our padrona has been very

ill. She is now well again, and came into our room the other day to pay us her compliments, sat down and told us the history of her illness, which was an 'arrabbiatura' with a lodger, who she conceived had treated her ill, and she thought it fitting to be so 'arrabbiata' with him that it brought on a fever. Richmond tells us it is a recognised form of illness with Italians, and that all of them under such an infliction will tell you their case, and expect condolences and obliging inquiries, just as much as if they called it nervous depression or spleen.

To Miss M. Rogers.

Rome : December 31, 1840.

My dear Marian,—I suppose my letters from Rome have somewhat set your heart at rest about the present chance of our turning Romanists. However, we got into a scrape yesterday evening at Lady Davy's. Hope, who is a sharp ready fellow, but who has not in any degree read up the controversy, thought fit (for which I have not yet nearly forgiven him) to plunge himself, in full conclave, into a controversy with Bishop Baines on our very most vulnerable point, the formal correctness of the proceedings at the Reformation, a point at which the Roman Catholics have laboured a good deal just at present, and which Bishop Baines plainly had crammed. I was talking with Sir G. Clerk next to him, and to my horror I heard what was going on and somewhat weakly stopped for a moment to listen and in a very slight way joined. I don't consider that I made a mess of it as far as my share went, which was merely putting in a word here and there to stop a thrust of old Baines, but it had the effect of increasing the audience, which was bad, and I must say that Hope, who was the combatant, must have seemed, though he was never fairly floored, to have the worst of it, and left on the minds of the spectators the impression that 'Puseyism' could not defend itself against Popery. I had no pity on *him* at all, and, after listening for some little time, fairly burst through the ring and retreated, having, as Hope declares with very much indignation, been looking blue and green and black for half an hour before. He declares I used him abominably, showing all the world that I thought him floored, but 'Que diable allait-il faire dans cette galère?' May it be a lesson to him! Baines is a clever fellow, thoroughly fluent and courteous, knows exactly when he has made a point and hammers it in. I hope this is a sufficient expiation for a certain exultation which I confess we did feel over the spiritual director at Milan.

I think I told you of the Carthusian Convent I went over with Hope and my friend Father Bruno. I suppose it is quite the case that they live very austere lives, but the horrors of their continual *jours maigres* are somewhat softened to me by hearing from my friend Mr. Pfyffer that *turtle* was *allowed*, that it was part of the ordinary food, and that they kept a stock of turtle in a pond or something of the kind on the premises. Also I was a good deal interested by a Franciscan convent which I went over with a lay brother, who had narrowly missed being sent as missionary to Jerusalem, a nice fellow (not of the lower class) but, it appeared to me, rather ashamed of his religion, which was not so well.

I have been trying this morning to get out of my scandal-monger all that I can about the state of parties among the ecclesiastical authorities here, which is not very much. I expected to find that the division was one of political views, *i.e.* that some Cardinals might be more liberal or more severe in reforming, or more disposed to exert Church authority against Kings of Prussia and Czars of Russia than the rest, but from all I can make out the division of the conclave appears to be between the Genoese and the Roman Party; the contest in the next Papal election is considered to lie between a Cardinal Patrizzi, who is the candidate of the latter, and Franzoni of the former interest. The latter is now at the head of the Propaganda (which is worked by the Jesuits), and both are said to be *good* men, but neither clever. My friend—who is very anxious to see the Romans educated, streets improved, thievery and dirt put down, the country tilled, and so on—says neither of them is sharp enough, 'buonissimi, ma buoni per niente,' as *temporal* governors of Rome. He would like to see Cardinal Micara Pope, who from his Capuchin education has 'seen the world' down to the dregs, and would unite the requisites of being an honest man and being up to the rogues. However, he would please no party.* Austria, France, Spain, and Portugal have, it seems, a veto on the election of the Pope, which is exercised in a curious way. The Cardinals, each with a chaplain and a servant, are turned into the Pope's palace to elect a new one; the entrance (as I understand) is *walled* up, their dinner sent to them through a kind of turnstile, and no one allowed to speak to them except through a 'grille' and in the presence of witnesses; then each of these four Powers has a Cardinal in their confidence who has a list of the persons to be vetoed, and if on collecting the votes any one of the forbidden seems to be getting a majority of votes as it comes near the critical moment he puts in his veto and a fresh start is made. But if any candidate has once got his majority it is too late for the vetoist, and he is Pope in spite of Austria's or any one else's objection. So if a majority of Cardinals quite understand each other, it has happened that they have been very sharp in their proceedings and whipped out all their votes before the gentleman with the veto in his pocket knew what they were up to, and so got in their candidate, and left him with his nose in the air. I believe the present Cardinals bear a fair character, and a few of them are said to be very good men indeed. I have heard Mezzofanti, the Cardinal who can talk fifty-six languages like fifty-six natives, spoken of as a man who would give the very shirt off his back in alms. His first discovery of his own talent for languages was, it is said, owing to his vehement wish to be of use as confessor to the mixture of all nations which composed the French army in the North of Italy when he was a poor priest at Bologna. He had great offers to take him thence, but refused them all till the Pope commanded him to Rome. They say that except in that one point he is not a clever man. My paper is finished, so goodbye to you.

Yours affectionately,
F. R.

---

* Gregory XVI. did not die till 1846, when the contest lay between Cardinal Lambruschini and Cardinal Mastai Ferretti (Pius IX.).

To Rev. J. H. Newman.

Rome : January 16, 1841.

My dear Newman,—Very many thanks for your most acceptable letter, especially, as always, for what you say about yourself. I don't remember what I said against Rome which you think wrong; I hope it was nothing insolent, or flippant, or self-congratulatory. I must own however to a strong aversion from her present form, which has been growing on me ever since I have been here. It is a wretched thing to be travelling among foreign Churches with the feeling that one must see faults in them in order to justify our own (Anglican) position; and I know I have had that feeling about me very strongly, and I dare say it has made me say things more bitterly than I ought to have done, particularly, I am afraid, in letters I have written since yours. All I can say is, I have tried not to allow it to make me believe lies. It is a little cruel of you to talk in that quiet way about inserting my 'most merciless criticism' on Sewell, [9] whose explosion is certainly most amusing. I shall be anxious to know if he deigns to express any feeling about it; for you make me remorseful.

I am *very* sorry to hear what you say about Bowden's feeling the winter. Cannot he get away?

As to my own proceedings, I am sorry to say I am as idle as ever, and begin to give up all hopes of being anything better while I am here. However, the last two or three days have been more worth having than anything I have seen before here. Hope has got himself introduced to a certain priest named Pentini, who is concerned in an interesting system of *retraites* for the poorer classes and soldiers, of which he is to show us the whole history; and on Tuesday he took us over the building, and gave us a lecture upon their proceedings. They are a society of twelve priests, incorporated by the Pope, but quite independent, with twelve (or more) working men

---

[9] This alludes, apparently, to a scheme of Professor Sewell's for converting the Irish, of which Mr. Church had written him an account in a letter published in Dean Church's *Life and Letters*, p. 26.

(without authority) under them, who simply buy a house large enough to accommodate about seventy people, with beds, a kitchen, a chapel and oratory, lecture room, and yard to walk in; catch their seventy men, partly with, partly against their will, and then inflict upon them eight or nine days of preaching, silence, meagre diet, finishing with confession and communion. When we went through the house they had got some fifty or sixty soldiers in hand. They came, we were told, of their own free will; but those who would not come of their own free will were forced to come. It seemed to me from his account as if it were fairly part of the military discipline to send them all once in so many years. When they went out, a batch (*muta*) of townsmen were to come in; and so, Pentini said, about twelve or fifteen hundred people passed through their hands during the year, with, on the whole, the very best results. Sometimes, he told us, men were sent who were known to cherish certain evil intentions, in order to have them worked out of them; and he showed us a stiletto hidden in a pipe, which had been given up after a few days of their discipline by a man who had been sent to them as known to be planning revenge on another. The society was self-elected, with no necessary connexion with the parochial system, and each '*muta*' required seven priests to manage it, the whole being divided into four roomfuls, and none ever left alone. Pentini himself seems a thoroughly earnest simple-hearted little man, apparently anxious to show everything, from the firm faith he has in its excellence; so I hope we shall see a good deal there.

Also I have been much amused at a dinner which we had at a convent of Franciscans at Albano, under the guidance of a certain tame deacon who is in Hope's employ, and whom I confess I respect as little as well may be, he being a regular 'Graeculus esuriens,' who professes himself ready to spend 'even his life' in Hope's service, and whom the said Hope has been obliged to prohibit from lying on his behalf, the man urging that profitable as well as jocose lies, 'bugie avvantaggiose,' are only venial sins, and therefore not to be accounted of. He 'fouls his own nest,' like Pugin, not a little. I can't make up my mind whether to be civil or rude to him; so alternate between the two, and catch it from my conscience both ways.

However, such as he is, he took us to Albano, and got us the above-mentioned dinner, and a very respectable one it was: we dined in the refectory, sitting all round the room with our backs to the wall. Three plates of meat (one being added on account of a feast-day), soup, cheese, and fruit. I can't say much for their polish or devotion (at grace), but they seemed to be good-humoured, and to be good friends with one another, and it was quite edifying to see the energy with which the whole convent set to work, when they had finished their own dinner, trying to make one or two pet cats jump for the remainder; the said cats, however, utterly neglecting the whole set of them in favour of one very dirty old lay brother, apparently the porter, to the infinite amusement of the unsuccessful aspirants.

To Mrs. Rogers.

Rome: January 26, 1841.

My dear Mother,—I think of leaving this place on February 25, going slowly to Florence by *Terni*, Perugia, Lake Thrasymene, Spoleto, and Arezzo, staying ten days or a fortnight at Florence, then a day at Pisa, then home by the Cornice road through Genoa (without stopping), Nice, Avignon, up the Rhone and down the Seine, and home, I hope, so as to spend Passion Week with you.

Richmond has just started back for England, to my grief, as I have not seen near as much in his company as I should have wished, especially in and about the Vatican. However, I hope to renew our acquaintance in London, and I shall get him down to Blackheath and make him give Kate some advice. I still have a few great sights in Rome unseen, but I think I have now *nearly* gone through all after a fashion and have before me principally the pleasant part of *revisiting* in Rome, and making a few excursions to the neighbourhood.

Yesterday, Mr. Leslie Melville took us to call on Waterton the naturalist, of South American crocodile reputation He showed us his stuffed birds, both finished and in hand. Hope asked about his terrible South American poison, whether it would kill cold-blooded animals. He said it would kill turtles, which are the animals most tenacious of life that he knew: 'Why, sir, there was a turtle that I had skinned and taken out his inside, and put in the glass eyes, and steeped him in corrosive sublimate several hours; Lord, sir, the next morning the animal bit my finger.' Also I was much amused at a history he gave me of his having gone into the Jesuits' church 'to say a few prayers' (he is, as he says, 'a good deal addicted to Popery,' *i.e.* the most thorough-going Roman Catholic in Rome), he put down his hat and went through his devotions, but found, when he rose, that a fellow had carried off his good hat, and left instead an old thing that he could hardly bear to put on his head; and then, on complaining to a Jesuit friend, all the consolation he got was the observation that he had only fulfilled one half of the Divine precept—' *Watch* and pray.' I will venture to say the Jesuit himself (Hope's friend G.) never fell into a similar omission.

On coming home from hearing Mozart's Requiem (January 28) I have just found Marian's letter, for which thank her very much. I had done very much what she seems inclined to in the matter of music, in which I shall invest a few pounds. I have ordered Pergolesi, also some trios of Clari's for S. C. B. I shall not stay here beyond Easter unless I receive a volunteer pressure thereto from Oxford (which I don't think likely) with assurance of the Provost's sanction, though, as you may suppose, I lick my lips a little at the thought of an Italian spring. I really have so wasted my time here that I don't feel as if I had earned any longer stay here. If I felt I was doing any good, getting up my subjects in a producible shape, &c., &c., it would be another thing. I think I was right in coming out here on the plea of health, but without either that or useful occupation I don't think Oriel Fellows ought to be amusing themselves about Italy. I may as well say, to prevent you from getting up an Oxford recommendation to me to stay, that a letter in answer to this cannot reach me here, and if I got as far as Florence on my way home I should not stop. I don't myself regret the loss of the Holy Week, for really the Roman Catholic ceremonies are so theatrical that I have no satisfaction in them and reproach myself for going (as I have done) simply to hear the music and see the sight. I have been as full of engagements here as you have been for the last fortnight; I don't think I have had three evenings without some engagement or other, ball, dinner, or evening party. The gayest balls I have been at are Madame Potemkin's yesterday week (Wednesday), the Russian ambassadress. But they are things which I confess bore me considerably, insomuch that last night I was fairly too lazy to go to one which I believe was rather a splendid sight, and for which I had *had* to buy a ticket on the Capitol.

To Rev. J. H. Newman.[1]

Rome : January 30, 1841.

My dear Newman,—I quite own that I am disposed to fix upon the faults of Rome. I know I have long felt so, ever since I began to feel that the controversy between ourselves and Rome was really pressing, and since I have 'fancied' that high estimate of her advantages was leading to a scorn of our own church. And I cannot complain of being distrusted on that account; I distrust myself, I know I am very likely not to observe their merits, or to give them proper weight. But I do think you are a little hard on my honesty when you set me aside as simply 'disqualified to be a witness of facts against her.' And again I think you are mistaken in thinking that it is 'their demureness' or 'their minute ceremonial' merely that is setting me against them. However, I will not inflict justifications on you, particularly as I have just plucked a letter which I had nearly finished to you for containing near two pages of them.

First, will you thank Pusey from Hope for his letter to him, and say that H. will write to him when anything is settled? From what he hears here, he thinks it will be difficult to get a good travelling collator; perhaps it will be necessary to get one from Germany.

---

[1] This letter is in answer to one from Newman, dated January 10, 1841, which is printed in *Letters and Correspondence*, ii. 323.

February 2.—Since writing the above I have heard from poor Abeken—'that Lutheran' as you remorselessly call him—that a certain Dr. Huyse (?), who has done some collations of Tertullian's 'Apologeticus,' would be a good and a likely man to be travelling rummager, and that being a Roman Catholic would not be any advantage except in Rome, and not very material here. However, all this H. will write about. I will bring home the collation of the 'Apologeticus.'

Hope has been rather taken with Bishop Baines of late, in spite of their encounter. We had a long and interesting talk with him during an hour and a half's walking up and down the Corso, and divers other public places where he would most effectually spoil our characters by being seen with us. It was in part the other aspect (I conclude) of what you at Oxford heard from Pugin. He was summoned here (by the Propaganda) for that Pastoral of his which we heard of in England, which certainly seems pretty strong against Mr. Spencer's prayers for the conversion of England in particular, and against new converts in general under that name. The charge attacks them for being abusive, and for setting afloat practices unnecessarily affronting to the English. And he complained to us in the same way of injudicious hot-headed people who would do just what was most shocking to English prejudices—silly books of devotion (as respecting the 'Sacred Heart of Jesus') over which the Bishop unfortunately had no control. 'Some' (of the 'converts') 'filled with the presumption of their ancient sect, and strangers to the humility of the religion they have embraced, commence their career by dictating to their spiritual rulers,' is his opinion on the unlucky converts. He is said (by his friends) to have gained a complete victory here, but the mere fact of having been kept here some months from his district seems something of a punishment. He spoke as if the old jealousies between seculars and regulars (Jesuits especially) were rising again, and especially on the subject of advowsons.

I hear from a friend of his (a Mr. Colyar, Roman Catholic) that there is some expectation of bringing the Abyssinian Churches into the Roman Communion. They have been in the habit of buying a patriarch when they wanted one from Mehemet Ali; the last he sent was a very bad one, a regular scamp, and, accordingly, when they found him out they deposed him : but Mehemet Ali would not take him back again, or, of course, give them another, so that all the functions of the Patriarch remained unperformed. Accordingly they have sent an embassy to Rome to say that they have always been in the habit of praying for the Pope, and that they hope he will send them one. Mr. C. winks and says he suspects there were some Jesuits in the neighbourhood. However, the Abyssinians are here, and delivered a discourse at the Propaganda at the Epiphany, when orations or poems were recited in some forty or fifty different languages—I believe, a most curious exhibition some of them. I have a suspicion this may be an old story to you.

The said Mr. C. also took us to call on a certain Cardinal Micara, of whom I think I have spoken before—a Cardinal who lives a Capuchin life, with no state, in the seminary of his diocese (Frascati), the *myths* of him being (1) that he has quarrelled with the whole Conclave, and will not enter their 'Congregations' till they have put down a certain Government lottery which exists here ; (2) that *if* he were Pope he would drive all heretics out of Rome forthwith. The *facts* are that he does attend the Congregations, and is not likely to *be* Pope. All seem agreed, however, that he has talent enough for most things, and daring for anything. Hope and I, now we have seen him, can't quite agree what kind of man he is. He seems to occupy himself with all manner of subjects : Russian statistics and the state of the marshes about Rome were the two which we came across ; also he is fond of fine paintings, and said to be a great theologian, but with all this, I thought, was a curious absence of refinement and dignity. Almost all the conversation was between him and Mr. Colyar (as was not unnatural, seeing Italian was the language spoken), and he carried it on in a kind of nudging, familiar, jocose way, which H. ascribed to shyness or to his not having made up his mind how to deal with *us* : I chiefly to a Capuchin education. I have seldom seen a person who gave me the idea of having much more 'go' in him. Mr. C. said that at one time the only English words he knew were 'Will you box ?' learnt from an Irish Capuchin, and with these he greeted the said Colyar whenever he called. He seemed to make me understand more than I ever did before great men whom one reads of, as carrying through life with them, through all their greatness, what the conventions of the world call somewhat low tastes.

I don't know why I have gone on prosing about this man, whom I have only seen once, except that he interested me a good deal, and that I have little else to say, and that I have given you data sufficient to set my opinions at their proper value—a piece of consideration, by the way, which I suspect you don't always give me due credit for, though really I don't know why I should say so, for I feel that what you say of my uncharitableness is just.

Hope asks whether you knew that a German Protestant named Dressel is bringing out here from the Vatican manuscripts (part only of which, it is said, Jacobson saw) a new edition of the Apostolical Fathers. The said Dressel has also taken a great deal of pains with collations of an edition of Prudentius which he wants to bring out, but it is questionable whether he has money enough to publish it himself. I have said I would suggest to you whether it could be made any use of for the 'Library of the Fathers.' He is a man well thought of here, for character and accuracy, by those who speak of him, has worked his eyes out, and is in distress.

Ever yours affectionately,
FREDERIC ROGERS.

To Miss Rogers.

Rome : February 6, 1841.

I must allow I shall not be sorry to get rid of Rome. The bad weather and continual parties, and calls on persons I shall probably never see again, have fairly tired me out. I feel as if when I began to move I must have some fine weather. I met at a party the other day M. Bethmann Holwegg, owner of the Castle of Rheineck at the mouth of the valley of the Brohl, which you probably recollect, and he recognised me as having been civil to him at Oxford ; so we greeted most amiably, and have exchanged invitations. He is an eminent man in his line (civil law).

We paid our visits to the Cardinals Micara and Mezzofanti. Micara was a vivacious old fellow with a kind of Capuchin good humour about him, but, with all his vivacity, capable, I could quite believe, of packing all heretics clean out of Rome, as some people say he would do if he were Pope. He would have made a capital picture with his red cap, Capuchin dress, long white beard, and bright keen eye. (I am afraid our going over to Frascati to look at him is quite out of the question.) And the Capuchin establishment in which he lives is a magnificent affair in extent, though of course as plain as possible in details, and quite unornamented. There is something, however, to me about the long corridors and quadrangles of the convent which is very grand and taking. Mezzofanti (the owner of the forty or sixty languages, I forget which) is a very courteous man, who talked English to us most fluently all the time we were with him, but without any particular talent.

February 9.—All plans to the right about face. I have just received a letter from Church insisting that there is no manner of necessity for my coming home for Easter, so I have indited a letter to the Provost, asking for more leave of absence, which I shall use to see Carnival here, then I think Naples, then through Rome again to Florence and Venice. So you may continue to address your letters here till the 4th or 5th of March, then write to Florence. One letter, perhaps, will have gone there as it is.

I have fallen across Mrs. Somerville several times lately, and like her uncommonly. I never met such an unaffected person with so much in her. Lady Adam is always exceedingly cordial, as she seems to be to all the English, but somehow I never find that we have more than a few words to say to one another; very *empressée* always but not much of it. And I am afraid last night I made rather a hole in my manners by staying after everybody else (but the Somervilles) talking to Mrs. S. By the way I dined last night with a very taking old German soldier, a Count Brühl, come to accommodate the Cologne affair, which they say here the King of Prussia wishes to have settled at almost any time. The party was only Hope, Count B., a M. Reumont, secretary of the

Prussian Legation, and myself, and a very pleasant evening we passed till it was time to be off for our respective evening engagements.

I have got rather a curiosity for you in the shape of an Italian love letter, written by the scrivano at the bottom of our staircase. I had suggested the notion to Hope, who accordingly, being the impudent man of the party, must needs one fine morning begin feeling his way towards getting the said letter, with our bland but tremendous 'padrona.' 'A good honest fellow the scrivano.' 'Yes.' 'How did he get on in the world? What did he do? Presumed he wrote a great many letters?' 'Yes.' 'Letters for the contadini of all sorts?' 'Yes, of all sorts.' 'From father to children, brothers, sisters, friends, &c.?' 'Yes, all that come; fathers, brothers, everybody else.' 'And lovers if they come to him?' 'Ah! ma non cattive lettere, non scrive mai cattive lettere, uomo scrupolosissimo—always takes care that the letters he writes should be "oneste lettere."' And it came too clear to be mistaken that the unfortunate Hope in one short moment had entirely knocked down all the little reputation we have scraped together during the last two months for steadiness and respectability, and was believed to have the most iniquitous designs on the poor scrivano's handiwork. However, on mentioning the story to my friend M. Pfyffer, he instantly volunteered to get the thing done, as he does everything else, and accordingly in two days we were in possession of a most approved specimen of the article required ('ma non cattiva,' implying honourable proposals), with all manner of illustrations plain and coloured.

To Frederick L. Rogers, Esq.

Naples: March 9, 1841.

My dear Father,—I have bid good-bye, almost for good, to Rome, without much regret. I have made one or two acquaintances that I like, but the chances are so much against my being thrown across them again that one does not gain much. In the last few days I made some acquaintances that I have liked as much as any people I have met at Rome, through a certain Oxford man named Anderdon; a certain German Count and Countess Hohenthal with *her* sister, a Princess Biron, good-natured, warm-hearted, and I should think superior people, and the ladies with the additional advantage of being very pretty. Mrs. Somerville's praises I think I have sung before. These are a few among some thirty or forty houses where I did leave or ought to have left P.P.C.s on leaving Rome. I have left a sad number of things unseen, my only consolation when people cross-questioned me being that I have dropt into one sight which is worth seeing, and extremely difficult to see, being the Villa Ludovici, including a magnificent statue gallery of the Prince Piombino, a man who refuses admittance to everybody, even Chantrey the sculptor, and the Pope! The Hohenthals, however, managed to get admittance for a party, to which Anderdon appended me; which was the beginning of our acquaintance.

I have been posting here with two Swintons, one a rising Scotch advocate, a very nice, frank, honest-hearted, fellow as possible, knows the Pringles of Yare, and Sir W. Scott's family well; but I can't make out much of our other Scotch friends; he has come abroad for his health, and brings with him his brother, who has insisted on taking up painting as a profession. The advocate meditates a visit to Oxford, where I shall like much to see him. One youth was a wild man from Ireland by name C——, utterly unlicked, but most entirely good-natured and charitable to all the world except towards a little tuft-hunting tutor of Lord Gifford's (who is travelling here) who has *apologised to him, C——, for not introducing him to society at Rome* according to a supposed promise at Florence; 'accursed villain,' 'infernal valet de place,' and such like, are among the epithets eulogistic which the remembrance of the insult elicits whenever it occurs to him, which it does almost twice a day.

We had three beautiful days for our journey here, which was for the most part along Horace's *iter ad Brundisium*, for writing which travellers to Naples should thank him much. The first day stopped at Albano to lionise, and slept at Cisterna (*Tres Tabernae* in Acts xxviii.), next day lionised Tarracina, 'impositum saxis candentibus (now red) Anxur,' lost Swinton's baggage from behind the carriage at Itri, a place famous for brigands, and had to pay a couple of scudi to some country people who had found it (probably before it was lost) on the road; and slept like Horace at Mola di Gaeta, under the Formian Hills and on the site (it is said) of the Villa where Cicero was killed. The third day a beautiful journey under the hills to Capua, and so to Naples.

To Rev. J. H. Newman.

Val Montone : March 26, 1841.

I have made what I suppose were pretty much your tours —round about Naples, to Paestum, Amalfi (by sea from Salerno), Sorrento, Capri and Castellamare. I am sorry to say I always fail to appreciate properly what I have heard much puffed beforehand ; consequently Pompeii disappointed me a little—even at Amalfi I must confess I was rather disappointed because it did not *surpass* my expectations. The *coast* between Salerno and Amalfi, and Paestum *did*. There is certainly something very pleasant in the way in which these places carry one back either to Horace and Juvenal (Virgil I have not with me), or to the time when I read them, I can't quite tell which. And lines which one sees now to be graphic haunt one in a pleasant way. I have been pursued for the last day or two by 'Liris quieta mordet aqua, &c.,' and 'Principis angusta Caprearum in rupe sedentis,' since I have crossed the Liris and seen Tiberius's Palace at Capri, a regular specimen of a magnificent vulture's nest.

I hear of a bishop in these parts (Neapolitan), of Avellino I think, who is what my cabman calls with much reprobation 'inquieto assai assai,' *i.e.* endeavouring vigorously to reform the clergy, and others too. The clergy, for misconduct, are without ceremony imprisoned in the Bishop's palace. Do you know exactly on what theory the distinction between offences of ecclesiastical and of civil cognisance are kept up here in the Papal States, the punishment being the same ? A man, as I understand, may be imprisoned for blasphemy, incontinence, or theft : but for the last by the police—for the two former by the Bishop. Is the Roman view of civil authority the utilitarian or the paternal? I think I mentioned that one of the Cardinals (Giustiniani, who is said to have been nearly elected Pope but vetoed by Austria) is also said to have used his episcopal authority of imprisonment at his diocese, Imola, to such purpose that it was thought expedient to transfer him to another diocese out of the ferment which he had raised in his own.

Rome, April 8.—A day or two since I saw a remarkable thing at one of the *retraites*, which I spoke of before for the lower classes, and which a priest named Pentini was to take us to. We went to hear him (in fact) preach to sixty or seventy soldiers who were in the *ritiro*, partly by compulsion, partly by their own will. We were present at one of a course of sermons which were to last the eight days of their being there. It happened to be the one on the Blessed Virgin. We were in the chapel and they in the next room with the door almost shut, so I could not hear distinctly, but I should not have thought it powerful—except that Pentini himself is an earnest, simple-hearted man and very energetic in manner. However, near the end of the sermon we were sent out of that part of the chapel, and shortly Pentini rushed in with all the soldiers in a body after him, who all threw themselves sobbing and groaning before a picture of the Virgin over the Altar, he standing at their head and leading the way in vehement ejaculations to her, mixed with a kind of shouting encouragement to pray on, and pray earnestly—much in the way, *mutatis mutandis*, in which you would cheer on men who were fighting: all the men going on sobbing loudly and apparently quite overcome—as ' Pray to her, pray earnestly, cry to her—you know not how she loves you—cry " Viva Maria ! " ' —and then there was a kind of low shout of ' Viva Maria !' (which with ' Viva Gesù !' seems common both as an utterance and as an inscription on the walls. I did not know it, though I suppose you do, from such books as ' St. François de Sales '). This continued for some time and ended with a short litany or some other office. He had told us that he considered this sermon was the most effectual of any to bend those who came into the place set against the discipline they were to undergo. The people, I hear, consider that great temporal curses are likely to fall on those who attend these exercises without being bettered by them. And accordingly there is much dread of going. Pentini himself certainly seemed to consider that manifest judgments had fallen on those who had relapsed after repentance there. A day or two before, I had heard two of the Jesuits' 'esercizi nobili,' which certainly did not strike me at all. . . .

We hear terrible rumours here about what is going on at Oxford [2]—Stanley with active curiosity, Smith of Trinity with distress, Hope with a manly anxiety, and I with a stomach-ache. Our principal authority is the 'Standard' with comments by the 'Sun.' Waterton, the mad ornithologist, calls you all 'the party that *won't speak out*,' *i.e.* Roman Catholics that won't own it. He has got hold of the 'Ecclesiastical Almanac,' now the 'Puseyite Almanac,' as he calls it (I suppose from his Jesuit friends who are 'taking notes'), and of course considers us all on the turn.

I have not seen very much of the ceremonies of last week, scarcely more than the fireworks, and the *miserères* of the Sistine Chapel, which certainly are very wonderful (they struck me like a wild singing of birds), though I do not understand the excessive impressiveness that they are said to have. The only things that the 'public' seem to have been impressed with this year were the benediction, and the Pope's manner of waiting on the pilgrims. I hear the Pope much better spoken of than I expected, and I have heard the current scandals denied in a frank unreserved way that looked true. The highest classes here are said to be far better behaved in point of morality than in any other great city of Italy. On my way here I saw one or two show convents (Trisalti, Carthusian, and Monte Casino, Benedictine), but much in the way a stranger sees Christ Church. At the strangers' table of the former I met a curious specimen of human nature, or rather of the Neapolitan country clergy, who amused me not a little, but will keep, as I am afraid you would row me for malice if I filled a letter with him. I shall be somewhat anxious for what I find at Florence from Oxford. Kindest remembrances to all.

Ever yours affectionately,
F. ROGERS.

---

[2] Tract 90 (on the Articles) was published in February, 1841.

To Mrs. Rogers.
Venice : May 9, 1841.

This place is delightful, and the Piazza di S. Marco, with the church (a kind of Eastern, Byzantine, half mosque-looking cathedral) and Doge's palace &c., beyond anything I could have conceived. I find myself there about twice a day, and I don't remember having enjoyed anything more than Friday evening, when a band began to play about sunset ; all the cafés, which almost surround the piazza, put out chairs, and all Venice came to walk about and enjoy themselves—shops gaily lighted up, and a beautiful starlight night. The delicious part of it is that *all* that you see there is magnificent and just as it was when the old Doges married the sea, and just exactly what it *ought* to have been—a magnificent mixture of the merchant and the noble, nothing at all of the feudal about it, nothing for defence, or putting you in mind of bands of retainers, nothing rough or unfinished, but a look of rich, well-managed security about the architecture, fine taste, no expense spared in detail, and no eyesores allowed, except perhaps one or two things, such as the standard holes, which had historical associations. Then the smaller canals are picturesque beyond belief, with a rich breadth of light and shade, and beauty of colour (even during the sirocco which is now blowing) quite wonderful to English eyes. And the luxury of sliding about in your most comfortable gondola instead of a dusty, muddy cab is no small addition to the enjoyment.

I have made this evening at dinner what I hope will be a nice acquaintance—a M. Thévenot, a French Carlist, who has been to Trieste, to visit the ex-Royal Family of France, and tells me that the 'Queen is coming to the Hotel in a few days, incog., to visit a friend.' Having told me this on a few minutes' acquaintance, he makes such a mystery of it that I almost suspect him of being an impostor, else I should say he was a remarkably pleasing, intelligent, manly kind of fellow and, curiously enough, he is in fact an old acquaintance, we having travelled together from Naples to Monte Casino about six weeks since, when he was much offended with a friend, a

fellow traveller, for admiring the country we passed through.
'Bah! tu es malade.' 'Tu ne vois pas clair ce matin.' But
I hear him coming to the door to take me out in his gondola.

May 10.—My friend M. Thévenot is certainly a nice fellow.
After the strict secrecy that he enjoined me about 'the Queen,'
I find her incognito only extends to travelling under the
title of *Duchess of Angoulême*, my to-day's gondoliers having
told me that the said Duchess and her nephew were to come the
day after to-morrow. M. T. gives a most enthusiastic account
of their virtues. She never speaks a harsh word of those who
have injured her, and the young Henri V. has much *esprit*, is
handsome, amiable, and rides like an angel on horseback. I
have struck up here and on the road an alliance with a
family hight Ruskin, the father a good, honest north-
countryman, and at the same time, London merchant; the
son an Oxford prizeman,[3] who draws beautifully. Also I
have just met the Hohenthals, to whom I shall go this evening, so that I find myself somewhat at home here. There
is something very amusing and agreeable in the way you meet
over and over again some of your travelling acquaintances.

I have just been over the inside of the Doge's palace,
Bridge of Sighs, &c. It is a terrible place, and more especially
in the change from the size and magnificence of the state
rooms to the prisons beneath, which are duly to be seen—
horrible places (though, they say, healthy), with almost more
wall than space in them, some with a gleam of daylight
(those for more ordinary criminals), the next story for those
who were taken cognisance of by the 'inquisizione' (as I
understood), *not Inquisition*, with lamplight coming to them
only through a round hole barred; and then below the level
of the canal those of the state criminals and some others which
they called 'casi reservati,' reserved, *i.e.*, for the Council of
Ten, with no light at all. Certainly, on the whole, taking into
account the position on the Canal, a narrowish and therefore
dark thoroughfare, and under all these magnificent counci
halls with nothing in them but rich paintings of glories and
victories and Doges and their virtues, and then the dreadful,

---

[3] Mr. Ruskin was then an under- and the first volume of *Modern Painters*
graduate. He took his degree in 1842, was published the year after.

quiet Venetian way of settling people's fate, they are as impressive places as I have seen. Ordinary criminals after condemnation were simply executed (in front of the palace, I think) in the sight of the people ; but the 'casi reservati' were made away with in those prisons, 'on the stone which you are standing on,' as I was told by the man who was lighting me through the narrow passages, when I asked him where the quiet executions took place.

May 12.—I have been rather more diligent in lionising here than in most places, though my good friend M. Thévenot spoilt a morning the day before yesterday. The pictures are very magnificent, not with the same touchingness that one finds about Perugia, &c., but rich golden flesh and drapery and bold light and shade. In that line I am much in love with Tintoret, a painter one never sees in England, but who seems to have painted in Venice almost as much as Rubens in Belgium. What perhaps pleases me most just at present is his originality; it is something so very refreshing after having gone through crowds of pictures, one just a little differing from the others of their school, to come slap on a man who has quite imagined a style for himself and thrown it off at once quite complete. For K.'s benefit, I will say that his style is generally strong effect of light and shade, with very bold contrasts and hardly any half tint except on the masses of light ; effect, however, not being of sharp contrast but of full richness. His shades are not veined with half lights like Rembrandt's, but dark masses, which, if he wishes to break, he breaks by a light as bright as any other in the drawing, only not so large (as *e.g.* in a glory round the head of a saint). And his great picture (the miracle of St. Mark, a slave whom a crowd are trying to kill with hatchets and stakes, which all break upon him) is in *colour* just what his ordinary pictures are in chiaroscuro. However, it is absurd writing to you about a painter that you don't know, only the more I think of that picture the more I am astonished at it. I can't conceive what could have put it into his head. I should say there was no mannerism in it, and yet that it was totally unlike any other style of painting I ever saw ; and the vigour of the drawing is quite up to the colouring.

I went to-day over the Arsenal, which has some interesting things in it; standards taken at Lepanto, which I liked because when one reads of bashaws, their tails, and Turkish standards flying in old history, it is satisfactory to have seen them and know exactly what they were like. Also some instruments of torture, the collar (as I understood) with which Carrara [4] was strangled; thumbscrews and other nice inventions for people who would not confess, taken from the Doge's palace, of which I have told you, a beautiful little model of the Bucentaur, and the actual chair of the Doge from it. All which things I don't consider as mere relics (for which I still profess not to care) but good solid realities which make you conceive history twice as well as you would without them. I regret every moment I do not know Italian history, particularly Venetian. Here I have, within sight of my window, palaces of Foscari, Barbarigi, Pisani, Grimani, and I may say Giustiniani, with nothing but a vague notion that people of these names existed in Venice, and did great things, without knowing what, except from Lord Byron. And by the way that gentleman does seem to enjoy the most extraordinary popularity here and everywhere in Italy. He is the first author every Italian priest or layman talks to you of. An Armenian to whom I brought a letter, and who showed me his convent, obviously thought it the great fact of his life to have taught Lord Byron. The Vitalis at Milan, a student I picked up at Padua, and the gondoliers here, all set to work talking of him immediately. N.B.—I have seen in the shops here 'Oliviero Tuuist,' 'scritto da Boz (Carolo Dickens), *e volgarizzato* (!) *da* A. B.' The notion of Oliver being put into the vulgar tongue, that vulgar tongue being Italian, seems to me rich. I should like to know Mr. A. B.

By the bye, don't be surprised at an artist of the name of Lear dropping in upon you some day to see if I have come back. But ask to see his drawings, which are beautiful. He is a friend of the Hornbys, and I told him I hoped we should see him some day on his way to them, and that, even though I am not at home, I hoped he would go in and make your

---

[4] Francesco II. da Carrara, surnamed 'Novello,' of Padua. He was taken prisoner by the Venetians and put to death in 1406.

acquaintance, telling him at the same time if he had his portfolio with him that some of you would really and truly enjoy looking at them. He was to have been my companion in the mountains about Subiaco &c., and the sketches (black and white chalk) are principally about Rome.

To Rev. J. H. Newman.

Innspruck : May 19, 1841.

I can't say what a satisfaction it was to me to receive Church's letter and your P.S. at Florence.[5] The whole affair has been to me like the bursting of a cloud that had been making me very uncomfortable, and it is quite a relief to fancy that it has gone off with so little damage. I suppose you feel yourself that the stopping of the Tracts is a thing of very little importance now, and, as you imply, things are on a truer footing. . . .

I hear from a French Carlist that the French Government is obliged to keep down religious education by a tax, *i.e.* that there are two systems at work, the Government one of *écoles d'enseignement mutuel* (of course purely secular) ; and that of the 'frères ignorantins.' Under the Restoration the Government patronised the latter, who accordingly got somewhat idle ; but since the Government of 1830 has discountenanced them they have become much more zealous, and there has been the great religious reaction, and all this, with the natural tendency of the French to oppose the Government, has made the 'frères ignorantins' so much preferred by the people that the schools of *enseignement mutuel* would fall if they were not supported by a tax, paid by every teacher on every pupil whom he takes, which (I think) goes to support them. He viewed the *enseignement mutuel* people as useful in their way, partly as a spur to the others, and partly as really 'authors of improvements,' but said they were in fact theorists, and the others were those who were used to have

---

[5] This letter from Mr. Church, dated March 14, 1841 (giving a full account of the feeling and the proceedings at Oxford), is published with Mr. Newman's postscript in the *Life and Letters of Dean Church*, pp. 27–34.

the reins in their hands, and knew how to manage children, and whom the people were used to.

The Tyrolese are really an uncommonly nice people. Anderdon told me that before you had been a day in the Tyrol you felt as if they were all your brothers—even without speaking the language—and really it is very true, and I do think it is not founded on fancy, but on themselves. There seems to be a mixture of obligingness and independence which is quite refreshing after the south of Italy, where one could not speak six civil words to a man without being asked for *qualch' cosa*. This place is, I think, the most beautiful I have yet seen, far beyond Florence, and to my mind without the enervating look that the beautiful Italian cities have.

At Verona I found as usual the Capuchins and Jesuits more thought of than the other clergy; my *cicerone* liked the seculars because they were *liberi*, disliked the regulars because they were *fanatici*, excepted in favour of the Capuchins because they were truly *pii*: explained that to mean that they did great penances and got up in the middle of the night to do them; they were not *fanatici*, because when people confessed to them they considered that true contrition was enough, and set very slight penances. The Jesuits, on the contrary, were *fanatici* inasmuch as they were not to be trifled with, and would not give absolution without good hearty penance. I was rather amused at the difference of Italian and English notions of fanaticism.

There is here (and elsewhere) a remarkable order called 'Redemptorists': their office is, when called on by a clergyman, to send some five of their body to preach and receive confessions in his parish for twelve days—in short, to head a kind of 'revival.' A good, simple-hearted friend of Hope's here tells me they produce very great effects, 'converting' whole parishes of *mauvais sujets*, and he said it did not cause any itching ears or discontent with their *curé*, as, firstly, they were not 'popular preachers,' but simply zealous, honest men; and, secondly (what seemed to me remarkable), that they often removed a cause of want of confidence between *curé* and people, for that they frequently found (so they told him) persons who, from fear of confessing to a person who knew them and was daily seeing them, had gone on, up to the time when the Redemptorists came, making false confessions, and confessed truly to these, whom they were never to see again. And he said that after this one good confession such persons did in fact put themselves under the *curé's* guidance in a way in which they (of course) never had done it before. They go principally to country parishes and were nearly coming to Wales, but had no one who understood Welsh, and so the opportunity passed. I was taken by my friend to see one to-day, but I cannot say much transpired, seeing the Redemptorist understood no languages but German and Latin—talking the latter not very well—and we were keeping him from his dinner.

I saw an account of 'No. 90' in an Innspruck religious newspaper (or periodical) translated from the *Univers*, and wished I knew German enough to read it. The delight with which my little friend here looks forward to the time when England with all her power of spreading Christianity will return to the Roman Catholic Church is so sanguine that it rather perplexes me.

I met Dr. Weedall (I think his name is), late head of Oscott College, again and again, and he has told me certainly a strange history. I ought to say that he is a person whose conversation is moderate and quiet and sensible, and so on, but with a strong dash of softness—or else he thought me very soft—as, *e.g.*, he talked with great satisfaction, and wished to impress me by talking of an *academia* or kind of *conversazione* held at Cardinal Orioli's on Good Friday evening, when the Cardinal read a paper on Latin prose, and others copies of hexameters, &c., and a celebrated *improvisatrice* named Rosa Taddei improvised on subjects connected with our Saviour's Passion. However, his history is that he stopped in the Tyrol to see two young women who are much talked of among Roman Catholics. They are said both to have shown a very remarkable piety from their childhood, and both early in life were attacked by very painful diseases which have never left them, and both have devoted themselves to a life of contemplation. In one this has passed into a continued ecstasy, except when commanded by her confessor (without whose direction she never makes a movement); she is continually on her knees in a position which Dr. W. describes as most beautiful and impressive, and one in which the mere natural force of the human body could scarce sustain her. When bidden by him, she lies down and gets up—which Dr. W. saw—and in a way which he says he cannot describe, but which seems to be without any of the effort which even a person in health would find it necessary to use (*e.g.* without unclosing her hands), and when bidden by him she eats a few grapes or a pear or some such slight thing. She never speaks to any one, but people are taken in to see her, and she seems to take a pleasure in seeing them. The other case is of the same kind, but that the ecstasy is not continual, and *I think* she speaks to strangers. She has not eaten or drunk *anything at all* for seven years, as her confessor testifies to Dr. W. Both have received the stigmata (which Dr. W. saw), and the latter also the impression of the crown of thorns, all of which cause them the greatest agony, and in the latter case gush out with blood (on Friday when they go over in their meditations the Passion of our Lord, and especially at three o'clock). The places where these two persons have appeared were places (like all the Tyrol, as I understood) where there was a great deal of piety, and their history has acted as a stimulus. How does all this strike you? I must confess to a *strong* prejudice against it. On the other hand I happened to go into a Tyrolese church the other morning (a feast day) while Mass was going on, and I must allow it is a thing to make one sad to see what may be, and is not, in the Anglican Church.

Döllinger and Wendischmann are being very civil, and Döllinger is one of the most taking people I have seen since I have been abroad.

All sorts of remembrances to all people, Church, Mozley Marriott, Johnson, Ward, &c.

Ever yours affectionately,
FREDERIC ROGERS

To Miss S. Rogers.
Oriel : June 27, 1841.

I find as I thought that that passage in Newman's letter to the Bishop of Oxford [a] which seems to throw the responsibility of the Tracts on the Bishop *was* put in to please him ; and that the whole letter was sent to him before it was published, and just sent back with a verbal notice of his ' unqualified approbation,' and then followed by a very kind and satisfactory note. The Bishop wished it to appear that *he had always kept his eye on the Tracts,* which in fact was tantamount (whether he meant it or not) to taking part of the responsibility, as far as *permission* went.

I suspect matters here will end in Church's tutorship being taken away. It is an uncommon nuisance for the Provost, as he loses two tutors by marriage (Daman and Prichard) this vacation, and so if Church goes he will be left with none but —— who is a blister to him. But it seems he cannot well help himself. Church was honest enough to volunteer telling him that he agreed with No. 90. The Provost said first he was a young man and did not know his own mind, which would have left things in a very uncomfortable position for Church as leaving it in the Provost's power to keep him (on trial) just as long as was convenient, and then pack him off on plea of being incorrigible, but since that he has had a talk, in which he proposed Church's keeping the tutorship but *not lecturing on the Articles.* This Church declined on the ground of the statute quoted by the Heads of Houses, which makes it the duty of tutors *to teach* the Articles. Then the Provost proposed laying it before the Vice-Chancellor : this Church also declined ; it being perfectly clear how the Vice-Chancellor would give it (against Church) and the Provost being perfectly competent to act by himself. So that the only effect would have been forcing from a University authority a strong judgment against No. 90. Now it is the Provost's move, and I suspect he is bound by some agreement among the Heads themselves not to keep a tutor under those circumstances (at least such an agreement has been asserted in print

[a] Bishop Bagot.

to exist, professedly on the authority of a Head), so that I suppose Church must budge. Probably it will end in Church keeping it for a short limited time, as a favour, till some tutors can be found to fill the places, if the Provost can submit to be under an obligation to the men he is turning out. He lately asked a good meek kind of man named B. (cousin of Pusey's) whether he agreed with 90, informing him that if he did he could not sign his college testimonials for priest's orders. B. in a great fright replied that he had no occasion for them, having already got them a year ago. 'But you will want them for that year.' No, he had been out of residence, and had accordingly got them from three neighbouring beneficed clergymen. So departed B. thinking the Provost had floored him excessively. The rest of the world, however, thought he had floored the Provost.

The Provost is obviously quite alive to the excessive in convenience of parting with Church at the present moment, which is amusing, especially if he is at the bottom at all of the agreement to expel tutors. I don't know which will be the martyr, he or Church.

To Rev. J. H. Newman.

Eliot Place : July 22, 1841.

As to the 'British Critic,' I confess myself out of heart. A line which shall satisfy Oakeley, Ward, Keble, and Wilson permanently seems hard to find, independently of the particular difficulties about Mozley. I am afraid your notion of my getting 'general influence' in the review is rather hopeless. I feel far too perplexed and mistrustful myself to have any chance of keeping together half-a-dozen different sets of writers all pulling ways which I don't understand. . . .

To Miss S. Rogers.

Oriel : Nov. 21, 1841.

My dear Sophy,—Your card has just arrived, and looks all that is beautiful. Pusey has been writing a most outrageously injudicious letter (which any one of his friends would have stopped if he had shown it them) in hopes of benefiting

Williams [7] by a plain statement of the case, and stating as matters of course and commonly known, first, that before party differences arose Williams was looked to by residents as the obvious man for the professorship, and secondly, that Garbett would not have been brought forward now to oppose him but for such theological differences. Now, both these things are in spirit quite true. The majority of residents *will* vote for Williams in spite of the strong cry against him, and he was publicly, and alone, talked of as the probable professor, principally of course among people of our own sort, but, I should think, in a way that must have come to the ears of most men, though certain sets do live so completely apart from others that, no doubt, they would not have heard it (I mean Heads of Houses, and hunting, noisy men, of whom there are still a residue here). As to the other assertion, it is clear that a set is generally being made against us (tutors turned out, &c.). The opposition to Williams is put on a theological ground by his opponents publicly, and as far as I hear almost universally, and the other candidate, Garbett, let Williams know that if he (Williams) withdrew in favour of a third person (Claughton) Garbett would not stand. This is explained in another way, viz. that against Claughton Garbett thought he should have no chance, whereas he would against Williams, but it certainly has a personal cut about it.

But on the other hand the head of Garbett's college,[8] it seems, had never heard of Williams as a candidate when he proposed to the college bringing forward Garbett, so he put forward a paper flooring Pusey with this fact, which you observe *does* floor (apparently) *both* Pusey's assertions, and talking about its being begun in 'generous rivalry' and then 'not being responsible for its having become theological.'

---

[7] In 1841, on the election to the Professorship of Poetry, vacated by Mr. Keble, there was a contest between Mr. Isaac Williams and Mr. (afterwards Archdeacon) Garbett of Brasenose. The opposition to Mr. Williams was, unfortunately, beyond a doubt due to the fact that he belonged to the Tractarian party and was a friend of Newman and Keble. Dr. Pusey's letter unwisely emphasised the point (which was not, however, avowed by the other side) that the fight was a theological one. The contest waged by pamphlets and letters, both at Oxford and in London, ended in 1842, when it was found that Mr. Garbett had most promises of votes, and Mr. Williams withdrew.

[8] Dr. Gilbert.

However, people were very angry with Pusey's letter *at first*, as dictation, and *because it was* Pusey, and this affair of Gilbert's has at present much heightened the bad effect.

To the same.

Oriel : December 12, 1841.

As to matters here I am afraid Pusey has knocked Williams's chance on the head ; I think he really would have got in if it had not been for that letter. And now, could you suppose it possible Pusey can hardly be persuaded not to write a *third* letter, which he wishes to direct at the universal recipient Jelf? I had to be called in and advise about the second, and never in the whole course of my practice did I undergo such a two days as were spent in the consideration of what should be said, a whole host of perfectly different opinions to be taken, Pusey himself dissatisfied with everything that was not grossly injudicious, and all of us in the most exceeding agony as to what would come, Pusey producing specimen after specimen each more dangerous than the last. And Gilbert's humbugging letter in possession of the field all the time, and getting additional credit every moment that it remained unanswered. However, I hope the answer has done pretty fairly, *i.e.* it has done no harm, which was all that could be expected.

I have had a short troublesome correspondence with Gladstone and Badeley, who wanted a compromise, they thinking that there was on the *tapis* a proposal to that effect from the other party. The people on the other side talk very big, and I suppose they really will beat us by some considerable majority ; but our numbers, if anything like all our promises come up, will be such as would secure an enormous majority in any ordinary case. The only thing that could save us would be some happy event which would make all the impartial people who want it not to be a theological contest rush up and vote on the merits of the question. But how they are to be worked up to such an act I don't see.

The moderate man was not myself but Palmer of Magdalen, whom you probably know of, who has accordingly, to show that he is not moderate, issued a letter to Golightly principally intended to 'anathematise' (his word) all Protestants and Protestantism and favourers thereof, archbishops, bishops, priests, deacons, and laymen, in a style which I should think might not be without a certain effect on the unlucky Williams's election. I really don't know why it is that everybody should seize this especial opportunity of going mad.

The Bishop of Winchester has again refused to ordain —— [one of Mr. Keble's curates]. Keble, of course, is very much distressed at it. I don't know what he will do. Professor Airey has been here for a day or so, and breakfasted with me this morning, with Johnson. What a queer fellow he is! He was amusing at breakfast; only he is plainly a lazy hand at getting up, and so was about three quarters of an hour after time, which does not always do in college.

I got up an unsuccessful attempt at Palestrina the other day; and pretty much gave up the notion of continuing it. One little thing, a kind of chant, very easy, I should like to try when we get home, in the reality it is most beautiful, and even played on the piano very fine.

I have not been seeing very much of anybody except Church, Mozley, and perhaps Donkin. The fact is, people are beginning to feel anxious about things, and I am glad they should, for it is not before they ought.

I think Sibthorp's conversion did good here in the way of frightening your young gentlemen who had been overready with their tongues. What do you think of 'Jack' Morris taking the sober line? Ward, Oakeley, and others go on pushing ahead, but many men are pulling up, Mozley, Ryder, Bloxam, I should say Pusey and Williams: of Keble I can't tell. I should think it almost impossible to say what strange changes of position may have taken place before three years are out.

On the whole matters look to me dreary enough, though one cannot but trust that things will be made to turn out right, if only people try to do right. If it were not for some indistinct feeling of that kind I should feel *very* blue.

Yours affectionately,
FREDERIC ROGERS.

To Rev. J. H. Newman.

12 Paper Buildings, Temple : January 4, 1842.

My dear Newman,—I hardly like troubling you about Williams's election, but I think somebody in Oxford should know the state of the case. A proposal to withdraw both candidates and letter of the Committee here will come down to the President of Trinity by this post. You will see the kind of thing it is. A letter, however, which I received from Gladstone this morning made me call on him, and I found him obviously set on getting the matter finished *quoquo modo* : if not by the withdrawal of both, by the withdrawal of one ; and urging the signatures of five out of seven bishops (members of Convocation)—the known sentiments of all, &c. —as motives in conscience for the withdrawal of one even if the other refused. He seems to have got them (especially the Bishop of Oxford) to sign, by the notion (on *their* parts) that their authority *would* put an end to the contest, Llandaff and Chichester (alone) refusing, because they wished a stigma thrown upon Williams. He insisted much on the Bishop's *real* wish that Williams would withdraw, and, as far as I understood, wished to establish that the presumption of the wish, arising from the mere fact of their signatures, was sufficient to bind us either to act on it or to take measures to draw out a more distinct statement, especially from the Bishop of Oxford. He seemed to think the Bishop of Oxford would be ready to give this.

I say all this because else it appears to me you might fancy things going differently from what they really are.

Yours affectionately,
FREDERIC ROGERS.

To Rev. J. H. Newman.

Temple : April 3, 1843.

My dear Newman,—I do not like to meet you again without having said, once for all, what I hope you will not think hollow or false. I cannot disguise from myself how very improbable—perhaps impossible—a recurrence to our former terms is. But I wish, before the time has past for such an acknowledgment, to have said how deeply and painfully I feel —and I may say have more or less felt for *years*—the greatness of what I am losing, and to thank you for all you have done and been to me. I know that it is in a great measure by my own act that I am losing this, and I cannot persuade myself that I am substantially wrong, or that I could long have avoided what has happened. But I *do* believe, if I may dare to say so, that God would have found a way to preserve to me so great a blessing as your friendship if I had been less unworthy of it. I *do* feel most earnestly how much of anything which I may venture to be thankful for in what I am is of your forming—how more than kind—how tender you have always been to me, and how unlikely it is that I can ever again meet with anything approaching in value to the intimacy which you gave me. . . . I should have been pained at leaving all this unsaid. But I do not write it with any idea of forcing an answer from you—nor does it require one —and I shall not attach any meaning to your leaving it unanswered.

Yours affectionately,
FREDERIC ROGERS.

CHAPTER IV

In London, reading law and writing for the 'Times,' and early official life (1842-1850)

IN the summer of 1842 Mr. Rogers began his work in London, reading law in the Temple, where he shared chambers with Mr. S. Wood, a brother of the late Lord Halifax. All his evenings, except on Sunday, seem to have been taken up by the task of writing leaders for the 'Times.' He has left an account of this work, which gives an interesting picture of the journalism of that day : 'I dined with Mr. Walter and his son in Printing House Square at five o'clock, and found that I was expected to write an article then and there on one of the subjects of the day. I protested my inability, not supposing myself capable of doing such a thing in less than a week. This was pooh-poohed. I tried, found it possible, and found also that I was expected to repeat the process next day ; same hour, same dinner, short conversation after dinner, then the subject was announced and I was left alone till tea-time, when Mr. Walter appeared, read aloud what I had done, with criticisms, and after correction carried off the copy to the printer. When the article was finished the same process was repeated, and when I was disburdened of the whole article I went home to bed. Gradually it appeared that I was expected to do this (*exceptis excipiendis*) every evening. And being, though an Oxford Don, not skilful in saying No, or in evading saying Yes, while Walter was an adept in the art of making you believe that you had pledged yourself to do what he wanted you to do, I found myself soon engaged to write a daily article, usually in the manner aforesaid, with a very liberal salary. I neither wanted nor expected one or the other; but there I was—engaged, with a month's vacation and occasional holidays, pledged to write six articles a week, and to eat five dinners in Printing House Square. Several rules or objects I laid down for myself: (1) not to write on Sunday, except in case of real urgency; (2) to strike a blow when I could in favour of the " good cause ;" (3) to substitute, as far as I could, satire for " thunder." The dinners I found such a tie that after the first year I gave them up. A new arrangement was made, and ultimately it was understood that I should send articles when required (*i.e.* about every day).

'It was a harassing work, partly from its continuous pressure, partly from a constant apprehension that my independence was being undermined. At the same time it was very interesting and amusing. In the first place you were not unfrequently crossing swords with notabilities by whom it was some credit even to have been attacked. Once I got such a notice from Sir Robert Peel. It was on occasion of his bill relating to banks of issue. I had read Jones Lloyd's and Hubbard's pamphlets on the subject—not to speak of ancient literature, such as Horner's famous report on currency —and felt myself capable of putting on the airs of a financial oracle. So I criticised, in an extremely patronising way, his great speech (founded, of course, on a thorough mastery of the subject), and proceeded to air my own newly acquired knowledge, under cover of supplying gaps in his argument. It was not badly done, and completely deceived Sir Robert, who, not seeing beyond the lion's skin, answered it in a tone of respectful deference with which he would have replied to some great City magnate.

'Then the phrase "monster meeting" was due to me. An immense balloon, called (I think) the "Nassau balloon," had been popularly christened the "monster balloon," and I applied the phrase contumeliously to one of O'Connell's immense out-of-door meetings. He accepted it, as the Netherlanders in old times accepted the nickname of "Gueux." "The 'Times' called it a monster meeting, did they? Well! monster meetings they should be"—and monster meetings they were for the future.

'Sometimes (though rarely) I saw or heard that what I considered a valuable thought had been accepted as such—as "that political economy busied itself too exclusively with the creation and not enough with the *distribution* of wealth," a view which must have been novel in 1844, as Laveleye spoke of it in the seventies as having recently attracted attention.

'It was less flattering, but much more amusing, to see how mere commonplace views on this or that subject were taken for granted at dinner parties for the next week or so. It sometimes happened, for instance, that, having to write an article, say, on a debate, I had had much discussion with myself as to the various handles by which it might be laid hold of—should I grapple with the actual subject, or criticise the characters of the speakers, or the tactics which underlay the question, or a particular quarrel which gave a liveliness to the debate, or the probable results, &c. ?—and, having chosen my handle, I might have had some difficulty in distributing my praise or blame. Not so my readers—at least, the average diner-out. They *talked* my article, as if there was no other point in the debate than that which I had selected, and no conceivable opinion but that which I had, perhaps doubtfully, adopted.

'Also I could be virtuous—not to the extent of airing any chivalrous or transcendental principle, but in a sober, reasonable, decent, utilitarian way. And be it observed that under cover of this cool reasonableness it is possible to give support now and then to a tolerably high standard of moral judgment.

'I really think I did a great deal to put an end to duelling; never lost an opportunity of making it ridiculous, and was favoured by opportunities for doing so. And after I had been at this some time (an early article about one Sir Nathaniel Wraxall was, I think, particularly successful), I was much gratified by some rather dull peer boring the House with a long account of some personal affront, because, he said, duelling had recently been made so ridiculous that a gentleman could no longer take that mode of righting himself.

'I was also successful (partly by these very articles) in making Printing House Square understand that there were other modes of affecting public opinion besides "thunder." Mr. Walter showed me one day with much satisfaction what he considered a compliment to my articles, in a letter (since printed) from Crabbe Robinson. The point was, to express his satisfaction at a new kind of article, which, instead of laying down the law, stated the case thoughtfully without dictating, though inviting, a particular judgment.[1] In some cases this might be—or, rather, certainly was—due to the fact that I did not feel sure (articles being often written on *ex parte* or possibly imperfect information) that one or the other opinion was right; and, indeed, it is the habit of my mind to escape from the responsibility of committing myself to a conclusive opinion till the case is quite clear, or till something has to be done. . . .

'People do not consider that in reality what they think the *dishonesty* (*i.e.* inconsistency) of a paper is often the *honesty* of contributors, each of whom is allowed to say what he really believes. Of course, in matters of serious principle the proprietors or editor ought to have their own views and admit

---

[1] The passage occurs in Crabbe Robinson's Diary, vol. iii. 237 (under the year 1843): 'Have you not remarked how much the style of the "Times" is changed now from what it was? One no longer sees those fierce declamations which caused Stoddart to get the name of "Dr. Slop," and the paper the title of "The Thunderer." It has become mild, argumentative, and discriminating. I wrote lately to Walter to tell him that I thought the paper better than it has been ever since I have known it—that is, thirty-six years. He thanked me most warmly for my encouragement and commendation.'

nothing else in their leading articles. But there are numerous cases in which they cannot have, and are not called upon to have, a settled opinion, and are quite right in leaving the matter to the writer.'

In 1844 Mr. Rogers began his official life, and gave up writing for the 'Times.' His first appointment was to the post of Registrar of Joint Stock Companies. The origin and nature of his office may be best described in his own words: 'An Act (unparalleled for the looseness of its drafting) had been passed—with good reason—for the registration and regulation of joint stock companies, and I was appointed to the office created for this purpose. I hardly had time to shake myself and two or three clerks into our building, and to get the necessary books and appliances, before the storm burst upon us. Every existing company had to register its name with us. There had been enormous frauds connected with joint stock companies, and the English law of partnership seemed made for obstructing co-operation and enriching lawyers. An Act was very properly passed to remedy these evils by facilitating incorporation, and enforcing (to a ridiculous extent) publicity. Every company thereafter formed had to register its name, and every change of name, certain particulars and every change in those particulars, every advertisement it ever issued, and every change in such advertisements; and to register an approved deed of settlement containing certain provisions held by the registrar to fulfil various conditions laid down by Act of Parliament. And all these things were to be registered promptly, so as to be ready for public inspection as soon as the company began to receive money. At this time—in 1844—the railway mania was in its utmost fury; every third-rate attorney seemed to ally himself to a third-rate surveyor, and to register two or three men of straw as "promoters" of some new railway in a country of which they knew nothing, in the hope of obtaining from would-be shareholders sufficient deposits to pay their own bills—the rest took its chance. Other speculations followed suit, at a distance, in their extravagance. I remember one man who came to inspect a register (on due payment of a shilling) with the object of selecting some two places between which no railway was yet proposed, in order that he might start one.

'I held the registrarship first under Mr. Gladstone and then under Lord Dalhousie; my real chief, however, being John Shaw Lefevre—the most amiable of men, also clear-headed, most industrious, of great literary accomplishments, a man of the world, and a thorough man of business. He was always cordial and friendly, though he could pull me up when I was careless, in a way of his own.'

Mr. Rogers seems to have succeeded in getting this Registration Office into order, but did not remain in it long, for in the course of the same year he was appointed Assistant Under Secretary to the Colonial Office and Emigration Commissioner. In 1846 emigration had so much increased that it became a matter of great public interest. It was not therefore a loss that his work was restricted to the Emigration Office as Emigration Commissioner with two colleagues, Mr. Murdoch being the chairman. 'We were responsible (1) for checking all the abuses which went on in private passenger ships, particularly such as carried Irish emigrants—and fever with them—to America; (2) for conducting in our own ships a large but intermittent emigration to Australia; (3) for doing the same for the black emigration to the West Indies; (4) for the examination (to the satisfaction of the Colonial Office) of the innumerable projects of emigration and land-take which were produced by the colonisation mania of the day.'

In 1845, having already given up his work for the 'Times,' he also resigned his Oriel Fellowship. By the existing University regulations he could have retained it, but he always intended to give it up as soon as he had any sufficient office or work which promised to be permanent. Curiously enough, his resignation reached the Provost of Oriel on the very day on which Newman announced his adhesion to Rome and resigned his Fellowship. From this arose a report at that time at Oxford—the very reverse of the truth—that Rogers had followed Newman to Rome.

In 1845, and for some time afterwards, he devoted much of his leisure time to the serious work of starting the 'Guardian,' in conjunction with a few of his most intimate Oxford friends. It was intended to be a Church newspaper of a higher order than the existing 'English Churchman,' and in some degree to carry on the principles of the Oxford movement as they were understood before the division in the ranks of those who took part in it. He has left in writing a description of the enterprise. 'Newman had joined Rome, and left those who had adhered to him headless, unorganised, suspected by others and suspecting each other; for nobody yet knew who would follow where he led. For a time a kind of perplexed hopelessness prevailed; who would trust us? or rather who could be expected to trust us, with such a fact as that our acknowledged leader, who, in our view, had systemaised the best practicable defence against Rome, had on full consideration pronounced his and our case a bad one? However, different people in different places picked themselves up and began to consider how they could take their share in the battle which they refused to consider as lost. Whether I was the first to start the idea of a newspaper, I do not know. Anyhow the idea was taken up by the knot to which I belonged, embracing James Mozley and Thomas Haddan, who, like myself, had written not unsuccessfully in the "Times," and Church and Bernard, who had signalised themselves in reviews. We, I think, comprised the substantial staff of the undertaking. That is, we tried to collect contributors and cash, but made ourselves responsible to each other for finding what was wanting in writing and capital. We expected to succeed in doing good, for it was something even to shake out a standard and seem not discouraged; and, in the event, to succeed financially. But we were totally inexperienced in the handling of a newspaper and in the conduct of business. We took the somewhat bold resolution of starting the paper ourselves, dealing directly with the printer and with Haddan's clerk as ostensible publisher and sub-editor. We made an agreement with some printers in Little Pulteney Street, and hired a room opposite the printing establishment, over the shop of a baker, where we could attend or meet to see what was going on, and where some of us spent the greater part of every Tuesday night correcting proofs, rejecting or inserting matter, writing articles on the last subjects which had turned up, giving last touches, and generally *editing*. Bernard, Haddan, and I, being in London, must, I suppose, have done most of this work, but Church and Mozley used to take their share, making use of a bedroom in my lodgings in Queen Street, Mayfair, whither I had migrated from the Temple. To these lodgings we used sometimes to return at four or five o'clock in the morning—sometimes, perhaps, later; for I connect some of these returns home with the smell of bread hot from the oven, on which I think we sometimes made our breakfast. It was on January 21, 1846, that the "Guardian" came into life (simultaneously with the "Daily News"); and for nearly six months we must have scrambled on, with plenty of help from writers of our own kidney, but in the lower departments we had no help but that of Haddan's clerk; and how we managed to get through the drudgery part I hardly now understand. Bernard and Haddan must have been indefatigable. In July 1846 we were lucky enough to find Mr. Martin Sharp to take the management of our affairs for us as publisher, manager, and ostensible editor; the higher editorial duties soon passed into the hands of Bernard. We received also literary help from many friends—Northcote, Coleridge, Mackarness, Burgon, and others.'

He goes on to trace the great and well-deserved success of the 'Guardian,' which followed increasingly a few years afterwards.

In September 1847 he married Georgiana Mary Colvile, daughter of Andrew Colvile of Ochiltree, and sister of his old schoolfellow, Sir James Colvile. At the end of the same year his uncle, Sir John Rogers, died, and his father, now Sir Frederick Leman Rogers, resigned his post in the Audit Office, and went to live on the family property to which he had succeeded—Blachford, near Ivybridge, in Devonshire.

To Miss S. Rogers.

Landerneau,[2] September 4, 1844.

My dear Sophy,—I suppose my father will have received my hurried note written yesterday immediately on receiving Gladstone's offer of the Registrarship of Joint Stock Companies. I am at present partly occupied in considering how I shall break the matter to Mr. Walter. I suppose my connexion with him may be considered at an end the moment I get a place. I like the notion decidedly as far as my own comfort is concerned. The only doubt I feel is as to its *permanence*, but as Gladstone says nothing about that I presume I am safe. I have given a distant hint at it in my note to him. At any rate if it offers a *fair prospect* of permanence it seems to me a thing to be caught at, because if I have an opportunity of doing work and making myself known to a few official people it will be much.

Now to my proceedings, of which I think I brought the history up to Landerneau. We found M. le Comte de Cadeille out, his daughter very Englishified and not wholly improved thereby; very anxious to be civil but not knowing quite how; the whole terminating in an invitation to dine on Wednesday. On Sunday (a very hot day) we lounged away the morning in rest, and walked in the afternoon to a place called La Forêt, where there was to be what is called a

---

[2] In Brittany, not far from Brest. He was travelling with Mr. Church.

'pardon,' *i.e.* a collection of the country people all round to hear vespers, a sermon, join in or see the procession, receive a benediction, and dance. There are sometimes great ' pardons ' hereabouts which people in danger make vows to attend, barefoot, half-naked, or otherwise as the case may be. Here the ceremonial is even greater, the people come from thirty or forty miles round, and the gaieties last three or four days; at Châteaulin (the place we last came from) there was a ball (*assemblée*) on Monday, horse-racing, foot-racing, dancing for prizes, &c.; at La Forêt it was only a small 'pardon,' but one of the most beautiful sights I ever saw. The church is a picturesque (and very characteristic) Breton church on the side of a hill, looking down on an arm of the sea, and surrounded by trees just so kept as to see the sea (or river as you choose to call it) and opposite bank through. The churchyard, full, almost crowded, with men and women in Breton costume ; the men in enormous *black* flapping hat, *dark jacket and trousers*, some sashes, some long hair down their backs, occupying one part of the churchyard ; the women in every variety of bright-coloured scarf and apron, very dark gown and brilliantly clean white caps, in the other part ; kneeling, standing, talking or lounging, according to tastes and the part of the service that was going on. The kneeling of all the people for the benediction which we saw from the top of the bank on the *upper* side of the churchyard was beautiful to look at, the crowd of white caps with a crowd beyond of black heads and jackets, and beyond that the sea coast seen through the trees, and all this seen between a frame of the church on one side and a picturesque Breton cross on the other. Presently one or two young fellows got up to the belfry by some steps cut in the roof of the church and set to work there ringing the bells. Out came the procession, the priests, women, crosses, canopy, a crowd of black-headed men and a crowd of white-capped women, and walked round the churchyard, the others kneeling as the Sacrament passed ; and then they are all separated, those who could stay at La Forêt to dance &c., those who could not (we among the number) to get home as fast as they could.

The next day, Monday, we went to Brest, intending to get out to the extreme point (St. Mathieu) ten or twelve miles further; but finding no carriage to be had, went up the Châteaulin river (which is very pretty) through the *Rade* (or Roads) of Brest which forms, I should think, about the most magnificent harbour in the world for steamers. We were put down a mile or two short of our destination (Châteaulin), and found the diligence full, the *coupé* being occupied by an English officer, a very civil and communicative old French gentleman, and his daughter. So we 'took our feet in our hand' and determined to walk our two miles, but hung about to look at a very picturesque and natural-looking dance that was going on—about a dozen young girls just come from the fête at Châteaulin, and rather more young men, arranged sometimes in two, sometimes in one line, having hold each of the other's little finger, and dancing, to the singing of two of the young men, a figure that (barring the running under arms) had more the effect of 'Thread my Needle' than anything else that I can think of. The song was like a somewhat monotonous English country dance, with a touch of the Ashantee. At last the diligence started. Church said 'Look!' and I saw the horses turning sharp the wrong way; in another moment the whole concern toppled and came smash down on its side; the postilion (as we heard was his habit) was drunk, the leader had been accustomed to go the other way and took the wrong turn, and between them this was the result. The people in the interior were soon out, but, as nobody seemed inclined to help those in the *coupé*, Church and I jumped up on the coach (the *door* side was undermost), the fools of Frenchmen holloaing out 'Ne montez pas sur la voiture,' and began to help out our friends. First came the Englishman, covered with blood, but only a little bruised, who proceeded to help the others; then the young lady, dreadfully cut about the face, her nose laid open, who (perhaps naturally) had lost her wits and, instead of getting out of the way, sat *in* the window, crying 'Sauvez mon père,' a thing impossible while she sat there; next the old gentleman, quite quiet, except that he too had been crying 'Sauvez ma fille,' covered with blood, very pale, and with an arm broken. The only other serious hurt seemed to be an old woman who complained of her shoulder, but more of the back of her head, which was bleeding profusely, a good thing as I supposed. She was travelling with her son (a soldier) and daughter, who seemed attentive but not alarmed. After much parleying the surgeon was sent for and arrived, and finding them in good hands we left for Châteaulin, having done what we could to help the young French lady in the matter of luggage &c. They had friends at Châteaulin, who, as well as the Brest brother-in-law, were immediately sent for. The next morning we met the old man *walking* into Châteaulin with his friends, weak but professing himself better, his daughter's face terribly cut about. But we heard very bad accounts of somebody, whom I take to be the old woman. The priest had been sent for, and had administered extreme unction and they expected her to die. I had no conception of her being so much hurt, and hope it is not true. She sat upright against a piece of timber slightly leaning against a wall, and was able to talk and walk, and help a little in making herself a sling for her hurt arm.

Tuesday we came here, a most beautiful drive, and after dinner drove to a professed ruin (the first regular humbug we have come across), which Mlle. de Cadeille in her injudicious goodness had provided for us, together with a copy of the *Nation* (Irish newspaper), a history of Landerneau, and of certain mines not far off.

To-day M. de Cadeille called, a friendly old gentleman, and has thought it necessary to send us to see the Landerneau racecourse ! he not being well enough to go with us. Conceive being boxed up in his carriage and packed off as if one was the Spanish Ambassador to such a place. However, it is curious. What think you of an old half-Druidical looking *cross*, opposite the great stand and between the bands of musicians on the top of an exposed heath ? We saw an interesting church on our way back, else I should say M. de C.'s civility was unfortunate. However, I must finish or I shall keep his dinner waiting. Love to all,

Yours affectionately,

F. R.

To Mr. Church.

October, 1844.

Dear Church,—All is right here. Lefevre exceedingly civil, not at all of a *don*, and has put me into the hands of a little lawyer named Symonds, now a Registrar of Metropolitan Buildings, who drew the bill and is up to details. Yesterday walked about with them choosing an *office*, probably close by here in Serjeants' Inn, and a *seal* of office. I shall soon be immersed in consideration of portfolios, *book-binding*, modes of *pasting documents*, *ruling lines*, managing clerks and messengers, drawing forms, &c.; at present totally at sea.

I have had two interviews with Lefevre, and am to have an enormous palaver with Symonds on Monday, and back to Lefevre on Thursday, meantime getting up Acts of Parliament and Blue Books.

I have an assistant and three or four clerks certain. Nobody knows or can guess the extent of work which is to be done; it seems to me likely to be enormous, and Lefevre tells me that with moderate industry I may in a month or two know more about the matter than any one else and be a person to be referred to by the Board of Trade on these matters 'which we know nothing about.'

To Mrs. Rogers.

Guingamp : August 28, 1845.

My dear Mother,—As you see, I am at Guingamp, but without very much to say yet. Lefevre thought there was no necessity for my staying in town, so I started from London by the 3 o'clock train, and from Southampton by the 7 o'clock Jersey packet. About 1 o'clock the next day we arrived at Jersey, changed instanter to another packet, and arrived at St. Malo about 6 o'clock. At 7 o'clock the next (Wednesday) morning I started for Guingamp, *viâ* Dinan and St. Brieuc. My travelling companion from St. Malo to St. Brieuc was a good-humoured, unaffected priest, successor of the Abbé Malais at the Hôtel Dieu at Rouen, who talked a good deal about the religious state of France. He gave a most tremendous picture of it, far worse than I was prepared for. Every one, he said, received their 'premier communion,' but after that never attended a religious service or received any religious instruction, and consequently before a few years are over are positively without any religious idea of any sort or kind. And he would not allow that there was much difference (at least in Normandy) between the country and the town. The rising generation, he said, are worst of all. And the schools (which everybody is almost obliged to attend, private schools not being allowed by the laws) are practically schools of infidelity. He has books to lend to the patients in the Hôpital, histories of Rome, lives of good men, &c. If he attempts to lend anything religious the patients tell him 'C'est bon pour les enfans.' However, he said he is sufficiently respected to be able to take possession of all *bad* books that he finds circulating there, though Government (under whom all these hospitals are) would not bear him out in doing so and have signified as much.

At 5 we[3] dined at St. Brieuc, and I transferred myself (there being no room in the diligence) to a most miserable little *voiture de retour*, which got me to Guingamp about 10 o'clock.

To-day I have taken a long walk up the Trieux and back again, and have been rather disappointed. The river is a quiet little trout stream running along a narrow, and not very deep valley, with a slight edging (generally) on one or both sides of water meadow, and beyond that of wood or heath, with rock breaking through occasionally; water mills every mile or two. This *might*, of course, be beautiful, but it is not even pretty owing to the want of boldness of form, and partly to the Breton custom of lopping up their trees like the most absurd of our hedgerow elm trees. I think I should say that the want of fine trees was the great mischief. I made two sketches only, one an attempt at water-colours, both failures, but the water-colour sufficiently near success to encourage me to try again. The day was *dull* and uniform (threatening rain), which made it hopeless for a beginner to make anything of colours. I think my attempt would have been much

---

[3] He was travelling with Mr. Mountague Bernard.

better if I had had the sun. I had it only for five minutes at the end, just long enough to show me the absurd mistakes I had made. Of course I collected a crowd of dirty children (at least the second time about eight or nine), some jabbering a little French and all a great deal of Breton, and having a great deal of fun. I ascertained that the name of the place I was drawing was Sainte Croix, and inquired the meaning of a phrase which they kept repeating to one another with infinite amusement, pronounced 'állapol ká.' However, they could give me no information except 'c'est ce que M. Maynard dit,' which would have puzzled me if I had not happened to see in a window that morning a set of infamously bad caricatures of which 'M. Maynard' is the hero. I certainly did not expect even the name of the polka to have made its way down to the dirty little children of a most miserable village in Brittany.

Yours affectionately,
F. R.

To Mrs. H. Legge.

Le Faou: September 8, 1845.

My dear Marian,—To-day (Monday) we have come into Le Faou, to see a 'pardon' at a place called Huelgoat, where there is a holy oak. It had, of course, all the ordinary features of a 'pardon,' the costumes were quaint and varied, but the scenery less striking than at the one I had seen at La Forêt. But a few peculiar features. People make pilgrimages to Huelgoat, and accordingly we had people walking barefoot or scrambling on their knees round the church, and water being served out to drink, at a holy well close by, at which also people came pressing to wash their feet and hands and say a prayer. But the oddest thing was the mixture of *fair* with the whole. The first thing was Mass at 11 o'clock. We went into the church to have a look at part of the service, preached in Breton, with much variety of tone and apparently very familiar; then the preacher sat down for a time in the pulpit and began talking to them (as it seemed to me) in a familiar expostulatory way; the women all in the nave, squatting down on the ground, a sea of white caps; the men standing in the transepts and sitting on benches, or on the steps of the altar—fine-looking fellows, generally with long hair down their backs and a dress something between a Swiss peasant and a gentleman of George I.'s time, very quiet and respectful (except a little whispering) but somewhat immovable. But after service there was the funniest sequel. Offerings are made at this place to a considerable extent, and those who can't give money may give what they can, a gay ribbon, an old coat, an ornamented child's skull cap, &c. Well, when mass was over, four long-haired young fellows who had been employed to go round the church and churchyard with plates for money, and who are evidently the wags of the village, got up on the steps of the cross in the churchyard, and without delay put up all these offerings to sale to the highest bidder. All the women collected round them and there was a quarter of an hour's high fun about all their ribbons, which, as it appeared to me, did not fetch any very extraordinary price, if indeed they were got off at all. Then came three or four hours' waiting till vespers at 3 o'clock. One or two cabarets opened (Greenwich fair fashion) opposite the church, and a few stalls at which you could get a certain variety of eatables and drinkables, there being one stall for each separate article. Bernard and I composed our luncheon as follows: we bought at one stall a roll apiece which we split, we then went to another stall where a dirty fisherman was frying small fish, of them we bought four (fried on the spot with incredible despatch), deposited them in our rolls and departed to sit down under a hedge to devour them with our fingers and pocket knife, then we came back again and bought a halfpenny-worth of wine apiece at a third stall and the same amount of pears at a fourth; being in all: rolls, two sous; fish, one sou; wine, one sou; dessert, one sou. And this seemed the general mode of proceeding. Then came vespers, I fear not quite so decorously attended, some of the Bretons having used the intermediate time to get very drunk. A second collection of money by the long-haired young gentlemen, and high romps with some young ladies to get their money from them; after service a procession, and all went home.

Crozon : September 11.

September 9.—Boat to a place called Landevenne on the Brest river. Walk about the country with beautiful views of the river reminding one of the view over the Alf at Prinzes Köppfen. Steam up the Aulne to Châteaulin, an old friend. At Châteaulin the next day we saw the tail of a fête, people dancing for a prize, and a general dance in the evening to the playing of the celebrated hautbois player of the country, a blind man named Maturin. This hautbois with a bagpipe accompaniment was the only music, and so far as I could see, it appeared pretty much going the whole day. What the players' lungs are made of I don't know, I suppose brass and leather like their instruments. About 10 or 11 o'clock we saw one playing to an increasing party of (then) ten or fifteen, who were dancing with an odd vigorous gravity in the middle of the high road ; at 2 o'clock he was playing to amuse the populace during the foot-races, for men and women ; at three o'clock he began playing to the prize dancers, general dancing began immediately, and about eight o'clock he was still playing in the thick of a hard shower. The dancing is highly funny, half the population of the town form themselves into strings of ten or twenty, and set to work cantering about a dusty *place d'armes* (which they call the 'champ de bataille' and entirely fill) with consummate care and deliberation, holding each other by the little finger and occasionally changing the leader after a fashion which I did not understand. How they managed to avoid utter confusion I don't know. But, as they did, the effect of these long lines coiling about, sometimes straight and parallel with each other, sometimes crossing each other and turning sharp round, was very quaint and rather pretty.

Quimper : September 12.

Yesterday we drove to a place called Crozon to see some beautiful grottoes and splendid coast scenery (rock) on a little peninsula south of Brest. This thoroughly answered : fine weather, barring a haze, and the things magnificent. Then a drive from Crozon here, where we have just arrived. It looks very pretty, but we have only seen it at night. But perhaps the most curious part of the Crozon business was the old scamp of a fisherman who rowed us about. He told us that at the time of the cholera it was fully believed by the common people that the rich ('the nobles' as he called them) had caused it in order to get rid of the surplus population, and that if it had lasted six weeks longer 'tous les riches auraient été égorgés,' a process which he seemed to regard with very tolerable complacency himself. He, I think, plainly believed that the rich and the physicians had been in a league against the 'malheureux,' having, he told us, himself heard the physicians say of a young fellow whom they were attending, 'Il faut sauver celui-ci, il fera bon soldat,' and he *was* saved. They did not know, he said, that he understood French, but he knew what they said. I asked him if the physicians could have saved more men if they had chosen, and then he stuck his tongue out and nodded grimly and made a quantity of contortions signifying 'Let them alone for that.' I think all fellows who are given to Jacquerie have the same way of leering and twisting their tongues about. This man was thoroughly ignorant, had been a sailor and present at the taking of a place of which he could not remember the name, but which turned out to be Algiers, was a long time understanding that London was the capital of England, but was no inconsiderable philosopher in a practical way, agreed with the rich that there were too many people in France, but thought the proper remedy was a *war*. Thought it might be no bad thing that one half of the 'malheureux' might be put out of the world by the management of the 'riches,' no use for the 'malheureux' to serve out the 'riches' in that way, they would only fall quarrelling who should have their goods; often had not bread to put into his children's mouths, but knew that he slept sound and had less 'chagrin' than a 'riche,' and finished by imposing on us most outrageously, after having shown us the grottoes, I must say, very well.

I should think it clear that, though the power of the priests is in full vigour, that of the seigneurs is wholly gone. In fact, without the law of primogeniture it can hardly exist. But the division of party seems to me to be between town and country. M. de Cadeille told us that the *campagnards* thought that the bourgeois had *done* them and got all the good things for themselves in the last revolution, and would take the first plausible opportunity of rising and pillaging the towns. This, however, is difficult, as they are all disarmed, while the town people are not. Half-past eleven o'clock. Good-night.

Ever yours affectionately,
F. R.

To Miss Rogers.

Colonial Office : May 28, 1846.

My dear Katherine,—Here you have my first Colonial *date*. The Order in Council is to come out to-morrow, at least to be made, and I *am* appointed here ; with a formal letter of proposal from Gladstone in my pocket. A precaution, I suspect, not wholly unnecessary or rather not at all premature, the Ministry being suspected of a considerable amount of ricketiness.

I am now in possession of a large first-floor room looking out on the park, but with the view rather the worse for certain trees before the windows ; badly furnished, but furniture has been ordered consonant with the dignity of an Assistant Under Secretary ; rather cold, which must be cured by fires, and having the inconvenience that I am able to hear most of the conversation of the clerks in the next room. This has to be cured by a large insertion of sawdust into the walls.

I had an interview with Stephen [1] on Friday and again to-day. He lectured me for about an hour on the mode of managing the Colonies, and my own position in the office, the features of the latter being that he did not look on me with jealousy or dislike because he looked on me as a probable successor, and that I was to understand that I was a cut above the clerks, and was to ring to have them sent to me when I wanted them. Conceive my telling the messenger to send me forthwith Philip van Artevelde (who is the senior clerk).[5]

---

[1] Sir James Stephen was then Under Secretary for the Colonies.
[5] Mr. (afterwards Sir Henry) Taylor.

To-day I came here to deposit myself at 2 o'clock, and was duly introduced to all the senior clerks, Taylor, our friend Murdoch, a Mr. Blackwood whom I have met at Gladstone's, with two or three others. I hear ominous words as to the dulness of my probable work; however, that must take its chance. Beginnings are always dull.

Hitherto I like Stephen. He is the most consecutive, or rather continuous, talker I ever heard flow, with a great deal in what he says, and singular precision of thought and expression and a spice of humour running through the whole. I also like the looks and manner of the people I have been introduced to. Murdoch &c. very friendly. What the juniors may think of the matter I don't know. *Nous verrons.*

I have also been to the Emigration Office to Wood and Elliott, both very warm and pleasant; we soon got our feet on the fender.

To Mrs. Rogers.

Steamer off Genoa: December 20, 1846.

My dear Mother,—To set your mind at rest about my *having received* Lord Grey's letter,[6] I write this, though I shall follow it and perhaps pass it on the road. I received that and your others immediately after having posted the letter in which I say I have *not* received them.

With regard to Lord Grey's letter your soul was prophetic. It is an offer of the appointment of Secretary of Governor at Malta with 1,500*l.* a year coupled with an announcement that he does not think I possess 'that peculiar aptitude for dealing with large masses of business' which would be necessary for an Under Secretary of State, and that therefore, in case of Stephen's giving up his place, he would not appoint me. He supposes that I accepted my present appointment with an understanding that I should succeed to that post, and therefore that he is bound to say this. I have written an answer which goes with this letter thanking him, begging to be allowed to

---

[6] Sir Robert Peel had resigned in June of this year, defeated on an Irish Coercion Bill, just after the passing of the Repeal of the Corn Laws. Lord John Russell had become Prime Minister and Lord Grey had succeeded Mr. Gladstone as Secretary for War and Colonies.

defer my answer till two or three days after my return to England, and telling him that no such understanding existed.

Of course, this announcement (though I could not suppose that any one would appoint me Under Secretary of State all at once) comes in a mortifying shape. But the question is, What is to be done with the offer? Viewing the matter personally the *pros* are: higher pay, less work, climate which would suit my health, and a work which would have probably more variety and more independence about it (I should think) than my present, which is simply that of legal cad to Stephen, also if, which I feel to be very possible, Lord Grey is right in thinking that my forte does not lie in dealing with masses of business, the taking a principal part in the actual management of a small colony might suit me better and show me to better advantage than having to deal with the paper work of the whole. I don't know whether it is a *pro* or a *con* that I should hope for the most part to have one of my sisters with me. Then the *cons*: removal from home, I mean from yourselves, and the chance both of missing higher preferment in England and of missing opportunities of being useful to the other members of the family. The uncomfortable part of the matter is that I am afraid it is in the nature of an intimation from Lord Grey that he would be glad to get rid of me if possible, and if his desire to do so took the turn of depreciating what I did (which, considering my inexperience and Stephen's position over me, it would be very easy for him to effect and almost impossible for me to meet) it certainly would make my position very uncomfortable. I don't think I ought to do anything definitive without writing to Gladstone, which I shall do by this post. I should be inclined to be much influenced by seeing what effect Lord Grey's letter had on him.

It is to be observed that, excepting Governorships, the appointment must be about the most eligible of all of which Lord Grey has the patronage.

To Lady Rogers.
Oxford : July 20, 1847.

Matters here are going on as was prophesied. We are ahead, but it is a near thing. The number of votes given to-day is (I think) 321 for Round, 362 for Gladstone, besides 200 others who have paired. A majority of 31 on 700 is not very large, but we consider this day has had adverse circumstances about it, and so are in heart for to-morrow. . . . One of the Roman Catholic converts has thought fit to tender his vote for Gladstone. They have stopped his mouth by insisting (as I believe without a shadow of law or right) on his taking the oath of supremacy. The unfortunate pleaded that his name was on the books, that no formal sentence of disability had passed on him, and that he had actually just paid his college dues, for which he produced the Bursar's receipt. However, they stopped him with the oath for that day, and now they find that, as he is in Holy Orders, they can blow him up by application of the 39 Articles, which if he does not subscribe on demand, he will, *pro facto*, incur every requisite disability. The man is notoriously as mad as a March hare.

To Rev. R. W. Church.
9 Park Street : March 3, 1848.

My dear Church,—I ought to have thanked you for your letter and the news in it long ago. But I half expected to have seen you in town as you promised. And now I write principally because if I don't write I sha'n't hear from you again.

I suppose the Præmunire negotiations [7] between Lord John and our friends have gone off into nothing. If it is so I am not sorry for it. I could hardly fancy anything coming of it, and in some way or other I do not doubt he would have got the best of it ; either he would have taken them in or he would have led them to do something which would have seemed to put them in the wrong.

[7] *I.e.* the correspondence regarding Lord John Russell's appointment of Dr. Hampden to the See of Hereford.

What do you say to Louis Philippe? It seems clear, or at least is thought so, that he could have put down the mob if he would have authorised firing cannon upon them. They say that the Duke of Nemours says that he himself besought him to give the necessary authority but the King would not. The D. of N. and the Princess Clementine embarked for England in the same steamer, both in disguise, and the Duke was only recognised by one of his children (who was with the Princess) hearing his voice accidentally and crying out 'Ah voilà mon papa!' Somebody passing the Princess (I suppose English) in the streets (in France) slipped a *ten pound note* into her hand—a curiously thoughtful thing to do. I don't know whether these latter matters have got into the papers. I believe they are Royal Family gossip, at least they rise in that direction.

The most alarming consideration to *my mind* in the matter is that if a war breaks out it will put an end to all Emigration. They must turn us into a War Department.

How curiously picturesque some of the bits are already, and how dreadfully parallel with the old story! Does it not strike you that Lamartine's life is in a very uninsurable state? I should think he would be one of the first to be knocked off the perch as time goes on, probably by the commandant, whoever he may be, of their new penniless brigade.

People seem rather anxious about Lord John's health, and beginning to speculate what is to happen if he slips off. Some say Peel is ready to take the command. A. Wood, professing to be in the secret, declares that he abhors the very notion. And some protectionists talk of the necessity of reunion against radicalism. They continue to talk of Goulburn (!!) as a leader.

To Rev. James Mozley

9 Ovington Square: April 9, 1848.

We are in a good deal of excitement here.[8] Ministers expect regular mischief: the Admiralty is filled with arms and marines. They say that the Chartists make no secret of their

---

[8] The Chartist gathering on Kennington Common was on Monday, April 10.

intention to have it out; and, especially, to attack the Government offices. The consequence is that we are all expected to appear at nine o'clock to-morrow, and to stay the night—dying at our posts if necessary. Guns are to be had on application at the Treasury, but only in case of special need (in which event of course not a soul would be able to get out of the house), and with a distinct charge that no one is to be trusted with a gun who does not know how to load and fire it—or who is likely to be in a very great fright. Elliot, my quondam chief, is extremely grand—like a man who feels himself in the face of an emergency to which he is equal—a mixture of the man of business, of presence of mind, of decision, and of light-heartedness. Another colleague fussy, anxious for orders: 'What are we to do? We must understand clearly what is expected of us' &c., &c. Downing Street preparing its mind for bloodshed, and for accepting assistance from the Emigration Office (which it is supposed, rightly enough, will escape notice in the bustle), in case they should 'lose any men!' Everybody is a special constable; and constabular rank is regulated by official rank —rather a fantastic notion, ὡς ἐμοὶ δοκεῖν. Some of the fat messengers and skinny copyists who are put in requisition, and whom I saw swearing to do their duty 'without favour or partiality, ill will or malice' (they say nothing about fear), pass ludicrousness.

Meanwhile the whole matter, at least the serious part of it, is in the hands of the Duke [of Wellington]; and I hear from people who are a good deal with him that they never saw him with his wits more about him. The plan hitherto has been to occupy the bridges, and so keep the mob to Southwark and Lambeth, but there is now a rumour that they have changed the locality of the demonstration to Primrose Hill. They obviously should have done this at first; but I cannot conceive that they can do it now without confusion. At any rate, it is odd if Feargus O'Connor out-generals the Duke. My artillery brother is on duty for Kennington Common, as adjutant; and I hear he has been riding over to reconnoitre the ground with his colonel. So I suppose they contemplate the possibility of a row on the spot.

I hear now it is to be a variety of small rows in different places. They say we are to have several days of it, Tuesday the worst. A French policeman tells Guizot, who tells the world, that he recognises in the streets the faces of many of the most forward people in the French fight. This I had heard said before. We had a report here, which proved false, that there was fighting in Ireland; but Irishmen say that the fighting there will depend on what happens here. Others say it will wait for an anticipated rise in Canada.

No ministerial rumours. Everything is merged in the mob.

Yours affectionately,
F. ROGERS.

To Lady Rogers.

Plymouth: May 31, 1848.

Our Irish workhouse girls arrived here by Monday's steamer from Dublin. I got to the Depôt just in time to see the lighter (or barge) arrive full of them—a very pretty sight it was, one of those picturesque barges with dark red sails full of 185 bright cloaks and shawls of different colours, clean and new, and they came out picturesque but not pretty. In fact, they are generally ugly and clumsy, though healthy and strong, but there was a certain amount of uniform about them which was pleasing. The Presbyterians from Belfast all in grey ill-made gowns and tippets—a kind of tweed stuff. Armagh bright brown and white printed cotton. Lisburne checked red shawls, &c., &c. They seemed generally glad to go. I only met with one that wished herself back again, a helpless kind of creature. But they were all excessively disgusted at the notion of being parted from their 'comrades;' they seemed already to have selected partners for the voyage. One poor girl was quite in tears at being separated from the other 'Lisburne' girls, and came to me to remind me that I had promised they should be all together. It turned out that her bag was inside out, which made her number (which was 91) look like 19. When she got to berth 91 there was her name nailed up in the thick of her friends, to her great joy. We have got about 70 Roman Catholics about the same, I fancy, of Presbyterians, and rather more of Church of England.

The Wesleyan matron I hope will do well when on board. She is getting on well with the sub-matrons, and has two daughters who will also be sub-matrons. Meantime she has been blundering about her luggage. It has not arrived, and in an hour or two the ship will be ready to start except for her. Luckily the wind is contrary (it has just become so), else we should have the 'Earl Grey' with its three masts, captain, crew, and 200 emigrants all waiting in port (perhaps losing the wind) for Mrs. C.'s portmanteau.

To Rev. R. W. Church.

Sydenham, 1849.

Work is slackening with me, and I am meditating something for the 'Christian Remembrancer,' but don't know what. Can you suggest anything better than 'Friends in Council,' Vol. II. ? I have not seen it yet, but think it must be (from what I have read of Helps's) a kind of thing I could prose about. You see the difficulty is want of eyes and of steady working time.

When Keble comes back from the Isle of Man you must find out what he has to say for himself. My wife gave him a letter to her uncle, the liberal Bishop,[9] who is a very frank, kind, and hard-working person, though of course Whig enough. From all we can hear they seem to have got on very flourishingly. The Bishop obviously considers himself to have got *rises* out of Keble about Miss Sellon &c., and I have no doubt poked him about a good deal. And I see no signs of Keble having given him the rough side of his tongue. Indeed, there is an honesty about him by which I can fancy the said Keble being much taken. But I should like to know. They seemed rather shocked at his ideas of discipline and could not stomach the idea of Bishop Wilson whipping (?) penitents.[1]

---

[9] Lord Auckland, then Bishop of Sodor and Man, afterwards Bishop of Bath and Wells.

[1] In Keble's *Life of Dr. Thomas Wilson, Bishop of Sodor and Man*, there is mention of the Bishop's strict discipline.

To Rev. Edward Rogers.

9 Park Street : August 11, 1849.

We have of course been going on quietly enough here. I find not much office work (of which I am glad) and I think the eyes are a little improving. Our principal event is a run down to Eton for Election Saturday. We betook ourselves to Pickering, who, of course, was all that was hospitable. We cabbed to Surly Hall, and got into his punt to see the fireworks, and very interesting it all was. The boys looked so like gentlemen, with so much freedom and no misbehaviour. It certainly is a noble nursery for an English university. No wonder gentlemen are not radicals. I really seem to myself to be almost thrown back into one's old steady-going or rather rampageous Tory ways of thinking by looking at the old place and the young people. Pickering gave a very good account of their behaviour, especially *in re* church ; and James Mozley, who spent three or four days there with one of the Hawtreys, was much struck at the tone (*inter alia*) of the speeches at Election Monday ; so much more serious than our 'Gaudes ;' and he was surprised to find that 'strong' men like Abraham [2] were viewed with so little suspicion or prejudice even by Dons and Provosts. . . .

You will probably have seen that Sir H. Jenner [3] has given judgment against Gorham on the ground that Baptismal Regeneration is the doctrine of the Church of England. People talked of a secession in consequence, but that is all nonsense, I take it. It is really, however, a very great point gained. It puts a large mass of heterodox people into a state of mere *sufferance*, to say the least, and probably will make them feel that they live in glass houses.

[2] Afterwards Bishop of Wellington in New Zealand.

[3] Sir H. Jenner was Dean of Arches. The question was whether the Bishop of Exeter (Dr. Phillpotts) could refuse to institute Mr. Gorham to the living of Bramford Speke, to which he had been appointed. Sir H. Jenner's judgment was reversed by the Judicial Committee of the Privy Council, and Mr. Gorham was eventually inducted.

CHAPTER V

Continuation of Work as Commissioner of Emigration.

To Miss Rogers.

London: June 12, 1850.

I HEAR no ecclesiastical or political news. There seems a lull in both departments. The report that Dodsworth, Allen, Henry Wilberforce, and some others are going over forthwith, does not seem *yet* true, though I am afraid it can be no more than a respite, which, if so, is worth little. Keble is getting, I think, very much put out at the Romanisers, *imprimis* with their attacks on Pusey, whom some of them who are gone do not scruple to describe as possessed by the devil. Perhaps this was mentioned by Church while you were with us.

G. has just told me an amusing story, which I dare say you have heard, of the Nepaulese ambassador who is the great lion just now. Passing St. Paul's he suddenly told the carriage to stop, and spoke a few words to a Hindoo who was sweeping the crossing, on which the man threw his broom over the churchyard, gaily got into the carriage and drove off. That evening the man was at Lady Londonderry's party dressed up in all sorts of magnificent toggery, and all the world was saying how much pleasanter it was now that the 'princes' had got an interpreter. Rather a sudden rise in life. A curious importation of Oriental ups and downs into the City of London.

To Miss Rogers.

9 Ovington Square: September 10, 1850.

Did I tell you that I made acquaintance with Edward Barnard, who acted as chairman to a dinner given by the

'Fire Annihilator Company' to which I was asked? He was friendly and amusing, talked a good deal of our family and more of Eton, and told some good old Eton and Colonial Office stories. The 'demonstration,' as they called it, of their 'annihilator' was certainly remarkable. They set on fire a long tank (I think fifty feet by six) of pitch, shavings, turpentine, &c., and when the whole was in a blaze ten or twelve feet high, two men with machines like large ill-conditioned watering-pots, walked slowly from one end to the other, just sweeping the fire out as they went. In the inside of their machine was a composition which when ignited threw forth a kind of steaming gas that totally put out any flame which it came into contact with. Then they set on fire a lot of combustibles in the between decks of a barge while the company were all walking on the deck, and just smothered it out in two or three minutes with these same watering pots, after allowing it to blaze up through the hatchways, sending up (I should think) twenty feet high or more of flame. Lastly they set on fire a lot of combustibles inside a *plank* house; and when the flame had broken the windows and was blazing out of every aperture, put the whole out with their pots *saving the plank walls*. Of course, the object was to get us to force passenger ships to carry their machines, which was perfectly obvious to one or two large shipowners who were part of the party, and one of them rather disturbed the harmony of the evening by gruffly protesting against having inventions fastened on them and tried at their expense; 'he didn't see why such a set was to be made at the shipowners, let the householders first be told that they must all supply themselves with annihilators and then it would be time to come upon the shipowners.'

Ever yours,
F. R.

To Miss Rogers.

Ovington Square: November 23, 1850.

In re the Pope, articles in the 'Guardian' (the last of which was mine, the one before Haddan's) express pretty much my views.[1] It is a matter against which the Church of England

---

[1] The Pope had issued a bull establishing a hierarchy of Bishops who were to take their titles from certain sees which he constituted. There were, of

may properly protest, but I think the great hubbub one of the most arrant pieces of humbug that was ever got up by a Whig Minister for his own ends. The more I think of it the more I think it so. How Lord John is to get out of his letter I don't know. Wiseman seems to me to demolish him absolutely. They say his colleagues dislike his skit at the Roman 'mummeries.' I expect there will be a patch up at the expense of the Church, and perhaps under the auspices of H. M., who is believed to have set it going. I don't myself expect so much harm to the Church from this kind of mere vulgar outbreak as from the distribution of Church patronage. The mob outcry will wear itself out and then common sense, as it does in the end, will get uppermost.

Manning, Dodsworth, and Aubrey de Vere are going together to Palestine. I suppose they will join Rome out there, at least I don't suppose any one would join Manning and Dodsworth who did not intend to follow them. I hear cases of disquiet every here and there.

However, I don't see any shaking in our clique; Keble is as firm as a rock and stouter in acquiescing in aggression against Rome than I ever thought to see him. There is a degree both of attack and of liberalism in my articles which I feared he would not approve. But he does wholly.

Mozley is setting to work with a book on Baptism. He declares there has been no *thinking* for the last twenty years, not even by Newman, so he is going to give the world his thoughts, which I am afraid will not wholly give satisfaction. As if we had not enough to torment us, he is bitten by St. Augustine's Predestinarianism. I believe Wynne *will* try to

course, Roman Catholic Bishops already in England, and it mattered little if they took their titles from Westminster &c., but at this particular time the claim of the Pope to divide England into dioceses seemed to some a dangerous aggression, connected (as to some extent it was) with the conversions which had followed the Oxford Movement. Lord John Russell very unwisely wrote a letter (on November 4), addressed to the Bishop of Durham, inveighing against the Papal usurpation, and against Tractarianism, in the strongest terms. A strong anti papal agitation with much bitterness on both sides was the result. Eventually the Government passed the 'Ecclesiastical Titles Bill,' which made it penal for a Roman Catholic Bishop to assume a title from any existing See. It was not a very dignified form of protest and as a piece of legislation was quite nugatory. It was repealed in 1871.

keep his All Souls Fellowship. But the report of ——'s trying to keep his rectory I take to be false. When I was at Abbotsford a letter arrived from him to say that he had resigned, and was there for a few days to pack up his things for a new residence, and (this was the object of his letter) wanted to know whether Hope could tell him anything about the cheapness of *cooking by gas*! Pound a monkey in a mortar and his monkeyism will not depart from him. . . . Northcote, I hear, is working hard at country knowledge and begins to know one breed of cattle from another; I hope he will get into Parliament.

G. and I went (with an order of his) to see the buildings of the Exposition.[2] It is a very remarkable sight. Something itself between a gigantic green-house and a gigantic railway station. But the singular part was the appearance of rapid rise that it had; so much space occupied, so many things going on, saw-pits, circular saws, forges, all kinds of carpenter shops, iron skeletons rising here, glass being put in there, holes for the foundation elsewhere. And the ingenious machinery for cutting into shape the window frames, each bit passing through almost as many hands as a pin does, all this gave a marvellous idea of promptitude and order. The thing itself is wonderfully light. One can hardly conceive its standing. Foundations it can hardly be said to have at all. Slender columns of iron set in pits about four feet square and two deep, filled with concrete, are all that the building is to stand on. I calculated that some of these columns would have to support *each* about seventy square yards covered with people and goods, independently of the building itself. We were there when the dinner bell rang (there are about 2,000 people at work), and the effect was like stirring an enormous ants' nest; there was a general bustle overhead on the roofs, galleries, &c., all clustering round the ladders, crowding, clambering, and sliding down, and streaming down all the aisles from the workshops and works.

[2] Sir Stafford Northcote was one of the most active commissioners for the Exhibition of 1851.

To Miss Rogers.

Ovington Square : April 1, 1851.

My dear Kate,—I hear that Lord John is after all in again with just the old set. I cannot help hoping, however, that he has lost a remarkable amount of credit and can't last very long. You will have seen by the papers all that has taken place and I can tell you no more.

I went, however, with Church (who has just left us) to the debate in the Lords last night. Stanley was excellent, so gentlemanly and natural.[3] It struck me very much how in all his behaviour about the crisis, he had been a thorough gentleman without losing any advantage which he was bound to take as a politician and the head of a party. The grounds on which, in the first instance, he threw back on Lord John the onus of forming a coalition Ministry seemed to me very well taken and well brought out.

I am not at present dissatisfied with the state of things. Stanley and Gladstone could not have coalesced with honour ; so I am glad they have not. I am also glad that the first great move has been taken, and that with so much weight and resolution against the Papal Aggression row, by Lord Aberdeen and Sir J. Graham. It cannot fail to have weight. And you will see that Stanley in effect gives the question very much of a shelving by the parliamentary inquiry which he proposes. Then he brings the question of Protection to an issue which is obviously intended to set it at rest. If he fails to get a Protectionist parliament next general election, he says, he and his friends are prepared to take it as a *fait accompli.* This will be a great stumbling-block out of the way, and it is a great thing that his party are made to feel the necessity of coalescing with some of the Peel party ; indeed, it almost looks as if Stanley wished to make them feel it. It was impossible, I thought, to gather whether he felt any bitterness towards Gladstone and Co. for not joining him (he was short but complimentary and dropped nothing) I fancy that the subs do.

---

[3] Lord Stanley did not succeed his father (as 14th Earl of Derby) till June of this year, but he had been called up to the House of Lords in 1844.

What I must rejoice at is that there is no Peelite and Whig fusion. I suppose Graham will before long join them, but I do trust he will leave his party behind him. How closely they do or do not hold together at present there is nothing at all, as far as I hear, to show. I ought to say that the papers have dropped the last sentence of Stanley's last speech which told very well. You will see that Lord Lansdowne attacked him for not believing fully the Ministers' statement of the reasons of their resignation. He replied by pointing out the hurried precipitate way in which it had been done; the noble Marquis was safe at Bowood all the time, a noble Earl (Carlisle) first heard in the City that there was no cabinet for him to belong to, the Lord Privy Seal, a relation of the Premier, was as ignorant of his intentions as of those of the Pope, 'and' (then he leant forward across the table and raised his voice like a person in thoroughly good humour with all the world and his own joke) 'and his noble relation didn't even pay him the compliment of saying, "*There's something that concerns you!*"' I don't know how the hit reads, but it quite told on the House, and I can't understand how the reporters missed it. There was good-humoured 'Put that in your pipe and smoke it' in his manner of doing it which was perfect.

My impression is that Stanley will have gained in public estimation by the really handsome, manly, and clever way in which he has done the whole thing. His tone was very conciliatory towards the Peelites, and I should hope (though I don't know) that a coalition with some of them hereafter was facilitated, rather than otherwise.

To Miss Rogers.

London: September 18, 1851.

I have had William Froude [4] for a few days here, but he is off to the Mediterranean to cruise with the captain of a steam ship of war. Among other things he is to go to Alexandria to see about the possibility of removing Cleopatra's needle, as the Pasha of Egypt has given in. We had a great

---

[4] The civil engineer, brother of Hurrell Froude and of James Anthony Froude

discussion as to what he should see in going through France and I flatter myself I have made out a very good fortnight for him. He had not time for the Exhibition, but took me through Maudslay's (the great engineer's) works. Most striking they are. The size of everything was wonderful, but what was most wonderful to me was to see punches and shears cutting through iron plates an inch thick like so much soap. To say that they cut it as quietly as scissors cut paper is below the mark. The shear (almost a foot long) came down and went through with a steady, tranquil, noiseless softness as if it met just with no resistance at all. Since that I have been trying to get up the cotton-making machinery in the Exhibition and have made some way towards understanding a mule and a power loom—wonderfully beautiful contrivances both of them. But I am shocked to find how close I must get to a thing to understand it.

The news of the gold in N. S. Wales is at last officially confirmed. Sir C. Fitzroy sends a sketch of one lump weighing forty-seven ounces. Thousands are off from Sydney, making a sensible difference, he said, in the population. Of course, many are wholly unfit for the work, and it did not appear how they were to feed or to travel along the 200 or 300 miles which they had to get across. Ships can't get off from the desertion of the sailors, and we here cannot get ships to go to Sydney (for that reason) except at the most exorbitant prices. I trust we shall make a better affair of it than California, but with a convict population to deal with I don't envy the Government. Of course, no one but Government has a right to lay a single finger on a single grain of gold; but there are not the physical means of preventing them from helping themselves.

To Miss Rogers.

London: 1851.

I was amused the other day at a police dodge, which I had never heard before, practised at the opening of the Exhibition. They had at the gate a bunch of detectives 'of all nations,' and as the *chevaliers d'industrie* of all nations came in, the police gave a sign, and the check-taker gave them a green instead of white or yellow card. When they got in, the employés were directed to show all the gentlemen and ladies with green cards into a particular inclosed quarter of the building, so that each 'swell' as he arrived was civilly handed on till he was finally shown into a family party of his own friends. Of course no exit was allowed. I can't help laughing at the thought of the fellows one after another coming in with their best behaviour on, and looking out for a place near a good victim, and becoming gradually alive to the fact that they were all old friends of a sort. It must have been worth while being one of the first comers, to have seen how all the rest took it.

I have lots to do, so good-bye. Love to all. I suppose you have seen in the paper Lady Buckinghamshire's [5] death.

Ever yours affectionately,

FREDERIC ROGERS.

To Miss Rogers.

Ovington Square: April 10, 1852

The official despatches from Victoria fully bear out the reports of the gold which you will perhaps have seen in the 'Times.' The Governor, Latrobe, seemed fairly appalled by it. He wrote that two tons a week were coming in, and seemed quite to think that there was no end to it. He now asks for ships of war, regiments of soldiers, &c. The Hudson's Bay people have also found some in Queen Charlotte's Island. If the Imperial Government are wise they will lay hands on part of that for themselves. But I hope they will have it worked through the Hudson's Bay Company, which will increase our profits.

All this is highly important as to the sale of Hoo.[6] I should be much more disinclined to sell now that a real change in the value of money seems so much more imminent. Before long I should think that, even in *anticipation* of this change

---

[5] An aunt of his wife's. She was a daughter of the first Lord Auckland, and would have been married to Pitt, but for the want of money on both sides. She married Lord Buckinghamshire five years before, and died nearly half a century after, the death of Pitt.

[6] A farm belonging to the Blachford property.

everybody will be calling in their *mortgages* and trying to exchange them for *purchases, i.e.* to turn their money debt into land. This, on the one hand, will *tend* to make it difficult to get or keep money on mortgage, and on the other will raise the price of land. But the former tendency will be counteracted by the rush of gold which will increase the quantity of money seeking some kind of investment.

To Rev. Edward Rogers.

London: February 23, 1853.

I write just now to finish my account of my dinner at the Duke of Newcastle's while it is fresh in my head. I was next but one to Lord Clarendon and opposite to the Duke of Leinster, Lord Carlisle, and Lord Lyttelton. Lords Carlisle and Lyttelton talked diagonally to Lord Clarendon and the Duke, so that I was in good company, and after I had been spoken to and said my little say, I was privileged to listen as one of the group. Lord Clarendon was *the* talker and most agreeable. Without many stories or elaborate *bons mots*, he had a neat way of capping everything and carrying it on, with just enough in his answer to make you laugh. They discussed a good deal different people. I shall just attempt heads of a dialogue about Lyndhurst and Brougham. They were lauding Lyndhurst and saying how genial and agreeable he was, especially in the House, and 'all without a touch of display or intention to exhibit.' Lord Cl. : ' Not a bit of it, he is just beginning his display ; he said to me the other day, " I *must* have a bill of my own. There is St. Leonards has six bills, all enormous ; then Brougham has three ; and little Cranworth, he has two. I *must* find something to reform, I *must* have a bill too." ' Then came Brougham's turn. Lord Lyttelton observed how he got on with half the sleep of ordinary mortals. 'He lives two lives, that man.' Lord Cl. : ' H'm. Yes, and one a very disorderly one. However, he's an uncommonly good fellow, no one would do more for a friend.' . . . But the best sight was after dinner. I heard behind me Mr. O'F., an Irishman just deserting from the Brigade, lecturing Lord Clarendon on the proper mode of governing Ireland, a regular case of veteran diplomatist *versus* impudent Irishman. Lord Clarendon was (and intended to be) the centre of a circle, with his shoulders well against the chimneypiece and his coat tails under his arms, and heard him out with the gravest of patiences. Mr. O'F. was telling him how Ireland should be conciliated by paying the priests. Lord Clarendon heard him well out and then began deliberately, ' You see unfortunately there is in this country a universal impression that the Catholic priests in Ireland are disaffected. People here think that they would one and all be very well pleased to see Louis Napoleon in possession of Ireland, or England either ' (then he got well upon his legs and fixed his eyes, which have a kind of cold glitter about them, very firmly on O'F., as if he could look, and was looking, clean into him), 'and don't you think that impression is well founded ? ' O'F. admitted it was, and very sad too, but then you have a state of things to deal with, and what is to be done ? Lord Clarendon (very deliberately and rather solemn) : ' It is with the greatest reluctance, after great hesitation, contrary to all my prepossessions, after the most obstinate struggles to avoid it, that I have come to the conclusion that nothing at all is to be done. Nothing is of any use. Every concession has been merely made a stepping-stone for a further demand, and it is plain that what the priesthood really want is not equality, but to be placed in the position now held by the Established Church.' Then he became rhetorical and rather violent. ' When was a government more just, more anxiously impartial, more thoroughly desirous to act without respect of parties than Lord John's administration of Ireland '(rather cool)' and how was it treated? With ' (*espressivo molto*) ' the grossest ingratitude.' O'F. acknowledged the merits of ' your Lordship's government,' but Lord Clarendon went on with a peroration which was only stopped by Lord Carlisle's offering him a seat in his brougham, which he accepted, and receded sideways, giving it to O'F. to the last moment, so that a reply was impossible. It certainly was no bad specimen of ' Put that in your pipe.' But the beauty was that, while the energetic outburst of feeling was going on, if you looked at Lord Clarendon's face you saw that iced cucumber was a joke to him in coolness. He was just keeping his cold sharp eye steadily fixed on the man, without a vestige of expression in his face except that of keen watchfulness. What he said was perfectly true, and there was every reason why he should believe it. But when you looked at his face you could not help saying, 'Now, you don't believe a word of what you are saying, and what in the world are you saying it for?' It was evidently intended that O'F. should communicate it to the Brigade, and I could only suppose it to mean, 'Now, the last time we had dealings together we prepaid you, and you sold us. Next time we don't intend to give you a single concession till we have got your votes.' On the whole it was certainly a good specimen of politico-diplomatic life and quite as good as a stage play.

The Duke of Leinster came up during the harangue and struck in. 'He had been a Liberal all his life, but a stand must be made,' &c., so I suppose the Ministers have made up their minds, having got the pick of the Brigade, to hold the rest at open defiance.

Ever yours affectionately,
F. R.

To Rev. R. W. Church.

Ovington Square: April 11, 1853.

I was glad to hear of your visit to Winchester, and had a kind of half hope, though not much bigger than a whole wish, that you might have come up to Oxford to vote for the Registrarship. I went; and made that an excuse for taking down a party, and getting a luncheon for them out of James Mozley. I think our people deserved a severe snub from their non-resident friends for so breaking up our interest as to give nobody a chance. Neither Cornish nor Rawlinson, *as matters stood*, were justified in going to the poll. Lake, I hear, kept Rawlinson in the field in spite of his appearing in the minority in the promises.

How the Protectionist party is knocking to pieces! Do you remember J. B. M.'s simile (in his article on Newman) of a ship sailing through floating bits of timber? Gladstone's position seems rather like it. The mere weight of his movements throws off all the trifling attacks of Dizzy and Co.—

they just knock against his sides and float off. I should rather like to know how far his budget was put forward because it was best abstractedly for the country, or what degree of skill had been used in making it 'go down,' *e.g.* buying the 'Times' by the free supplement, Manchester by the legacy duty on land,[7] &c. &c. The landholders (as S. F. N. says in the 'Guardian') have not got much but an argument, which, too, he will not allow them to use.

To Rev. R. W. Church.

Ovington Square: Dec. 29, 1853.

My dear Church,—You are too bad; Thursday is *the* only day in this week before Friday on which I dine out. Why in the world did you not come on here at once from Sparkford, instead of pottering back to Oxford, where you cannot have anything to do? A bed is exceedingly at your service. If you would take it we should at least see one another on Friday morning. Do come.

The Ministry is a bad job. I don't know what to expect. But I have expressed myself fully in the 'Guardian.' If Gladstone has anything Conservative in him, he will find it difficult to remain in a Ministry which must eventually be thrown on Radical support. But he is so really powerful a man that whatever shakes, and delays, and loss of time there may be, he must come up near the surface. I expect he will show the best—*i.e.* most politically powerful—side of himself as Chancellor of the Exchequer. Pursuing details is so much his power, if only he is not run away with by it. I think, if it is not a paradox, he has not poetry enough for the formation of a first-rate judgment. He has an immense mass of knowledge most methodically arranged, but the separate items must be looked for in their respective boxes, and do not float about and combine. The consequence is, not merely want of play, but that crotchety, one-sided, narrowish mode

---

[7] In Mr. Gladstone's famous Budget of 1853 the additional stamp required for supplements was taken off, and a single stamp of a penny covered the whole copy, whatever its size. The stamp duty was abolished two years later. The same Budget of 1853 introduced the succession duty for real property.

of viewing a matter uncorrected by the necessary comparisons and considerations, which people call ingenious and subtle and Gladstonian. He looks at the details, not the aspects of a subject, and mastered it, I should imagine, by pursuing it hither and thither from one starting-point, not by walking round it. And financial subjects will, I suppose, bear this mode of treatment better than any other. When they don't bear it, they bear it down with a kind of tangible power which makes onesided views impossible.

What do you say to the formation in the Cabinet of a Graham, Palmerston, and Molesworth party?

To Lady Rogers (Lady Blachford).

Feb. 5, 1854.

Edward drove me over to Kingsbridge in the dog-cart, where, after waiting some three hours, we saw the proceedings. Sir Stafford Northcote's speech was a repetition of his Newton one, which has been printed and circulated, with certainly the most admirable effect on the election. Everybody on the Low Church side is rather more pleased than one likes with the disclaimer of Puseyite parsons. Northcote apologised for it to me by the necessity of the case and the absurd extravagance of the Newton parsons, and said he had taken the opportunity at Exeter of setting himself right by abusing the laity for the fifth of November riots. The people were dull and one could not see that they were on one side or the other during the speech, which was fluent, clear, but without any special points. The fencing afterwards was much better. He is capital at that. He just hits at once those good-humoured answers, which with an agreeable, amused manner are 'the right thing.' One man started the opposition on the Tory side—an honest old stuttering tradesman, I should think, of what people call 'the right sort.' He told us he had always been a C—C—Conservative, or rather a T—T—Tory, ' that the hon. baronet was evidently a man of great ability, and, he believed, an honest man, and was going to be our member,' but what he didn't like was these four names, Courtney, Acland, Kennaway, Durant. 'Did the hon. baronet know that Sir T. D. Acland always voted against the other three county members?' N. 'No, indeed, I don't!' 'The hon. baronet must know that.' N., with overpowering innocence and urgency, 'No, indeed, I assure you I don't. There are certain questions respecting Free Commercial policy, which certainly Sir Thomas Acland does consider settled, and others hitherto have not, &c., but, &c.' 'Then does the hon. baronet know that Mr. Durant proposed a Whig candidate for Totnes?' (Durant sitting behind laughing.) 'Well, now he has seen the error of his ways, for, you see, he is proposing a Conservative.' 'Well, all I can say is I should like to have seen the name of Sir John Buller there.' 'Well, so should I, but surely Mr. —— would not have had the member for the county do so unconstitutional a thing as to put his name, &c.' Then came a Radical who wanted answers to these questions: 1. Ballot, 2, I forget, 3. whether N. would support the law of Primogenitureship.' 'Primo-how-much?' from the crowd. N. 'I will take the last of the three questions first. I am an eldest son, and I think the law of Primogeniture a capital law. And I think if I didn't take care of my own interests, the Kingsbridge electors would think I wasn't very well able to take care of theirs.' 'I want to know, if all these boroughs are disfranchised, whether the hon. baronet will vote for giving Kingsbridge a member?' 'I think I must wait till after the election before I answer that question, and then I shall see whether the Kingsbridge electors are sufficiently enlightened to send a member of their own to Parliament.' Northcote speaks at Plymouth to-morrow, and at Totnes on Tuesday. I shall not be at home till Wednesday morning.

To Rev. R. W. Church.

Ovington Square : March 16, 1854.

So you went up to vote against Pusey, the Heads, and the 'Record.' I got rowed by J. B. M. for not going up, but I own that residents seem to me to manage their tactics so ill (cases of Rawlinson and Hansell) that I have ceased to obey their calls, and certainly don't intend to do so unless either I have a strong conviction of my own, or our party is *united* with a prospect of success. My brother Edward had to go up and vote in duty to Pusey against his convictions so far as he had formed any.

People seem to me in an odd state about the war, perhaps because I am so myself. Nobody has any genuine enthusiasm about it, but a discontented cry of 'I suppose we must,' caused by a factitious indignation against Russia. I hear it said that the Emperor's proposal a year or two ago was that we should take Candia and Egypt and he what he liked, to which we replied that we could not entertain the idea of dismembering Turkey. Then Sir H. Seymour left St. Petersburg in more or less of a huff, saying he must take care that the whole truth (meaning about another matter) must come out, that the Emperor then thought he meant the publication of their secret negotiations, and so took the initiative in order to take off the edge of *our* publication. The result is that he has placed us at liberty to publish what otherwise would have remained confidential. Meanwhile the military people and Rothschild persevere in saying it will all come to nothing. Lord Raglan, that there will not be a shot fired, but the whole settled by manœuvring. Lord Seaton's is the same story. Others, that the Russians announce their intention to make the war *defensive*: whether this involves holding the principalities, *non liquet*.

Also rumours of great quarrellings in the Ministry. The 'Press' is trying hard to cocker up Lord John into holding hard by his Reform Bill, by which they flatter him that he will outlive Peel. *Reform* is to stand in the eyes of posterity with Magna Charta and the Bill of Rights, and Johnny to be greater *leading Opposition* than serving in the Ministry. Report is pretty distinct that he, Graham, and Lord Granville, if anybody, are the three (alone) who would quit office rather than the Reform Bill. But people are hardly to suppose that the remainder can hold office without them.

I had an amusing run to Devonshire to do what I could for Northcote; and certainly it is very pleasant on such an occasion to find yourself inheriting a family influence even though not a very large one. In only one case did I hear the idea of politics broached, it was always that 'I always have voted with the family and intend to,' and this in one or two cases from little landholders, *not* tenants. I asked whether our asking for votes would be considered *intimidation*, but it was clear that far from this it was considered a friendly compliment. We were told every here and there that '—— says he would vote with your honour if you or Mr. Edward would ask him,' all very flattering to one's self-importance. It makes me understand (not justify) the tenacity with which people cling to *extent* of encumbered property.

I have been reading 'Dante' and 'Anselm.' They are most excellent, and make one wish, like the 'Guardian,' that you could find time to write a history of something. You really owe it to yourself. It is provoking to feel that you are wasted on these 'Guardian' articles, good as they are for the paper and probably (I confess) better for your pocket than your first large production.

To Miss Rogers.

Ovington Square : March 28, 1854.

Of course, people are in a flutter (more than excitement) about the war: especially 'my colleague' Wood, who is evidently anxious to have a finger in the war pie, not unnaturally, as so many of his relations are in the thick of it in different ways. He took me down yesterday to look at a transport which is taking artillery from Woolwich. We just came in upon them as they were hoisting the last horse or two in. And a very pretty animated sight it was. I suppose you know how it is done. The horse is put in a sling, craned up twenty or thirty feet into the air, where he plunges and kicks out to his own satisfaction, then in that position wheeled round till he gets over the hatchway and let gently down through the said hatchways to the bottom of the ship, where the men are waiting to rush in upon him and mob him into his place. The arrangement is this. The hold had a good broad passage down the middle with a row of horses each side, nose inwards, packed as close as they could be. It looked all very comfortable at the moment when we saw it, but one thought what a turmoil there would be when the ship began to roll and plunge. They were separated each from each by bars padded more or less, and there were pads also behind, bars also in front, so that they had not much *room* for being riotous.

We fell upon Sir Hew, who was civil, asked after my mother and discussed matters. They have sent off some ships already. Each is complete in itself and is to make the best of its way to *Gallipoli*.

Wood tells me that when Lord Raglan and the rest were at Paris the Emperor expressed great surprise at the rapid way in which we had got all our men to Malta, and said they could not do it. Satisfactory to our authorities; only we have not got our horses, and I understand that till they arrive the infantry might just as well be in London.

Our Oxford affairs are getting into a considerable mess. The younger party of our friends have taken up University Reform, and have in conjunction with Gladstone pretty much framed the Government bill. On the other hand, Pusey (who draws with him Keble and Marriott) has joined the heads in thinking it revolutionary, and now on Friday I receive dunning letters from Mozley and Rawlinson to come up to vote against a petition which Keble and Pusey and Marriott will agitate for. I don't know whether it is sneaking, but I shall simply not trouble myself to go. I don't care enough about the bill *pro* or *con* to vote against either section of my friends. It is not good enough or bad enough for that. It seems by no means impossible that it may be simply shelved by the war.

Was not the secret correspondence amusing? It is not often that one has such a peep behind the scenes. Sir H. Seymour must evidently be a sharp fellow, he sees so clearly the real English of things, and is so prompt (at least on his own showing) in taking advantage of openings.[*]

I am glad to see by to-day's proclamation that we give up the great 'neutral bottom' question, *i.e.* that we don't profess any longer to touch Russian goods in neutral vessels. It will tend, of course, to prevent us from choking the trade of

---

[*] This refers to the proposals which the Czar made to the English Ambassador, Sir H. Seymour, for partitioning the dominions of Turkey, as being the goods of 'a sick man.'

any country with which we go to war. But, after all, I think every step towards making war less generally disagreeable is a point gained.

To Rev. R. W. Church.

8 Park Street : May 25, 1854.

My dear Church,—I sincerely congratulate you, first on receiving a son and heir, secondly on receiving him on the same day as Martin R. Sharp, and thirdly on Her Majesty's birthday. Is he to be named Victor? Give my kindest regards to Mrs. Church and the little gentleman, and let me know some time or other how they are getting on. I had my usual birthday dinner last Saturday and was lucky in getting a good deal of talk with the Duke, Lord Hardinge, and Sir Hew Ross (the Lieut.-General of Ordnance). They all seemed (in spite of the 'Times' Commission) proud of their arrangements, and the Duke said that a friend of the Emperor's (of the French) had been telling him that Canrobert from Gallipoli and the military authorities at Paris are complaining how much worse off their soldiers are than the English who came out with their tents and their beer and every comfort men could invent for them. Lord Hardinge was severe on the people who wanted *chairs* in their tents, and observed that for some years they had no tents at all in the Peninsula, till a year or two before the end of the war the Duke got them. He thought the Czar's conduct of the war 'very disgraceful, coming up bullying to Kalafat, concentrating masses of troops, and all the rest of it, and then being obliged to shorten his line and fall back.' I tried him on Omar Pasha. But he did not very much respond; a clever man, but had made his line of defence much too long. I suggested his success, on which he observed that a man sometimes got a good deal of credit by the blunders of his opponents.

Also I made Sir George Grey's (New Zealand) acquaintance. He goes out in the independent Church (of England) line, which he considers almost necessary to support society in New Zealand. In this and other things he said that he was very much struck in coming to England with the way in which we *lived for the present*. In the colony whatever you do or plan is calculated with a view to what it will or ought to be twenty or fifty or a hundred years hence. Here nobody looks a year before them.

I suppose this is very true, especially as regards Government. Indeed, I never have been able to see how a really representative Government could be far-sighted except in the way of removing obstacles to the natural action of the society. People have not in the mass patience enough, or faith enough in any of their representatives, to endure anything that is only to have *prospective* advantages, involving of course large present sacrifice.

I have also just shaken hands and exchanged words with Selwyn.[9] Just what he was in the fifth form at Eton. I was much struck with his way of walking up and down talking to his old and some new friends : there was a kind of lofty frank independence and $\pi\alpha\rho\rho\eta\sigma\iota\alpha$ about it, rather like a savage yet very like a bishop, a combination of humour and dignity and unaffectedness and elasticity that recalled one's old feeling of having got hold of a great man, long lost. I must finish.

Ever yours affectionately,
FREDERIC ROGERS.

To R. W. Church.

Ovington Square : Sept. 15, 1854.

My dear Church,—At last I am discharging my very bad conscience of the letter I owe you, and, I am afraid, without much prospect of writing a letter worth receiving. Till lately I have been at work either on things which it was difficult to put off, or on the largest question I have had yet, being little less than a Legislative Declaration of Independence on the part of the Australian Colonies. The successive Secretaries of State have been bidding for popularity with them by offering to let them have their own way. And in professed pursuance of these offers they (New South Wales, Victoria and South Australia) have sent home laws which may be shortly described as placing the administration of the colony in a Ministry dependent on the representative assembly, and

[9] The Bishop of New Zealand.

abolishing the Queen's right of disallowing Colonial Acts. What remains to complete colonial independence except command of the land and sea forces I don't quite see. I shall be interested to see what comes of it. It is a great pity that, give as much as you will, you can't please the colonists with anything short of absolute independence, so that it is not easy to say how you are to accomplish what we are, I suppose, all looking to—the eventual parting company on good terms.

Also I have been getting Keble to compile a prayer-book which we shall put on board all our emigrant ships. I shall send you a copy to look at when it is printed. I am rather proud of it, though only the channel.

I am afraid Keble is a good deal put out with Gladstone; he writes severely and substitutes 'Mr. Gladstone' for 'W. E. G.'[1] If I could be sanguine about what people call 'things in general,' *i.e.* about our own strength, I should be sanguine about the effect of the University Act, Dissenters and all (not that I would have supported the latter part). I can't help thinking that if Dissenting tradesmen begin to send their sons to Oxford, it might chance that the effect would be just that the Church would appropriate some of the best blood of Dissent, the very people who would otherwise be most effective against her.

To Lady Rogers.

Ovington Square : August 2, 1855.

Wood tells me that somebody (I think Lord Hardinge's son) has been dining with Pélissier and says that the Department of Works has run up for him a fine house and garden, with reception rooms, smoking pavilions, clocks, carpets—in short, all the Parisian *meubles* and luxuries that can be invented, simply on the notion that it is appropriate to the condition of a commander-in-chief. And this while Layard and the 'Times' were abusing Lord Raglan for having a cottage for himself and staff.

---

[1] It is noticeable that this circle of intimate Oxford friends nearly always wrote of one another by initials, J. H. N. (Newman), J. B. M. (Mozley), H. W. (Wilberforce), &c. In many cases the full surname has been substituted for the convenience of modern readers.

To Right Honourable W. E. Gladstone.

9 Ovington Square: August 15, 1855.

My dear Gladstone,—I cannot help writing to say (if it is not impertinent) how very much I am hoping that you will print your speeches on the war.

People seem to be gone mad, but I hope not so mad but that they are capable of being gradually affected by truth. And I don't know where else they are likely to get it. I am afraid I am asking you to increase your chance of being stoned. But as I see you are well quit of London for your holiday, your martyrdom is at any rate respited till next session.

I cannot say how much satisfaction I felt in reading in your speeches all (and much more than all) that I had myself been longing to hear said with effect.

Ever yours sincerely,
FREDERIC ROGERS.

To Right Honourable W. E. Gladstone.

8 Park Street: October 12, 1855.

My dear Gladstone,—I must thank you for sending me your speeches. I had observed that they were published, but did not know where to get them. It was a great satisfaction to study them again. They put the world in your debt, a good deal more, I am afraid, than the world is likely to acknowledge.

The average specimens of the public whom one meets are still, even when they profess themselves anxious for peace, so terribly exacting in their terms.

I see by a note that you have sent to this office that you are looking into the progress of Emigration. Is there any special point on which we are likely to be able to give you information?

Ever yours sincerely,
FREDERIC ROGERS.

To Rev. R. W. Church.

Blachford: November 28, 1855.

My dear Church,—I have but half a morning for lots of letters which ought to have been written long ago, so I must despatch you summarily. George Mayow [2] (you know whom I mean) writes that Windham was appreciated before the Redan business. Col. Wood told him (Mayow) that he (Wood) was in command of a battery [3] when they found the Russians almost on them, skirmishers among their numbers. The Captain asked W. what he was to do; W. told him he could not retire, but, seeing Windham, galloped up to him to ask assistance. Windham was Sir G. Cathcart's quartermaster (qu. general?) and had been sent by him to order up Torrens's brigade to succour his disastrous advance, which he was doing. Windham looked for a moment, said 'Yes, I see,' and shot off to Torrens to ask for a regiment or two. Torrens (knowing Cathcart's straits) hesitated for a moment, when Windham (his junior officer) said that as senior on the staff of T.'s commanding officer he ordered him officially to send up two regiments to save the battery. It was done, and Cathcart before he was killed approved it. But, as Mayow writes, a man must have tolerable nerve to force down the throat of his senior officer a movement which both of them know to be directly contrary to the instructions he had received from the common superior, whose authority he appropriated, and when both of them also knew that superior to be in the utmost extremity. What strikes me most is the entire confidence he must have had in being right, and on a snap judgment.

Ever yours affectionately,
F. R.

To Rev. R. W. Church.

Park Street: March 18, 1856.

My dear Church,—I am glad you and Mrs. Church like 'Dorothy.' [4] The characters seem to me very good, also the

---

[2] Colonel Mayow was Major of the 17th Lancers in the Light Cavalry Charge at Balaclava.

[3] At Inkerman.

[4] A novel by his sister-in-law, Mrs. Paul.

gradual accumulation of bereavements and depositions on Dorothy and the mode in which Lance's return after a long absence brings sharply back on you the contrast between what was and what is, is very good. . . . We have finished Orme, which is admirable. I was quite struck, on taking up Froissart for the first time the other day, to see how much it reminded me of Orme. The mixture of chronicling with lively graphic touches and descriptions, the mutual consideration of the great belligerents for each other, abject population, floating bodies of mercenaries, vast variety of minute movements and individual feats, are quite remarkable. And the contrast between Edward III. and John Company only makes it better. Certainly the Frenchmen *did* mess it. We are now on Macaulay. How absurdly diffuse or rather minute he is! It seems constantly as if he had some one touch which he could not resist, and gave you a couple of pages of trifling detail in order to avoid the appearance of lugging it in head and shoulders.

Did I give you a couple of Crimean stories I got from Wood? I shall repeat them on the chance.

His brother-in-law, Col. Brownrigg, was aide-de-camp to Brown when they took Kertch, and was sent by him to ask Col. Autemarre (the Frenchman in command) to stop plunder. The answer he got was: 'Mais, mon cher, je ferai tout mon possible pour le général—tout mon possible: mais vous savez bien que je n'ai fait la guerre qu'en Afrique, et là, mon Dieu, *on tue toujours les habitants.*'

The other was the account of a horse artillery man in Colonel Wood's troop, a fine fellow six foot high, who was taken at Kinburn. He seems to have pleased the general in command, and was had up to be shown to a party of Russian officers and gentlemen. One came forward from the rest and questioned him in very good English. 'All the men in his troop were not of his height?' 'Yes, he was pretty much the average standard' (terrible lie). 'How many strong did your troop land?' 'Well, sir, when we take Russian prisoners, we don't ask them these questions' (lie again) 'and I shouldn't like to get my comrades into a scrape. I'm in your hands, sir, but I hope you won't ask me any questions.' Well, he

was told he needn't answer anything but what he chose, then
'Would he like to go to England?' 'No, he would rather
go back to stay with his comrades as long as they stayed in
the Crimea.' 'How long was that to be?' 'Why, sir, we
expect to be there *five* years.' The Russian pricked up his
ears at this: 'What was to keep them five years in the
Crimea?' 'Why, sir, we think in my regiment that the
nation won't be satisfied till they have made the enemy pay
the expenses of the war, and we don't think we can bring him
down to that under five years.' This amused the questioner
greatly, and he told it all to the rest, and after a little more
talk told the man he should be sent off by the next vessel
that went to Odessa to go back to 'his comrades,' which was
accordingly done; and it appeared that the inquisitive gentleman was no less a person than the Emperor. This was the
man's account, and I suppose was roughly true.

My brother [3] has been back at Woolwich for the last few
weeks. He is getting steadily better; but it will be a long
time before he is strong again. One feels a continual fidget
lest he should be doing something absurd and making himself
ill again.

To Rev. R. W. Church.

1856.

It is astonishing to me how little people talk of politics.
I suppose the Gladstone and Disraeli combination means a
large amount of mischief. But there is no keenness about it
in those people whom you meet. It seems as if people really
did not much care who was in, so long as they were not bored
by Income Tax or otherwise. As for the Chinese war, which
seems to me one of the greatest iniquities of our days, nobody
seems to care sixpence about it. I was half alarmed, by the
way, the other day, lest I should be found responsible for it,
by allowing to pass the Colonial Ordinance under which Sir
J. Bowring has been making a fool of himself.[6] It was our

---

[3] His artillery brother, Henry, who had returned from the Crimea dangerously ill.

[6] The clause providing for the registration of vessels which could hoist the British flag and claim British protection was the only warrant which Sir J. Bowring (Minister at Hongkong) had for the outrageous bombardment of Canton. It came out afterwards that even this

business to report that it should be referred to the Board of Trade; and if instead of doing so we (or rather I) had reported it unobjectionable I might have had the reflection that a blunder of mine had been a link in the chain of causes of all this slaughtering. I was relieved to find, however, that we were all right. I cannot help suspecting that our friend Dorney Harding has got rather into a mess, though it is one which John Bull will pull him through.

I have been reproaching myself for some time for doing nothing for poor people, and have begun (*faute de mieux*) reading aloud to patients in St. George's Hospital now and then. I do so wish I had a turn for it; but I have never felt visiting of that kind anything but an annoyance. And this revives all the dissatisfied shyness that I used to feel in former times at such things. Is there any medicine for such a moral diathesis?

. . . .

I have been reading Newman's letters on Universities (printed first in a newspaper) and have been rather struck by his ingenuity in proposing an *avenir* for Ireland. He feels that some rivalry with England must be got up, and that as far as governing power goes John Bull must in the nature of things be lord and master over Pat; of course, though, they could not be otherwise: 'tu regere imperio.' But he holds out the bait of an intellectual supremacy which shall make Dublin the Athens of modern civilisation, the centre of mind and letters to all who speak the great English language, which is overspreading the world. And really it seems a bright idea. One hardly sees what might not be made of Irish invention and brilliancy if it would submit itself to a good intellectual training.

But he seems to me terribly behindhand in supposing that by merely establishing a centre of Catholic learning he can draw all the world after him as people did in the middle ages. He seems quite to forget that barbarous ignorance

---

clause did not apply, since the 'Arrow' had not been registered at the time, and was a Chinese vessel both in law and in fact. Leading politicians of both parties, among them Mr. Gladstone and Mr. Disraeli, joined in condemning Sir J. Bowring's action, which was approved by Lord Palmerston.

and the inaccessibility of centres of learning are not the evils of the present day, and that he himself has to fight, not with the ignorance of the people, but the rivalry of Queen's Colleges; in fact, that sharp fellows and educational institutions are rather a drug than otherwise. However, it is very interesting.

How does Montaigne get on; and when does it come out? I am glad you are publishing at last with your name. I don't call *re*-publishing the same thing. . . . . .

Ever yours affectionately,

F. R.

To Miss Rogers.

8 Park Street: Sept. 9, 1856.

I have been reading Wiseman and Newman's 'Callista' and 'Fabiola' (both worth reading), and I think I must review them slightly in the 'Guardian,' though I have not a great deal to say. One thing I am mightily amused with, which is the marked way in which Wiseman (whose scene is laid under the persecution of Diocletian) brings into light the old Christian families in whom the faith was hereditary and who had furnished in each generation their martyrs to the cause. All his principal martyrs are hereditary Christians, while an impracticable convert, who is all for flying in everybody's face, courting martyrdom &c., is the 'Judas' of the story, betraying his brethren—is punished—repents and is restored. Newman's great character, on the other hand, is St. Cyprian, who is delicately made to point out how he is a convert and how all the apostates were hereditary Christians, who are described as almost universally torpid, only to be roused in fact by the martyrdom of a convert. Wiseman gives a good deal of interesting topography and Christian antiquities, and a lively plot with some absurdities, and some beautiful incidents or passages. Newman gives some very fine scenes and very fine characters with a good lot of sharp satire, somewhat wanting in delicacy of touch. It is odd how both of them fire on heathenism almost as a living personal enemy—Newman most vigorously, as he hits at Protestant England (the nation rather than the Church) over the shoulders of Pagan Rome.

To Rev. R. W. Church.

8 Park Street : December 10, 1856.

I have been trying, at the instigation of Moberly, of New College, to get your name into circulation for the Ecclesiastical History professorship. It seemed extravagant to suppose that Lord Shaftesbury would allow Lord Palmerston to appoint the Proctor who vetoed the censure on Newman. But there is some good always, I think, in putting a man's name about. However, I could do nothing, as I imagine Stanley is to be the man. So at least, affirms Bonamy Price.

I have marvellously little to say for myself. Indeed, I feel a most aged inability to care about things except the little matters I have in hand myself, official prospects, Blachford buildings, and cuttings and plantings and exchangings, and altogether what intimately concerns self. As to office, it seems more and more clear that I am to go to the C. O., and more and more doubtful when it will happen. Not just yet, certainly, and in time anything may turn up. For the present, I suppose, I shall have an easyish time of it here for some time, plenty of opportunity for doing something else if I had it in me. I am beginning to think my own liberalism will come to a crisis one of these days. I got into a controversy with Keble about divorce, and am besides half afraid to think of looking him in the face from feeling so out of his line on the Denison case.[7] I am only glad you and Bernard are able to treat it as you do, but I confess the Articles seem to me insuperable, and it is a very unpleasant feeling that if I told Keble the truth I should say that his subscriptions are inconsistent with what I understand to be his belief. And I must say that St. John vi., taken as a prophetic exposition of the

---

[7] A charge had been made against Archdeacon Denison in 1854 that a sermon preached by him the previous year contained doctrines about the Eucharist which were inconsistent with the Articles. Judgment was pronounced against him by the Diocesan Court of Bath and Wells on October 22, 1856, with sentence of deprivation. The Court of Arches, on an appeal, in the following year reversed this decision, and absolved Archdeacon Denison from the charges, on the ground that more than the prescribed time had elapsed between the alleged offence and the beginning of the action.

sacramental doctrine, and culminating in ἡ σάρξ οὐκ ὠφελεῖ οὐδέν, seems to me to carry you out of the stream of thought which culminates in Roman or semi-Roman doctrine.

Have you looked at Helps's 'Conquest of America'? It is well worth reading, except that it really makes one boil *too* much. The unbridled treachery and ferocity of the Spaniards passes all I had imagined. And somehow it is, to me, more terrible to see Christians cruel to heathens than *vice versa*. There is the triumph of martyrdom on one set of accounts to set against the dreariness of successful cruelty, but here the crime of the tyrants is greater and more one's own, and the compensation of the persecuted less. It makes the Papal act which handed America over to the Spaniards a terrible deed. There is such a contrast between the stupendous power which is affected in such a transfer, and the utter want of qualification for its proper exercise, which is evident in the act itself and all that followed on it. However, I must be off. Kindest regards to Mrs. and Master Church.

Ever yours affectionately,
FREDERIC ROGERS.

To Lady Rogers.
August 26, 1857.

My dear Mother,—I think I got as far as *Chambéry* in my last letter, which, as far as I was concerned, was somewhat of a failure. It is exceedingly prettily placed, among good Savoyard hills, but the heat made the smallest distance formidable, and so there was hardly any getting out of the town, and in the evening we were seduced by a laughing little chambermaid to go and see what she called 'la vogue,' which is supposed to be a kind of *guinguette*, and expected to see the world and his wife nicely dressed and looking fresh and gay; but it was a mere stupid crowd, disturbed every now and then by a procession of men arm in arm, with a noisy drum at their head, going up and down the town with a vague intention of amusing themselves or somebody else (it was hard to see which), but without quite sense or spirit enough to make a row. Besides I got cheated at Chambéry. Next day a drive to Ugine, a beautifully placed village, at one end of a mule ride which leads to Sallenches. We came into Sallenches after dark (near 11 o'clock), and next morning, getting out of the inn door, I got my first view of Mont Blanc, blazing white with flying clouds, sometimes hiding more, sometimes less, of his head. Georgie and I had a pleasant morning walk on the side of the valley *opposite* to Mont Blanc, getting fine views of him (broken by clouds) from time to time. Next day to Chamonix, by a fine valley with some wild defiles, and noble views of the different groups of ' Aiguilles ' which form the real beauty of Mont Blanc. I fancy Mont Blanc to be a magnificent mass of pointed peaks, of which the highest are so high up and so close together that the perpetual snow has actually *buried* them. But, however that may be, the peculiarity of Mont Blanc is that the two summits, the *Calotte* and the Dôme du Goûter, are flat lumps, like the ordinary shape of an English granite pile, while they are supported by a most beautiful forest of peaks advancing out in all directions, and forming a kind of pinnacled wall round the great snow field, through which the ice pours down into the low country wherever it finds an opening. Our first great expedition was to the *Flegère*, a point high up on the side of the valley opposite to Mont Blanc, from which you see its whole line spread out right and left as far as you can see, the white domes above, but not greatly above, everything else, and the *aiguilles* stretched out in front of them in a kind of battle array, graceful and beautiful beyond everything, with the great glaciers pouring through them here and there like enormous cataracts. That evening we crossed the Glacier des Bossons and the next day crossed the Mer de Glace. S. was unequal to the Bossons, G. and E. were unequal to the Mer de Glace, but nobody went off without seeing a glacier and standing on it. It is certainly very wonderful. The immensity of the mass of ice is striking, the deep light blue which is discovered by any chasm or new fracture of the ice is almost unearthly (there are no blues, however, tell Kate, equal to the Rosenlaui), and where the ice passes over a great fall in the ground it breaks into a magnificent imitation of rocks and waves (' pyramides ' they call them on the Glacier des Bossons), but to me they were more the satisfaction of a curiosity than actual *enjoyment*. From the Isère, the Flegère, the Tête Noire, and Vevey, I seemed to myself to be sucking in pleasure. But on the great torrents of ice one seemed rather to be examining and taking in something very wonderful, though, no doubt, the peaks in which you were enveloped *were* very beautiful too. I think that a glacier is not a thing for *idle* enjoyment. I suspect the true pleasure of the ice is in hearty exertion, when a man feels that he has a good day's work before him and is doing it.

To Rev. R. W. Church.

8 Park Street: November 16, 1857.

So we are inside Delhi and Lucknow, at last. I suppose it will hardly do to ask what we did when we got in, at least to Delhi. It must have been a frightful business. I feel what you say about the heathen. These facts seem to sweep away one's sickly faint view of the Ammonites and such people, and to suggest a wholly different and more terrible picture of the deserts of a heathen nation. It is curious how these realities (to use the cant word) seem to drive people back on a Jewish state of mind. I mean how people jump at once to the idea of bloody and sweeping punishments administered to a whole community, for example or amputation's sakes.

I hear that the day before the telegraph came in the Government sent Sir F. Thesiger, who has a son-in-law (Colonel Inglis, in command), daughter, and grandchildren there, a despatch from Colonel Inglis to Havelock which must (of course) have been received here by last mail. Colonel Inglis said that he had taken the command with 300 fighting men, that these of course had been reduced by casualties, that he had then 20 guns bearing or playing on him, that all were on half rations, and had enough to last them at any rate till the 24th, and hoped they could hold out till then, that he thought the enemy did not know the state they were in and that, to prevent their learning it, he had not allowed a single message to be sent out except this despatch, and that if Havelock wished to communicate with him he had better send a *verbal* message by any native whom he could trust, with the password 'Agra.' I suppose he must have felt when he sent this that it was likely enough to be the last message that any Christian would receive from any inside the fort.

When Thesiger told my friend this, he had just received in court this post's telegram, 'Lucknow relieved,' and of course was in a swim of excitement, and rushed home, leaving all his causes to take care of themselves (if they came on) and begging somebody to make what apology or excuse he could . . . . I have just come back from attending the funeral of an uncle whom you may recollect near Southampton—General Rogers (then Col.), the last of my father's brothers.

CHAPTER VI

Mission to Paris on the Coolie Question, 1858, 1859

SIR F. ROGERS spent a considerable part of these two years in negotiations in Paris about the terms on which the French should be allowed to import coolie labourers into their colonies. He has left the following notes of the manner in which the negotiations began:

'The English nation, while its own interests are not very visibly and gravely concerned, has a strong vein of philanthropy, but it is in regard to negro slavery that this feeling has so taken hold of the people, and is so powerfully organised as to become a political influence. Partly on this account and partly also, I doubt not, from genuine conviction, Lord Palmerston had taken up this particular question, and felt himself bound to assist, if possible, certain plans of the French Government for conducting an immigration from the West Coast of Africa to the French negro colonies, which was supposed to have hitherto covered a disguised slave trade.

'The French Government, pressed by its planters, did not venture simply to suppress this, and, I take it for granted, replied to a remonstrance by pointing to our own coolie emigration (which it had for some time been my special function to superintend). At any rate, Lord Palmerston, then Premier, and Lord Clarendon, then at the Foreign Office, suggested to the French that, if they would give up their African emigration, they might be allowed to take coolies from India to their colonies on the same terms (*mutatis mutandis*) as those on which they were taken to English colonies. Neither the India Office, nor the Colonial Office, much liked this arrangement, because it appeared probable that, since we had not been more than able to protect the coolies in our own colonies, we should be less than able to protect them in those of France ; and so the evil of quasi-slavery might exist, the responsibility of it merely being transferred from the Foreign Office (which was bound to protect the Africans) to us, or rather to the India Office, which was bound to protect the Indians.

'However, the first step was that the French should understand what would be the terms to which the planters would be bound to submit in importing coolies from India, and I was bidden to call on Persigny. Persigny was on the whole much pleased, and in course of time desired that I should be sent to Paris to be examined before a committee of which Prince Napoleon, then Minister of the Colonies, was chief, and then settle the details of the question.

'Persigny struck me as not having much in him ; he liked to talk as if he were conducting large affairs with large views, and at the same time was competent to descend into the minutest particulars ; but he did not show that grasp of principles in their practical bearing which makes what I should call the "man of capacity," and which saves principles from becoming loose and airy, and details from becoming petty, as they do in the hands of political and commercial projectors, who overwhelm you with one or the other project without impressing a man of sense with any certainty that it will work as it is expected to work. Some time afterwards I happened to speak of him to Lord Stratford de Redcliffe, as not having much impressed me (Lord Stratford having just been staying with him at a country house). He said that Persigny had nothing in him, no *suite* in conversation, or tact : " He said to me " (and he drew himself up ferociously as he spoke) " he said to me, ' Milord, on me dit que vous êtes deux personnes, dans la conversation rien de plus charmant : mais touchez aux affaires ! eh, voilà le lion Britannique,'" and his lordship straightened his neck and opened his eyes and closed his lips as if he felt himself the British Lion and had just had his whiskers pulled. This was in driving from Saltram to Mount Edgcumbe. Driving back I was touched by a little bit of sad poetry. We were crossing one of the Plymouth creeks, and saw two small sails, one in deep shadow, and the other white with the sun upon it. Lord Stratford just pointed them out to my wife, with the words "Hope and disappointment;" he spoke sadly, as if he had some real reason; on the other hand, he certainly had some cause for feeling satisfied. . . .

'The negotiations were interrupted when the French war in Italy was imminent and gave the French something to think of. However, it was taken up again after the conclusion of the war, and I was again sent to Paris to proceed with the convention—this time with M. de Chasseloup Laubat. He was a talkative, quick, handy fellow, and we got through the work rapidly and in a friendly way. The only hitch was his great anxiety to get into this convention a special mention of Nossibé and Mayotta, two places of which I had never heard, but which turned out to be places in Madagascar,[1] where the French wanted to get a specific recognition of their acquisitions.

'. . . . . The convention was some time after concluded, as I had settled it; I imagine, with scarcely an alteration.'

To Lady Rogers.

January 1858.

My dear Mother,—A few lines written in a hurry to inform you of a new 'commissionership' which has fallen on my head (unpaid of course)— I am now commissioner for settling in conjunction with a French Commissioner the regulations under which coolies may be taken from British India to French colonies.

Wednesday evening I got a note from Labouchere saying that he and Lord Clarendon had settled this mode of pro-

---

[1] Two small islands off the north-west coast of Madagascar. Events which have happened since the above was written supply more clearly the motive of this insertion.

ceeding;[2] and yesterday evening I got a note from Lord C. to Labouchere, forwarded for me to open (in his absence) and act upon immediately, saying that M. de Persigny was quite satisfied with that mode of proceeding, 'that if he had known where to find Sir F. Rogers he would have called upon him and made his acquaintance,' but, that not being so, he wished Sir F. R. would call upon him at the French Embassy at half-past two 'to-morrow,' *i.e.* to-day. To the French Embassy I am accordingly bound; and I suppose I shall be introduced by M. de Persigny to my colleague and antagonist in the negotiation. The French are, I believe, excessively anxious not only to get the thing done, but to get it done *immediately*. So I suppose I shall be spurred on, or dunned furiously. At present I don't know my own position, and not only go without a shadow of instruction of any sort but without a distinct view as to what instructions I must or can get. And (between ourselves) I am not likely to get much from Labouchere, and am likely to be a kind of central point to be battered by all the conflicting interests—French, West Indian, East Indian, Foreign Office, philanthropists, sugar-manufacturers &c.—so I look at my future with 'awe mixed with jollity.' Mind, this is not to be talked about just yet— I wish diplomacy were not so wholly new to me. As to knowledge of the subject, I am at least a one-eyed man among the blind, I hope.

Ever affectionately,
F. R.

Happy New Year to you all.

Miss S. Rogers.

January 3, 1858.

My dear Sophy,—You come in for the account of my interview with M. de Persigny. At half-past two, of course, I presented myself and was shown in; he is a pleasant-mannered man, much younger than I was prepared for, as I fancy (or fancied) him an old Louis Philippe official, agreeable-looking, and anxious to set to work. It soon appeared

---

[2] Mr. Labouchere (afterwards Lord Taunton) was Secretary of State for the Colonies, Lord Clarendon Foreign Secretary.

that he intended to do all the work on his side himself, and
he was somewhat disconcerted at hearing that I had no instructions, till I told him that however I knew enough about
the matter to enter upon it, and that probably we might
facilitate matters by going over the ground. Accordingly we
started, he at once taking for the heads of the negotiation a
certain paper that I had concocted for the Foreign Office
while I was laid up with rheumatism. The paper, I think,
was pretty clear and complete, and as it was done off-hand
without papers I think I got credit for it (a mere enumeration
of regulations). I was able to throw off on the first point
with what he considered a great concession (at least I
volunteered that I personally thought it ought to be conceded),
and, as my ground was that the contrary course would eventually lead to heart-burnings between England and France,
that gave occasion to a little oration on his part on the
general desirableness of avoiding paltry points of collision
between two great nations. Then we went through the
points : one point he (as they say) 'tried on' about which I
had thought and was prepared for him, then he at once gave
in (he never argued a single point, or for a moment, but
merely occupied himself in ascertaining what we would
or could give, generally assenting and noting quickly any
point that might be material in after-discussions). Then
on some provocation or other he made a speech, as if it were
to imbue me with the views with which the Foreign Office
ought to be indoctrinated (and, of course, had been) in the
general treatment of the question. We, the English, had had
our triumphs in 1815, and our enormous progress since had
given us the supremacy in this and that, commerce, &c.
Therefore we had that supremacy to lose and nothing to gain
by war. France, under a new dynasty, which wanted con-
solidating, also required peace till she was firm on her legs.
A liberal mode of dealing was the way to preserve peace. In
the matter of Bolgrad [3] (here he could not remember the name

[3] The Russian plenipotentiary at the
Conference of Paris claimed Bolgrad
on the River Yalpuk, a little north
of the Danube, and the Isle of Serpents, which would have commanded
the approach to the Danube. England
and Austria, wishing to keep the Russian frontier away from the Danube,
stood out against this (though France
did not) and eventually gained their

of the place, and had to boggle and apologise for five minutes in a way which interfered with the effect of the oration), the Emperor was wrong (very confidential was it not?)—quite wrong; he had given an offhand assent to the Russian proposition without seeing what depended on it. Then we, the English, thought he was Russianising, which was not the case, and he had to get out of the scrape as he could. In fact, he frankly owned to Lord Palmerston that the whole was his fault—a blunder. But then a nation cannot go on time after time confessing itself wrong, and it would be very unfortunate if a quarrel were to arise by requiring such a thing. This is ambiguous and oracular. The sense is this. The French Government have promised their colonies to revive the slave trade (in substance), the English make such a row about this that it may lead to war or something like it, unless the dispute is evaded. The French Government is too far pledged to *give in visibly*, whether wrong or right. But if you will let us get emigrant labourers from India instead of buying slaves in Africa, we will give up the African enterprise and tell our colonists that we have made a capital bargain for them, and so we shall be out of the mess altogether.

All this is *sous-entendu*, and, I suppose, was all said to me in order to impress me with the feeling that I held the fate of Europe in my hands and would imperil it if I did not somehow or another come to an understanding about this same emigration. And I must admit that this sort of humbug, even though one sees through it, has a decided effect on the temper with which one gets into the matter.

Then I raised a point on which I felt a future difficulty was coming, sooner or later. He said then, for the first time, that his Government had instructed him that the obvious mode of getting over it was *inadmissible*. Then I explained that something effective we must have. He agreed, and then we concurred in a proposition, he admitting its propriety (indeed, I think it was his own suggestion) but reserving it

point. The frontier between Russia and Turkey at that point followed the River Yalpuk, leaving Bolgrad to Moldavia, and, of course, also the Isle of Serpents. This was settled early in January 1857.

for his Government. All that I said or did was, of course, so reserved, as I told him I had no instructions.

However, he evidently considered (and he was not far wrong, I think) that the affair was practically so far settled ; and we made little rough notes of what we had agreed, he taking a copy of mine, which, I suppose, he sent off to Paris. At least he worked like a man whose mind was bent on settling this particular question without an hour's more delay than he could help. He tells Lord Clarendon the Emperor is *determined* to have labour from one place or another, and that at once.

He is not like any English worker that I have seen. There is about him a quick promptitude in getting through questions one by one, without forestalling or going back to anything, which is unlike an English official, who is either a clerk or a great man. He worked like a union of the two— *more* of the clerk, but having the authority to speak and settle things (generally) off his own bat that a chief has. And yet he worked like a man who was to give an account to a chief of what he had done, and would be held accountable for letting the matter he had in hand sleep or miss its way. I should say perhaps more than anything else of him that he was 'thoroughly alive.' It is too soon to say he was *very fair*, else I should say that also. There, now you have a full, true, and particular account of my introduction to diplomacy.

I must be off, so good-bye.

Ever yours affectionately,

F. R.

Of course all this is not to be talked of—*cela va sans dire.*

To Rev. R. W. Church.

8 Park Street, Westminster : January 14, 1858.

My dear Church,—I certainly wish very much that I could have a talk with you, especially as I have come out in a new shape. At present I am engaged in an 'English Commission' with M. de Persigny, a plan about Coolie Emigration, which presents some considerable perplexities, and, *Dis quoniam propius contingo*, have seen some little bits of fun which you would enjoy if I could talk them over with you, but are hardly spicy enough to be potted in a letter. I am in a somewhat absurd position, pretty much without authority or instructions, but dealing with a subject of which I certainly know more than anybody else, at the same time hemmed round by superior authorities, who, little as they know what the details and rights of the matter are, know what they want and have traditional and incompatible views. The French Government are, I imagine, determined to have their way; the Foreign Office determined that the question should be settled; Labouchere is torn about by divers influences which must, under all circumstances, prevent his standing upright, but is subject to a Colonial Office influence adverse to what the French (if they see their way as clearly as I suppose they do) will insist upon. The India Board[4] have drawling, minute, obstructive ways, that will stop the whole thing, I should think, if nobody runs over them. Then the matter is one which, if it gets wind, will bring down on poor Labouchere's head, in a state of fury, the West Indians, or the humanitarians, or both.

I was greatly amused at the (as yet only) interview with de Persigny—he is very pleasant and, as somebody called him, '*coulant*,' but different from any English *chief* that I have seen. He unites with a certain amount of a chief's authority much more of a head clerk's mode of going rapidly and with knowledge through the successive points of a case, never anticipating what is coming or going back to what is past, or showing ignorance or hesitation as to what he had and what he had not power to conclude. But what struck me very much was that he seemed to work (I cannot analyse my reason further) as if he had a master in the cupboard watching him and seeing that he lost no point in anything. Also I was greatly amused at his endeavours to make me imagine by one or two set orations that the question at issue was one on which it was of such deep importance that England and France should not fall out (becoming withal confidential), that no small difficulties should be allowed to interpose themselves &c. &c.- all this being peculiarly apposite or

---

[4] The old Board of Control, now within a few months of its end.

inapposite (as you choose to view it) to my peculiar function, which was that of framing details which he was likely to dispute, on a matter in which I was supposed to be cognisant of details. I should say that the thing was well done, except that he did not make full allowances for my being a matter of fact Englishman instead of a Frenchman of expansive views.

To Lady Rogers.

January 20, 1858.

I have seen Persigny again (we talk English with a phrase or two of French). He apparently knew that I had finished my work and that he must wait the leisure of the Court of Directors, but he sent for me because he wanted to tell me what the Paris people objected to, and I was reassured to find that he was *with me* and against his own Government. It is rather amusing to see how each department wants to keep itself clear of difficulties. The Minister of Marine, ' qui est un peu partisan ' according to M. de Persigny, wants on behalf of his colonies to make sure of a supply of coolies and so to charge *us* with the collection, and blame *us* if we fail in doing it. I say : ' *We can't collect enough for ourselves*, and won't promise for you what we can't perform. If we do, you will certainly turn upon us and say we have not given you fair play. Go and collect, if you can, for yourselves. It will keep us better friends in the long run if when you fail you have clearly no one to blame but yourselves.' This last sentence (being clearly true) touches the *Ambassador* who will be troubled to compose French and English quarrels, just as the Minister of Marine will be troubled to allay Colonial complaints, and so I may fairly hope the Ambassador is in earnest (as I think he is) when he professes himself to side with me. He was very friendly and seemed as if he did not wish to get rid of me. But when I got up to go away he perched himself like a little bird (he is more like a cock robin than I thought him at first) on the top of his fender with his back against the chimney-piece and went on discoursing about our business. I was much amused at one point which I tried to make. The French pack their emigrants and ships *twice* as close as we do, and yet they have had very good passages.

Of course they object to imposing on themselves our strict law, and I want to come to some compromise, so I tried to find what would pacify them, and suggested 50 cubical feet *par personne*. This posed old Persigny, who wanted to know what it meant; and betook himself in a vague perplexed way, like a puzzled linen-draper, to a measuring tape which he began to pull out, and measure distances in the air as if that would help him. So I explained that 50 cubical feet was 6 feet long 1½ feet broad and 5½ feet high, or, to make the matter more intelligible, if he would imagine the whole ground pretty well covered with human beings lying at full length, and 5½ feet of height above them, that would be the thing—'and,' I added, 'I don't think you can well give a man less than *that*.' I shall not easily forget the mixture of disgust and astonishment and amusement with which he burst out, 'Sacré-Dieu! non! they will all be sick' (or rather '*seek*') 'too,' on which I began to repent me of having given in so much, and tried to retrieve a point or two, with what success remains to be seen.

To Lady Rogers.

February 2, 1858.

I have not written to you my last communications with Persigny. On the 21st I received notice that the Court of Directors[5] had approved my articles, and so I took them off at once to him, and on the 23rd he despatched them in a modified shape (in some respects) to his Government, giving me warning of one or two objections, which (as I could not yield to them myself) the Government would raise.

Since that time I have heard no more of him—I dare say that the exchange of shots, which must have taken place about the 'attentat'[6] on the Emperor, does not dispose them to proceed very cheerfully or zealously in the negotiations.

---

[5] The powers of the East India Company lasted till June of that year.

[6] Orsini's attempt at assassination on January 14. This was followed by Lord Palmerston's 'Conspiracy to Murder Bill,' drawn up in consequence of representations from the French Government. The Bill was right and desirable, but unfortunately the English nation had lost its temper over some stupid inflammatory speeches of officers in the French Army, who talked about

He was personally very civil and easy throughout, though keen in working for what he considered his Government would object to. I have no doubt I shall have a lot of objections to meet when it comes back.

He read me a long list of the 'Minister of Marine's' objections to what I may call my requirement, that the French should collect emigrants for themselves instead of throwing it on the British Government, and of his own reply which was characteristic and amusing. The civil deference with which the objections of the 'Marine' were magnified and evaded was very French; and an elaborate argument that the *cordial and bona fide* co-operation of the English Government might be counted upon because the success of the scheme was the only way in which Lord Palmerston could escape from allowing the French emigration from Africa and so incurring the pressure of public opinion, 'which is so susceptible *à cet égard*' and of '*la Société Biblique*' (which was made to figure as a great political power), was wonderfully characteristic of a French view of English manners.

I tried to say something civil about the attack on Louis Napoleon; but did not make much of it, and his mode of dealing with my little sentiment, a kind of significant shake of the hand at parting, without words, was explained when I saw afterwards in the papers what he had been saying to the Lord Mayor the same or previous day.

To the Rev. R. W. Church.

February 20, 1858.

My dear Church,—My French negotiations have come to a fix. After all the drawing up of details and canvassing and inquiring, the French Government require a preliminary which according to my views is absolutely inadmissible, and so the matter stands—Persigny pledged to my view, and professing much anxiety to get over the people in Paris (where he now is), but the 'Ministre de Marine,' who I

'pursuing the assassins to their stronghold' [England]; so the Bill was rejected, really on the absurd theory that it was truckling to the French.

imagine sees more clearly the actual view of the case, stoutly opposed to concession unless we can *guarantee* them what they want to get—which we can't do. Persigny gets more insignificant as I look closely at him, but very friendly and amusing. He read me a good many of the Paris comments on my articles (some grossly unreasonable) and observed on the spirit of mistrust, especially on some which concerned particular proposals of 'Sire *Rogers*'—'apparemment on vous croit un Ogre par-là'—told me how the Emperor and he had to combat all these natural jealousies in France, just as English Ministers had in England, and how he would get at the man in Paris who had drawn the papers, 'the Sire Frederic Rogers of Paris,' and see whether he could not come round him. I wish you could have seen him, sometimes perched on the top of his fender, with his shoulder-blades just leaning against his chimney-piece, and extending his arm like a man who was extending protection to all French subjects in all parts of the globe, to give a weight to a peroration; of course, all this was especially confidential. I should think in every point of view it must all come to an end now. I don't half like, under present circumstances, calling on his *locum tenens*.

Pam has got, in a degree, his deserts. There are lots of things (as I think) to be said for any one else in his situation, but none for him. He has been making capital of the unreasonable arrogance of the English, and passed himself off as the man who was to make all the world submit to it, and upset or outbid anybody who was for reasonable dealing, and now *he* has to be reasonable, or more, to foreign powers and make a case *against* England.

I think if I had been the Opposition I would have contented myself with protesting *in speeches* against the omission to answer Walewski, without coming to a vote on it. It is a mere censure without any practical object; and according to the old principle you should not censure (by vote of the House of Commons) unless you can *replace* a Ministry, which I apprehend the Opposition cannot. Also I confess I dislike inexpressibly House of Commons meddlings in foreign negotiations.

However, I can't deny a satisfaction for the moment in the result.

Ever yours affectionately,
FREDERIC ROGERS.

To Miss Rogers.

8 Park Street: November 8, 1858.

I have been so busy that I forget whether I have told you about Gladstone's mission, not that I have much to say, except that I have come across him and Sir Edward a little, from having to draw up his commission.[7] It was very absurd to see them talking it over, Gladstone's clear dark eye and serious face and ponderous forehead and calm manner was such a contrast with Sir E.'s lean, narrow face, and hurried theatrical, conscious kind of ways. Of course, my affair was merely with form and language, knowing, in fact, nothing of the substance of what was being done, but people are characteristic even in their way of treating that. They both originally wanted (Gladstone, I suppose, principally) to give the mission a *diplomatic* character, the Ionians being, under the treaty of Paris, a 'free and independent State' under our 'protection.' But *that* I had to fight against, and, indeed, on looking into the matter, it would have been as absurd as a matter of form as it plainly would be as a matter of substance.

I have seen a good deal of Lord Carnarvon about that and other matters. He is very friendly and extra confidential, and I think will have not a bad judgment when he gets a little more to know his ground and have confidence in himself. Both he and Sir Edward work very hard, Sir E. writes perfect volumes by way of minutes, and then tells me that he learnt two great maxims in life, one to write as little as possible and the other to say as little as possible.[8]

However, I must get to work; so good-bye.

Ever yours,
F. R.

---

[7] Mr. Gladstone was sent as special High Commissioner to the Ionian Islands to inquire into the complaints which the people of those islands made regarding the Protectorate of Great Britain.

[8] Sir Edward Bulwer Lytton (the first Lord Lytton) was Secretary of State for the Colonies; Lord Carnarvon was Parliamentary Under Secretary for the Colonies.

To Lady Rogers.

November 9, 1858.

My dear Mother,—I forget how much I told you about Gladstone. I have had to do the technical part—drawing his commission and writing his introductory letter. He and Sir Edward Lytton are obviously Philhellenes, and, I should say, disposed to think that we have treated the Ionians rather arbitrarily. This I take to be true; but on the other hand I imagine that it is difficult to treat such a pack of scamps otherwise.

In 1815 we acknowledged them as a 'single, free, and independent republic, under a protection,' and the King engaged to employ peculiar solicitude in looking after their internal organisation and administration; then we or our Lord High Commissioner required them to pass a constitutional law, which, under the forms of a republic, really gave our Lord High Commissioner despotic power, and this power he exercised until lately when Lords Grey and Seaton[9] gave them a real voice in their government. This they have used to job astoundingly and rebel occasionally. We, on the other hand, have shot the rebels, and resumed somewhat of our despotic sway.

The people all, I imagine, hate us, and wish for union with Greece; but a good many, apparently, in Corfu think that English despotism is better than English or Ionian anarchy, and would be satisfied to get back quietly to the old strong rule. Meanwhile all our own knowledge respecting the state of feeling &c. in the islands comes either from what we see of the noisy democrats, who are probably a bad set, or what we are told by our own toadies, who are likely enough to be worse. So the appointment of an able and unprejudiced Commission of Inquiry is a likely thing enough to be valuable.

Sir Edward and Gladstone wanted to make the mission a diplomatic one—*Envoy* as well as Commissions—and Sir E. L. made a ridiculous speech, sawing his arm up and down as if I was the House of Commons, and holding

---

[9] Lord Seaton as Lord High Commissioner, Lord Grey as Secretary for the Colonies in 1848.

forth about the 'Statesman' whom he would wish, if he could
(Gladstone was not avowed), to procure for the work. But
on examination it was pretty clearly ascertained that this
could not be, and it was accordingly given up Then I had
to draw the Commission, and was brought rather pleasantly
into council with Gladstone and Sir Edward (it was pretty
clear who was the better man) on the final alterations.

As to the coolie business, I supposed it to be stirring
because the Foreign Office came to me to look up some old
papers. But Louis Napoleon's manifesto [1] was quite a surprise.
I don't know whether or not they will make use of me—I
don't think that the French would desire me. Persigny
might, but he is out, and the Paris people look on me as a
perfect enemy. I think our people would wish to use me if
they were sure I would not be troublesome and thwart the
project. I don't know that there is any reason for making
any further mystery about my having been engaged with
Persigny in the negotiations to which his Imperial Majesty
alludes. I have done nothing about it except to send in to
Lord Carnarvon one or two outstanding letters which ought
to be in the hands of any one who takes charge of the matter,
simply that he may know that he has all that has passed,
and to enter a little warning on one point which wants
reconsidering.

I was glad to see old —— , who, with his white moustachios
and stupendous hunched-up shoulders, looks like one of the
savage smelters in Retsch's 'Fridolin,' putting the unjust
steward into the fire.

To Miss Rogers.

Nov. 22, 1858.

My dear Kate,—I write to say that I find on my table a
letter from the Colonial Office inclosing one from Lord
Malmesbury to Sir E. B. Lytton, saying that the French

---

[1] The Emperor, in a letter to Prince Napoleon on October 30, said that he would no longer permit negro labourers to be taken from the African coast : ' If their enrolment is simply the slave-trade in disguise, I will not allow it on any conditions ; ' and he desired that his minister should try to obtain Indian coolies as free labourers.

Government have requested 'the presence and assistance of Sir F. Rogers' in Paris as soon as possible, that he, Lord M., has spoken to Lords Derby and Stanley, who consent, and that he would be much obliged to Sir E. L. 'to allow and direct Sir F. R. to call at the Foreign Office at 4.30' to-day.

Sir E. L.'s private secretary incloses it, writes that Sir E. B. L. has answered that I cannot be spared from here until the end of the week. I am afraid I may hardly be able to write after I have been at the F. O.—there probably will then be much to say. So I finish off at once.

Ever yours,
FREDERIC ROGERS.

To Miss Rogers.

Nov. 25, 1858.

My dear Kate,—A line only to say that I have just seen Lord Malmesbury, who wished me to go off this week, and had partly promised that I would. So I have been to Sir Edward, and got leave to be off on Friday. My instructions, I suppose, are simply to present myself to Lord Cowley—that is all he tells me to do.

The object professed is to give all possible information to a Commission, at the head of which is my old friend Persigny.

Ever affectionately,
F. R.

To Lady Rogers.

Château de Chantilly : Nov. 28, 1858.

My dear Mother,—G. will probably send you on my first letter, so I shall not repeat, except to say that I found in getting to Paris that Lord Cowley was then with the Emperor at Compiègne, and was living at Chantilly (the Ambassade in Paris being under repair), and Lord Chelsea, whom I saw, told me I could not do better than go down and spend the Sunday with him there. Accordingly I got down by an evening train in time for dinner, and, as Lord C. was not to be home till late (12 o'clock at night), had dinner and a pleasant evening with Lady Cowley, two of her daughters, and a governess—Lady Cowley very hospitable and friendly. This evening I have seen Lord Cowley, who is too busy to have anything to say to me till the morning, when we can talk over our own affairs; meanwhile I have been looking a little over the premises, and am now waiting for a summons to take a lionising walk with Lady Cowley.

The Château was the hunting palace of the great Condé, but the larger and more magnificent part was destroyed in the Revolution, leaving a kind of appendage called the 'capitainerie' (in the style of the Tuileries), which is the present château. Condé's stables (holding 170 horses) remain. And the whole plan certainly has a grand look of Louis Quatorze magnificence remaining. The inside is said to have been fitted by Watteau, and very beautiful in its way; the room in which I am writing (my bedroom) is a little circular room, about twenty feet across, with all sorts of painted ceiling and gilt adornments, with alternations of painted wood and gold pilasters and shawl-like hangings, medallions, &c.; and looking out in front on a large piece of artificial water, which wanders about the house as if it might once have been a moat, with some idea of defence; but had afterwards been enlarged and Louis Quatorzified. The basement story, or, as they call it, 'the foundation,' of the old palace remains, and there is a kind of faint similarity to a fortified house in the outline both of it and the water, in which I can contrive to imagine that the taste of the great general may be visible. The terraces are very grand indeed, smaller than those of the Crystal Palace, but more beautiful, and evidently the *real thing*, out of which the Crystal Palace terraces are blown out. It is on a flat, so there is no view, except just upon the grounds, which seem to be according to the French park fashion—avenues, vistas, &c. The whole is backed by the Forest of Chantilly, of which one just sees the edge, looking like a belt. It went from Condé to the Duc de Bourbon, then to the Duc d'Aumale, and then, on the forced sale of the Orléans property, was bought by Messrs. Coutts, it is said, for the Orléans family.

Back again from my walk. The stables are certainly a sight—more like a cathedral than anything else, if one could imagine a cathedral strictly *à la Louis Quatorze*—they certainly impress on one's mind a notion of the way in which the great princes of the blood did things then, also relics of the old festive way of going on; a group of would-be picturesque cottages, including a mill, where the gentlemen and ladies used to picnic in the dress of Dresden china millers and shepherdesses, and a labyrinth, in the centre of which luncheon for two was laid every day; both the cottages (the *hameau*) and labyrinth are in decay.

Watteau seems to have been a hanger-on to the Condé clique of his day, and in one of the rooms there is a caricature of Louis Quatorze and Madame Pompadour as monkeys. (Condé was always in opposition.)

The village is a queer place—largely inhabited by a population of English jockeys. In front of their windows is the great race-course of France, where there are races four or five times a year (the principal one being called 'the Derby') and constant training; and, of course, English trainers and jockeys are in request, and a set of them have fairly naturalised themselves here. I find my room is an imposture, being fitted up, not 'siècle de Louis XV.' as I supposed, but only by the Duc d'Aumale. However, be that as it may, it is a gorgeous little affair; I ought to have seen that it was too fresh for an antiquity. Lord C. at luncheon rather short and grumpy— I hope nothing has gone wrong. I am glad to hear from him that they have seized the fellow Guernsey that stole the paper from the Colonial Office. The subs. were rather in a state of indignation at its not having been done before. He was to have been off to the United States on Friday or Saturday, and I suppose that made them feel that it must be done.

To Lady Rogers (Lady Blachford).

Hôtel du Louvre: November 29, 1858.

Half-past seven P.M., Hôtel du Louvre, dinner just finished, dressing-gown, slippers, wood fire, and a long evening. . . I had a very pleasant time at Chantilly. The place is very pretty and full of character, and Lady Cowley fond of showing it off—at least, apparently so. On Sunday I was agreeably surprised to find that they had a chaplain and two services for the benefit of themselves and the colony of English jockeys and trainers who have been collected at Chantilly, leaving time for a goodish walk between services (along the old waterworks of Condé and Lenôtre) and odds and ends of time enough to read the Emperor's 'Idées Napoléoniennes'—an interesting book under the circumstances, with a good many striking thoughts in it, and a good deal of useless effort to fight against facts. The idea running through it is that the Empire was in Napoleon's view the only practicable school by which the French could be educated into freedom. . . .

Business was soon despatched; in fact, I was merely in the first instance to answer questions, though in so doing we may probably work some way towards an understanding. I understand that Prince Napoleon[2] is to do the business himself (like Persigny), and, I suppose, at Persigny's suggestion desired that I personally should be sent over. But there seems to be a hitch of etiquette. Walewski protests against any communication between England and France in Paris except through him. But nobody wants him, the particular matter not being, I suppose, his affair: so, as a compromise, he insists that I should see him *before* I see Prince Napoleon, but as he is not forthcoming in Paris till Wednesday I am idle to-morrow; and Lord C. has written to the father of his private secretary, who is a famous lioniser of Paris, to give me a helping hand in that way. I expect to hear from him. On Wednesday Lord C. is coming to Paris, and will take me to Walewski; after that I shall, I suppose, be free for the Prince, and business will begin. It will probably last two or three days, so that I am not likely to get away this week, and Lord C. says that if it comes to *negotiation* I shall be wanted again. Lord Cowley is a mixture—sometimes dry and silent almost to forbiddingness, and sometimes very communicative, and cordially communicative, only of what he wishes to be known and repeated, but with the appearance of talking freely and giving his opinion. Of course, the Embassy view of everything is in relation to its own work. 'Everything that tends to blow the coals

---

[2] Prince Napoleon ('Plon-Plon') was Minister for the Colonies.

between England and France is detestable. Montalembert is a trumpery fellow, absolutist at heart, and merely set on notoriety. The Government have most imprudently fallen into a trap and given him his wish. Nobody in Paris cares twopence about him, his book, or his prosecution.'[3] Lord C. seemed to think that the French had very little confidence in any of the old Louis-Philippist school of statesmen, and said that the Emperor had said to him more than once that if he could find any Minister in whom France could have real confidence he would make any sacrifice to get his services. The first part seems likely enough, for I suppose that all the world knows Thiers to be a regular scamp, and Guizot, though honest himself, to have been a regular fountain of corruption to others. *Au reste,* 'any sacrifice' is a loose way of speaking that may mean anything you choose, but I can easily imagine that the Emperor hands the government of the country over to unknown men who are staunch friends of his own, *partly* because he believes the old school to be in sober truth not a bit more trustworthy, and therefore not worth the sacrifice which he would have to make for them.

This morning (Monday) I left Chantilly, got here between two and three, and what with a call at the Embassy, shaking into shape at the Hotel, and luncheon, did not manage to get more than a walk along the Quais before dark.

No use for the cocked hat, but I suppose it was safe to bring it.

To Lady Rogers (Lady Blachford).

Paris : December 3.

As far as I am concerned this week is *simply lost.*

I imagine there is ill feeling between Walewski and Prince Napoleon, and W. is affronted at having the matter pass over his head. He has first interposed generally, next he has appointed Lord Cowley to bring me before him on Wednesday (yesterday), then to-day (Thursday), and now he professes to

---

[3] Montalembert was prosecuted (November 25, 1858) for having published the pamphlet *Un Débat sur l' Inde,* in which he contrasted English liberty with the system of government under the French Empire. The judges sentenced him to a fine of 6,000 francs and six months' imprisonment; but the Emperor gave a free pardon.

be detained with the Emperor at Compiègne till Saturday and pushes off my interview till Monday. Lord Chelsea says this is the kind of thing he does. Meanwhile, I suppose, the Colonial Office will growl. Luckily I left a clear table, except what I have with me, and I hope nothing is accumulating. I am not really wanted. . . . December 4. All different. We really are of such importance that we shall have our heads turned.

'S. A. I. le Prince Napoléon ayant appris que Sir F. Rogers était arrivé à Paris, le Prince désire vivement qu'il soit entendu aujourd'hui même' (being about 4 P.M. already) 'par la commission d'enquête sur l'immigration. La Commission se rassemble à cet effet ce soir au Palais Royal. Si Sir F. R. veut bien s'y présenter à neuf heures du soir, il sera reçu par le Prince et introduit à la Commission. L'entrée au Palais Royal est Péristyle Montpensier. Des ordres sont donnés à l'huissier. Dans le cas où Sir F. R. serait dans l'impossibilité de répondre aujourd'hui au vœu de la Commission, le Prince désire vivement en être informé, soit directement, soit par l'intermédiaire du Commandant Ferri Pisani, son aide-de-camp, Secrétaire de la Commission, demeurant au Palais Royal.

C. FERRI PISANI.

'Paris &c. &c.'

So you see in a few hours I shall be fairly landed. I intended to have kept the grand letter (addressed to Lord Cowley), but as Lord C. wants it back again as his protection against Walewski, you see I waste time in copying it. I went to Ferri Pisani with Lord Chelsea, and having ascertained first my way, secondly, how I am to address the Prince (who is to be my questioner), I am now waiting for first my dinner and next *neuf heures*.

To Miss Rogers.

Paris : December 5, 1858.

My letter was broken off by a letter from the Embassy inclosing one to Lord Cowley (I suppose) from the Prince's aide-de-camp . . . . appointing 9 o'clock when I should be received by the Prince and introduced to the Commission. Well, of course, off I went, was shown into a magnificent room at the 'Ministère d'Algérie' into which came the Prince (short, stout, intelligent-looking and *very* like his uncle) and Persigny. The Prince received me courteously and Persigny cordially, and after a few words took me into the next room, a large, long, handsome room, with a large, long table with about twenty Frenchmen, sage-looking and solemn. The Prince took his seat on the centre of one long side, with Persigny on his right, and put me opposite to him and began his questions—I tremble for my French and still tremble at the recollection of it—but there I was with the Prince upon me in the first instance and, to say the truth, as cool as a cucumber. 'Nous causerons ensemble,' was the way he put it, and the notion was throughout of giving it a friendly conversational character. Well, before long, others began to strike in with their questions, one or two who really wanted information, and some who wanted to show off themselves— one in particular, although he had got up the question of Mauritius very well. Then arose larger questions of general immigration policy—views of the British Government and so on—reasons *pro* and *con* for African emigration, and little half-impatient discussions between the Prince and members of the Commission, I being the mark at which every one who wanted to make his point fired his first arrow. 'Si Monseigneur me permettra, je ferai une question à Sir Rogers,' or 'je rappellerai à M. Rogers une question à laquelle il a déjà répondu, mais qui me paraît demander quelque développement,' and so on. I got sometimes horribly confused in my French, and then they told me to speak English. Many of them understood it, and the Prince, I think, *well*. This lasted for about an hour and a quarter, when the Prince rose and led the way into the room in which he had received me, Persigny half followed, expressing a hope that I was authorised to negotiate, but then falling back motioned me to follow alone. Then the Prince repeated that he wished very much I would get authority to begin negotiations at once—that we might despatch it all in a fortnight if the matter were really pressed on, and after a little talking in this strain shook hands very courteously; afterwards I came back to ask whether I should be of any further use at present, as giving more *information*, explaining that I had work to do in London. He told me, no, that they had got my 'autorité' for the points on which they wanted it (so that now I might run back at once, but that Lord C. is back at Chantilly, and I must, I suppose, get his leave (I wrote to him the result of the interview). Then with another rather pointed handshaking, we each went our way, he back to the Commission, I out as I came.

I would give two and sixpence to know that I had not grossly exposed myself: there was a calm courtesy about their mode of dealing with my flounderings in French which is alarming to look back upon—though it was particularly reassuring while the process was going on.

The one point which keeps me is that I was appointed for Walewski on Tuesday, and when you miss an appointment with a somewhat unwilling appointer you have a chance of messing the whole affair. So I half incline to run down myself to-day to Chantilly, and find out what will be the best way of managing. I ought to have a few days in London before coming back to take up the negotiation, else the C. O. will be grumbling.

To Lady Rogers.

H. de Veuillemont : December 17, 1858.

As you did not have my last great interview you shall have this—a more nervous one than the other. I was duly informed, as I told you, by Lord Cowley that the Prince and Benedetti were to take me in hand. In the course of the day I got two notes, one from a M. Belling, the Chef de Cabinet as it is called, to Walewski ; another (provoked by a note of mine) from Ferri Pisani telling me to go to the Prince's private residence, 18 Avenue Montaigne, at 9 P.M., which seems to be his time for doing this kind of things. Well, away I went, but first, like a goose, thought it was *Rue* Montaigne, and got set down at a most ill-looking and shabby, dirty *porte cochère*, then, like a double goose, not seeing instantly that I had somehow gone wrong, and being a few minutes too soon, sent away my *voiture* and walked about till 9 o'clock. Well, when 9 o'clock came I rang at the bell and got into a still dirtier yard, with nobody but an old woman, from whom I ascertained my mistake, and had explained to me that I was to 'traverser les Champs-Elysées' and so on; so off I posted, not knowing really my way, being in the dark and horribly disgusted at the notion of being too late. Again I went wrong, but at last, with many askings (not being able to read numbers), got safe to the house—an hotel standing alone, with a sweep in front. There I found to my great satisfaction that the Prince was still at a Ministerial dinner, and was shown into a small room, where a big, yellow-haired and bearded, round-faced, tall, broad, black-coated man came to divert me, a kind of majordomo or master of the ceremonies he seemed to be. So we talked of London and Paris, fogs &c., till we heard the Prince had come. Then I was shown into a library—tea table and tea-urn hissing, Benedetti requesting to be introduced, study table with three ominous-looking sheets of foolscap and blotting paper, laid out, and with a little complimenting, got to work. Well, we went over the whole ground and got matters pretty much to the shape in which they were left with Persigny— that is to say, we see the future points of battle. The matter is to be brought into a more definite shape, and then we are to be at it again on Wednesday. These proceedings seem to be rather like a *table d'hôte* dinner at the Hôtel du Louvre. We get through the courses fast enough when they come, but there is an enormous pause between them; I am not sure, however, that it is more than necessary, seeing that everything has to be well considered and by divers people probably. Meantime this looks long; on Wednesday we may come to some conclusion (or not), on Thursday I shall write (I suppose) referring the points of difference home; these will have to be considered by Lords Malmesbury and Stanley and perhaps Sir E. Lytton and their respective advisers. They must agree on something and send it back—then a fresh touch of conference here—then a fresh reference home—which perhaps I may take home myself in person. This seems the least that can happen. The interview was curious. The Prince, I should think, affected a good deal of his uncle's ways; he is loud and declamatory, disposed to bear down opposition, but (to me) very civil, and not indisposed to infuse a touch of satire into his declamation; quick in seeing things, but not always catching a fine point. Benedetti, on the contrary, is quite

O

courteous and insinuating and would make you suppose that
you were wholly agreed in substance, and only differed as to
the position of phrases and turns of expression—never run
away with by any of the Prince's misunderstandings and quietly
keeping all straight and warding off fights about nothing. At
the same time both the one and the other gave me very distinctly indeed the impression that it was necessary to look
sharp, and very hard work it was. When you have a man
that talks rather loud and long in English you have a great
advantage, because, while he is battering you, you can give
him a half attention and compose your own answer and study
your position. But when he is talking French your (or at
least my) whole attention is necessary to be sure that you
understand him, and so all that is said has to be said (in
fact) much more off-hand. Also you have to consider when
you speak, not only what you ought to say but what you can
say and how; all which, when it is really necessary, if you can
help it, not to make a false step, gives one a kind of feeling of
being hurried through all the different subjects which arise
and are despatched, so that really I hardly felt that I had
recovered my breath till I had slept upon it. It was like
having a battle with two dogs, one great open-mouthed
barking fellow, who was making all sorts of noise and demon-
strations in front, while an extremely quiet bull terrier was
very composedly walking round you and about your legs with
evidently the deepest interest in your calves, but, withal, the
greatest propriety of demeanour.

However, we were all very civil, and after about two
hours of it (which carried the matter as far as it could be
carried at present) I was dismissed, leaving them (I suppose)
to talk it over by themselves, and Benedetti (as he declared)
to read and note twenty-five despatches. I got home about
a quarter to twelve o'clock, and having only had a cup of tea
at the expense of His Imperial Highness had a good comfortable talk and tea with Edward and went to bed.

I can't say I like the work altogether. It is interesting
but an unpleasantly anxious interest. It is very unpleasant
to deal with people who you feel want to trip you up, and
understand their work—that is, the method of proceeding—

better than you do, and very unpleasant to feel what tyranny and loss of life may be inflicted on thousands of people by a false step. I get rather nervous and almost shaky when I think of this part of the matter. But even little meddlings of this kind help one to understand historical people. I think I feel a little how Roman and Venetian ambassadors must have felt in the presence of great men. When you really come to work, it is astonishing how the difference of personal rank vanishes in the feeling that whatever *you* may be, there is a big nation behind you.

To the Rev. R. W. Church.

Paris, Hôtel Veuillemont : December 26, 1858.

On Thursday I got an invitation to dine on Christmas Day with His Imperial Highness. His hotel is an extremely handsome Villa rather Pompeian in style; consistently classical, with the necessary modifications to make it Parisian. The dinner was very choice, rooms and lighting splendid, and the party made up, half of grand official-looking gentlemen, and half of Algerian officers (one being General McMahon, the man who stormed the Malakhoff, and is now military commandant of Algeria); of the rest I found out nothing, except my old friend Benedetti, and a young Prince of Schleswig-Holstein, who is on the wide world here, and who turned out or rather whom I knew to be an old friend of James and Charlotte Colvile's at Calcutta. It was pleasant to see the style of such a dinner (to say nothing of eating a variety of remarkably good things): the rising from dinner instantly on finishing, and proceeding to the very handsome drawing-room where the whole party instantly set to work on their cigars, the Algerians walking up and down the room in twos as if it was a guard-house or the deck of a steamer, was a new style of thing. But otherwise except when the Prince or Benedetti took me in hand on our business there was nobody to talk to except my little Prince, who introduced himself. To say the truth, I think the Frenchmen might have been a little more civil. I had entirely to start the conversation, almost to force it even to my neighbours at dinner. There was no species I will not say of *effort* to make the foreigner at home, not even of inclination to meet him half way. If it had happened in England I should just have called it English *mauvaise honte*, and I really half think some of it may have been so; at least, there was about one or two of the soldiers a great want of that ready prompt look that one associates with a Frenchman, almost the manner of men who were not quite sure that they were in their place; perhaps they only felt that they were not quite the men to do the honours of the Prince's drawing-room; anyhow I wish they had been a little more agreeable.

I had a longish talk on business in the course of the evening with the Prince, his secretary and Benedetti, with a certain amount of general talk. The Prince professes himself a *Radical*, 'plusqu'un radical' in matters of free trade, but I suppose unable as yet to carry out his views; an admirer of Bright, 'who in a year or two may be Minister, qui sait?' I should think he would have a good deal of pleasure in overcoming opposition and bowling things over. Just now his game is, I fancy, to consolidate his own power as Minister of Algeria and the Colonies; shaking himself free from all Ministers of War, Trade, Foreign Affairs, &c., and managing his own matters and all things 'ad colonialia' without communication with anybody but the Emperor. He was asking to whom I now reported my proceedings, or, what he thought synonymous, who was Colonial Secretary. I explained that, though I was attached to the Colonial Department, I communicated on this matter with Lord Malmesbury; on which Benedetti (turning to *his* chief) struck in with an 'of course,' in which again H.I.H. replied by something which was a mixture of grunt, chuckle, and horse-laugh. 'H'n. Moi, je ne communique' (that was not the word) 'qu'avec le parlement, c'est à dire Napoléon Trois.'

To Miss S. Rogers.

Paris: January 4, 1859.

You will see by the papers that the Emperor has given the funds a kick by a short speech to the Austrian Ambassador. After a word of personal friendship for the Emperor of Austria he added, loud enough for every one to hear, 'but I am sorry that our relations are not good.'

I must have expressed myself ill about Prince N. He is pointedly civil and cordial to me. What made his party rather oppressive to me was that the other Frenchmen did not pity my solitude when I had no friend nigh.

To Hon. Mrs. Legge.

Paris : January 9, 1859.

My dear Marian,—I intended to have given you an account of the Napoleon's dinner No. 2, but in the first place it was not very eventful ; and in the second place I thought it would have enabled me to get back to London at once, and so see you before long. However, I have been baulked in my hope to get off this evening, and so have an hour for a letter.

I only met this time Benedetti and Ferri Pisani (the Prince's secretary). Prince Napoleon rather likes to talk, I think, of the prospect of England's being radicalised by Mr. Bright, for he was again upon that subject. Also he cross-examined me a good deal about English official salaries and talked about official arrangements. I forget whether I told you that at the former dinner he was attacking Benedetti about the number of Foreign Ministers that ought to be supplied by the Foreign Department, and I laughed and said, 'Voilà, monsieur, les réformes que chacun fait dans les départements d'autrui.' And he turned round quite eagerly and said 'Mais je les fais dans le mien,' and went on, on the point. I believe he is a good deal engaged on 'administrative reform' as we should call it. This time he was attacking bureaucracy and bureaucrats, partly by way of chaffing Benedetti, and declared that he had nine about him ; one was an engineer (Pisani, a *chef d'escadron*, I observe), another something else, but none (I understood) the practised official. On the other hand, Benedetti was giving in names of old hands in the Algerian Department, as much as to say, 'Ah, with all your new men it is the old clerk that does the work.' However, it was a business affair altogether; we talked a little business in the grand drawing-room (looking very different from the day in which it was blazing with candles), then went in to dinner, then back again to the drawing-room, when the Prince went to sleep sitting on the sofa with a cigar in his mouth, a thing I never saw before, then adjourned to the library to settle some business. The only touch of character that I remember was explaining (as he likes to do) the difficulty he has in forcing this treaty down the throats of the old sailors and the Colonial party. 'Je vous dis, il fallait le faire enfin par ma volonté. Il fallait dire absolument: Je le veux.' And I dare say he did.

Now there are some little alterations to be settled, and he wishes to see me again on them. So I am waiting without knowing when he will appoint me. I have heard nothing from him yet, though Pisani hoped I should not be kept over Monday.

I suppose you have seen in the papers the Emperor's speech to the Austrian Ambassador. I understand from those who heard it that it was a little softened in the publication. It was: 'Je regrette que nos rapports soient mauvais, mais vous direz à l'Empereur que mes sentiments personnels envers lui sont les mêmes.' The Servian question was considered ugly, but that seems by the papers to be settled. But the real point is, of course, Italy. That is always in a combustible state, and I suppose any encouragement from England and France would set it in a blaze.

We have just been looking over the Hôtel des Invalides —nothing to be compared with Greenwich Hospital in any point of view, least of all in the cleanliness of the wards; the smell of the one we looked into was enough to knock a man down. Also a look at Napoleon's tomb. It appears, however, that he is to be moved to St. Denis. I don't wonder at it. We went there on Saturday (the most interesting and beautiful thing I have seen here), and it seems at present a kind of standing protest against all that has happened since the expulsion of the Bourbons. It is the custom of the church (where, as you know, the kings of France are all buried) that there should be an altar in mourning, as it were, for the last sove-

reign buried there. It is now in mourning for Louis XVIII.
Of course, this is natural enough—seeing Charles X. and
Louis Philippe both died in exile. But it has a kind of
ominous look which the present Napoleon, I could easily
fancy, would like to remove. So, I observe, thought a little
French Legitimist whom we met this morning at Lady Elgin's,
and who was introduced to me as Professor of Hindostanee and
one of the few remaining Gallicans in the French Church. It
was rather curious to see the way in which he felt himself
deserted by his Church, and looked (I think) with a species of
charity accordingly to the English. He was greatly disgusted
at the substitution of the Roman for the Parisian Liturgy
which is in course of taking place. At present, the Parisian
Liturgy is in actual use, but the Pope has ordered (as I
understand) the substitution of the Roman, and the Ultramontane ecclesiastics have contrived to suspend the printing
of the Parisian; so that a person cannot at this moment
buy a copy of the Mass service as it is actually performed
in the churches of Paris. What an inconceivable state of
things! M. de Tassis cries against the *weakness* of the
bishops in giving up their old service. But I suppose it is
really that they are Ultramontanes and like it.

To the Rev. R. W. Church.

Ovington Square : January 17, 1859.

My dear Church,—Here I am back, but only for a few
days. After I wrote to you, and some offs and ons had taken
place, I was summoned to dine again with the Prince Napoleon
on business, just himself, his secretary, Benedetti, and myself.
Well, we went through matters again; one or two small objections were partially removed; and then I proposed to come to
London with their amended project in my pocket to push it
through as fast as I can. Accordingly, I arrived last Thursday
and am to go through a course of Secretaries of State: Sir
Edward, Lord Stanley, and then Lord Malmesbury. Lord S.
will, of course, be the man who will settle in substance all the
Coolie part of the matter; and I shall not be surprised if the
decision on one point which he has already arrived at stops

the whole affair. However, I am to get my instructions complete on all points (probably something in the nature of an amended project), and shall try to be back by the end of this week, when Prince N. will be back from his marriage at Turin. That seems a wretched affair.

I don't know that my further experience of the diplomats added anything to my first-sight impressions. They go on, one plausible and the other blustering, and I certainly have had quite enough of them. Nap. was very curious about our official arrangements, salaries, &c., disposal of patronage by the Indian Secretary of State, and so on, with a great idea that Bright is to become a great man, a Minister (which I told him was likely enough) and a Prime Minister perhaps. Also he professes himself a great 'radical' in the matter of 'libre échange,' takes credit, rather like a great boy, for pushing in that direction, and wants to get compliments from our Ministry on a little advance in that direction which he proposes to make in the convention. On the whole, however, it is a great bore being with people with whom you have to fence, and with whom, though you wish to get on well with them for a purpose, and are glad to have seen them, you would be best pleased to have no further relations. Intercourse is such a dull thing if you neither have nor wish to have friendliness in it.

Did I tell you of our visit to the Bourse? I think not. We were sent up a staircase into a gallery or loggia from which you look down on a great square hall containing some 2,000 or 3,000 people. As we were coming up the stairs (Edward and I) we heard a most tremendous clamour, and supposed some extraordinary uproar, a man being torn in pieces, or something of the kind. But when we had got up so as to see it all, and had partly mastered what was going on we realised that this was the normal state of the Paris Stock Exchange. At one end of the room was a small ring framed off as if for a prize fight, round this was a larger one, outside the larger was the public in a dense crowd, inside the smaller one nothing and nobody, but in the intermediate *annulus* were about seventy or eighty brokers crowding to the edge of the inner ring, and everybody making bargains across it with everybody. It seemed a kind of confused mêlée of auctions, everybody being indiscriminately seller, buyer, and auctioneer—clamouring, gesticulating, taking notes—I think this was the most absurd thing I saw in Paris; the most interesting, if that can be called in Paris, was the Church of St. Denis and the monuments of the kings. I think I must go the round of it again.

Ever yours affectionately,
F. R.

To Lady Rogers.

Sunday : January 23, 1859.

My dear Mother,—The last I told you was, I think, that I was to go through a course of Secretaries of State. First I went off to Sir E. B. Lytton, who was in Cabinet—and packed off to him a note to say I wanted to see him and Lord Stanley together or apart. No answer came to this, and I waited accordingly some three or four hours (an hour after dinner time) till at last out he came. He does not like the affair, I should think, feeling that the colonists will be upon him about it (which I don't think they will—I seem to see my way about that) and that he will generally be involved in squabbles and troubles and things that he does not like, and that the other Ministers are stronger than he, and will put upon him and take the halfpence and leave him the kicks; and so he expresses a strong personal objection to this and that provision, and then draws in his horns with a kind of querulous 'unless wiser persons than I should take a different view'—like a man who is afraid of being snubbed for having an opinion of his own. The end is that Lord Stanley[4] was to talk to me about it; so the next day I was off to Leadenhall Street to find his lordship, was told he was again at a Cabinet, found out he was not, was recommended to rout him up at his private house before 10 A.M. next morning, and ended by losing a

---

[4] Lord Stanley (the late Lord Derby) was Secretary of State for the Colonies in his father's Ministry which came into office on the defeat of Lord Palmerston's 'Conspiracy to Murder Bill' in February 1858, but he was transferred to the India Office (which he had just taken over), and was succeeded at the Colonial Office by Sir E. Bulwer Lytton. The India Bill was passed in June 1858. The East Indian Directors met in Leadenhall Street.

second day and writing a note asking an interview the next day. In the evening, he sent for me in a sudden way to the Colonial Office. I told him the then main question, and got him to my views about them—with a little reluctance—(which was all the better for me) as I want backbone. He was pleasant, and soon decided the matter, made his notes on a sheet of note-paper and stepped off at once to Lord Malmesbury [5] whom I tried to get hold of the next day. He was, however, at Windsor, and appointed me for Friday, when I saw him. He strikes me as a sensible but rather dull man wishes more to get the matter through than Lord Stanley does, and so is inclined to give up as much as possible. Of course, this is natural enough, as he is not responsible for the coolies. With him I regularly went through the treaty clause by clause, putting my questions as I went on and getting definite answers as far as I cared to get them. Of course, he could not know about details, but he rather took my views about them, making, however, some good suggestions, which nevertheless will, I think, hardly be sufficient to escape what is perhaps the great difficulty of the whole, the getting an 'effectual renunciation of the African Free Emigration' as it is called.

From him I went to the 'Treaty Clerk' at the Foreign Office, and from that time I cannot complain that the work has stood still. In the afternoon I was translating the French draft convention, altering it in the proof; in the evening he was overhauling it; in the morning I was settling off some Colonial Office business with Merivale,[6] till he came to me with his work done; the rest of the morning I was resettling it with him, or getting up information at the Slave Department of the Foreign Office. From 6 to 9, B. and two clerks were making three fair copies while I was dining, and from 10 to 12 I was again revising and writing a note to Lord Stanley, while they, I hope, were dining or supping. To-day (Sunday) I have delivered my letter at St. James's Square, but find Lord S. out of town, and this evening I dine with Harding at

---

[5] Foreign Secretary in Lord Derby's Ministry, March 1858–March 1859.

[6] Mr. Herman Merivale had succeeded Sir James Stephen as Under Secretary for the Colonies.

his desire (I suppose prompted from above) to talk over the subject with him. G. told you of this little saying of Lord M.'s: 'It will be a feather in your cap if you can get it done in time for the Queen's Speech'—but I am afraid it is impossible, I almost despair of getting off on Tuesday. And I cannot see how the French objections which are sure to arrive can possibly be disposed of, at the usual pace of work, in the eight days which remain between Wednesday the 26th and Wednesday the 2nd.

And now I want you to do something for me—which is to send hampers of game &c. from Blachford to the three young men in the Colonial Office who lost their dinner and kept their wives waiting in despair, in order to make three copies of some thirty articles for me in a hurry.

To Lady Rogers.

Hôtel Bedford, Paris: January 30, 1859.

My dear Mother,— I had a desperate scamper at the last all in a bustle, and had, after passing Tuesday night in the steamer and railway, to sit up till one o'clock on Wednesday night helping to make a copy of the convention in French and English for Benedetti. A wretched concern it was, as a matter of caligraphy I was perfectly ashamed of sending it to him. However, I gave it to him the next morning. He simply received it asking few questions, and treating it as not impossible that it should get into the Queen's Speech. But I hear Lord Cowley 'scouts the idea' of its being possible. Meantime I conjecture it to have gone to Turin to the Prince, in which case I calculate I cannot hear of it until to-morrow, and that only in case he answers by return of post. Seeing that the Queen has to say her say on Tuesday it appears unimaginable that it could be got into shape and sent to London, approved, then signed and initialled here, and the news of the signature and initialling sent home between the two days; the only possibility is that our draft is accepted wholly, which will, of course, ease matters. . . .

In the afternoon I went with Georgie and Lady Augusta Bruce to look at an infant school and one or two old houses in or about the Rue St. Antoine. Sully's old palace very pompous and characteristic of the man, massive, substantial and overloaded with ornament; and the old palace of St. Paul inhabited by Louis XIII., well worth seeing. There are not many of these old spots about Paris, and so one values what one can get.

We are pretty comfortable and tolerably cheap here. The main evil is a portentous woman who dines steadily at the *table d'hôte* and talks the loudest, most self-satisfied, and most utterly abominable French that I have heard for a long time. I could hardly have imagined anything at once so bad and so unhesitating; I have never seen her at fault for a moment, and she not only talks but dominates in French.

To Miss Rogers.

Paris: February 3, 1859.

It seems my matters must wait till Prince Napoleon comes back with his bride, so I suppose I shall not get off before the end of next week, if then. Lord Cowley is also clear that I must be presented, and as the Emperor fixes the time for such things that may be another delay. I understand that the convention *is to be*, so I may perhaps have a dinner at the Tuileries. If they were to fête the Princess Clotilde and would ask me to one of their gaieties it would be a sight worth seeing, though in some respects rather sad.

The principal event lately has been a dinner with Lady Augusta Bruce,[7] a friend of Georgie's, at her mother's, Lady Elgin's. The dinner was merely among themselves and Baillie, an attaché who married Lady Frances Bruce. But the event of the evening was the coming in of an old gentleman, Comte de Bruce, who had been page to the Comte d'Artois *before* the French Revolution. He was, of course, a refugee, and was placed, by the interest of Lord Elgin,[8] in a regiment commanded by young M. de Bouillé, and so saved from the semi-starvation to which emigrants

---

[7] Afterwards married to Dean Stanley. She was then living with her mother in Paris.

[8] The Lord Elgin who brought home the 'Elgin' marbles; he was grandfather of the presen Viceroy of India.

generally were reduced. He has the most grateful recollection of this, and pays it off to Lady Elgin, whom he has lately found out, to his great satisfaction. She, poor lady, is paralytic, without speech, and only expressing her meaning or wishes by inarticulate sounds and gesticulations. It was very touching to see the reverent old-fashioned way in which he took her hand and kissed it coming in and going away. He was, as he said, a Scotchman, living abroad by permission of his sovereign: *i.e.* under a letter given by Charles I. in 1633 to one of his ancestors, a cadet of the Elgin Bruces. Lady Augusta regularly set herself to set him going upon old times and away he went. We had been reading the very period in Carlyle the evening before, and I cannot express the strange feeling it gave one to hear this old gentleman quietly dropping his allusions and sentiments in the easy familiar way of personal knowledge, just on the points which we had been previously reading of, as history, not *of* but before the Revolution. It was as if a man had started after dinner with ' I remember Julius Cæsar saying to me just as he was going off to Gaul.' Lady A. asked him whether he had not once borne Marie Antoinette's train, and he answered in the kind of half modest, half self-satisfied disclaimer of a man who wishes to keep the credit without appearing to make more of himself than he deserves. ' Ah, c'était un hasard. La Reine était allée voir Mesdames Tantes avec Monsieur ' (Mesdames Tantes being the daughters of Louis XV. whom Carlyle mentions as having stuck to him on his death-bed, and the Count being page to Monsieur, afterwards Louis XVIII.), ' et son service n'était pas là, ainsi il fallait '—that I should carry her train. ' Ah, Mesdames Tantes étaient très aimées de la Reine et de tout le monde, parce qu'elles étaient très bonnes et toujours très bonnes pour moi, puisque Louis Quinze aimait beaucoup mon oncle. Quand mon oncle se retirait de son service, il disait : " Tous mes bons serviteurs me quittent." ' Then Lady A. tried to make out whether in the years '85-6-7 there was in the Court any of that vague apprehension which one might have imagined, and there was a kind of curious familiarity, a matter-of-courseness, which seemed to carry one back like a shot, when he said with half surprise : ' Mais non, c'était avant l'assemblée des notables.' He told us that he was in the antechamber when Cardinal de Rohan passed through to the King and was arrested on his way out; and he looked at him with all his eyes because he had never seen a Cardinal before. He was still at that time page to Monsieur, and he described how he and his fellow pages were well treated by the mob. 'On aimait ma livrée parce qu'on croyait que Monsieur avait des idées populaires, mais les pages de Monseigneur' (Charles X.) ran the risk of their lives in going into Paris (Carlyle again). He said that de Rohan was arrested by one d'Agoust, major in the Gardes du Corps, with some of his brethren, who were all so much employed in that kind of work that it was said to be a family of 'bons chiens d'arrêt.' They have a descendant in Paris, a little insignificant man, as the Count de B.'s daughter was making out. 'C'est donc le nain de la famille,' said the old gentleman; 'ils étaient beaux hommes, les d'Agoust.' Then he explained that from his pageship he was promoted into the army, the regiment (I think M. de Bouillé's), but not the detachment, which was to have taken charge of the King on the flight to Varennes. Lady A. observed that that affair was 'mal mené,' and he answered quite quickly, like a subaltern standing up for his colonel, 'Mais M. de Bouillé ne le mena pas mal,' and then went off into a panegyric on M. de Bouillé; how when he was Governor of St. Lucia and an English frigate was wrecked there in time of war, he helped them all he could, and would not make them prisoners, and sent them home, saying that it was not the French army that beat them but the elements; how the English merchants gave him a sword and pistols at the end of the war to show their sense of the generous way in which he had carried it on; how, when he was over head and ears in debt and the King determined to pay his debts for him, he thanked his Majesty and requested leave to draw on the Treasury for 100 crowns, his debts being nearer 50,000.

Then we came to more modern times, and were greatly amused by his answering with the slow deliberation of a man who feels he is going to say something heretical, almost shocking, 'Moi, j'avoue, j'ai un peu de respect pour Napoléon' (then, very distinctly, to prevent any misconception); 'je veux dire

Napoléon premier.' People should have known what France was then, to know what he did for it. ' Nous devons à lui que la chrétienté existe en France.'

To Miss S. Rogers.[9]

Paris: February 5, 1859.

My dear Sophy,—Lady Augusta Bruce is a treasure, and her idea of a dinner party is a good one—four persons to a plain dinner, and at the dinner or in the evening one person who is really worth meeting. The day before yesterday she gave us a M. Mohl, a German by extraction, Professor of Sanscrit, hater of the French official hierarchy, as they call it, and above and beyond all, of Louis Napoleon, but naturalised here for thirty years or so, and a person of extreme fun. The evening (or the best part of it) reduced itself into an account of all his adventures while in the National Guard. I wish I could give you them; but, in the first place, I cannot remember all, and next, half the fun was in his vigorous and lively way of telling it, and his very good but strongly accented English. I will try, however, and you must fancy all his sayings in French or German-English—every syllable equally accented, foreign words here and there, English familiar phrases slightly diverted from their uses, and so on, but fluent and pointed. Imprimis, he was obliged in 1830 to enter the National Guard, and, abhorring it and all that belonged to it, set himself in the first place to consider how, without subjecting himself to any penalty, he could get out of it. The best way which occurred to him was to get a copy of the 287 articles of war, to put them up on the wall of his room, and to make himself such a perfect master of them that by a proper and constant use of them (being a man of talent, industry, coolness, and infinite humour) he might make himself so utterly insupportable to everybody as to tire them into turning him out. H. will fully appreciate the extreme wisdom of his proceedings; though it seems to have cost him twelve years' labour to accomplish his object. However, here are two or three of his anecdotes

[9] This letter has already appeared in print. It was published in the *Spectator* after M. Mohl's death.

—supply foreign accent. 'Now I will show you how they did things in those days. I will tell you about the man who was assassinated. While I was on duty at night in the Corps du Garde, a man came rushing in to say there was a terrible thing —they were assassinating a man in the Rue Cherche-Midi. Well, instead of our going out as fast as we could to help this man who was assassinating or assassinated, the officer says to me, Go immediately and tell the Commissaire de Police : he lives in the Rue Grenelle, under a red lamp. Well, away I go and find my Rue Grenelle and red lamp and I make a great noise at the door for a long time. At last a head with a nightcap comes out at the window and asks me what in the world I want. "The Commissaire de Police," say I. "Well, I am the Commissaire de Police. What do you want?" "There is a man being assassinated in the Rue Cherche-Midi." "Which side of the gutter?" says he. Well, I did not know about one side or the other side, so I say at once boldly, "The right side as you come down the street." "Ah," he says, "that is in the other arrondissement ; go to the other Commissaire, No. — Rue ——." So away I go, with my man being assassinated all the time, and I find my other Commissaire. "Which side of the gutter?" says he. So I thought at any rate I will stick to my story, and I say, "The right side coming down the street." "Ah," dit-il, "cela me regarde. But how long is it since they have been assassinating him?" "About three quarters of an hour," say I. "Ah, then he is dead by this time. We must get two men and a stretcher to carry him away." So we get two men and a stretcher, and I went with them, for I wanted to see whether the man was on the right side of the gutter or not ; and we found him lying stone dead in the gutter. But he was more on the right side than the left, and he was stabbed through the heart, so the three-quarters of an hour did not signify. But this is the way they do things here.'

Then came instances of his own mode of performing military duty. You must remember that in Louis Philippe's time, the Line and the National Guard were doubled up, as it were, every sentry consisting of one Liner and one National. He had begun by giving us an account of the 'gōne' or 'gōhn' (gun) which had been issued to him, incapable of going off, and bought cheap from the Tower of London because the English wanted to get rid of it. This 'gōhn' played a great part in all his adventures. 'One day, when I was going down to take my twenty-four hours' duty, I thought how I should get through the time, and as I was going down, I stop at a bouquiniste, what you call bookstall, and bought a dozen brochures or so, to read till I go home again. And when I get to my post I put my " gōhn " carefully away in my sentry box and sit down to read. There was a little dwarf wall under the archway by my sentry box—a wall round the corner to prevent the carriages coming on the *trottoir*—so I spread out my dozen brochures on the dwarf wall, and I choose out the one I like best, and I sit down among my books and I begin my reading. Well, presently I hear a gentleman go by on horseback who talks to the soldiers, and seems very much discomposed; but I do not pay any attention, and when he is gone, up comes the soldier and says, " National, you are in a scrape ; vous donnez scandale." "Why should I be in a scrape ? " says I. " Nous verrons." Well, presently I hear a noise, and I look up and I see our capitaine running along without his cap, and carrying his sword in his hand to run faster, and he runs up to me and he says, " Mais quel scandale ! Quel horreur !" " Mais quel scandale, capitaine ? " lui dis-je ; " qu'est-ce qui est arrivé ? " " Mais c'est vous—c'est vous—est-ce que c'est comme ça que vous montez garde ? Où est votre fusil ? " " It is safe in my sentry box," say I. " Et vos livres ! est-ce donc que vous tenez ici boutique de bouquiniste ? " " It is only something for me to read. I cannot wait here all day doing nothing." " Et vous restez toujours assis comme ça ? " " Mais oui—I have not the force in my legs to keep always standing." " C'est un scandale, vous dis-je—c'est un scandale." " Mais qu'est-ce qu'il faut donc faire, capitaine ? " And as he was a reasonable man, I got him at last to consent to a compromise. I had found out by this time which of my brochures was worth reading and which were not ; so I agreed that I would take my " gōhn " out of my sentry box, and I would put there in its stead my eleven brochures which were not worth reading, and I would sit on my dwarf wall and put my " gōhn " between my knees, and go on reading my twelfth brochure.'

Another in the same spirit: 'One day I was told to stand sentry under an archway to prevent the carriages from passing under it. But I find that the masons had made a scaffolding and a wall, and a great mess altogether, so that a dog could not pass, much less a carriage; so I sit down, and take out my newspaper and spread it out before my eyes and begin reading. Well, before long I hear somebody chattering and sputtering behind my newspaper, and I turn down the top and look over it and see a capitaine of the line in a great rage, and he says, "What are you about? What do you suppose you are here for?" "I am here," I say, "to prevent carriages from going through; mais je les en défie, donc je cultive mon esprit." And so we fell into an argument, and at last says he, "But with that newspaper before your eyes you cannot salute an officer as he passes." So I say to him quite quietly, "Y tenez-vous, capitaine?" and that put him out of himself. "Votre nom?" me dit-il. "Je ne pourrais pas vous le dire." "Mais vous connaissez votre nom?" "Mais vraiment cette occupation me rend si stupide que je ne pourrais rien dire avec certitude. Demandez au Corps du Garde." Now I must tell you there was one thing about which we Nationals all agreed, that nobody should get any information at the Corps du Garde. "Who is the sentry at the gate of the Tuileries?" "We do not know." "Let me see the *feuille de service*." "There it is, but it will tell you nothing, for the Nationals are always exchanging duties, and the changes are not entered." And so it was that my capitaine went away and I heard no more of him.'

Lastly you shall have his crowning exploit, after which they never put him on duty again. The law authorises the officers to call out National Guards for twenty-four hours' duty; but they used to add on to this two hours extra, calling them out two hours before the duty begins, for drill and parade. Our friend knew and did not like this; so he presented himself two hours after the time appointed, and quietly took up a position ready to fall in when the parade was over and the Nationals dismissed to their respective posts. 'When the parade was over, the colonel saw me standing at my ease, and that I had not been parading with the rest (which was as plain as a pikestaff) and asked me why I had not come before. "Because," say I, "the law only allows you to call me out for twenty-four hours, and as I know you will not send me away before 11 o'clock to-morrow, I have not come before 11 o'clock to-day." "Ah!" says he, "la garde nationale se perdra par les raisonnements." "Toute chose," lui dis-je, "se perd par son ennemi naturel." Then he tells me that he will give me double duty, and I tell him that I must submit, but that I shall bring an action against him for *abus de pouvoir*. However, he gives me double duty at the gate, which is now blocked up, from the garden of the Tuileries on to the Seine. Well, there I went, and as there were a great many of my friends going to and fro there, I begin talking to them, when a little gentleman with a fine cane begins a conversation with me. "Well, National, it is a fine day; how do you like being on guard?" and after a word or two he says: "You do not seem to know me." I say, "I have not the honour of your acquaintance." Says he, "I am the colonel of your regiment." Say I, "And I am the National Guard whom you ordered to do double duty this morning, and if you are a colonel (he was in plain clothes) you ought to know that it is an offence to speak to a sentry on his post, and I therefore arrest you for it, and will trouble you to walk into my sentry box till the corporal comes round to let you out." "Ah!" says he, "that is a *plaisanterie*." "*Du tout*," says I; "je ne plaisante jamais avec la baïonnette. Go into my sentry box or the soldier opposite will put his hand on your collar and put you in." He did not like this at all, as he was one of the fine gentlemen of Paris, the Duc de Grammont, I think, and he did not want to stand like an ape behind me in my sentry box, for all his fine friends to laugh at when they passed. The only thing I wondered at was why he did not sink into the earth. For what could he do? He had before him a man with a gun in his hand, with the law on his side (for he was *dans son tort*), and his mortal enemy. So he made a great fuss about it, and at last I let him go, telling him he had better not be so strict to other people another time. After that I was never called out to do duty again.'

Yours affectionately,

F. R.

Hôtel de Bedford : February 14, 1859.

My dear Edward,—I went last night to the ball given by the Préfet and Municipality of Paris at the Hôtel de Ville to Prince Napoleon and the Princess Clotilde. Never did I conceive anything so beautiful. The Tuileries is a thing wholly not to be spoken of in the same sentence with it. In the first place, it is not in a suite of apartments that you are, mind, but in a palace—upstairs, downstairs, galleries, staircases, corridors, saloons, small sitting-rooms or cabinets; here and there ball-rooms, here and there refreshment-rooms; servants in white liveries everywhere about, telling you which way to go; and all in a blaze of light. The main ball-room has a magnificent gallery, about (I should guess) 200 feet long, the sides formed by a row of Corinthian columns, white and gold, projecting from the wall, with rich satin damask curtains between each, and in front of each a large chandelier —thirteen compartments, making on both sides twenty-six chandeliers in all. Then above that the usual kind of ceiling, only so high as to give room for a second row of windows on one side of the room, and a gallery—a kind of triforium, you may say—on the other. This was the grand ball-room; to this there was an ante-chamber, smaller but more beautiful, the upper gallery being not so much set on the ceiling, but a kind of loggia, only with caryatides instead of columns— from this above I saw the entry of the prince below. But *far* more beautiful was what I call (by way of distinction, for *room* it was not) the music room. First fancy yourself in a quad as big as a small Oxford quad, the said quad being made up of a colonnade all round below and a second colonnade all round above, the lower colonnade ornamented by marble columns, the upper by statues standing above each column; above both a tallish roof with dormer windows, in the form of the Hôtel de Ville at Rouen, but with Renaissance details. Then from the top, or nearly so, of the roof of the quad, starts a fresh roof which shall cover in the quad; then put a rich carpet on the ground, with curtains in all the apertures of the colonnade, richly dressed centgardes at the side of each column, lamps in the hands of all statues, chandeliers in front of each arch, lamps in close line along but below the banisters of the staircase, so that up to the very top there was no mysterious darkness (three stories high, remember); and then under the staircase a plentiful fountain playing, the water rushing up, falling into basins, and then rolling out of sight over two or three steps among yuccas, camellias, and all sorts of flowers and evergreens, with a great gurgling and coolness. No plaster or painting, but all that you saw honest stone, and marble, and carpet, and damask, and all the galleries crowded with brilliantly dressed people, leaning their elbows on rich velvet hangings, to look at you below. Of course all these galleries were part of your range, and the people in them not spectators, but *you*. The company with jewels, and artificial flowers, and silks, and satins. Then in another place you came on a low, long gallery, broken in by columns or piers with nothing but trellis-work and roses (real *bona-fide* creeping or trained roses about you). Then perhaps a second great Louis-Quatorze ball-room; then a pleasant room, all light-blue hangings, light-blue curtains, light-blue chairs, pretty and ladylike; then you dropped on tea and ices; then different forms of staircase, differently treated in point of ornament. The only defect was that before long you found that you had wholly lost your bearings, and became unable to get back to any place which you wanted to reach—up, down, in, or out—and could only recognise an old friend when you came upon it. I hope it will be open to the public to-day, in which case I shall go to have a look at it by daylight—a sad falling-off, but it will be like looking up one's analysis for Collections. The blaze of light in these places is astounding.

To Miss Rogers.

9 Ovington Square : February 28, 1859.

I have not much to say here, except that Sir E. B. Lytton is in a great quandary about a committee on West Indian matters, which has been asked for by one of the race of Buxton. Everybody is agreed that it ought to be stopped, but it is by no means so clear that it can be ; and if it can't, why, then, Ministry must not try. If it is given, of course I shall have to appear to give the Government account of the immigration, which will be the main object of attack. Lord Carnarvon had a great talk about it with me last Thursday, wishing to know what sort of case I considered we had. I think we have a very good one, and told him so, and that I had no fear of the committee, though I quite agreed that it would be very troublesome, and ought to be quashed if possible ; but that I did not think that Government should oppose it with an obstinacy that looked like fear. 'Do you feel sure that we shall have an overwhelming answer to everything that is brought up ? ' 'Overwhelming is a big word, and nobody can tell certainly what they may bring up ; but I feel sure that, before a fair committee, the immigration can, on the whole, be thoroughly justified and shown to have been successful.' 'Oh, we must get something better than a fair committee. Well, I think I understand now where we stand and what to be about. Thank you very much.' And so we stand for the present. I suppose the committee will be given, and am not without a certain curiosity about the result. If it comes, I shall not be altogether sorry.

I suppose I am safe here till Lord Cowley comes back from Vienna, and then it is of course a chance what happens. If they accept bodily the draft which they have in their hands, which is hardly probable, or if they refuse it bodily, which is hardly possible, after what the Emperor said to Lord Cowley —I shall not go back. But if, which is most likely, they refuse some changes of detail, accepting in the main, then I shall have to go. I don't know whether Georgie told you that Lady Augusta Bruce wants me to put up at Lady Elgin's, which will be pleasant. And this I shall do, for some days at least, unless her spare room is occupied by one of her brothers. I shall have the profit and pleasure, probably, of seeing some nice French people, and shall have the satisfaction of feeling that I really shall be useful to them in the evenings in helping to amuse poor Lady Elgin. I can't say I look with any pleasure to renewing my acquaintance with Plon-plon ; that marriage of his really makes one sick to think of. I never heard a man so generally abused. Probably he will have little to say to me.

I have my hands pretty full, and so am taking the opportunity of Sunday evening to write, and shall put up at once without waiting to see what to-morrow produces. Love to all.

Ever yours affectionately,
F. R.

To Lady Rogers.

Colonial Office : April 29, 1859.

My hands are pretty free. There is a flow of easy work—not very heavy nor yet very light—and Lord Carnarvon is very pleasant to do work with. He makes me feel that he relies on me and likes making work. And it is pleasant to have to deal with a person who sees the absurd side of things as much as he does. He certainly has the advantage of not being anxious. He was breakfasting with Gladstone yesterday, and tells me that Gladstone is furiously Sardinian. He—Lord C.—is as furiously Austrian, has read the whole history of the Revolutionary War to test Austrian character, and finds that under all their terrible trials they never once broke faith or shuffled with us.

You will see that the 'Times' is finding out all sorts of bad omens—sales of charts, &c., &c. No doubt it looks as if a terrible time was coming. However, I think our people are inclined to brace themselves up to it. Taxes will be their *first* test. Certainly the war is not of our seeking. I hope the big wars which we don't seek may not be coming as a punishment for the little wars that we do.

Wolfe tells me that the elections are going on very Conservatively. Four gains to-day. G. Hope and Vansittart at the head of the poll at Windsor, others I don't remember.

Ever yours affectionately,
F. Rogers.

May 3, 1859.

My picture gives satisfaction.[1] We were amused at an old gentleman who was looking at it while we were laughing about it behind him, and catching the idea, accomplished a

---

[1] His portrait by the late Mr. George Richmond, R.A., was in the Academy exhibition of 1859.

very gradual 'right-about face' so as to get a look at the original. But unluckily, just as he had accomplished his artful object, I quite unconsciously wished good-bye (to A. and S.) and ran off—a loss for him.

I have read 'The Bertrams,' a wretched book. The part about Jerusalem is really too offensive to be read. He means to satirise the coarse way in which people take their pleasure about holy places, and so he himself, in the very act of doing so, makes literary capital out of it. It is just as if a fellow were to draw a smart, lively description of some disgusting outrage which had been offered to his wife or sister, and print it in the newspaper by way of shaming the offender.

I am not very sensitive, I think, in many things of that kind. I mean I often defend people who are accused of profanity for satirising or exposing what is profane. But this is indefensible. The Waddington is well drawn, though disgusting. It brings out very well the dangers of that strength of mind which enables a man or woman to act steadily on a principle, instead of allowing themselves to be carried away by a feeling which after all may be a truer guide than the principle. In her case, of course, the principle is pride and worldly prudence.

But it illustrates, I think well, the danger of being strong enough to overrule your instincts, especially, perhaps, in a woman.

To Rev. R. W. Church.

Paris: Hôtel Castiglione.
September 4, 1859.

My dear Church,—*Eccomi.* After bringing me up from Blachford, the Ministers could not make up their minds, and kept me for a fortnight in London while they were deciding pretty much what, if there had been less cooks to the broth, might have been settled in two or three hours, and I might have visited you comfortably after all. I had my interview with Lord John,[2] which was rather amusing. He is very courteous, with a pleasing smile and dignified manner; but his small

---

[2] Lord John Russell was then Foreign Secretary; the Duke of Newcastle Secretary for the Colonies

size is almost droll, when you are receiving orders from him, or answering questions. He asked me a question or two—let me talk—talked about some old doings of his own respecting emigration, and let the conversation rather drop, without indicating clearly whether he wanted me to be off or not—a mistake, as I think, of great men, who are entitled to keep you as long as they choose, and send you away when they have done with you. However, I considered that 'When you doubt, be off,' and acted accordingly. I believe he really is a shy man, and does not know how to do a thing of that kind easily. His manner was a good composed one, which did not let out much, and quite friendly, but in the solemn line; and his talk rather too much on the 'I did so and so.' Well, at last I got off and have been about ten days here. I am now doing business with Chasseloup Laubat, the Colonial Minister, who is certainly rather an amusing contrast with Lord John and the Duke of Newcastle, lively good-humoured, frank-mannered, a great talker, seeming to tell you much and expecting you to be equally open with him, and liking a triumph in the way of chaff. There was in our English draft an error of copying—3 for 5 instead of 5 for 3; there was also what was worse—an absurd bull in point of language, the consequence of making an alteration in a principal phrase, without altering what hangs on to it. These he inflicted on me in the most unrelenting way (all very good-humoured). I think he must have made me a present at least half a dozen times of the clerical error. I see him again to-morrow and dine with him on Tuesday. I have often thought of writing to you to see whether after all you would come over here. But there is such a continual uncertainty about my stay that I never can fix on any plan which will last for more than a few days. At first I thought the matter would go off wholly and at once, but it has fallen back into its old state of hammering out details. I suppose I can hardly be off under ten days from this time. But there is no telling. Things might take a turn which would send me to London off-hand, or keep me here for weeks. The Emperor, it is said, wishes it decidedly to go on, and as Lord Cowley says: 'Any point on which you and Chasseloup can't agree is to be referred to him.' I felt rather tall at being so near the great man of the age. By the way, Lord C. mentioned as a thing that 'ought to be known' that at the beginning of the Crimean war the Emperor proposed that England should send one fifth of the troops, the whole to be under the command of a French general, while France should furnish one fifth of the ships to be under the command of an English admiral; to which Lord C. replied that that was all very well in the abstract, but made the objection 'Our soldiers will serve honestly under your general, and so far so good. But I defy you to name a single captain in the French navy who will honestly serve under an English admiral;' to which Louis Napoleon replied: 'Be it so; but see where you are driving me; if you will not take my proposal you are driving me to increase my fleet. And take my word for it, that in three or four years you will be complaining of the very increase that you have forced upon me.' I don't know that it quite bears out the inference that Lord C. desired to draw from it, but it certainly shows remarkable foresight.

His (the Emperor's) view now is, arm as much as you like; every independent nation has a right to arm as much as it thinks necessary for its own security. 'But I think it very hard that you should throw the blame on me, and say that you are arming against me.' Lord Cowley says that the Emperor was greatly disgusted with the apathy of the Italians. The French took with them into Lombardy 28,000 stand of arms, expecting a popular rising, and that they would be able to distribute them among the insurgents. They were able to distribute 500. He also mentioned, as true, the story that an Italian town which had welcomed, in great triumph, the French soldiers, pulled down the tricolor and ran up the Austrian colours on a rumour that the French had been beaten. So you see your view of the relations between the Emperor and the Italians was pretty correct. It is really a curious spectacle, the working up of the little Italian States. I suppose we shall now soon know what is to become of them.

I was too late for all the military fêtes here, not crossing until a week after they were all over, and the soldiers despatched to their garrisons. I hear that Paris was uncommonly glad to get rid of the Zouaves and Turcos, and that the soldiers themselves did not at all like the affair, but would much rather have been sent off to their garrisons, instead of being whisked up by railway to a dusty camp, and there made a spectacle of for the Parisians.

To the Rev. R. W. Church.

Hôtel Castiglione :
September 23, 1859.

My dear Church,—Here still, and I don't know when I am to get away.

We have had some amusing interviews with Chasseloup Laubat. I told you of his luncheon on a lump of sugar, of which he offered me a part, and of his talking almost three and a half hours at a rush, and of our agreement in not liking the job which we had to settle. Well, the Emperor settled that the thing was to go on, and so go on we did, and are getting over the details with some small difficulties hanging about us, and one apparently insuperable ahead. I am struck rather with the *kind* of difficulties which arise ; they seem to be matters of phrase or language—the peremptory stringent mode of drafting, which is English, seems to hurt their feelings ; they want to be treated like gentlemen in legal documents. But then it is sometimes not perfectly clear whether this extreme susceptibility is not a contrivance to keep open loopholes. There was an amusing specimen of our mode of proceeding in the very first article. It stood (at the desire of Prince Napoleon) that the Indians should be at liberty to emigrate freely to the French colonies. I objected that they should add 'sous les conditions ci-après stipulées.' The matter seemed one of mere language, and so was treated ; till at last M. de Chasseloup Laubat, being driven into a corner, let out that the Prince at the council had made a great puffing and blowing about this clause, explaining that the influence of France was conferring on the poor Indians, who had hitherto been cramped up in their country, the 'liberty of emigration.' 'Mais le Prince nous a dit que ' &c.

On which I instantly replied that I thought the Indian Government, if that view of the matter were suggested to them, would reply that they did not make stipulations with a foreign power for the good government of their own subjects, that they knew what was good for them, and would of course do it, but would not be inclined to admit of foreign meddling ; on which, with a kind of half laugh, half shrug, he said : 'Ah —mais—nous autres Français, voyez-vous, nous allons porter partout la liberté (action of hands in the air) pff—pff—comme en Italie.' Shrug again. And so the matter dropped and I hope is settled.

Another *mot* amused me. He had been very critical both on our draft (which we were rash enough to have translated into French at the Embassy) and on the frequency of my *petites choses*, small stickings in of words and phrases which seemed to me necessary to make the thing as watertight as it ought to be. And I had told him that this was all very well for him who was a Minister of State to pick holes in the work, but that it was not so easy a matter for me who was but representative of half a dozen Ministers who were not always quite agreed among themselves. And I had asked him whether the French had the proverb of 'too many cooks.' Presently we came to one of the awkwardnesses which had been imparted into the affair by the translation made by an Attaché. My friend stopped : 'Puisque trop de cuisiniers font mauvais potage, qu'est-ce qu'il en arrive, quand les marmitons s'en mêlent ?'

Another thing was too horrible to be laughed at—at least almost. I had written home and to you about his talking three and a half hours. I had also told Lord Cowley, who told me that he did not know him, that he got on very well, but that he was a great talker. In the middle of one of our colloquies, *à propos* to nothing very particular, he broke out 'Est-ce que vous avez dit à Lord Cowley que je suis bavard ? Lord Cowley ne me connaît pas, n'est-ce pas ?' I was aghast, as you may imagine, thinking for a moment whether it was only his conscience that made him suppose that I had said it, and mine that made me suppose he had heard it, or whether Lord Cowley had betrayed me to Walewski, and Walewski had thereupon chaffed Chasseloup, or what had happened. The concurrence of thoughts 'Lord Cowley ne me connait pas' seemed like a repetition of the Chantilly talk. Nothing better occurred to me than to look surprised (in which there was no difficulty) and to say 'Je lui ai dit que nous avions beaucoup parlé.' And I must say that I wish it had not happened.

We have been to Fontainebleau twice, and we were lucky enough to cut in for a stag hunt. I wrote a long account of it home, which I think would amuse you, and if you would send this to Blachford and ask them to let you read the Fontainebleau stag hunt, it would be an exchange profitable, I flatter myself, to both.

I must finish, so good-bye. Kind remembrances to your wife; mine sends her love. We are very glad to hear so good an account of you all.

Ever yours affectionately,
F. R.

To Lady Rogers.

Paris : October 21, 1859

I have dined twice at the Rue de Lille, meeting Baillie both times and M. de Fresne last time. We were a little prosy. He is of course very hot about Austria and the good Austrian government of Italy and had a fight with Baillie. He told a revolution story, which, however, sounded to me (coming from him) a little got up. The revolutionary authorities were anxious to get hold of a priest who was in the habit, contrary to law, of visiting the dying and administering the Sacrament, and some blackguards settled that one of them would affect to be dying and send for him, and then they would catch him in the act of performing the office. They accordingly sent and he came, but when he came up to the bed he said, 'Mais comment? vous êtes trop tard, l'homme est mort.' And so he was. The others were so alarmed at what seemed a judgment that from that reason (or from the criminal act not having been performed) the priest escaped.

To Lady Rogers.

Paris : October 24, 1859.

I have been rather often at the Rue de Lille by invitation or otherwise. I was talking yesterday with Mlle. des Pomarets of the *first* emigration, which she greatly disapproved, taking her views from her father who stayed to be put in prison, while his brother stayed to be shot. Certainly it seems a regular desertion of their posts, and what was worst they jeered at as *cowards* those officers who did not emigrate, sending them spindles and broken swords, till at last they bullied them into following their example, and leaving the King alone. His useless character seems to me the only excuse for those who ran before it was necessary. She said that when her mother, after the troubles, came back to her estates (vineyards in Burgundy), she found the cellars stocked with all the wine of the last few years which the tenants had gone on making and putting by for her against the time when she would come back and take it. All the time the priests were taken away from them, they assembled regularly twice every Sunday at church, and the oldest read the service. She said that so it was in places (as Auvergne) where the landlords were good *as a class*, but where some were good and some bad, the good had to suffer for it, with the bad.

To Miss Rogers.

8 Park Street : January 13, 1860.

I have nothing special to say since my last, except that I have not much office work to do just at present, and so mean to give the 'Guardian' a help.

I met Sir Charles Macarthy yesterday, a clever fellow, Colonial Secretary at Ceylon. He is just from Paris, where he appears to have been living with the Orleanists, Thiers, Cousin, &c., who are furious with Louis Napoleon for his attack on the Pope. Considering that Louis Philippe was no Churchman, and that Cousin and Thiers are probably both unbelievers, of course the cry is a mere attempt at party advantage. A French naval officer told him that there was a moment when an invasion of England might have been possible, but that in a few months it became a most doubtful possibility, and that now the very idea was ridiculous, that no French naval officer would dream of viewing such a thing as possible. Thiers declared that nobody had even thought of it; others (*i.e.* my friend, M. Mohl) nudged Macarthy and told him that Thiers might say what he pleased, but did not himself believe what he was saying. There were certain flat-bottomed boats, said by Thiers to be built for navigating the Loire; by others, for the benefit of the English coast, which was the main point in discussion. Love to all.

Ever yours affectionately,
F. ROGERS.

To Miss Rogers.

8 Park Street : February 14, 1860.

My work here seems to be leaving me just now. I have been coming for the last few days, almost to go away again. Before that I had a rush of work, owing to a hard and interesting job, which has the effect always of keeping me at work on itself for a week or so, and then piling up a heap of light work to be disposed of when it is gone. But now all that is cleared off; and at this moment, twelve o'clock, I have absolutely nothing to do. My hard job was on the question whether the natives of New Zealand should be managed by the Home Government or handed over to the colonists, and if the former, how ?—a question well worth working at, and I think I sent them a creditable report. I start with Merivale a little against me. Of course I am for keeping the matter for the present in the hands of people responsible to the Crown.

Gladstone's speech seems to have been a great success and his scheme is well spoken of in the City; I suppose he will carry it. But I have been very angry with the Government for Sir G. C. Lewis's disgraceful mode of handing over Bryan King to the mob. That he is an obstinate fellow is no answer.[3]

---

[3] Mr. Bryan King had been Rector of St George's in the East since 1842. In 1856, on the question of Eucharistic Vestments, and other matters of ritual,

I was rather glad to find the other day that A. C. had been much shocked by the profane abuse that the Ultramontane papers are heaping on the French Emperor, and one is glad to see in moderate Roman Catholics a tendency to separate themselves from the firebrand party. The thing that shocked her was a kind of parody of the Passion, Louis Napoleon standing for Pilate, and his wife saying to him, 'Have thou nothing to do with that just man' (the Pope). I believe there is a good deal of division among them on the subject.

As far as we are concerned, I think the personal attitude of the Irish Roman Catholic members gives us reason to wish that the Pope had no temporal authority. Here are a number of members who are going to vote steadily against the Ministry, not because they think the Ministry have done anything bad for England, not because they think badly of their principles of foreign policy, but simply because they give their vote with reference to the temporal advantage of a foreign Prince, and not with regard to any other point of right or wrong or any really religious principles of English policy whatever.

Of course injustice is injustice, and it is not to be defended. But certainly one may well wish that a state of things which induces members of the Legislature to take such a line did not exist.

---

he and his curates, Mr. Mackonochie and Mr. Loudon, were violently attacked by the Evangelical Party. His church from time to time during the next few years became the scene of disgraceful riots, Bishop Tait having in vain tried to persuade Mr. King to make some concessions (*Life of Archbishop Tait*, vol. i. p. 230; Loudon, *Twenty-one Years in St. George's Mission*, p. 227). Sir G. Cornewall Lewis was Home Secretary, and so far answerable for the non-interference of the police.

CHAPTER VII

Under-Secretary for the Colonies, 1860

IN May 1860, Mr. Merivale was transferred from the Colonial Office to the Secretaryship of the India Office, and Sir F. Rogers was offered the post of permanent Under-Secretary for the Colonies. With the Colonial administration, in which for the next ten years he had so large a share, his experience of fourteen years as an Emigration Commissioner had already made him familiar. His chief, when he accepted this post, was the Duke of Newcastle, Secretary of State for the Colonies in Lord Palmerston's Ministry.

'The Duke of Newcastle,' he writes, 'was an honest and honourable man, a thorough gentleman in all his feelings and ways, and considerate of all about him. To me he was always kind. He was stiff, so that you would never say anything to him because it came into your head. He respected other people's position, but was sensible of his own; and his familiarity—friendly enough—was not such as invited a response. It was said of him that he did not remember his rank unless you forgot it, and the expression well hit off his relations to subordinates. In political administration he was painstaking, clear-headed and just. But his abilities were moderate; and he did not see how far they were from being sufficient for the management of great affairs—which, however, he was always ambitious of handling. It was said that Peel looked to him as a future Premier, and it was thought that the Duke expected it. The failure would have been terrible, as was seen from his administration of the War

Q

Office, where he showed himself unequal either to managing affairs himself or to choosing confidential advisers who could manage them for him. When the Duke of Newcastle died in the year 1864, he was succeeded at the Colonial Office by Mr. Cardwell. Cardwell was just and kind, clear-headed and hard-headed, industrious, very accurate, and enormously safe, especially in regard to matters of which the House of Commons might have cognisance. In fact, he seemed always to feel on his trial before the House of Commons; and I have occasionally felt that his dread of a parliamentary scrape sometimes supplied the place of thorough force of character. He had a fine instinctive sense of what " would do " in that point of view, which made him invulnerable to specious fallacies in the opposite sense. And it is to be remarked that in nine cases out of ten his guide would be a true guide—the House of Commons seeing in ordinary cases what is not honest, or not for the public interest. He could deal well with masses of business, and bring order out of disorder. He knew his own mind and worked steadily towards his point; but—which was odd for a hard-headed man—did not always distinguish a plausible from a substantial result. He took pains not to make enemies, and bore no ill-will to his opponents.'

To Miss Rogers.

London : May 4, 1860.

My dear Kate,—Very many thanks for your letter. I am, as you see, installed here in Stephen's old armchair, and have just had all the interviews with the senior clerks, telling them about the division of business. We, Elliot and I, have divided the work between us a good deal; he taking North America and Africa, and Mediterranean; I taking Australia, West Indies, Eastern Colonies, Ceylon, &c. I also taking legal matters everywhere, and he military and convict matters everywhere. But it remains to be seen how all this will end.

F. R.

To Lady Rogers.

9 Ovington Square : June 17, 1860.

My dear Mother,—Sunday, and I have had a day to myself, and this very wet Sunday I take the opportunity, like a good boy, to give some account of myself.

The work goes on much as it did. I rather hope now for a little relaxation of the storm, one or two important things that have taken up time being, for the moment, disposed of But there is plenty ahead. Just now I am well off. I have brought with me the only thing that had to be done when I left the office on Saturday, and hope to have it done before I leave for the office on Monday. I may consider while I am walking down that I have my table clear. The satisfaction of this is that I have gained rather than lost in my work. It is not more than I can do, and I hope I do it well. This however remains to be seen. You will have seen by the papers that we have New Zealand troubles ahead. The clergy of the English Church out there think us (the English) in the wrong, I fear. But the official accounts, coming through a Government well inclined to protect the natives, seem to show that great care has been taken to keep us in the right, and that we are so. He, the Governor, asks for 8,000 troops, which is of course absurd. However, you need not say that. I see very little of the Duke [of Newcastle]. The Duke works at home, comes down about three, is off to the House of Lords about four, and probably has two or three appointments in the meantime, so that it is very difficult to catch him at all, and you must dispose of what you have to say shortly and clearly when you do see him ; so far, perhaps, no bad thing. But then, when a thing has to be passed in a hurry, amended in progress, and so on, the absence of your chief or his inaccessibility is worrying. However, he is very ready to accept your conclusions, very clear in his own directions, and extremely careful (which I respect very highly) never to throw back on a subordinate any shadow of responsibility for advice that he has once accepted. I think I have observed this in more than one thing. He is a good deal brought to, I think, when his advisers differ, and rather catches at the notion of getting fresh advice, as if the *bulk* of advice made it easier to decide, sometimes without seeing that the advice he seeks is on his own principles less valuable than what he has got. He is oddly dilatory about patronage, even when he has substantially made up his mind (as I understand); he seems to hesitate at making the plunge, and goes on letting the idea simmer in his mind. Just now he is keeping various Governors expectant in a state of anxiety.

I take it for granted that you know about G.'s Drawing Room. She looked 'very nice,' as William (the footman) told her. After having a good look at the side view (she sitting in the middle of the drawing-room in a circle of beholders) he did not content himself with it, like the more modest maid-servants, but moved round to get a front view, looking in a composed kind of way, as you would at a statue or a wild beast, or anything inanimate or irrational, and then gave out 'I am sure you couldn't look nicer, my lady.' Church and I almost burst out laughing, but restrained ourselves till he had got out of the room. Since that time he has asked to have a boy under him.

To Lady Rogers.

January 29, 1861.

What do you think of the last from the United States? Sir E. Head[1] read me a letter from an eminent Boston man describing the state of things as hopeless. Fifteen Slave States almost certain to go, and nobody knowing whom to follow or what to do. 'There is anarchy in men's minds,' he says. As showing what is going on, Sir E. H. showed me an extract from a newspaper, being an address signed by the Senate and Representatives of Maine and by 19,000 other persons, praying the Queen of England to effect the annexation of *Maine to Canada*. And the Consul at Boston writes to Engleheart that people there are talking of New England uniting with Canada to form a kingdom under a Prince of the Blood Royal. Think what the old heroes of Bunker's Hill and the men who pitched their tea into Boston Harbour would say to this, within a hundred years of their liberation.

[1] Governor-General of Canada.

However, don't talk of this, for though public in the United States, our people here may not wish it talked of. Head said that of course it must be all a lie, but that it was impossible in the present state of things to disbelieve anything.

To Lady Rogers.

Undated, apparently August 20, 1860.

G. will have told you that Chichester Fortescue,[1] being in a great fright that his Bill (New Zealand) would be abandoned, took me, as a bottle-holder, to an interview between himself and Lord Palmerston. We were duly shown in, and found his lordship writing and sealing letters, in the midst of such a heap of papers, books &c., as I should have thought sufficient to make the transaction of business impossible. He set us down, finished his sealings, directions and so on, and then sat himself down, put his hands between his knees and assumed a kind of fixed resigned look, drooping his shoulders and sinking his eyes like a man who was to undergo a shower-bath. Then (it being understood that Palmerston was in doubt about proceeding) Fortescue began, and, as I should say, rehearsed his speech for the House, stating the case and invoking me occasionally. Pam, when he had done, put one or two (pretty searching) questions and listened carefully to the answers (rather deaf). He said in a kind of obedient way, 'Well, then, I have got my lesson; and I shall say that alterations will be made in the Bill that will remove any of the objections, and that the Government will state the

---

[1] Mr. Chichester Fortescue (Lord Carlingford) was then Parliamentary Under-Secretary for the Colonies. The Bill, as introduced by the Duke of Newcastle in July 1860, was for the protection of the aborigines, to establish, by imperial authority, a local council on which should devolve the revision of the native laws and the arrangements respecting the sale and purchase of native land. This passed the House of Lords, and the second reading in the Commons was fixed (as this letter says) for Tuesday, August 21. But there was opposition in Parliament and in New Zealand (chiefly in the southern island), and on that day Lord Palmerston announced that the Government would not proceed with the Bill so late in the Session. It was intended (see *Times* of April 20, 1861) to re-introduce it next year, but the New Zealand Bill (passed in May 1861) dealt only with the division of the provinces in New Zealand. (See also p. 228.)

reasons for introducing it on Monday ' (now put off till Tuesday), and then got up, and we got up and went off in our cab. I had expected a kind of arguing and cross-examination, and the whole thing was despatched by Pam in such a free and easy way and with so little trouble to himself (except hearing F.'s speech) that as soon as we got into the cab I burst into a fit of laughter, in which F. joined. Then I asked, ' Well, what do you think he thinks of you and your case ? ' ' Oh, I don't know,' with an amused look. ' I would give something to know. I should say his impression was that it would go down with the House of Commons,' and then he laughed and said : ' This is being behind the scenes.' He had quoted to Palmerston with great force a passage in favour of his present proceedings from a despatch of Lord Carnarvon's. ' Of course I shall read that in the House,' as if that were the testimony of an enemy. So when we got into the cab I told him that that despatch was my writing, so that when the Whig Under-Secretary quotes the Tory Under-Secretary in favour of the Whig measure it will be in fact quoting Sir F. R.'s despatch as a hostile testimony to the merits of Sir F. R.'s Bill. I told him this and he laughed and said, ' Behind the scenes again.' He is very pleasant and uncommonly plucky, for we have the whole world against us. I can hardly believe even now that it will pass. It is fixed for Tuesday evening. Sir J. Pakington and Adderley speak against ; Lord Robert Cecil and Bethell (Attorney-General) for. Bethell is quite keen and a valuable help.

To Rev. Edward Rogers.

Colonial Office : February 23, 1861.

I got an immense buttering from the Attorney-General (Bethell) about that paper which I wrote at Blachford on Ionian Consular Jurisdiction—' an *admirable* paper—I can assure you I mean what I say—an admirable paper—a perfect knowledge of the subject—very well put together and felicitously expressed—complete as a Jurist—a lawyer—and ' (some word implying the political treatment of the subject). He harped rather on the ' Jurist ' part of the matter, which is a character I rather ambition. He took occasion to explain to me 'there is *jus, lex,* and *forum. Jus* is the principles of natural justice, especially as embodied in international law. *Lex*, the written law defining offences and rights. *Forum*, the mode of procedure and jurisdiction of courts.'

I really shall soon begin to think that V.'s friend was right and that I am a profound lawyer, or at any rate that, by a judicious amount of silence and a judicious choice of occasions for lecturing, I may support that character.

To Lady Rogers.
April 12, 1861.

What do you think of the Cooly business turning up again? I was called on yesterday by a delegate from Réunion, who is in London trying to push things through. I am amused to see how 'the cat jumps.' This Réunion man is full of concessions, has the firmest reliance on English good faith, &c., &c. At one of his proposals, however, I asked, ' Qu'est-ce qu'en diront MM. les Délégués des Antilles ?' when out came the truth. Réunion, being close to India, and seeing what has happened in Mauritius, wants coolies and cares little about Africa ; the Antilles, being far from India, wants Africans and cares little comparatively about coolies ; consequently the Réunionists are hot to push the treaty through (having already got five ship-loads), while the Antilles abuse us and it, and would stop it if they could. Now this Réunion man appears to have got hold of the French and Foreign Office, and I dare say will push it through.

To Lady Rogers.
May 10, 1861.

I have just been interrupted by a little M. Imhausen, ' Délégué de l'île de Réunion,' who has come over to push the Cooly Treaty, which seems approaching a conclusion (as it has seemed for the last two years), and prays me to restore him to his family (now in Paris) by expediting matters. ' Vous me rendrez à ma famille,' with an affectionate enthusiasm, and then enlists my sympathy by appealing to my paternity. 'Vous, Monsieur, qui êtes le père de ce traité ; on l'appelle toujours dans les départements de Paris le traité Rogers.' I can't say I wish to ride down to posterity on the back of that convention. It is enough to have ridden it into the Colonial Office, and now I should like to change my horse.

To Miss Rogers.

Nov. 1861.

My dear Kate,—War in earnest, I am afraid.[2] Sir E. Head has just been here talking about what is doing to put Canada in a state of defence. They are proceeding just as if war was declared, as far as preparations go. You see the Yankees have dealt us their slap in the face just as the St. Lawrence is frozen up and New Brunswick covered with snow, so that it is not so easy to say how anything ought to be sent.

The only hope is that the bankers and substantial men in the U.S. may be strong enough to send Seward to the right-about, and then knock under. But it is much more probable that before our mission arrives they will have committed themselves too deeply to recede—or at any rate to recede in double quick time—which I apprehend we shall demand.

Of course Canada is in danger, but a few thousand English soldiers (and there are a few thousand in the North American provinces) will do a great deal till more come. I hear Col. Lysons is likely to be sent—however, don't talk of that till you see it—I hope he is fit for real work.

Pam goes about saying he is not going to be bullied, and I suppose *is* not. Mr. Slidell says that the lieutenant who boarded the 'Trent' said, 'Oh, John Bull would do as he had done before, he would bark, but not bite.'

They say the lieutenant who had to seize Slidell and Mason was a Southerner, who had been dining with them at Havannah, which accounts for his saying that it was the most disagreeable job he ever had.

The American proceedings, as a matter of policy, seem to me so wild that I cannot but half think that Seward feels himself going (they talk of very strong opposition growing up to him), and wishes to be turned out on the ground of affronting England ; in which case, of course, he would go out

---

[2] Slidell and Mason, the Commissioners from the Southern Confederate States, were taken by force by Captain Wilkes, of the American Navy, from the British West India Mail Steamer 'Trent,' in November 1861. The Guards were sent to Canada, but the American Government gave up the commissioners, and the danger of war passed.

as a mob hero with a capital chance of coming back again on mob shoulders, saying that all the mischief had been done while and because he was out of office.

Ever yours affectionately,
F. R.

To Lady Rogers.
March 4, 1862.

We had a pleasant Sunday (as we always have) with the Taylors. I like him more and more. He certainly has an enjoyment in being considerably unlike everybody else, more perhaps like a Capuchin friar than any other animal.

He amused me by an anecdote of Lord Melbourne. In his (Lord M.'s) Cabinet, Lord Grey (then Howick) was objecting after his manner to everybody's draft of a proposed certain despatch, and at last Lord M. pushed a sheet of paper to him, and said, 'Well, then, in God's name try your own hand upon it.' Lord Howick wrote a sentence, then altered it, then expunged it, then crunched up the paper and threw it down, then *da capo* with another sheet of paper, all which Lord Melbourne allowed him to do for some time without interruption, and when he came to a short pause struck in with 'Ah, I thought so—you see now, when you have nobody to contradict but yourself, you are done.' Not a bad Cabinet interior. I told Taylor I did not know whether I wished to be again under Lord Grey, and he said, 'Oh, depend upon it, you would like it very much. I should like excessively to see you together. You would get on admirably now.' . . . The last thing almost I have been upon is a ponderous quarrel between the Governor and the Bishop of ——, in the course of which the Bishop, thinking himself insulted, told the Governor that he would have to answer for it to a 'Higher Power.' The Governor, a soldier, taking it for granted he meant the Duke of Newcastle, proceeded at once to lay the matter before the Executive Council, in order to appear with fresh support before his Grace, and in a subsequent despatch informed us in a tone of something like complaint that his Lordship '*now* says that when he referred to a "Higher Power" he did not mean that he would report me to your Grace, but that God would judge me,' evidently not quite persuaded in his mind that the explanation was not an afterthought.

These quarrels often make me think what a capital post a Roman Proconsul had. 'If it were a matter of wrong, reason would that I should bear with you. But if it be a question of words and of your law, see ye to it, for I will be judge of no such thing, and he drave them from the judgment seat. And the Jews took Sosthenes and beat him. But Gallio cared for none of these things.' I wish we could afford to wink at the Governor and Bishop horse-whipping each other. As far as I see, it would do both of them good, and I shall get the Duke to go as near it as ever I can with due regard to his character.

To the Bishop of Oxford.[3]

June 30, 1862.

My dear Lord Bishop,—I am rather afraid of being misunderstood about your Bill, a copy of which has just reached me.

I, of course, think it is a just claim of the English Church to be allowed to consecrate Missionary Bishops, and as a Churchman I shall be extremely glad if your particular Bill passes as it stands.

But I think that in your Bill the State is entitled to take this objection—the Bill proposes to invest a Bishop in a Mahomedan country—say of Mecca—with a statutory relation to the Church of England, that is to say, to attach him remotely, but really, to the constitution of this country of which the Church is a part.

Now, this Bishop of Mecca is not a mere Bishop of English congregations, but a Missionary Bishop bound in that capacity to make war upon Mahomedanism, which is, on the other hand, part of the political constitution of the Ottoman Empire.

Now, the Ottoman Empire having been to a certain extent admitted into the family of nations, is it according to the comity of nations that the English Parliament should take under its wing an organised attack on the constitution of

[3] Bishop Wilberforce.

that Empire? The Pope, no doubt, does it in England, but first he does it under shelter of certain principles of toleration, which we profess, and which it appears to me are sufficient to cover his aggression; and next we, notwithstanding, quarrel with him for doing it.

You will answer that the Crown may, under your Bill, prevent any such complications by refusing its assent to the creation of any Bishopric which is calculated to cause them.

This is one of those answers which is good or bad according to the animus of the person to whom it is addressed. A rash or careless Minister may authorise the erection of an Anglican Bishopric in a place where its erection would be politically unjustifiable. The question is whether the advantage (of setting the Church going in a missionary direction) justifies the risk of an ill-advised appointment causing a complication with a foreign country.

Personally, I think it does (and therefore wish well to your Bill), but if I held the well-being of the English Church a matter of little importance to this country I should think differently, and should think that the Parliament had a right to some more distinct guarantee (to speak as a politician) against the abuse of the powers of consecration.

Even personally I prefer our colonial principle of proceeding, the principle, namely, of leaving Bishops to consecrate in virtue of their inherent spiritual powers, and leaving the consecrating and consecrated to arrange for themselves what shall be their relations to each other. In this case, the State is subject to no responsibility (colonial Bishops being no part of the Constitution), and is therefore entitled to no control over the missionary operations of the Church.

I should therefore have liked best to see a Bill (though it would have been perhaps very difficult to draw one) which would merely have permitted the Church to create an Episcopate beyond the limits of the Queen's Dominions, leaving the relations of that Episcopate to be formed by mutual consent without any statutory aid or the necessity of any Royal assent.[4]

---

[4] Some account of the accomplishment of this will be found at the end of Chapter viii.

But I repeat, in default of this, I should consider your Bill as likely to be of great advantage, and wish it success.

Yours sincerely,
F. ROGERS.

To Hon. Mrs. H. Legge.

Venice : October 13, 1862.

Rainy journey to Milan, rainy morning at Milan—rainy journey to Padua. Then we had a beautiful morning to look at Padua, which is not, I think, sufficiently highly rated—the famous Giotto frescoes are, of course, valued properly. They are the only Giottos that I really feel myself to appreciate. And they derive great interest from the fact that Dante was with him while he painted them, and that from the style of their beauty Dante might have painted them himself—there is that curious mixture of beautiful finish in essentials (in D. harmony of verse, appropriateness of language, and precision of thought) with a rude carelessness of conventionality when it interferes with the vigorous expression of an idea, which seems to me characteristic of Dante, or (what is partly the same thing) a power of realising a conception and putting his whole mind and soul into the expression of it. I should like to see (except that they would be so entirely spoilt by being taken out of the context) a series of heads of our Saviour taken from these frescoes. They would in themselves almost be a *résumé* of the Gospel. Two which are almost contiguous are, I think, the most impressive : the expression of our Saviour receiving Judas's kiss, and of our Saviour telling the women of Jerusalem to weep for themselves. The first is like the sentence of the Last Judgment; our Saviour seems to look through and through Judas. It is an habitually sad face, but there is no emotion of sorrow ; it is simply piercing and unrelenting as if there was no use in thinking of what might have been, respecting a man whose day of mercy was past. I could fancy Dante suggesting the treatment and sitting by dissatisfied with the sketches till his idea was exactly realised. The other is all tenderness ; the expression of sorrow for their sorrow, and of seeing what was coming upon them more clearly than they did themselves, is perfect and beautiful, and also (I should say) quite Dantesque. Still more so the raising of Lazarus—Lazarus standing straight up, ghastly and surprised, like a ghost in swaddling clothes (tied hand and foot), the two sisters crawling (I really can hardly use any other expression) at our Saviour's feet. On the whole it is a most interesting sight if you stay long enough before it, as in some slight degree we did.

The city is beautiful from the number of old palaces in decadence, and the profusion of colonnades supported not on piers but slight marble columns; and a shrine of St. Antonio is, I think, about the most beautiful thing of its kind I ever saw. I wonder it is not more praised. There is a certain reflection of Venice in Padua (substituting colonnades for canals) which makes it also interesting. The type is similar, and it strikes me, as I write, that part of what I most admire in St. Antonio's shrine it has in common with St. Mark's.

To Sir George Grey.[5]

Colonial Office: November 26, 1862.

My dear Sir George,—I inclose a letter from Wirima Repa[6] to his grandfather, which perhaps you will be good enough to forward to its destination. I inclose also the copy of a letter from Captain Tremlett, in whose charge he is, which appears to be satisfactory. We are somewhat puzzled to know what to do next with the boy. At present he is in the 'Impregnable' in the harbour at Devonport, with two or three hundred boys who are in training for the Royal Navy; he is looked after by one of the petty officers, with whom he messes; he is clothed differently from the rest, and has one or two privileges, and a certain amount of private and pocket money. Captain Tremlett represents him as anxious to learn English (our main point just at present), affectionate, but rather mortified if not a little passionate when anything is refused him, fond of dress and of games of chance, holding himself aloof from the other boys (which is perhaps as well), pleased with notice and generally contented.

---

[5] Then Governor of New Zealand.
[6] Wirima Repa was the grandson of a Maori chief, who wished the boy to be placed at the disposal of the Queen. As will be seen by the following letters, the poor boy's life was short.

This does tolerably well for the present, but he is said not to fancy the sea and to show some turn for drawing and machinery. It seems to us here that it might be very useful, if possible, after two or three years to send him back to New Zealand, with some such knowledge and habits as would render him useful to his countrymen. But there is great difficulty in finding a place in which he will acquire these, when he has outgrown the 'Impregnable,' *i.e.* when he can write and read English a little and speak it fairly well.

It is rather late to ask you the question, but it would much assist in dealing with the boy if we knew your views about him, and particularly what teaching would be likely to make him most useful in New Zealand when he gets back—a little surveying, mechanics, working in wood or iron, agriculture, navigation?

I am afraid he will hardly be advanced enough in English to raise these further questions before we get an answer from you to this letter.

Believe me yours very truly,
F. R.

To Rev. Dr. Lowe.[1]

December 13, 1862.

Dear Sir,—Mr. Mozley informs me that I may communicate with you respecting a young New Zealander who has been sent to England by his grandfather, one of the principal chiefs on the English side, or, rather, beyond comparison the most important and trustworthy friend we have ; and whom the Duke of Newcastle wishes to send back to his country, after two or three years' residence here, with something of European knowledge and improvement.

He is a lad of sixteen or seventeen years of age. I should think, both from what I saw and from what I hear of him, that he was susceptible of kindness, and that he had much quickness of observation (as to such things as flowers, family likeness, simple mechanical contrivances, &c.). He speaks (or spoke in last September) very broken English, but understood fairly those to whom he was accustomed ; he was

---

[1] Headmaster of Hurstpierpoint School.

inclined to be contented and to form attachments (probably not very strong ones). I hear he is anxious to learn, fond of dress, and that he stands somewhat on his dignity—which is as well, seeing he is at present among a set of boys picked up anywhere, being educated for seamen.

When I saw him he could write a little, but, strange to say, could not read. He was also inclined to try his hand a little at drawing. So much for the boy.

What I should be very glad to ascertain is whether you think you could take him in hand, what you would propose to do with him, who would be his associates, whether the place is healthy (a very important point), and what would be your terms.

The difficulty, I suppose, would be in assigning to any class a boy so big and so untrained. My own general notion would be to teach him first reading, writing, arithmetic, and manners; then some useful art for which he showed a taste (I mean not so much the manual aptitude as the principles and rationale of it, so that he would bring his own knowledge to bear on his countrymen); neatness of hand, such as it may be, together with something or other for which he may show special aptitude in the way of accomplishments, say a little physical science, history, drawing, and music—anything, in short, that it was possible to hope that he would pursue for his own amusement, and with which in after years he might infect his wife and children.

Yours,
F. R.

To Lady Rogers (Lady Blachford).

Clumber: January 2, 1863.

I duly arrived here about five o'clock, having fallen in with the Reeves.

The dinner party were the Reeves, a Colonel and Mrs. Sherwin Gregory (neighbours), and myself. The next day were added the Speaker (Denison), and Venables—a clever pleasant fellow whom you may know by name.

I have spent my leisure time in walking (declining a gun) —partly alone, partly with Venables, partly with the ladies and men shooters. Yesterday a dull day, made the place look dull. To-day is beautiful, and makes the place produce a different impression. It is very ducal, and much what you might expect. The country is made up of low undulations at a slight gradient—the top of the hills or ridges not being higher than the top of a good-sized house. Along one of the valleys runs a stream (which becomes ultimately the Idle), which has been stopped up in one place and widened, for, say, a mile and a half, into a lake ; the banks are wooded, and planted park-like fashion ; and close on one side of the water is Clumber, a heavy house with stately terraces running down to the water.

The rooms are very grand ; library beautiful ; drawing-room and dining-room to match. The drawing-room, recently furnished with white satin walls and sky-blue curtains for the Prince of Wales, is certainly very stately and fine ; so are the plate, the statues, the horses and carriages, and the pictures. But it is all a kind of George III. grandeur—imposing without much interest. The Duke yesterday lionised us over house and grounds, which are all of a piece ; a characteristic picture hanging in the hall gives a key to a good deal. The picture is of horsemen, gamekeepers, and dogs, and it comprises the great-grandfathers of the present Duke, of the present Duke's gamekeeper, of his assistant gamekeeper, the ancestors of his spaniels (the Clumber breed, who will not thrive anywhere else), and the ancestors of his pointers. In fact, everything but the horses appears to have been hereditary.

To Lady Rogers (Lady Blachford).

Clumber : January 4, 1863.

The Duke is anxious to be friendly and to do all his duties to tenants, neighbours, friends, &c.—kindly, I fancy, to real intimates, or in matters which call for real feeling, but in the matter of the 'small change' of feeling, what small talk is to conversation, he is somewhat *dépourvu*.

I think I described the place. It is very characteristic of the possessor. Very little natural advantages, a reasonably nice river stream, low slopes, indifferent timber—all swollen into a sheet of water and spacious park by their connexion with the dukedom. The house ducal, the talk ducal, the dinner ducal; the collection of silks, satins, and diamonds in the large drawing-room with satin hangings, after dinner, strikingly ducal. It rather decidedly impressed me in its pompous way, the more so because there was no large party, but merely a few persons looking magnificent, and as if it was not necessary that they should be a large party. Not, so far, the kind of thing I like, but the kind of thing to look at as a stage play.

I renewed my acquaintance with Venables, a clever fellow, whom I knew at Cambridge, and who writes the political articles of the 'Saturday Review.' A fellow of a clear, calm, rather biting turn of mind, and no nonsense, whom I intend to cultivate. A thorough Liberal, I imagine. I also met the Reeves; he is the editor of the 'Edinburgh,' who knows everybody, has seen a good deal, and consequently has a good deal to say which is amusing to hear. I picked up a fair amount of their little odds and ends, which are pleasant to hear but hardly worth writing, and not very easy to remember.

One thing amused me from hardly knowing whether it was a passage of arms or not. The clerks of the Privy Council were Charles Greville and William Bathurst. The place is, of course, one of importance. When Lord Derby came in, as Reeves told us, Charles Greville declared he would never attend the Council till the Conservatives went out, and so put it off on William Bathurst, who delighted in the dignity of attending. 'Ah,' said the Duke, more inclined, I imagine, to side with the Conservative Peer Premier than with the Liberal official—' You know how Derby took that. He said, "What on earth can you suppose it signifies to me what footman brings up the coal-scuttle when I ring the bell?"'

I did not think it necessary to consider whether I was bound to appropriate any part of the indignity, and so only chuckled.

The Duke said, to report a somewhat improper sentiment, that one of our Ministers had complained to Louis Napoleon that he was playing fast and loose with us; to which Louis Napoleon replied: 'I can assure you I wish nothing better

R

than to be faithful to England as my wife. I must confess I like to have another power from time to time as my mistress.' There is something for us to make what we can of, considering the nature and habits of the man. Love to all.

Ever yours affectionately,
F. R.

To Rev. Dr. Lowe.

February 13, 1863.

Dear Sir,—I have not written to you on the subject of Wirima Repa the New Zealander, partly on account of his illness, which has frightened us, lest we should be obliged to send him back to New Zealand. At present he is better, and I think it possible we may be able to keep him over the summer, sending him back in October or thereabouts; another winter here would be plainly imprudent. The fear is of consumption—he has been troubled with cough &c., and an obstinate sore in his leg, now better, but apparently more or less constitutional. This may affect your readiness to take charge of him for a few months. And it may still make it impossible to send him to Hurstpierpoint. But I will write to you again on the subject unless I hear from you that what I have now said makes it impossible for you to take him. We should be glad to place him in your hands, if you were ready to take him and his health appeared to allow of it. In answer to one of your questions, he is a Christian, and a good docile, reverent one, fond of reading his Bible (in Maori), and not without desire to be a missionary—on the understanding, however, that this is not to interfere with his fighting the Waikatos, for which also he has a taste.

What his *capacity* is I do not know, but he is evidently extremely amiable and affectionate. He has a good deal of quiet dignity when with the other boys on the 'Impregnable,' who are not, and whom he feels not to be, his equals—their principal point of contact being the game of draughts, in which he excels. He now, I am told, understands English perfectly, but does not speak with ease.

Yours faithfully,
FREDERIC ROGERS.

To Miss Rogers.

March 18, 1863.

My dear Kate,—It seems an age since I have written what can really be called a letter to Blachford, and now I have an idle morning just fit for the purpose. I had a very sharp touch of work from the latter end of last month; since that time I have had, what in the ordinary course of things would be easy work; but there have been a few blank days, more or less of holidays, which, though easing the work as far as comfort was concerned, kept me in a sense pretty well employed. (Drawing-room—Princess Alexandra—journeying to Hurstpierpoint.)

I suppose G. will have told you all about the two first. The last was a journey to an institution on High Church principles for middle-class education, to which we shall send young Wirima Repa. It is just the place for him'—a collegiate building in a high healthy situation, with 300 boys of different ages; a cheery, good-hearted head-master and wife who will notice the boy; a kind of pupil-teacher, who can be more or less told off for him; the run of the country (no bounds); and, what he will much delight in, a rifle-corps in the school, which will have to appear at a review on Easter Monday or Tuesday. The head-master's wife was a Miss Coleridge, and will therefore have aboriginal tendencies, being cousin to Patteson, the Bishop of Melanesia.

My employment during the end of February was in a great measure the drafting a long New Zealand despatch which was moved for by Adderley in the House of Commons before it was sent off—in a great measure before it was written—and which may make a row here and there. I may almost say it has been written three times; first, a year or so ago, next in January last, and thirdly in February last. The Duke of N. criticised the January version as too didactic—'like what they find fault with in Stephen - but better '—a compliment with which I was not ill-pleased—whatever it may be worth. Then it went through a revision of my own in consequence of fresh news from New Zealand, then a revision by Fortescue, all of which took a good deal of the sting out of it, and, I half think, a little the coherency. It remains, however, a complete treatise. Fortescue read it all to the Duke and myself in its final form for approval, and I was disappointed with it. Then I read it myself and liked it better. What the rest of the world will say to it I do not know. I think I shall send it to you when it comes out (though in itself it is not a kind of thing that would interest you) as the most elaborate 'State paper' I have yet produced.

The truth is that I doubt whether it ought to appear in the form of a despatch at all. It is rather an attempt to obtain from public opinion in England support against the public opinion of New Zealand which ought by rights to be got by a speech in the House of Commons. But to say the truth, I don't feel that I could get my own views (such as they are) well before the world in that way, and, as I attach a certain amount of importance to them, I have put them out in this way at the risk of making the Duke look like a lecturer. I hope, however, that this will not be the effect. For the New Zealanders have happily given me lots of handles for all that I wanted to say, so that, though I may be tedious, I can hardly be accused of being uncalled for. Also the occasion is an important one—a regular turning-point, in regard to colonial policy as regards military defence of colonies.

We have been getting through Kinglake's 'Crimea,' which of course you will get in due time from Mudie. It is excessively entertaining; his sketches of character are admirably amusing, especially when you know the men (Gladstone, Duke of Newcastle, and Lord Stratford) and can separate the genuinely good hits from views which have more or less an ingenious partiality or caricature.

I think, however, it is what I should call a wicked book. First it does not admit of war as a terrible necessity, but rather writes it up as a noble amusement like fox-hunting. At least, this is to me the spirit of the book. Next it is a reckless attack on the French Empire, that is (in spite of all his efforts to make a distinction), on the French nation. His friends say that he feels that, knowing the truth, a duty is laid on him to speak it. But there are many ways of speaking the truth, and the policy of the book with regard to the French is a cold bitter desire to sting, rising, with regard to the Emperor and his generals, to a burning hatred and desire to destroy. All this is put out with the most finished possible deliberation, the author being evidently quite careless of the effect it may produce in engendering bitter and angry feelings between England and France, and desirous if possible of inflaming the French feeling against Louis Napoleon, without (I must believe) any distinct view as to what is to happen as a consequence of this inflammation.

His monster account of the battle of the Alma is as interesting almost as a novel (if you deliver yourself up to it), but it requires very careful reading, and is provoking from the long deliberate episodes which he inflicts upon you sometimes in the very crisis of affairs. I should call it *very instructive* in a military point of view to a non-military reader, *i.e.* (like William Greig's account of the Battle of Waterloo) it gives you by its detail a real comprehension of the value of lots of things, which in ordinary military histories you see stated roughly and have to take for granted, as matters of tactics or military detail, which an unprofessional reader has to pass over in faith. Colonel Hood's manœuvre appears very clearly.

On a careless reading the whole will (I should think) appear a mass of confusion. But this is only from the tremendously complicated task which he has undertaken. And with care you can get at a distinct idea how (in his view) each separate regiment (almost) of the French and English army acted, and how all their proceedings bore upon each other. But then you have to study 300 pages. I should think that you must take at least two or three times as long to read the account as it took the armies to fight the battle. Then, to be sure, they were 100,000 men and you are only one. Love to all.

Ever yours affectionately,
F. R.

To Lady Rogers.
Summer, 1863.

I suppose G. or somebody told you how Wirima Repa went down to Osborne to see the Queen, very ill, poor fellow, and of course with much fatigue, and came back delighted with his opportunity, but in a state of dignified disgust with his countrymen * who went down with him, and who, from his account, would seem to have drunk more than was good for them, and made more noise than was by any means to be desired. The Princesses showed the Maori women over their own private rooms, and the Queen had Wirima in for a little talk after she had disposed of the rest, and finally sent them all (him inclusive) a little autograph of her own, her signature and the date of the visit, on note paper with a black border about an inch broad—a pleasant memento enough for an affectionate boy. Altogether the visit was a great success—having been a great object—which is not always the case.

Ever yours affectionately,
F. R.

To Lady Rogers.

September 1, 1863.

I had a very pleasant day at Birmingham, though I look back at it as you do at some exciting novel—I hardly know with more pleasure or pain. Newman was, of course, extremely affectionate, asking after you all, and hearing with interest all I had to say (I delivered your message and Sophy's), and going back with great pleasure and feeling to all recollections of old times, conversations &c. But I cannot express the melancholy feeling which the whole view of his situation (with Ward's comments) has left on my mind. There he is almost alone in a large house with none of his old friends about him, overworked, and that in a way which is not his own line—not what he had expected or planned for himself or for which he seemed fitted, thrown away by the communion to which he has devoted himself, and evidently sensible that he is so thrown away. He talked freely as if it were old times again about his former and present plans—the translation of the Bible, which for a time was committed to him and then fell out of his hands—a

---

* These were some Maories, who had been brought over by a speculating showman. The Colonial Office interfered, and arranged for their entertainment, and for their return to their own country.

project of writing on 'Reason and Faith'—his school—
projects of Catholic University and the question (which
divides them) whether it is better to effect, if possible, a
lodgment in Oxford or Cambridge, which is his view, or to
set up a separate University, which is Manning's, and the
majority's—and the inability of his own people to understand
what a University in his sense of the word (derived from
Oxford) really is. He set me criticising his beginnings towards
a church, and, though there is much I did not like, I happily
hit more than once on a thing to admire warmly, which made
him stop and look at me hard in his old amused way and
ask, 'Now, do you really mean what you say?' 'Certainly.'
'Because, my dear Rogers, that is my own.' And once or
twice, after talks of this kind (quite in the old way) as we
were walking rather quickly from place to place, he leading
the way, and so, not talking, he was left to follow his own
thoughts for a moment, I caught a kind of impatient and
half mournful 'Ah, tzt' (you know the sound, though I can't
spell it), which seemed to say, 'Why is he not with me, why
can't I be often talking to him in this way?' Then we
talked about various matters, Birmingham habits, Birmingham villas, architecture, Ward and his eccentricities (I saw,
sitting with Newman and his two followers, that a joke at
Ward's expense was not unacceptable, and it was a pleasure to
get a good hearty laugh out of him in the old fashion). He
gave me the whole day (dismissing rather shortly Lord Henry
Kerr, who dropped in) but evidently did not desire that I
should come again on Monday, so I started by an earlier
train (9.30) and got here in time to do a little work.

To Miss Rogers.

18 Radnor Place : October 10, 1863.

My dear Kate.—Our Maori proceedings have somewhat strange and perplexing. In the first place you know
that we were told that Wirima would start on Wednesday
morning, then this was put off to Thursday, and luckily
—for poor Wirima frightfully overwalked himself (being left
alone for a short walk), came here hardly able to stand, and

at 11 o'clock, when I went into his bedroom to see that he was all right, we found him suffering so much that we sent for the doctor, who at once poulticed him and dosed him for an attack of pleurisy. Next day he was better, but hardly thought himself able to see Mr. and Mrs. Pomare.[9] However, I forced them on him (in his bedroom); his coming to luncheon was out of the question, and at last it was agreed that Mr. Pomare should stay with him and see him off. So we were at once saddled with 6 feet 3 of savage, in addition to poor W. However the six feet three packed themselves up on an armchair. He seems to have looked after him very nicely, though I was rather alarmed to see the window left open all night upon a pleuritic patient (the alternative was being baked), and on the next (Thursday) morning he was far better. The doctor thought, not only that he was fit to embark (which we had doubted), but that the voyage would do him more good than anything else could do him, and that there was really a chance of his reaching New Zealand. Well, on Thursday morning off I started with my two Maories to the Emigration Office. . . . . .

But on arriving in the City I was informed that the ship's surgeon (the very point on which we were particular) had cried off, that the ship could not start till the next day, and that W.'s cabin (a very good one, I understand) would not be ready for him until then. So what was to be done? . . . . .

Of course all things are possible, though all things are not convenient; and the question was whether to go back, which would have been to W.'s great disappointment, for he was keen to get on board. However, at last, I settled to put them into the hands of the Emigration officer—a kind sensible fellow, who would take them to Gravesend, bed them there, put them on board the next morning. . . . I have not yet heard the result.[1] They ought to have started yesterday, and, if so, ought to have let me know. But I believe they are in good hands.

---

[9] The Pomares belonged to the party of Maories whose reception by the Queen was mentioned above. The Queen was Godmother to a child who was born to them in England.

[1] Wirima died on the voyage to New Zealand.

To Rev. E. Rogers.

1863.

I dined yesterday with Goulburn, and met Ward, of Balliol, who was enormous fun. He is full of stories of his own priests, some rather good; but what most interested me was his account of Newman, which was very sad. He disposed of as absurd (I have no doubt with truth) the statements that Newman was dissatisfied in the sense of being shaken in his belief. But it appeared clearly that he is entirely a fish out of water—that he has practically broken with the old Roman Catholics—that almost all even of his old friends have left him—that he thinks very ill of his own health, and that his principal interest now is in his school at Birmingham, about seventy or eighty sons of converts. The main difference appears to be as to the manner of education. Newman is for a system like our public schools and universities—with great freedom of life. Accordingly while he was at Dublin College it transpired that some of the collegians had been going to plays, and had been hunting in pink. This is wholly contrary to their system, which is one of close surveillance and rigid discipline, and the Archbishop held forth to Newman for half an hour and an hour about it. ('Very narrow-minded man, you know, Archbishop Cullen, but excellent good man—and in this case, you know, quite right, I think.') 'But then,' as he says to Ward, 'what can I do when Dr. Newman just listens to me without speaking, and then says, "I will think about it," and then everything goes on just as it was before?' There is an internal evidence of truth about this which places it beyond doubt. One sees the stony expression of Newman's face. Well, thereupon they turned him out, greatly to his own mortification, and, of course, having given up the English Church for the Roman, and England with his English friends for Ireland and the Irish, it must have been galling and sad to be sent back again to the place with which you had broken all or almost all your ties.

Ward implied—almost used the expression—that N. considered that his real life had come to a close in 1845. But then one knows what Ward's ideas are worth.

The Roman Catholics describe Newman as a *mauvais coucheur*,—bad bedfellow.

Ward said that St. John was the only man who had stuck to him. Dalgairns had quite left him—I suppose for Faber. On the whole I came home very sad about him, and much disgusted with Manning, Faber, Wiseman, *et id genus omne*.

He seems to be writing a great work, 'Faith and Reason,' I suppose on the ground of belief in everything. It will be a good work (I do not doubt) when it comes. It occurs to me that Church would very much like to see all this. But I have no time to write it him; would you send it him?

To Miss Rogers.

18 Radnor Place : July 12, 1864.

Of course you have been in a certain amount of excitement here about the vote of no confidence. The reports were up and down for a long time : at the last people expected a majority of about ten, and the eighteen was a triumph to the Ministry. As you see, the Conservatives gained some eighteen Irish Roman Catholic votes, with whom Dizzy is always supposed to be coquetting ; *per contra*, they lost a few Conservatives who were disgusted at the Catholic alliance. The Whig Evangelicals sent out a manifesto to their co-religionists (it is said) calling on them to come out from among the Papists, and some obeyed the call and voted with Palmerston. Northcote, by whom I sat to see the lamentable conclusion of the Eton and Harrow cricket match, was talking politics to Lord Cawdor, and both agreed that they wished to be quit of the Irishmen. 'Every Irish vote we gain loses us an English one.' That is one of the bones of contention between Diz. and his party.

Cardwell told me that he thought the speeches also told on the division. One man said when Pam got up, 'Now my vote depends on this speech,' and voted with Pam. He said that Brand (the Treasury Whip) told him that he considered that Dizzy's replies frequently sent votes to the Ministry, *i.e.* that people were disgusted at his rhetorical slash, and took it out by voting against him. They now talk of the Ministry being safe until next autumn, which seems to me rather rash, considering how little anybody can calculate on Pam's life, or foresee what will happen if he dies or throws up, and Gladstone steps forward to lead the Commons, or to obstruct any one else who is put forward to lead. I imagine his speech to have been a considerable success—once or twice I have heard the expression that it 'crushed the debate.'

As I have said I spent a morning (being rather easy just now) in seeing the end of the Eton and Harrow match. I had no notion what a pretty thing a cricket match was. The Harrow fielding was beautiful—no fumbling—but every fellow stopped the ball as if it stuck to his hand the moment they touched. I hear the bowling was very good also, but that I had not eyes to see.

To Miss Florence Nightingale.

December 6, 1864.

Dear Madam,—The abuse of supplying liquors to Indians and aborigines is, as you may suppose, no new matter of regret—perhaps I should say despair—to this office. Laws have been passed against it in Upper and Lower Canada, in Vancouver I., in New South Wales, Victoria and Queensland, New Zealand, and, I think, in West Australia. Police regulations of the same kind exist in S. Australia.

But the difficulty is not in passing laws but in enforcing them; and considering the difficulty of enforcing all that ought to be enforced, even in this old, well-organised country, against the unwearying pressure of pecuniary interests, it can easily be imagined what is the difficulty of preventing publicans from doing as they like in young democracies where the machinery of Government is meagre, population scattered (as in the Australian bush and Canadian backwoods), and perhaps a large seaboard is the scene of a more or less illicit coasting trade.

I dare say that more might be done than is—much more. But the wishes of the Home Government are perfectly well known in such matters, and the temper of the colonists (at least, in large colonies) is not very tolerant of Home interference. I fear, therefore, that the Secretary of State could do little more than remain on the watch for opportunities, which would enable him to stir the question, and keep governors alive to their duties. This is rather an unsatisfactory conclusion, and I heartily wish for myself that I saw my way to anything less unsatisfactory. But I am not aware, at the present moment, of any colony in which a movement from the Colonial Office would be likely to do any good.

Yours very faithfully,
F. ROGERS.

To Lady Rogers.

December 11, 1864.

Mozley, as you perhaps know, is going to preach what are called the Bampton lectures at Oxford, and has taken Miracles as his subject. He is very like himself, thinking away like a steam engine of 100 horse-power, and whirling you along with him if you will let him. However, he came here more to pump than to talk, and I held forth on Metaphysics like a demon. I did not know I had so many. I shall be curious to see what he makes of it. It is the subject of the day, and he might do the world and himself any amount of good by a really first-rate treatise.

To Miss Rogers.

18 Radnor Place: December 23, 1864.

My dear Kate,—We have been unusually quiet since we got home, except as to family company. Partly, I believe, because I was getting rather sluggish and averse to the trouble of composing a dinner party: partly, I suppose, because other people are reserving themselves for later in the season.

Cardwell is happily absent, though not so much as I could wish. He is very friendly, but his fidgets are a great torment. The constant presence in his mind of the House of Commons and the Leader of the Opposition is a terrible nuisance. And after a despatch is drafted with sufficient clearness to give all necessary instruction and sufficient prudence to be perfectly defensible (because right) against any reasonable attack, he will go on for half an hour revising and modifying and paring off edges in order that it may offer no handle; sometimes, as I think, to the disadvantage of the despatch as a matter of administration.

'I have been a good deal interested by the proposed American union. We have had the principal man here, the Canadian Prime Minister,[2] to talk it over, and of course it was interesting to understand (though of course seeing through his eyes) the position of affairs. The great difficulty is to arrange for a real union of the five provinces (Canada, New Brunswick, Nova Scotia, Newfoundland, and Prince Edward Island) on terms which shall make the Central or Federal Legislation really dominant, so as to make one body politic of the whole, and yet to provide security to the French Canadians that this dominancy would not be used to swamp their religion and habits. Then, as it is not, of course, desirable (or is supposed not to be so) to legislate specifically for Lower Canada, there is to be a scheme which gives too much to the individual provinces, but leaving it to the British provinces to effect a clear amalgamation by degrees. This, as you may suppose, renders the affair rather wanting in neatness and scientific character. But I suppose it will push through, as all parties are agreed in desiring to launch a 'British America.'

Ever yours affectionately,
F. R.

Extract from a letter to a Colonial Governor.[3]

Your suspicion that you are over-full in your despatches is, I think, just. Their exuberance, so to call it, gives them rather an appearance (which is, of course, disadvantageous) of being written for the public, not very well informed and anxious to be amused and interested, than for a Secretary of State anxious to deal rightly with the subject in hand, and desirous above all things of having succinctly, prominently

---

[2] Sir John Macdonald. There is a fuller account of these matters at the end of chapter viii.

[3] This was written in answer to a letter asking for criticism of despatches.

completely, and once for all brought before him the information (including, of course, state of opinion) which is requisite to guide his judgment, and the impressions of the Governor on these facts. I mean that reiteration, reflections, historical illustrations and quotations &c., necessary and instructive to a general reader, are easily overdone in the transaction of business.

Then there are two or three points on which I should lodge what is called, I think, a 'caveat.'

1. General fulness of statement is no compensation for the omission of an important fact or consideration ; sometimes even it has the effect of overlaying the significant fact.

2. It is no doubt a Governor's clear duty to give the Secretary of State his honest opinion and honest information; and it is his *right* also to do so for his own protection. But a Governor is often under a temptation to do more than this, and so to express his own opinions as to *appear an advocate* for the views held by those about him (and by himself), although by so doing he may add to the practical difficulties of the Government here.

3. It is impossible for a Secretary of State to ignore information which comes to him from newspapers, individuals, or elsewhere. What he can do and ought to do, and what it is the rule to do, is to give the Governor (or Colonial Government indirectly) the opportunity of explanation. If a request for explanation is treated as a censure (as I think you and your ministers treat it), all this information (which it is, I repeat, impossible to exclude, often impossible to leave unnoticed) will be doing its work silently and uncontradicted, than which nothing can be worse for the Governor and the Colony.

4. No doubt the colonists, or some of them, are angry with us. They may have some good reasons. It is not for me to say they have not. But they have some bad ones. One is this : some of their friends are continually trying, while disclaiming argument or controversy, to do the work of argument by insinuating in papers intended for the public facts which we think untrue, and arguments which we think delusive. We do not like our flank being thus turned, and

justifiably, as I hold, protest sharply against such insinuations, recalling what, if we are right, is the true state of affairs. This has a tart appearance, but it is the doing of those who provoke it.

Another bad reason is that the Secretary of State is unhesitatingly represented as saying sometimes what he has cautiously avoided saying; sometimes what he has expressly disclaimed (there is, I think, a splendid instance in a paper you sent me lately), or as implying or believing a fact when he only asks a question. The representations of course become current; the original on which the representations are based does not. And the consequence is, of course, a popular impression against the Colonial Office. . . .

I am writing on post day without time to be short, and unluckily without your letters before me, so I may not have chosen my words very properly, or have said exactly what I wished to say in answer to your letters.

Yours sincerely,
F. ROGERS.

To Rev. E. Rogers.

1865

I think Charles Buxton has rather disgraced himself in his writing about Eyre.[1] My notion is that Eyre was really justified in viewing the matter as a most dangerous rebellion to be crushed at all hazards, and I expect to find his first measure right. But I doubt whether he will be able to show that he pulled up the rude reckless system of execution and other punishment as soon as safety was substantially restored, and he might have recovered his head. And I am clear that he has not felt sufficiently the painful and terrible character of what he and the officers acting under him have done.

---

[1] Mr. Eyre (previously distinguished for his adventurous journeys in Australia) was Governor of Jamaica. The rising of the coloured population was, as may be gathered from the letters which follow, a serious one; and it could not be questioned that his prompt action saved the English residents from grave danger; but it was judged that he had carried his severity farther than was necessary, and that his punishments had been too summary; and he was recalled.

As to the numbers of blacks killed our evidence at present is :

1. Official despatches which do not show more than 200 or 300, but do not negative the idea that very many more have been killed one way or other.

2. A loose statement in a private letter that 'I should say 1,000 had been killed.'

3. A triumphant statement in a Jamaica paper that 2,000 have been killed. A report of the naval officer in command that 1,500 would be a moderate estimate.

4. An oral statement of a dissenting minister and manager of estate who was in the thick of it, and assisted at some of the courts-martial, that many more than 2,000, say 5,000, may have perished.

So that the matter is vague and terrible enough. I am very anxious to see what this mail brings from Eyre.

To Rev. E. Rogers.

1865.

My dear Edward,—Church found a point superfluous in your Hebrew, but as the mistake was John Rogers's[3] and not the printer's, he left it unaltered. Your title-page professes to be a facsimile, not a revised edition. He read the two sheets

---

[3] Edward Rogers was publishing *The Life and Opinions of a Fifth Monarchy Man, chiefly extracted from the writings of John Rogers, preacher.* This John Rogers was an ancestor, father of the first baronet. There had been a constant family tradition (a curious instance of the development of myth) to the effect that 'their ancestor had been Dean of Christ Church in Dublin, imprisoned by Cromwell in Carisbrooke Castle for his loyalty to Charles I.' The truth, as Sir E. Rogers found, was that John Rogers, though the son of a Prebendary of Ely, was ultra-puritan and a preacher of the Fifth Monarchy. He was presented by the Parliamentary Commissioners with some of the confiscated revenues of Christ Church in Dublin in 1651 for such time as he should be minister for the puritan congregation there : he was afterwards imprisoned by Cromwell in Carisbrooke Castle, and treated very harshly, but it was because he went too far *against* earthly monarchs—in fact he was denounced for praying that God would 'hasten the time when Christ should reign and we shall have *no other Lord Protector.* Let our faith have so much of the grain of mustard seed as to say *to that great mountain* " Be removed " and it shall be removed.' Antony Wood called him ' a conceited pragmatical fellow,' and Cromwell said to him, 'You will talk, I see, though it be nothing to the purpose.'

and was clearly of opinion that there was nothing in them which ought to be omitted. I was glad of this, for though he did not know how much more of the same kind there was, and so far saw your extracts at an advantage, yet he did not also know how they were introduced, and so saw them at a disadvantage. He was also clear that an account of R.'s doctrine and discipline was indispensable. I really think you could not have been shorter, unless you intended to write a wholly different kind of book. He understands that he is to review it. . . .

Mrs. ——'s relations with her maids are rich. She was describing one who was a breaker of china. At last she broke three things in one day. 'So I said to her, " You are ill, Jane, you want some castor oil." The maid stared and was astonished. " Your hand shakes, you want some castor oil, Jane." The maid took it as a joke and grinned. But when bedtime came, the upper maid was duly summoned. " Jane is ill, and wants some castor oil; come with me and I will give it out for her." ' . . . Mrs. —— appeared at the bedside with a quite inflexible determination, explained that Jane was ill and did want castor oil and must take it. She did take it, and no further breakage occurred from that time to—I don't know when.

Ever yours,
F. R.

To Lady Rogers (Lady Blachford).
July 18, 1865.

Almost before I got to Oxford I found it was all up with us.[6] When the railway omnibus stopped at its first hotel waiter and boots told us that Hardy was 200 ahead, evidently too great a start to be made up on the last day's poll; and when I saw Bernard, he told me that the Committee had actually telegraphed to Gladstone that the seat was lost. To-day will *somewhat* reduce the majority, but the poll is not carried on with any hope of reducing it materially. The numbers will be rather above 1,700 on one side, and about

---

[6] The members for the University had been Mr. Gladstone and Sir William Heathcote. At the election of 1865, Mr. Gathorne Hardy (Lord Cranbrook) took Mr. Gladstone's place.

1,900 on the other. The total number of voters is about 4,150. . . . It is a great bore. All the consolation is that Hardy is not a bad man, certainly the best opponent that Gladstone has yet had. Gladstone will, of course, try South Lancashire, but with very much diminished chance of getting in. . . .

It is astonishing what mistakes men will make. One actually sent up a voting paper certified properly by a magistrate to have been signed by the voter in his presence, but not signed by the voter at all. Some persons have been troubled by a scruple of conscience in cases where the paper was insufficiently executed, considering that after such a failure they cannot conscientiously affirm that they have 'signed no other voting paper' (which they are required to do) and have written up to the Committee for advice. The answer has been—'Sir, you are mistaken in supposing that you have signed a voting paper. You have indeed attempted to do so, but you have signally failed. There is therefore no reason,' &c. Gladstone has sent down an admirable farewell letter, short, dignified, and feeling, almost enough to make some of his opponents repent of their votes, I should say.

To Miss Rogers.

Radnor Place : November 25, 1865.

My dear Kate,—I have had my first interview with William Forster. He is certainly a rough diamond, as strange a contrast to Fortescue's polished, almost feminine, manner as can well be imagined. But he seems a clear-headed, thinking, and not wrong-headed man, ready for work and very friendly. He began at once, when we were alone, asking after all the family. . . .

I see he is a regular universal suffrage man, or something near it, by his speech at Bradford, which by the way did not appear to me to have much in it.

We are expecting our Jamaica news with some anxiety. The soldiers seem to have made wildish work of it, and Eyre's hanging a member of the Assembly by court-martial, sending him from Kingston for the purpose, is rather startling.

The Dissenters are preparing a most furious attack on the local Government and soldiers. They intend to try to make out, I fancy, that Gordon was an obnoxious champion of the negroes, whom the Government hated, and took this opportunity to get rid of. Of course they put themselves on their defence and pelt as they are pelted.

To Right Hon. W. E. Gladstone.

18 Radnor Place : December 18, 1865.

My dear Gladstone,— I ought to have thanked you some days since for the copy of your speeches which you sent me. Parts of them almost brought the tears to my eyes on re-reading them in cold blood. But personally glad as I always was to have you at Oxford, I cannot help feeling that you are better where you are. The position of having to do good to those whom you represent, in a manner which they do not conceive to be good, and that, not once or twice, but as a consequence of certain differences of view on matters of wisdom and equity which are sure to be always reproducing themselves, is a position which would drive me mad, and from which a man who is to govern the country ought to be released.

I confess, however, that I hope to find that you differ from some of your present constituents as to *ends*, almost as much as you differed from some of your late constituents as to *means*, if at least it is fair to call democracy an end and Church ascendency a mean.

Yours very sincerely,
FREDERIC ROGERS.

To the Rev. R. W. Church.

Colonial Office : January 2, 1866.

My dear Church,—What do you say about this? You see Gladstone is a good deal smitten by the book ' Ecce Homo,' and would be glad to see it well reviewed. I should imagine it would be very much in your line. Try it. It is, I hear, or rather you see, an exhibition of our Saviour's character and mission from the merely human side, not denying, but carefully excluding, the idea of His divine attributes.

I should imagine it would require much care to do justice to its value as an exhibition of *part* of the truth, so as yet to warn people effectually against so riveting their eyes on that part as to become insensible to its essential incompleteness.

——'s 'something beyond human being needed' is an uncommonly feeble conclusion to arrive at.

I can easily believe that there may be Unitarians (and this man may or may not be one of them) who love and revere Christ, believing Him to be mere man, with greater depth and fervency than many of us love and revere Him, though believing Him to be God. And one would desire to do justice to such men, *utinam nostri essent!* What one would desire is that such men's works should be so exhibited as to lead Unitarians and others forward instead of leading Churchmen backward. And this would be done in this case if (to put the matter extravagantly) any one would write such a book under the title of 'My Lord and my God' as would furnish an inseparable second volume to 'Ecce Homo,' so that no one who bought one would think his book complete without the other.

However, all this is said in the dark, as I have not seen the book, I have heard of it.

Why will you not come to town? There are so many things, it seems to me, that I should like to talk to you about. The Jamaica business is most terrible. The doings on both sides appear in truth to be rather worse than better than what you see in the papers. Only that consideration suggests excuses for the whites which are wholly wanting in the case of the blacks. It is really terrible to see human nature naked.

Ever yours,
F. ROGERS.

To the Rev. R. W. Church.

January 25, 1866.

My dear Church,—What Newman says about his views on the present state of things is a reflection on what I said on the author of 'Ecce Homo,'[7] that one of his aims was the 'moral elevation of your (the Roman) Church.'

He replies with general truth—no—not moral, but mixed moral and intellectual, 'a narrowness which is not of God.'

Again, his anticipations for the future, as to a fresh aspect of doctrine opening out, seem to me rather an answer to my suggestion that 'Ecce Homo' was aiming at establishing a basis of doctrine without assuming inspiration in any technical sense.

I understand him to amuse himself by taking all the privileges of sham mystification with me. 'I have sent for the book,' *i.e.* he said to somebody, 'Just fetch me "Ecce Homo," I want to see what it was in the forty-eighth page that opened Rogers's eyes so wide.'

To Right Hon. W. E. Gladstone.

18 Radnor Place : February 18, 1866.

My dear Gladstone,—If you have twenty minutes to spare next Sunday do cast your eye through Newman's two sermons sixteen and seventeen of the volume called 'Sermons on the Subjects of the Day,' headed 'The Christian Church an Imperial Power,' and 'Sanctity the Token of the Christian Empire,' particularly pages 256-58, 263-5, 273-5, 284, 287. And observe not only the particular thoughts but their grouping and relation to each other.[8]

'If he be not Bran he is Bran's brother.'

Yours sincerely,
FREDERIC ROGERS.

---

[7] Sir John Seeley published *Ecce Homo* in 1866 without his name, and many incorrect guesses at the author were made at the time. It is remarkable that (as appears from this and the next two letters) two of Newman's most intimate friends, both very acute critics, discussed the probability of Newman himself having written *Ecce Homo*.

[8] Coincidences, partly of thought and partly of style, may be observed, if the passages referred to are compared with the chapters in *Ecce Homo* on 'Christ's Royalty,' 'Christ's Credentials,' and 'The Conditions of Membership in Christ's Kingdom.'

To the Rev. R. W. Church.

18 Radnor Place [February 1866?]

My dear Church,—I am so possessed with the idea of the book being Newman's that nothing will drive it out of my head, not even this letter, though it is not in style like Newman, and as you say mystification is carried very far. Why should you not give your name? and why should you not give Macmillan leave to print your article if he likes? Be the author of 'Ecce Homo' who he may, I should (if I were you) like to have established a relation of personal friendship with him. I think it is really ungracious to refuse. It clearly accepts your interpretation of the book so far as belief in the Divinity of Christ goes, on which you express a positive opinion. But it does not say *I am a Roman Catholic*.

I have been reading your Hooker by snatches. I like the preface very much, but I see that when you warm to your work, and involve yourself in a sentence in which you really wish to give force and vivacity to what you have to develop, you still run to substantives. I think you are quite right to do in your fashion what requires to be done best.

Hooker's melody is beautiful certainly. One has a curious feeling in reading it, that it is such a full grandiose exposition of truth with such odd assumptions as evidence of matters which in the present day are almost exploded, at any rate that have to be stated with proof or apology by a member of the aristocracy of intellect.

The style of the writing brings to my ears the lines

> 'A solemn air, and the best comforter
> 'To an unsettled fancy.'

Just at the present conjuncture of religious belief, would a sketch of the counter-Church heathen revival of philosophy and morality be interesting. I could fancy some curious parallels. An essay on Origen, for example, or Julian the Apostate.

Ever yours affectionately,
F. ROGERS.

CHAPTER VIII

Last Years of Official Life, 1866-1870

IN June 1866 Lord Russell's Government was turned out by Lord Dunkellin's amendment to the franchise bill and Lord Derby became Premier. Lord Carnarvon was the new chief at the Colonial Office. 'Lord Carnarvon became at once a friend more intimate than Cardwell, both because there was more warmth in him, and because there was the bond of a common feeling in Church matters. He was a great contrast. He had not Cardwell's hard-headed desire so to do the work that statesmen, and Parliament following statesmen, should see it was well done: but he had more of a generous desire to effect worthy objects, and also more, I think, of a wish to shine before the public and to distinguish himself in the ordinary sense of the word. His failing was rather too much self-consciousness, and a disposition to be caught by showy schemes. He was not the least afraid of the House of Commons, a great recommendation to a chief in the eyes of his subordinates; but on the other hand, being in the House of Lords, though he was less afraid of what the House of Commons would say or think of him, he was less able to control what they could do to him and his measures. He was friendly to everybody and particularly so to me both as a chief and as a companion. It was curious, that though he was fully aware of his own abilities and desirous of receiving credit for them, particularly in his measures and public appearances, he was given to take a second part in conversation, always wishing rather to draw out others than to speak himself. Accordingly I used to find myself lecturing him almost in the tone of an old college tutor, which is after all a little the same position as that of a Senior Under-

Secretary. When Cardwell retired he gave his opinion (without any suggestion from me) to his successor, Lord Carnarvon, that I ought to have assistance, which was given me in the person of Henry (now Sir Henry) Holland,[1] than whom it was impossible to have a more delightful subordinate: prompt, intelligent, conciliating, regular, always ready to help, never making difficulties, and having that quickness to perceive the characteristic or amusing side of business which goes far to make work into play. Not only did his industry take work off my shoulders, but his companionship lightened what remained. He had a kind of pleasantly impulsive rapidity, which in some men leaves an impression of want of solidity; but his judgment was very good, and he would stand to it. He had at once that openness of mind which would make him, as a member of a department or a party, alive to the force of adverse arguments, and at the same time that intelligent flexibility which enables a man to turn the flank of differences, and to continue to act not less cordially because on one point there was a hitch. When Lord Carnarvon left the Disraeli Ministry with Lord Salisbury and General Peel, on the occasion of the 1867 Reform Bill, he was succeeded by the Duke of Buckingham, a thoroughly honest and kind-hearted man, with a rough but friendly manner, not without shrewdness, and clear-headed, but with a natural turn for detail which he had indulged as Chairman of a great railway, till it injured his capacity as a Minister. . . . The Duke of Buckingham was followed at the Colonial Office (when Mr. Gladstone became Premier) by Lord Granville, the pleasantest and most satisfactory chief of those under whom I served. His merits as a chief were, that he trusted his subordinates in matters of detail, that he saw his way clearly and would act vigorously in what may be called ministerial as distinguished from departmental policy, and he was ready to act with promptitude and authority in matters which none but a chief could handle, matters requiring action in the House of Lords or the Cabinet or the Treasury. And in a diplomatic kind of way he thoroughly enjoyed the characteristic and amusing side of business.'

[1] The present Lord Knutsford.

To Lady Rogers.

Colonial Office : July 4, 1866.

Lord Carnarvon has made his appearance. Cardwell has had him here to talk to, and called me in to be bottle-holder. I was much struck by Cardwell's mode of going through the state of business. There was such an evident wish simply to ease matters to his successor and facilitate in every way the transaction of business.

Both were very kind to me, and Lord C. almost instantly asked about distribution of work, and seemed surprised to find that I had what I have to do: on which Cardwell spoke up (having left something to the same effect in writing) and said that he should be prepared to support any step for taking the legal busiuess away from me, as a relief that concerned the interest of the public. Lord C. meets me here to-morrow at 12 o'clock to take up what most presses.

How those poor Austrians are getting slaughtered![2] It is heart-breaking. I should suppose that the end of the Austrian Empire was fairly come, were it not that they seem to be so wonderfully tenacious of life.

To Lady Rogers.

October 9, 1866.

I have had a pleasant Sunday at Highclere. Sir Henry Storks,[3] a certain Major Skinner, a Ceylon official, a very fine fellow, I should think, of the 'valuable old public servant' sort, two New Brunswickers, the Oxford notoriety Mansel, and his wife, and a young brother—Auberon, I think, is his name—whom I liked greatly, and a young private secretary who was cordial and energetic in doing the honours of the house.

---

[2] The Battle of Sadowa was fought on July 3.

[3] Governor of Malta. The year before he had been sent out to Jamaica as President of the Commission to inquire into the events which took place in the governorship of Mr. Eyre. His work there was over, when Sir John Peter Grant was appointed Governor of Jamaica, and he returned to his post at Malta. He was Lord High Commissioner of the Ionian Islands at the time of their cession to Greece, in 1864.

Storks is always pleasant. I never came across a more complete man of the world—a man with all his wits about him, never slighting or quarrelling with anybody—never committing himself— determined to succeed in all he attempts and to let alone what cannot be effected—ready and quick-witted in conversation, never without his answer to any thrust you make at him—plenty of good sayings and stories—talking such French, it was a pleasure to hear the sounds, and I should think as good Italian—a scientific appreciation of a French cook, and of the proprieties of a dinner—thinking London even in November better than the country, and plainly professing that if, as the 'Autocrat' says, 'good Americans when they die go to Paris,' he would be content to throw in his lot with them.

If there is one thing he would like just now, it is that the Pope would take refuge in Malta during his government: I think I see the grave courtesy with which he would receive His Holiness, with a perfect appreciation of what was due to the Chair of St. Peter from the representative of the British Crown in Malta, and *vice versâ*.

I am not sure whether he has strong affection or much imagination. However, he is, I should think, a capital master, a capital servant, a capital ally, and a capital companion.

To Lady Rogers.

18 Radnor Place: November 2, 1866.

My dear Mother,—I cannot get from under my pressure quite, but I must not delay in giving you an account of my last Highclere visit till I have forgotten it all.

I had offered myself for Sunday and was accepted, and pressed to come on Friday to talk over some business for Saturday's mail. . . . I had unwittingly offered myself to meet the Salisburys and the Disraelis. It was a piece of luck, for Lord Carnarvon had first asked me on the previous Sunday when I was engaged. The other guests were a young cousin, Edward Herbert, Graham the private secretary, and Verdon, a Melbourne Minister. I planted myself next Edward Herbert, a pleasant, intelligent Viennese attaché. . . . Dizzy was either much out of humour or assumed the mysterious; silent and sullen-looking, as far as I saw. He is certainly a most remarkable-looking fellow—eyes, mouth, chin, hair, everything; but he is far more massive and powerful-looking than I imagined. The caricatures give me a notion of something rather insignificant. There is nothing at all of that—nothing puny, or merely acute. . . .

Next day Saturday. I had some very pleasant walking with Edward Herbert and was greatly amused at an interview with a gamekeeper whom we met. The gamekeeper was got up in such gilt and velveteen as almost made one take off one's hat, and was full of dissatisfaction at the leave given to tenants to kill hares, and looking forward with a grim satisfaction to 'his Lordship' having next year to send into Newbury to buy leverets for the table; then he burst out on the farmers. 'Right good shots, sir; some of them will kill their fourteen or seventeen hares a day; there's ———, the best shot in the neighbourhood, just as good as any gentleman as has been brought up to it.' He was altogether of opinion that a Tory Government was an unmixed evil, 'made his Lordship entirely neglect the game, and no getting him to listen to anything.'

At breakfast and luncheon I found myself next Mrs. Disraeli. She insists on being heard and seen and 'keeps up the ball;' rather thinks herself the life of the party. Seeing out of the window a piebald cow in the park, she insisted that every one all round the table should wish for something (I suppose you know the superstition; I did not), overriding and smashing all the little private neighbourly conversations. Lord Salisbury wished for 'sleep' and explained himself to wish for 'the power of going to sleep when he was bored.'

On Sunday I had two delightful walks; the day was perfect and the place lovely, and I liked my companions—Graham in the morning, Auberon Herbert and Verdon in the afternoon, and partly Lord Carnarvon. I was almost tempted to join their smoking party after bedtime.

On Monday I found myself (without being treated with anything but the most entire friendliness) rather hustled off—*i.e.* sent by a rather slow, very early train—when there was another an hour later, and faster. However, I had every reason to be satisfied with the result, for it appeared that the Disraelis were going by the last train, while Lord and Lady Salisbury, Verdon and Edward Herbert were going by the first. The Highclere party had a carriage to itself, and we were really neither more nor less than a jolly party.

I have not told you Lord Salisbury's story about the Duke of Malakhoff and his pheasant. He (Malakhoff) was at a battue at Strathfieldsaye and shot nothing, much to his disgust, and when the day was over it appeared that he would be extremely put out unless he was allowed or enabled to kill something ; so, in spite of all the gamekeepers could think, feel, or say, a pheasant was procured, tied by its leg to the top of a post, and Malakhoff was put some thirty yards off with a double-barrelled gun. It was supposed that he would thereupon and from thence take two shots at the bird. Not a bit of it ; he loaded his two barrels, walked close up to the pheasant, put the muzzle close to him and discharged both barrels into him with ' Hé! coquin !' The next day the Duke of Wellington told the keeper that Malakhoff was a great man who had smoked to death 500 Arab men, women, and children in a cave, to which the gamekeeper replied, ' Like enough, your Grace, he'd be capable of anything.'

To Miss Rogers.

18 Radnor Place : November 2, 1866.

My dear Kate,—I am much elated to hear of the flowering of another Sikkim rhododendron.[1] Oddly enough, I had just been admiring at Stowe what I took to be Sikkim rhododendrons and trying to make out whether any of them were the same as ours. It looks a beautiful flower, and it gives hopes that the others may come on one by one.

Stowe is a magnificent place, ducal in the highest possible degree. But, after the fashion, I suppose, of the last century, everything seems sacrificed to pomp. There is one perfectly magnificent suite of rooms running from one end of the house to the other. Here is the south front. (Sketched on the letter.)

---

[1] A present from Sir Joseph Hooker, brought from the Himalayas.

In front, a terrace garden, and in front of that a splendid lawn with trees on each side (pierced for one or two views) sloping down to the water at the bottom, and facing the opposite slope of the valley. But (for the sake of the architectural façade) not one of the south bedrooms along this grand south front look out to this great view, but look out over the leads, or sideways, and the domestic dining-room and the Duke's study are down in the basement, so low that I think they can hardly see over the terrace flower-beds, on which they look, to the view beyond. The other side of the basement is offices, and all that part of the house seems intended for it, for you have to go through dreary cellar-like vaulted corridors to get at the Duke's study. However, for entertaining crowned heads it is admirable.

I disposed of what I went down for, pretty much to my satisfaction, or at least got the instructions for it, and must finish off to-morrow. . . . The Duke seems to be endeavouring to recover as he can the mass of beautiful things that were sold to pay his father's debts. He showed me some miniatures (in which they were rich in old times), one of which (the great Duchess of Marlborough) he had bought back. It was lamentable to see the masses of empty brackets that were formerly filled with majolica. The ceiling and wall decorations were very fine; they were done by Italian artists in about 1780. I rather like to see the internal decorations of that date—after the Louis Quatorze had a little worn out.

To Lady Rogers.

Colonial Office : May 8, 1867.

The Ministers, I fancy, are well pleased with themselves about Luxemburg. What seems to me to be feared is that Louis Napoleon is putting off the evil day till he has got a sufficient armament of breech-loaders. I confess I do not much fancy extending our guarantees. Storks has just interrupted me with a call. He says that in Paris a week ago the talk was all of war, and that the Prussians (he hears) look on the Conference as an insult; in fact, that war is to be. I cannot imagine that we shall be foolish enough to guarantee

Luxemburg. Storks thinks that Prussia would like a little more time for preparation as well as France, and that the French *élan* will carry it at first, but not at last.

To Lord Monck.
June 6, 1867.

My dear Lord Monck,—I have sent on your letters and enclose some copies of the Union Act. I wish you heartily a pleasant voyage and a prosperous time in Canada.[5]

It is a great occasion and there are few things I should like better than to be at your elbow during the launch of the new ship.

Yours sincerely,
F. ROGERS.

To Lady Rogers.
June 15, 1867.

My dear Mother,—Yesterday evening a small 'immediate' despatch box came in from the Duke of Buckingham, and the lock being out of order I had, in great perplexity, to commit the atrocity which shocked John so much, of breaking it open, imagining Fenian invasions of Canada, an insurrection in Heligoland, and 'what not.' However, it turned out to be information that the Ministers and their Under-Secretaries would be presented to the Sultan[6] at half-past three to-day, and that he would take me if I was duly rigged out at 2.45.

And now I have just come back from making the Commander of the Faithful's acquaintance. The rooms of Buckingham Palace look, I think, more grandiose than I had expected from seeing them in the evening, and of course there was the usual approach through the handsome staircase with flowers &c., &c. Then all the party collected gradually, Ministers dropping in one after the other, and one or two Turks sprinkled among them. The Duke introduced me to Fuad Pasha, the Grand Vizier —who shook my hand with a certain

---

[5] The Act for the Confederation of the North American Provinces was passed in March 1867. Lord Monck was going out as the first Governor-General of the new Dominion of Canada (then including Upper and Lower Canada, Nova Scotia, New Brunswick and Prince Edward's Island). The first Dominion Parliament met at Ottawa in November of that year.

[6] The Sultan Abdul Aziz.

empressement—a keen-faced old man, with (I should have said) a touch of the Greek in his physiognomy, red fez, blue frock coat richly embroidered with lots of diamond orders, and red trousers. Then after a time we were arranged in a semicircle, the door of the inner room was opened so that we saw his suite and speculated about what they were, and after a time he came forth at the head of them. Their general dresses are modifications of Fuad Pasha's, but there were one or two Albanians (beautiful dresses they are), red cap, gold tissue scarf, white kilt with some bright scarlet showing below it, and handsome leggings.

Then he made his round, began, and had some conversation with Lord Derby and the two or three chief Ministers through Fuad, who seemed to translate everything, shaking hands with them at the end. Then he came round and stood for a moment or two before each of us second-chops, looking more or less agreeable, while Lord Bradford said to Fuad, 'Sir Frédéric Rogers, sous-secrétaire des Colonies,' and Fuad said something to the Sultan, and I (as every one else) bowed, and Fuad said on behalf of H.I.M.: ' Enchanté de faire votre connaissance.' Then he swept off again with his suite into his inner room.

He is a handsome-looking man, pot-bellied, with a quiet, heavy, and perhaps rather languid expression, but a dignified manner, not at all graceful. The whole affair *from* Downing Street *to* Downing Street took an hour.

It is a thing to have done to shake hands with a Grand Vizier, though Grand Viziers are not what they used to be. And I am certainly glad to have had a good look at the Sultan.

There, I thought I would give you this while it was fresh in my mind, and now I must set to work again.

Ever yours affectionately,
F. R.

To Sir Henry Taylor.

July 6, 1867.

I thought the debate on martial law went well as to the principle. I think we (the Colonial Office) are quite right on the point on which Cockburn denounces our view (viz. that in emergencies a man is to suspend the law, trusting to an act of indemnity).

The essence of the difference when run home appears to me this: I say that a man in authority is to do his best to put down a rebellion, trusting that if he acts honestly and defensibly in general an act of indemnity will be passed to cover all that he has done.

Cockburn says that a man in authority is to endeavour to put down a rebellion by such means, and by such only, as a jury of his countrymen may be expected in each separate case to accept as rendered lawful by the necessity of the case.

His view seems to me to have every possible disadvantage.

It absolutely paralyses every man who is not prepared to risk his own life and reputation; for how can he tell what a judge and jury will pronounce to be the measure of necessity recognised by law? And next it does not provide for a just determination of the question, for it is almost certain that a jury in such critical circumstances will be of such stuff that either it will indiscriminately condemn every officer, or it will indiscriminately acquit every officer, or it will be absolutely incapable of agreeing on any verdict. A Government and Legislature subject to the pressure of public opinion are far less likely to be unfair.

Ever yours,
FREDERIC ROGERS.

To the Rev. R. W. Church.

18 Radnor Place: March 21, 1868.

I have just read Bernard. I do not see much harm in what he says, except that he appears to me rather given to advocate the particular step which the Liberals want for the moment, without considering what next; or rather, without considering whether the next landing-place is more stable than that which he proposes to leave.

If he only means that colleges may be relieved from Acts of Uniformity, but should remain at liberty to impose tests of their own, being consistent with or in the spirit of their Statutes, I am not disposed to differ from him in the abstract.

But I wish the Church party had coolness and wisdom and determination enough to see when the stand ought to be made with the utmost available resolution. I should be quite ready to abandon outworks, if only I were sure that somewhere or other in the rear we were shutting gates and pulling up drawbridges and mounting cannon.

What would be encouraging would be the way in which the early Church, with all its abuses and absurdities, which I suppose had begun to be pretty vigorous, had bottom enough to throw off all the shallow intellectual speculations and philosophical morality of Alexandria &c.

Ever yours affectionately,
FREDERIC ROGERS.

To Lady Rogers.

Highclere Castle : August 9, 1868.

My dear Mother,—Here we are for a Sunday. We stay till 2 o'clock to-morrow, Monday, when we must be off for me to sign letters &c. at Downing Street at 5 o'clock. G. perhaps told you of my Committee on military matters. There has been a great difficulty about a garrison for the Straits Settlements, what it was to be, who was to pay, &c. Sir H. Storks and I met and settled it to our own satisfaction. But as the Horse Guards (not to say Treasury) were concerned, the War Office sent us a letter to propose *officially* that the matter should be referred to a Committee of one representative from the Colonial Office, one from the War Office, and one from the Horse Guards, meaning Sir H. Storks, Sir Hope Grant, and myself. Storks and I are *bouleversés* by an announcement from Sir Hope that nothing would induce the Duke of Cambridge to consent to our plan. However, at last we agreed on something.

The point was that Storks and I wanted to have nothing from the Horse Guards but 150 British artillery men, and that the colony should provide for the rest armed police. But the Horse Guards said that British troops could not stand sentry in the tropics, therefore that if we had 150 white artillery with guns, magazine, &c., we must have 150 black troops to stand sentry over all this, and then the black troops would also have to stand sentry over themselves, and that this would require another 150 black troops, 300 in all. Then the question was how and where to get these black troops. The Horse Guards wanted *not* to reduce a Ceylon coloured regiment and use that ; Storks wanted to reduce it and save money. Indian regiments had not enough white officers, the Ceylon regiment could not keep up its privates, and so on. However, at last we settled to hire a regiment from the Indian Government. Of course *I* did not care where it came from so long as we got it, having only to take care that faith was kept with the colony, a pledge having been made that it should have so many men for such a sum of money.

Well, this being our report, we all met. The Duke of Cambridge's manner is uncommonly taking and pleasant and frank. But somehow or other he had a jolly big-dog way of blurting out things that made me inclined to laugh, and I felt that if there were not a desk between him and me I should get into a scrape.

The question arose, and the Horse Guards were to tell us, what amount of troops were *necessary*. I should have meant by this, what amount of troops were wanted to give the colony such protection from mobs, neighbours pirates, &c., in time of war as we undertook to give. But the Horse Guards never seemed for a moment to entertain this view, their single idea was, what sentries were necessary, and how many men were necessary to give these sentries five nights in bed out of six. . . .

This [a proposal of Sir J. Pakington's] entirely threw over poor Storks (whose face visibly lengthened), and I must say H.R.H. saw it like a shot, and got up from his seat: 'Ah, ah ! that'll do capitally. Just put that into writing,' and then went over to Pakington as if he was going to stand over him with his fist till he had done it. I fairly laughed (with my face I mean) this time, and as he was now above the box which screened me he caught it, and I thought I was in a scrape. Not a bit. 'Ah, I see Sir Frederic smiles, but *I* always think there's nothing like black and white.'

And so it was all put down, and the last I heard from Storks as we broke up at the door was: 'And here we are, just where we were before.' True enough perhaps for him; for the Duke of Cambridge had done him. But the rest of the world knew where they were, and now we shall have to battle it out with the colony. I hope my view on that head will be found to hold water. If not, I shall have to draw as long a face as he does.

To the Rev. Father Newman.

18 Radnor Place: December 3, 1868.

My dear Newman,—I put off answering your letter till I heard from Doyle. I have not yet got through Gladstone's autobiography, nor some other things which I began with hopes that are disappointed. Of course, as you say, some of his friends think it injudicious, and I am not sure that it is not injudicious on that very account. One great weight which Gladstone has to carry in the political race is a *character* for want of judgment; and every addition to that is an impediment.

I am prepared to find that, if it is not injudicious, it is an act of the same kind as the Maynooth secession from Sir Robert Peel—*i.e.* a manifesto or manifestation to be appealed to hereafter, when he moves on the English establishment, as he now appeals to the Maynooth move in explanation of his policy towards the Irish establishment.

Ever yours affectionately,

F. ROGERS.

To Miss S. Rogers.

18 Radnor Place: December 20, 1868.

I like my chief[7] very much. He is very pleasant and friendly, and I think will not meddle beyond what is required to keep us clear of political slips. G. told you of what Cardwell said, that he had told Lord G. that with him at the head

---

[7] Lord Granville. Mr. Disraeli resigned early in December after the General Election of November 1868, and Mr. Gladstone became Prime Minister. Lord Granville was at the Colonial Office till Lord Clarendon's death in 1870, when he moved to the Foreign Office.

and me as the 'motive power,' the office could not go wrong ; and then when I acknowledged the compliment said, ' Oh, it is just the truth.'

I am just making a general reform as to my own business, a horizontal instead of vertical section of the business, so that I shall have all the top, and others all the bottom (this is a rude way of saying it) instead of dividing the world between us : Asia to me and Africa to Sandford. . . .

Sandford * I do not see much, but like what I see. He is a good Churchman, which I am uncommonly glad of, and seems to be going steadily at his work in a businesslike painstaking way. He meets my reform half way, though rather depressing his position, and with perfect pleasantness.

There is no political speculation that I hear. Gladstone is so strong that there is not much room for speculation. The younger Radicals I imagine are very angry at not having a better share in the places. You see they have all been pushed into second-rate places, Forster, Ayrton, Stanfield, Bruce and Childers being the only men who get a real lift. *They* are men who are both regular ' county families,' and steady-going fellows with no turn for revolution. Egerton (the late Conservative Under-Secretary of the F. O.) was loud in his praise of the way in which they had helped the incoming Conservatives with information, each in the department which he had managed, to transact their business at starting, really anxious, not for party advantage, but for the proper transaction of the business of the country. On the whole I think the Radical element is depressed to the utmost limit of prudence. Page Wood's appointment is of course excellent.

To Right Honourable W. E. Gladstone.

Colonial Office : January 8, 1869.

My dear Gladstone,—There is nothing in Church's reasons to cause ' permanent uneasiness ' except so far as they indicate that he is not getting better of his most unreasonable habit of declining everything.

---

* Mr. (afterwards Lord) Sandford was then Assistant Under-Secretary for the Colonies.

It seems, from a letter that I got from him this morning, that when he wrote his Irish Church articles he made up his mind that he would not be the better for them, and (in a spirit which other people have acted on within the last thirty years and got called crotchety for their pains) determined that if you came into power, one of your first acts should not be to give him anything. He said the kindness of your letter shook him greatly, and that he never refused anything with so much regret, but that he felt after all that there was no real reason for changing his decision, and was only vexed at the appearance of repelling a kindness, and the impossibility of explaining to you.

It appears to me to the last degree unreasonable, and I half feel that I myself as his friend owe you an apology. For if every honest man is to act on his principle, how are you possibly to fill the high places of the Church except with place-hunters?

Yours very sincerely,
FREDERIC ROGERS.

To Lady Rogers.

June 19, 1869.

My dear Mother,—I don't know that I have anything special to say, and sit down because I have a few minutes to spare.

Our Foreign Office party went off very splendidly. It is certainly a royal sight. The staircase, which my sisters will remember, well lighted and filled with finely dressed people going up and down was magnificent, like some great Paul Veronese painting alive, only that the dresses are all of such light colours. We always meet the same friends at these places, Hollands, Forsters, Mowbrays, Palmers, and generally politicals. Forster was full of praises of the speech of the Bishop of Peterborough,[9] never had such a treat in his life; he enjoys a good cut and thrust, on whichever side it comes, which I like in him. I praised Thirlwall's speech (St. Davids). He said yes, but he did not half like to see a Bishop deserting

---

[9] Bishop Magee—against the Bill for the Disestablishment of the Irish Church.

his position and his order. He certainly has a great, grim allowance of an adversary's merits which is amusing.

Lord Granville, of course, was somewhat disgusted with the mess Bright had got them into, said it would lose some votes, and told me what he himself was going to say with some fun.[1] Lord Salisbury's interruption was curiously happy (as a hit); it exactly put into his mouth what was the very next thing he was going to say. I thought his plan of (I suppose) snubbing Bright's ungentlemanliness, by appropriating the attack as one on *himself* as well as the other Lords ('unwisdom' and 'childish tinkering'), was very like him. I wonder whether John Bright saw the snub. . . .

To Lady Rogers.

18 Radnor Place : November 1869.

My dear Mother,— . . . I don't know that I have much to say to amuse you on your sick-bed. I expect we shall have some fighting to do in the Parliament about the colonies next February and wish we had some one stronger in the Commons than Monsell. However, we have Gladstone well with us: and he is, of course, a host.

Just now we are rather perplexed by an insurrection in the Red River (Hudson's Bay Territory), which comes just at an unlucky moment, as the whole transfer of that great territory to Canada was on the point of taking place.

The official news came here in a long (cypher) telegram on Friday while Macdonald [2] (who is for the moment in charge

---

[1] At a meeting in Birmingham on June 14, 1869 about the Irish Church Bill, then before the Lords, a letter was read from Mr. Bright (then President of the Board of Trade) in which he reflected on the capacity of the House of Lords, and hinted that if they delayed the passing of the Bill, people might be led to inquire what was the 'special value' of the House of Lords as part of the Constitution. Even his own party felt that such a letter from a Cabinet Minister was, to say the least, indiscreet. A discussion was raised in both Houses on June 18. Mr. Gladstone in his reply took occasion to say that he had himself steadily discouraged public meetings on the subject then before Parliament, and that each branch of the Legislature might justly feel jealous of any attempt to interfere with its liberty of discussion.

[2] The late Reginald Somerled Macdonald, well known as an explorer of the High Alps. He was then a clerk in the Colonial Office, and private secretary to Sir F. Rogers.

of the key or *de*cypher as it is called) and Merivale were dining here. As we have been worried by all sorts of rubbish, Fenian threats, murder of Prince Arthur, and so on, Macdonald was full of zeal about starting off at once to decypher it, leaving his dessert behind him, and I was so affected by his flyaway rodomontading ways that for a moment I was going to let him go, when Merivale grimly grumbled to the rest of the company, who, of course, were waiting the result, 'All this is bluster and brag, you know.' This restored my presence of mind and I told Macdonald that he need not hurry himself. He says, if it had been at Stowe or Chandos House he would have had to be off in a jiffy. When I went to bed, however, I was a little fidgety and was rather reassured by receiving a note from Macdonald at breakfast time to say it was only this insurrection which he had heard of long ago. Meantime, of course, it gives us a little trouble, framing a proclamation and firing it off by cable, discussing with the Agent of the Canadian Government, who may not like to take over the property with the tenants in such a state, and so on.

Edward will remember a despatch I drafted at Blachford to turn the flank of some fellows who are trying to set up an anti-Downing Street Colonial Conference. It seems to have answered its purpose, for I hear they complain that till that despatch went round they got nothing but favourable answers, and now they get nothing but unfavourable. They are, as may be seen by the papers, agitating to the best of their powers, but I think we shall beat them. . . .

I am afraid the Archbishop of Canterbury [3] is dying, and of course every one is speculating on his successor. . . . Lord Granville was asking me whom I thought the best man ; I said (or at least wrote after consideration) Claughton. But, of course, he is out of the question as being a Tory Bishop.

As times go I should not be ill pleased with Jacobson whom I have heard mentioned. Lord G.'s criticism on *him* is that he is a man who is always looking as if he was going to say something uncommonly shrewd, but it never comes. Edward will probably tell you that it is a whimsically good picture of him.

[3] Archbishop Tait. He recovered and lived nearly fourteen years longer.

I should doubt whether Wilberforce would be allowed to have it, nor should I myself be exceedingly pleased at the appointment.

To Miss Rogers.

Walmer Castle : September 19, 1869.

My dear Kate,—Here I am, as you see : very pleasantly housed and on the mend. I am getting stronger, though not very fast. . . .

The house is a strange place, a Henry the Eighth fortification ; four round corner towers, with a moat round them turned into garden, and in the middle a central tower with a deep passage almost amounting to a small moat, but now turned into passage. The great round tower is the habitable part of the house with certain additions and subtractions, and the turnings of the passages and shapes of the rooms are beyond understanding. I give you a general plan of our bedroom and dressing-room. . . . The corner towers are batteries and make an extremely pleasant terrace overlooking the sea and Goodwin Sands, with swarms of vessels : I counted upwards of 100, Lord Granville thought there must be 150 in sight. Our party is : Lord Granville himself, who is full of talk and anecdote ; Lady Granville, friendly and pleasant ; her mother, Mrs. Campbell of Islay, and Meade ; so that we spend our time agreeably. It is a pleasant run of anecdotes which are characteristic, told with great freedom, and pleasanter perhaps from the persons they relate to than they would be as a mere matter of humour or oddity. I remember two about his own family, *i.e.* his mother. His father, he said, with all his experience, was to the last shy and silent, but very fond of society. His mother cared little about society but was perfectly prompt and self-possessed, and he had one or two stories of her readiness from third persons who were by. A lady came to one of her Paris parties, and she said to her neighbour, ' I know that woman, but I never invited her here.' The lady approached and the friend wondered what would happen ; when Lady Granville received her with the most affable and cordial ' Enchantée de vous voir ici, madame, invitée ou non invitée.'

She had large parties, omnium gatherum, and small special parties, principally French. A pushing lady attacked her at the omnium gatherum, and told her that she lived herself so much among the French that she hoped Lady G. would invite her to one of her small parties. Lady G.'s answer was prompt, compact, but in the most affectionate cadence—'No, *dearest* Mrs.——.' The two together amused me. And last night we had a regular string of Cabinet and other stories, just of that kind of calibre, perhaps scarcely capable of retailing but very pleasant to hear run off.

Yesterday we drove over to Sir Walter James's, Bettishanger, pretty gardens &c.; to-day we are to walk to Deal Castle (if a heavy shower does not prevent us). The country has some tolerably pretty spots on the north but is generally very dull; to the S., *i.e.* towards Dover, it is evidently better. I must finish.

Ever yours affectionately,
F. R.

To Miss Rogers.

Colonial Office: May 5, 1870.

As you see by the 'Times,' we are for the moment in a state of satisfaction as to our Red River difficulty.[1]

Lord Granville's statement seems to me very good and judicious. The rocks ahead are connected with the murder of Scott by Riel. I do not understand how Riel fails to see that he is liable to be tried for his life for that little transaction. Nor do I see how the Government can avoid so trying him if it once gets its hand on the reins. If this breaks upon him he must either (1) ask an amnesty, (2) oppose our troops while they are clambering and wading their way through the lake country, (3) run away; and in the two last cases he will have to consider whether it would be more

---

[1] After the Hudson's Bay Territory was transferred to Canada, Louis Riel headed an insurrection of the Red River Settlement (now Manitoba), seized Fort Garry and claimed that the Settlement should be separate and independent. A successful expedition was led in August 1870, by Colonel (now F. M. Lord) Wolseley, against the insurgents, who submitted quietly.

satisfactory to him, like the Greek brigands, to finish off by murdering a few of his opponents.

From all we hear, no *Canadian* Ministry would dare to give an amnesty, and if the question rises it will rise on the entry of our troops, under *Imperial authority*, *i.e.* it will fall on Sir J. Young as an Imperial officer to settle it, and he will ask us.

What would be most satisfactory in the abstract would be to hang him. What would be most for the future peace of the country would be that he should run off with such Hudson Bay furs and other valuables as he can lay his hands upon.

I saw a man yesterday who saw Scott shot (from a distance) and repeated all the horrors of his being alive for some hours after being nailed up in his coffin, and then the coffin being opened and his being despatched.

I breakfasted the day before yesterday with Lord Granville to discuss the difficulties of the expedition with Laurence Oliphant .... who on the strength of having been in the neighbourhood (at Lake Erie) thinks himself capable of advising everybody. The croakers are rather tiresome. Luckily Lord G. has a laudable impassibility to croak when he is once in for it.

Sir John Mitchell, late commander-in-chief, is sending us long memoranda to show that the route is impracticable, to which the answers are: 1. that Canada has spent 100,000*l*. in improving it since he saw it; 2. that at any rate it was not impracticable to Annie Colvile,[5] who did it in its worst state. ....

---

[5] Wife of his brother-in-law, Mr. Eden Colvile, who was Governor of the Red River Settlement from 1849 to 1852. Mr. Colvile's district included Vancouver Island on the other side of the Rocky Mountains, and in one visit to Vancouver he spent four months in getting there, travelling every day and all day by the lakes, with portages, and down the Frazer River, with no companions but the Indian canoe-men. On the return journey he took a shorter route (with more snow-shoe travelling over the mountains, and less canoe) which occupied *only* three months. He had arranged to meet Mrs. Colvile at Fort Garry, in the Red River Settlement, and she was to start from Montreal on a given day. They came into Fort Garry from opposite directions on the same afternoon.

To Miss Rogers.
September 25, 1870.

I saw Monsell fresh from France. He is a devoted admirer of Trochu, who, he says, is a religious Breton of the Montalembert school, a determined, honest, first-rate man. He had seen him when he went through Paris early in August. He says what struck him was the fixed expression of sadness which never left his countenance or changed in the least, like stone, though he was speaking with great eloquence and animation. It was a long time before the Emperor's Government could make up its mind to employ him, and only in extremity. Till the 'personal government' was gone he was most desponding, now (he implied) he felt that at least France was free to exert herself.

You see that Lord Lyons has brought the King of Prussia and Favre together, which is a step.

To Lady Rogers.
Binsted Wyck: " October 16, 1870.

My dear Mother,—You will like to see the enclosed. Please to send it back. I have written something for his Lordship on the bombardment, rather too rhetorical, and wanting to be chastised before it is sent, if it is capable of being sent to Bismarck, and I am waiting to see what comes of it.[7] I expect it may be useful in furnishing some phrases or single thoughts, but that it is too undiplomatic to be capable of use bodily. I have not got hold of the Foreign Office slang or the diplomatic proprieties. I am afraid he is rather bad with his gout. His last letter to me ended ' Yours goutily, G.'

I am glad to be in relations with him again—of course, this is all the deepest of secrets.

My draft hinged on the consideration that as bombardment had been useless at Strasburg it would be wanton in Paris, and therefore a blot on an otherwise noble history (that

---

[6] He was staying with Mr. Wickham, the present M.P. for East Hants.

[7] He had been asked by Lord Granville (now Foreign Minister) to draft suggestions for a despatch from the English Government to the Prussian deprecating a bombardment of Paris.

of the present war) and of course a spring of inextinguishable hatred between France and Germany for generations. . . .

This is a very pretty place, and our host and hostess are so pleasant that it is a particularly agreeable visit. . . . The features of the country are broadish valleys with coombes running into them, at the head of one of which and on the hill the house is placed—one of those houses that have grown up like Blachford, but into a shape more according to modern taste, with gables and oriel windows, with a terrace in front and water meadows, which form the two sides of the coombe below, and a sweep of distance with a front ground of woody slopes beyond. The meadow, fringed with wood, on which I am looking, has a good deal the look of an 'alp,' one of those little pastures which you find in Switzerland ; and, to give it more of a Swiss taste, he has put one or two bells on his cows, which he says they like very much, and which he has been extremely proud to find useful, as in a foggy morning and on a great irregular zigzag run of meadow it helps the dairyman to find out where they are. We are surrounded by friends, Rickards and Palmer, and I think others within a few miles. . . .

I intend, if as I suppose I am asked, to dine with the Lord Mayor on November 9 to hear what Gladstone says. I suppose he will say something, and it will be a very goodly dinner.

Ever yours affectionately,
F. R.

To Lady Rogers.
October 21, 1870.

What a mess those Frenchmen are making of it ! I must say that, though I keenly desire peace, I find it impossible to have much sympathy with such a set of vapourers as those at the head of affairs or those to whose silly vanity the leaders are obliged to pander. I do most heartily sympathise with and pity the poor peasantry who have to pay for it all. Georgie was reading me yesterday a long letter from a French lady in Sedan, sister of the Protestant minister there, which was full of pathos. But one is used to the horrors, and I think what touched me almost most of all was the grief of a poor peasant woman who was bringing her pet cow to be butchered. 'Oh! madame, la pauvre bête, elle s'est opposée, elle ne le comprend pas, et puis je l'avais élevée de la mère et elle ne connait que moi. Ah, mon Dieu, quel malheur, tout ! ils prennent tout ! il faudra donc mourir de faim !' This was said to the writer, Mlle. Gulden, who is nursing the wounded, relieving the starving, and so on. She is full of gratitude for what the English are doing, in money or otherwise ; says the Prussians are individually well behaved and steady, some officers 'tout ce qu'il y a de plus poli et convenable,' but the system and Governor frightfully grinding and hard. One Prussian officer who calls on them (the Guldens), and often spends the evening with them, 'apporte lui-même de l'argent aux pauvres incendiés de ce malheureux Bazeilles.'

She says she found some of the poor people of Bazeilles paid to look after the Bavarian wounded and doing it with the greatest kindness, not charging their miseries on the soldiers, but saying 'c'est tout Bismarck.'

And in their case it was the soldiers, Bavarians, who she says are not bad in themselves, but after battle ' n'ont ni frein ni loi.' It is a remarkable letter, so strangely just and measured, and accepting what has passed as a judgment on them all for their lying, luxury, and frivolity.

I should like to know whether she is an example of the old Huguenots. Sedan, you remember, was the Duke of Bouillon's headquarters and of course the great Protestant stronghold.

Ever yours affectionately,
F. R.

To Lady Rogers.

Walmer Castle : October 31, 1870.

My dear Mother,—We came down in the train with a Prussian attaché, or Secretary of Legation, Count Kuserow, who was bound, like ourselves, to the Castle, and is staying here with us. The rest of the party are : Mr. Fullerton (husband of Lady Georgina Fullerton, the novelist, Lord Granville's sister) and a Mr. Wetherall—Roman Catholic like

Fullerton, and a clever man—a clerk in the War Office, and of the Döllinger and Acton school; editor or something of the kind of the Roman Catholic Anti-ultramontane Review which the Pope at one time censured.

The Prussian is a Prussian all over: civil, self-satisfied, correct, continuous in his conversation, speaking English correctly and with ease—but *tant soit peu* heavy. Of course, he precludes a good many subjects; but yesterday morning, when he was out of the way, Lord Granville began about the war. He said that he had more hope of peace than the newspapers, though, of course, not sanguine; that when both Governments desired it there was always hope that it would come, and that both did desire it now. He observed that it was all very well to talk of England going for nothing, but that here we had all the neutrals ready to do what we liked, France of course anxious, and Prussia, after all its cries against neutral mediation, not ill pleased that we should come forward. He said he heard from surgeons and others that the German army had had quite enough of it and wanted peace. (And Herbert of the C.O. told me that a sister of his passing through Germany found people also of that mind. All cried out for peace, and told her that we (the English) did not know what they had suffered in loss of lives.) They evidently hide the amount of loss. Kuscrow implied that Bernstorff had no relatives lost, but Lord G. was down on him at once with a nephew here and a wife's cousin there, and other family losses. And it must be so. There is a good hope that it will sicken them.

He says Bismarck hates us as a centre of constitutionalism, and affects to depreciate us as powerless—'an old red rag.'

Lord G. evidently has no love for the Prussians, and is a little inclined to make the best of the French—always except the Duc de Grammont.

I have been in the habit of defending the French on the ground of Grammont's volunteer to Lord Lyons of a written declaration that if so and so were done 'tout l'incident est terminé.' But he, Lord G., quotes Grammont as saying that there were twenty ways out of it, but that Le Bœuf would have the war, declaring that he was ready. So Grammont upset the coach.

The Empress seems to have said to Lord Cowley that it was due to the weakness of the Emperor—*i.e.* this not insisting on his own opinion, which was in favour of peace. She added, ' I admit that I was too warlike. . . .'

I was amused at a saying of old Brunnow, the Russian Ambassador. He observed to Lord G. that Thiers had gone round to all the neutrals, just so as to avoid the dangers of the siege. Lord G. said the same thought had passed his own mind, but that he had dismissed it as improper and unjust. ' Moi pas,' Brunnow replied ; then he added : ' Moi, j'aurais fait autant ' (pause). ' Il n'est pas donné à tout le monde d'être héros ' (pause). ' Il y avait Régulus.' To appreciate it you should know the look of the man—a great, big, old, stumping mountain—with a great sallow ponderous face, but a dry twinkle in his eye, which lighted up at the whimsicality of going back to some 300 B.C. to look for a man to whom it had been given to be a hero.

G. was amused at a little passage of arms between Lord Granville and Kuserow. She, Lady Granville, and Kuserow, were sitting talking at one end of the room after dark, and Lord Granville was working in the other corner, when they heard him say in his most velvety voice, ' I see that 30,000 rifles and 200,000 cartridges are being shipped in the United States for France.' (Of course, you know that Bismarck is getting up a feeling in Germany against England for allowing the export of arms &c., in which they are quite wrong, as our doings are consistent with international law, and just like what Prussia did for Russia during the Crimea.) Kuserow said, ' I hope we shall catch them before they reach France ' (pause) ; then Lord G., ' I wonder when you intend to make a remonstrance against it.' Kuserow then took up the gauntlet and began explaining somehow that there were obligations between us and Prussia which did not exist with the United States (pause again) ; then Lord Granville, silkier than ever, ' What I don't quite understand is when you changed your minds.' The Prussian was quick enough to catch his meaning, laughed, and said, 'Ah! you mean about the Crimea,' and shut up.

He—Kuserow—is a great Bismarckian, and apparently considers that there is to be a remodification of German parties, Bismarck (as I infer) giving up the old 'Specific Prussian' party, as it is called there (the 'Chauvins' of France, and 'Codini' of Italy), who are for mere Prussian objects and unmitigated absolutism, and placing himself at the head of what we should call a 'Liberal-Conservative' party, with German (as distinct from Prussian) objects. All I can say is that, if his memoirs are true (which Kuserow says they are in the main), it will be a considerable change.

He dropped one thing, which seemed as if he expected an arrangement between Prussia and Russia embracing Constantinople. Dawdling about on Sunday, he picked up a volume of Macaulay's Essays, in which he described the Parisians at the entry of the Allies in 1814, in a way which was a wonderfully severe and accurate anticipation of their behaviour now. Presently he came up again : 'I am falling on one remarkable thing after another. I find what I never knew before' (he had taken up Cobden's political writings) 'that Cobden advocated abandoning Constantinople to Russia,' and he proceeded to announce that he should buy the book.

An agreement to that purpose between Prussia and Russia is, as I suppose you know, what France threatens us with in case we neglect to help her.

Lord Granville showed me a letter from Count d'Haussonville sending most warm thanks for Colonel Loyd Lindsay's 20,000*l.*, but pouring scorn on our diplomatists (English) and Government for their inaction : 'On rit d'eux.' They think they can flout us into folly, as they would be able to flout one another.

There, it is getting to luncheon time, and my eyes are complaining. We stay here till to-morrow, when Lord and Lady Granville go up to town themselves for a fortnight.

Ever yours affectionately,
F. R.

P.S.—When Lord Canning went to India, he dined with Lord Ellenborough to be coached. Lord Ellenborough said he would find the work unremitting. 'Most men,' he said, 'grow a beard when they go to a hot climate; I did not, and I found my practice valuable, for while I was shaving was the only time I had to throw my mind on the whole of India.' He declared that he had never read over a despatch which he had written except that which was a reply to the despatch recalling him. Lord Granville asked the Prussian which they thought the best general, Prince Frederick Charles or the Crown Prince. He said that no one gave the Crown Prince credit for military ability till after the Danish war; that he then greatly interested himself in the soldiers, went about among them, and so on, and then got a command and credit in the Austrian campaign; but he said (cautiously and justly) that you could not judge which was best till you set them to manœuvre troops without a *chef d'état* at their elbow. At present each has close to him one of the best generals in the Prussian army.

To Lady Rogers.

18 Radnor Place : December 14, 1870.

My dear Mother,—We had a pleasant dinner party yesterday. Doyle was very amusing: one story is worth repeating.

Talbot, the head of Keble College, is a very good scholar, but a bad driver. The other day he took out Prince Hassan, the son of the Khedive (as they call him now), who is getting an Oxford education to fit him for the Pachalik at Cairo— and upset him into a ditch. The next day, driving out again, he caught up Liddon taking his constitutional, and pulled up to ask him to take a seat. Liddon also pulled up, and replied, 'What! intendest thou to kill me as thou killedst that Egyptian yesterday?'

I got into a great fight right and left about Gambetta, whom I believe to be a most abominable impostor. To prove him a great man, one of the company told the story that when he was a boy his father sent him to a Jesuit school, he declaring that if he was sent he would put his eyes out.

U

He was sent, and before long the tutor wrote to his father that the boy was very ill, and must be looked to. When the father came, he found that the boy had put out, by some means or other, one eye, and announced that if he were not taken away he would put out the other, on which the father yielded.

It seems that he was as little able to take care of himself then as he is to take care of France now, and that what he should have done to himself he is doing to France. It has lost one eye, and he is putting out the other.

The Foreign Office are, I am afraid, in anxiety about this Luxemburg business. It seems to me very ugly, not so much on account of Luxemburg, which does not signify to us, as from the menacing way in which Prussia announces her intention. It seems as much as to say, 'We are determined to quarrel with you; Russia has given you a kick, and somehow or other you have managed to satisfy yourself with a half apology; take this from us; and if this kick is not sufficient, we will try another.'

I hear from a German by extraction, who has lately been through Germany, that the nation is terribly tired of the war. This ought to be all in favour of peace.

Ever yours affectionately,
FREDERIC ROGERS.

To Lady Rogers.

18 Radnor Place: January 12, 1871.

My dear Mother,—Yesterday I had an interesting afternoon with the Stanleys, who asked Georgie and myself to meet Père Hyacinthe at tea, half-past five. There was no one but him, so we had a real talk instead of just being introduced and saying some *banalités*. The defect of the proceeding was that I found myself talking instead of listening, which, though good exercise in French, was not what I wanted; but somehow or other I found myself in for it. I think the Père was rather tired of being trotted out. Anyhow they began on Newman, whom he had just been visiting, and whom, I think, he wanted to understand. That set me off, and Stanley kept putting things in that made me more and more go on. What I now think he wanted to judge of was how far Newman would be prepared to join in any manifesto against Infallibility (not that he so put it), and Stanley wanted so to turn the conversation as to illustrate that point. He had made up his mind that Newman would not take a leading part in any such move, whatever he might think, and could not have been encouraged by what I told him of Newman's almost superstitious desire (as it used to be) to obey authority implicitly when it would speak out.

However, at last he began to talk himself about the Infallibility—the *dogme* as they call it—and the Council. He said that the Council originally had passed a decree condemning all Protestants as unbelievers, deists, atheists, and everything else that is bad (which I imagine the Pope does annually), and that they would not hear with patience, and hardly hear at all, Strossmayer the great liberal Archbishop on the other side, almost hooting him. But that Baron Arnim, the Prussian Minister, asked what he was to do if this were passed and published. The Prussian Government wrote back, Leave Rome, in that case, at once. This he told the Pope, and the decree (or whatever they call it) was heard no more of.

He thought the war was in favour of Infallibility; that if men had had nothing else to think of, they would have thought of that, and there would have been discussions taking place, and opinions settled while the questions were fresh and people's minds open. But he thinks that in a year it will be an old story and people will be reconciled to the *status quo*, *i.e.* to the new doctrine as established.

He seemed to expect nothing from the Bishops (except perhaps Strossmayer), not a great deal from the clergy, but an opposition widespread but more or less what he called *sourde* among the laity, and a disbelief in it wider than the opposition, what he called a *schisme latent*.

He did not speak of the war, but I hear he told the Stanleys (with whom he is living) that the exasperation in France was demoralising. He said he had received a letter from a *moderate* man, who expressed his hopes that the King of Prussia would be assassinated.

He is rather a short man, broadly made, with a broad but even-cut face, with a well-proportioned, powerful look, dark hair with a touch of grey, eye dark and intelligent rather than thoughtful or piercing, and a fresh healthy colour—rather what I should call an intelligent Belgian physiognomy than a French one.

There was no touch of vapouring or pretence, nothing of the platform or showy conversationalist. . . . .

Ever yours affectionately,
FREDERIC ROGERS.

To Miss Rogers.

18 Radnor Place : January 30, 1871.

I do not know that I have much that is cheerful to tell you, except what you see in the papers, which is certainly a very great relief. What the 15th of February is to produce for France, God knows. Peace I take it for granted—a republic, I suppose, but under whom ? Never I suppose was a great nation called on to pronounce on its own fate with so little notion whom it could trust, or whom it ought to place in the saddle. I cannot imagine their adhering to Gambetta, or he to them. It becomes material to ask now, what was the 'pact with death' to which he told us he was party. It seems at first sight that Death will have a right to consider himself ill-treated and thrown over.

I am very glad the Prussians do not enter Paris ; there is, I will not say a generosity, but an absence of ungenerosity about it which is a shade better than I expected : no doubt, they are themselves too anxious for peace to risk driving Favre and Trochu further into a corner.

You see Mozley is Regius Professor of Divinity. Gladstone sent for me to talk about it, and asked me what I thought of M.'s prospects as a Professor. Then he began on me about my retirement. 'Surely you are not going to' etc., 'having made for yourself such a position as you have,' and then he said that all my chiefs spoke so highly etc., and when I afterwards used the phrase that they had all been 'very kind to me,' he said in a kind of ' Marry, come up ' way, 'I should think so.'

I keep thinking that in eleven hours (it is now 1 P.M.) I shall be entitled to retire on a pension.

W. Froude is up and down here, about an Admiralty commission on which he is sitting. It is to discuss, as far as I see, ship-building in general, shapes, armour, sizes, etc. etc. He seems to like it much and says that the sailors and men of science of whom it is composed work well together. It is to be hoped they will keep us straight, and make our ditch impassable to Prussians or any one else.

Ever yours affectionately,

F. R.

To the Rev. R. W. Church.

18 Radnor Place : February 1, 1871.

Gladstone said to me of you, ' His refusal of the Worcester Canonry was from a most generous feeling, but it was very unwise.' Of course I am aware that it was not a question of what is called 'wisdom,' and I more entered into your feelings about that refusal than, I think, about any other. But putting it together with what had just passed, it made me understand what old placemongers say, that it is such a step to have something that is worth giving away. The Worcester Canonry *a valu* the Professorship to Mozley. You remember the old Cardinal who, with no recommendation, had had all the ' best ' things of the Roman Church, and told some one who wanted an explanation, that he had never spoken evil of anybody and never refused anything.

So we have come to the opening of the last Act at Paris. I suppose the revocation by the Paris Government of the delegation to its Bordeaux offshoot is required by Bismarck. But what will it lead to? Gambetta will scarcely consent to be left *en l'air*. And if not, shall we have peace in the North between Germany and what Germany considers the lawful Government, and fighting *in esse* or *posse* between Germany and what Germany considers in the South an unauthorised collection of brigands? Or will the National Convention really meet and make peace?

How the history of parties and countries in the present day illustrates the way in which the personal qualities of bodies of men bring their own rewards and punishments with them, by guiding them in the choice of their guides. The French and the Conservatives desire to be deceived and to say what it is pleasant to say, to think what it is pleasant to think, and to hear what it is pleasant to hear, and are a prey to Gambetta and Disraeli. .... And yet has not the genuine enthusiasm of the Italians for each other's freedom produced on the whole a degree of respectability in the government which was hardly to be expected from men whose *raison d'être* was (from one point of view) to take what did not belong to them?

To Miss Rogers.

March 13, 1871.

Perhaps you saw that some of Cook's excursionists were caught at Paris. Miss —— was one of them, and after the massacre thought it high time to make off, so with a kind of English hobbledehoy who was attached to her (as a companion, not a lover) she took her bag and posted off to the railway station.

They met a lot of insurgent Nationals marching along the *trottoir*, who called out *Chaussée, Chaussée*, but the English youth, not understanding that he was expected to go into the gutter, held on his way. On this the front fellows brought down their bayonets upon him, to which action, without yielding ground, he replied by the ebullition ' I say, mister, don't you go poking at me.' Something, I suppose (and can easily conceive), in his manner set the Nationals in a violent fit of laughter, and they let him have his way. I call this maintaining the character of England in every sense of the phrase.

To Miss Rogers.

Athenæum Club: May 19, 1871.

My dear Kate,—Here I am half-way home, after having finally quitted my room in Downing Street. It has been an odd feeling of pain and pleasure. It is a real pleasure to be free, and a real pleasure to be so kindly parted with. I have either sought or been sought by nearly all the members of the Office, and have heard a complimentary amount of regrets. The packing up of books and burning papers and handing over of memoranda is a dismal kind of ceremony, and parting with work in which I have been for so long—I may almost say exclusively—occupied, and with men with whom I have contracted such friendly relations—now of so many years' standing—is pathetic, so that just at present the retrospective and rather sad side is uppermost. And when I feel that tomorrow I shall wake to a holiday, the thought suggests itself 'And what shall I do with it?'

However, I shall be a good deal surprised if that lasts long.

Work for the last two or three days I have really had none, but the succession of interviews—at first rather reviving—has got a little tiring, and I feel as if I could not set my mind to considering whether I have anything worth telling. I incline to think I have not.

Ever yours affectionately,
FREDERIC ROGERS.

In 1871, at the age of sixty, he resigned his post and retired on a pension. It is believed that Lord Granville particularly desired him to fill the post of Under-Secretary for Foreign Affairs. But he did not wish any longer to continue the heavy strain of official work, a strain which he had felt the more from the constant weakness of his eyes, and he held to his purpose of taking his well-earned rest in country life. It happened too that at this time his mother died, and this made him the more anxious to settle down at Blachford and carry on the management of the property which had been hers since his father's death.

At this point, when he finally severed his long connexion with colonial administration, a brief account of colonial history as it came before him, extracted from notes of autobiography which he left, will be useful both to indicate the opinions which he entertained and to explain some of the letters which follow.

'The matters which come before the Colonial Office are by the nature of the case in great part official details and controversies even of the most petty kind It is, of course, a great thing that in all these controversies, whether between private persons and officials, or among officials themselves, the Colonial Office should maintain a reputation for justice, as an accessible Court of Appeal. And this gives interest to small cases. And it is more interesting, though more rare, to watch the development of principles. Two such I should particularly note as having established themselves during my acquaintance with the Colonial Office—colonial self-government, and the emancipation of the colonial Churches.

'Fifty years [a] ago the colonies were divided in general into two classes—Crown colonies, in which the Crown was almost absolute, and colonies having representative institutions, that is to say, colonies in which money could not be granted or laws passed without the consent of an elected assembly. The executive government was in all cases alike composed of permanent officers appointed by the Crown.

'To this limitation of the colonists' power the Canadians first objected, and it was determined in Canada and the other N. American colonies to establish what is called responsible government, under which the executive government is composed of persons who command the confidence of the local legislature. This is, of course, the English Constitution —the Governor, like the Queen, being obliged (except in a few matters of Imperial interest) to endorse the action of his Ministry, and being unable to exercise any authority without them. The full extent of the principle thus conceded was not at once understood, nor did it extend beyond N. America: for the establishment of such institutions in the West Indies (where certain representative institutions existed) would have been ruinous, and Australia was as yet comparatively unimportant.

'But wherever there was a vigorous and heterogeneous white population, a demand arose, which it would have been impossible, if it had been advisable, to resist, for this form of government, which, as in America, unavoidably and rapidly developed into practical independence : the Governor (the only remaining link between the colony and the mother country) being in essentials little more than the ambassador

[a] This was written about 1885.

of a great State to a weaker, with which it is on terms of close alliance, and which relies on the protection of the more powerful.

'On the other hand the mother country, while abandoning all local authority, soon began to decline the responsibility of local defence, and has withdrawn her troops from British North America, Australia, New Zealand and the Cape Colony. This great establishment of colonial independence cannot (as I think) be justly or wisely or possibly arrested.

'Of the growth of the Australian colonies, and of their independence consequent on that growth, I had been witness at the Emigration Office. During the fourteen years I had been in that Office, I had been concerned with my colleagues in sending out upwards of half a million emigrants to Australia and New Zealand. When I joined (in 1846) the population of New South Wales, including the then unimportant district of Port Philip, was considerably under 200,000. Before I left the Emigration Office (in 1861) it had risen to nearly 800,000. Its wealth had increased *pari passu* and so had its independence. The Australian colonies had received responsible government, had enacted their own constitutions, and, excepting that they were not entitled to repeal Imperial statutes expressly intended to apply to them, had become free from all practical interference with their legislature. Of this constitutional progress (extending to all the Australian colonies, and embracing at last Western Australia) I was especially cognisant, as having to examine and report on all their laws.

'The moral difficulty in the abandonment of all this authority was the difficulty of securing the protection of coloured races, who are always exterminated by Anglo-Saxons in temperate climates, and yet are incapable of receiving more than an illusory share in the government.

'Lord Grey was possessed with the idea that it was practicable to give representative institutions, and then to stop without giving responsible government—something like the English Constitution under Elizabeth and the Stuarts. He did not understand either the vigorous independence of an Anglo-Saxon community or the weakness of an executive which represents a democracy. So events took their own course, and left his theories behind.

'When the natives were so few that they gave no trouble to the colonists, matters went on without a check. Complete independence in local affairs was given, and British troops were withdrawn. But in New Zealand and the Cape it was otherwise. In each of these colonies the colonists required our protection, and the question arose on what terms we should continue it, or whether we should withdraw it.

'In New Zealand the danger arose from the desire of the colonists to acquire land, and the growing indisposition to part with it, except at increasingly high prices. The Government proposed the establishment of a kind of land court, composed of the Governor and a few persons in whom the natives would confide, and acting, not under the authority of the colonial government, whose capacity the natives at that time distrusted, but under that of the Queen, whom they respected.

'This was approved in the Colonial Office, and a Bill, prepared by me, was introduced into Parliament, but rejected without division, because it was held that the colony was entitled in that, as in other matters, to manage its own affairs; from which it followed that they were to have absolute power of bringing on wars of which we were to pay the cost, and that they would be under a constant temptation, which they were not likely to resist, to pick a quarrel with the natives, and clear them out at our expense.

'Simultaneously a war did break out—provoked, I should say, by high-handed dealings of the colonists—which led to the employment, with little credit to us, of ridiculously large bodies of troops, the destruction of the tribe which was most advanced among the Maoris in civilisation, and whose territory presented the greatest temptation to cupidity, and the appropriation of their land. For myself, I at once made up my mind that there would be no quiet for ourselves or safety for the natives until our troops were recalled and the colonists forced to rely on their own resources, and to try mild and just methods rather than violent ones. . . . Eventually the last regiment was withdrawn, and we had no more trouble with the Maoris.

'The case of the Cape was very different in one respect. In New Zealand the colonists were equal in number, or nearly so, to the natives, and were increasing, while the natives were diminishing ; there was therefore no reason why they should not be forced to defend themselves. In Africa the natives were far more numerous, and increased, when not thinned by war, faster than the colonists. And, the executive being still, according to Lord Grey's policy, in the hands of the Home Government, it was possible to exercise a very efficient control on native policy. The colonists seemed to require more protection for themselves, and allowed the Government to protect the natives. But here difficulties arose in the general government. The finances got into disorder, and Sir P. Wodehouse declared that the Home Government (*i.e.* himself) could, with the existing constitution, do nothing. He was told that if he could prevail on the colonists to reform the constitution so as to give the Crown the requisite power, he, and they, might do so. . .

'If, on the other hand, the government were changed to a "responsible" government, the question was whether (as troops would not be supplied to a responsible government) this alteration would not be the signal for native war. But it was thought—and I think that events have not at present disproved the supposition—that the white population was sufficiently varied in their interests and sufficiently intelligent to avoid native wars if they must pay for them ; and it was decided that they should have responsible government. . . . [At the time of the Zulu War] this policy was reversed, and the system was re-introduced of war carried on at the expense of the British Treasury. . . . [Since that period] it was decided that we might safely give the government of the colony to the colonists. The final step was taken by Lord Kimberley after I left the Colonial Office.

'I had always believed—and the belief has so confirmed and consolidated itself that I can hardly realise the possibility of any one seriously thinking the contrary—that the destiny of our colonies is independence ; and that, in this point of view, the function of the Colonial Office is to secure that our connexion, while it lasts, shall be as profitable to both parties, and our separation, when it comes, as amicable as possible. This opinion is founded first on the general principle that a spirited nation (and a colony becomes a nation) will not submit to be governed in its internal affairs by a distant Government, and that nations geographically remote have no such common interests as will bind them permanently together in foreign policy, with all its details and mutations.

'This being so, and a colony being regarded as the seat of a nation, the Colonial Office presented an interesting set of successive developments, by which the seed grew into a forest tree. First there was, as I have described, the personal government of the Governor, instructed by the Colonial Office; then came a purely legislative council, nominated by him; then a part of this legislative council became the instrument of an informal kind of representation, a means of feeling and in some degree conforming to public opinion; then part of it became elective—a minority, but an influential minority; then came the separation into a nominated and an elective chamber (called, as I have said, representative institutions); then responsible government, placing the executive in the hands of persons practically nominated, as in England, by the community; then, in Canada, the addition of status and weight given by confederation.

'The scheme of confederation floated about for some little time as an idea. Among other persons who took it up was a Mr. Howe, a popular leader in Nova Scotia. But it took no substance till it was adopted by Sir John Macdonald, the exceedingly able Premier of Canada. In that colony the French were so large a minority (if indeed in mere numbers they were a minority) that government became almost impracticable, and he adopted the idea of confederation with New Brunswick and Nova Scotia, separating, however, Upper and Lower Canada, so that the French should be predominant in the latter —their own province—while the union of New Brunswick and Nova Scotia would make the British predominant in the Union. This involved a new constitution containing guarantees sufficient to ensure that the dominant party in the "Dominion," as it was to be, should not be able to withdraw the privileges given to the French province of Lower Canada. In this arrangement the French agreed, and their leader, Mr. Cartier (afterwards Sir G. Cartier), joined Macdonald in a ministry which was to carry it into effect. They framed an Act to be carried in the Imperial Parliament, and a large deputation from the proposed four provinces, with Macdonald (and Cartier) at their head, came to England to settle details with the Secretary of State. The delegates were ministers of their respective provinces, the legislatures of which addressed the Crown praying that the Act might be passed.

'But meantime Howe had changed his views. His enemies said that he did not see his way to such advantages for himself as he had hoped for in confederation. At any rate, he was not in the delegacy nor in the provincial ministry. And not being so, he agitated the province 'through its length and breadth," and came to England loaded with petitions against a change which would transfer them—the most ancient and loyal North American colony—from the allegiance of the Crown to that of a Canadian ministry. All this was done in the most approved platform style, and he spouted in public and interviewed in private with all the usual evidence of being the mouthpiece of the people of Nova Scotia. True, the people through the legislature had expressed themselves differently, and their ministers were pressing confederation on the Home Government. But there was all the usual evidence that the people had changed their minds, and that Mr. Howe was the people.

'However, he could not arrest the progress of the negotiations. It was, I should say, under Mr. Cardwell's rule that the project was matured; but it was during Lord Carnarvon's secretaryship that the deputation arrived. They held many meetings, at which I was always present. Lord Carnarvon was in the chair, and I was rather disappointed in his power of presidency. Macdonald was the ruling genius and spokesman, and I was very greatly struck by his power of management and adroitness. The French delegates were keenly on the watch for anything which weakened their securities; on the contrary, the Nova Scotia and New Brunswick delegates were very jealous of concession to the *arriérée* province; while one main stipulation in favour of the French was open to constitutional objections on the part of the Home Government.

'Macdonald had to argue the question with the Home Government on a point on which the slightest divergence from the narrow line already agreed on in Canada was watched for—here by the French, and there by the English—as eager dogs watch a rat hole; a snap on one side might have provoked a snap on the other, and put an end to the concord. He stated and argued the case with cool, ready fluency, while at the same time you saw that every word was measured, and that while he was making for a point ahead, he was never for a moment unconscious of any of the rocks among which he had to steer.

'The measure was settled and passed easily through the House of Lords, introduced in a good speech by Lord Carnarvon. This done, or soon after it was done, Lord Carnarvon left office, and was succeeded by the Duke of Buckingham. One day, probably while the measure was passing through the House of Commons, the Duke came into my room and said: "Well, there will be no more difficulty over Nova Scotia." The measure passed, and all the colonists returned home. I was curious to see what was to become of Howe. And what became of him was this.

'On his return to Nova Scotia he convened a meeting of the leading malcontents, and he made them a speech. He told them that he had left no stone unturned in England to give effect to their wishes, but the statesmen, without distinction of party, were unjust and inexorable. That the time for words was over, and that for deeds was come. That if they intended to assert themselves, they must do it as did the Fathers of American Independence. That he had drawn up a declaration, pledging all the signatories to resist confederation at the cost, if necessary, of their lives and fortunes. This he was ready to sign the first. And this was the course which he was prepared to recommend. But if they were not equal to this, then a mere resistance of talk was idle, and they would do well to make the best of a situation from which there was no escape, and, throwing aside local jealousies, to endeavour to obtain in the new confederation the weight which properly belonged to Nova Scotia.

'Of course not one of the agitators had the most remote idea of perilling a single dollar, much less life and fortune, in defence of their colonial isolation, and the second alternative was unanimously adopted. Mr. Howe, with the applause of his fellow citizens, accepted an appointment from Government

'So much for the development of the self-governing colonies while I was at the Colonial Office. I had soon come to the conclusion that the endowment of the colonial Churches was not a matter to be calculated on, and my fear was that in the vain attempt to perpetuate the advantage which these Churches derived from their connexion with the Crown, and the comparatively small endowments which they possessed, either alone or in common with other Churches, they would be led to make such sacrifices of their ecclesiastical independence as would interfere with their energy and stability. . . .

'As endowments were one after another cut away, I succeeded in persuading successive Secretaries of State that Churches might be allowed to organise themselves, a matter in which there was much traditional jealousy; that the appointments to bishoprics to which the State contributed no endowment should be left to these Churches; and, finally, that the form of creating bishoprics and appointing bishops by letters patent should be abandoned. In the colonial Churches, as in the colonial civil government, the changes which have taken place (almost entirely within the period when I was connected with colonial matters) are worth noticing. Formerly there were colonial bishops appointed *during pleasure* by the Crown under letters patent, asserting very unambiguously the extreme form of royal supremacy. These bishops were paid from imperial funds, and outside the limits of their dioceses the English Church was represented by a few State-paid clergy, supplemented insufficiently by the S.P.G., with a grudging assistance from their people, and in Canada with the considerable support of the "Clergy Reserves."

'About the year 1843 Selwyn refused to accept the Bishopric of New Zealand unless the appointment was made for life, and the rampant Erastianism extirpated. This was done, but the Crown still retained the creation and appointment of bishops, even after Miss Burdett-Coutts had set the example of instituting bishoprics without State aid. The independence of colonial Churches suffered from two jealousies —one, the apprehension that if the Church organised itself it would prove a troublesome and exacting power; the other, lest ignorant or heterodox men ordained by colonial bishops should, through our system of patronage, find their way to English preferment.

'Thus there was a strong official and ecclesiastical feeling against any organisation in the nature of a synod, and against taking the colonial episcopate from under the direct control of the Crown. It was felt by some of broader views that emancipation was a corollary of disestablishment, which soon began in the appropriation of the Canadian Clergy Reserves. Of the bishops some, like Gray and Selwyn, were keen for independence, and, with more or less judgment—Selwyn with more, Gray with less—organised their Churches with a view to it. But when it came to the question of creation by letters patent, and all the opportunities for official delay and obstruction and meddling, they did not generally like to give up what they considered the dignity of being the Queen's Bishop. When I became Under-Secretary for the Colonies, I found the Duke of Newcastle quite prepared to go with me, and Fulford, the Primate of Canada, fully realised the advantages of a free hand. The initial processes were going on everywhere. But he with my help, and I with his, first clenched the matter in Canada, when, Palmer being happily the leading law officer and Phillimore, I think, Queen's Advocate, I got the Colonial Office to announce that colonial Churches would be left to elect their own bishops, subject to the necessity of obtaining what the Prayer Book calls "a mandate" from the Crown, if they were consecrated in this country by an English bishop.

'What is certain is, that under the new system—that of free action unaided by the State—the colonial Churches have increased greatly, and the number of the bishops perhaps rather unnecessarily. (I almost think that the chaplain of St. Helena must have, or must have had, a Bishop to himself.)

Hence, at the time when I retired from the public service, the colonial Churches (with one or two exceptions, which I think no longer exist) were as free as the Episcopal Church of Scotland to regulate their own affairs, to choose and increase the number of their bishops, and to obtain consecration in the colonies if they pleased. The old letters patent were swept away.

'But the existing law of England had been framed by ecclesiastical lawyers, who had a strong jealousy of colonial orders, and an extreme devotion to Crown supremacy, and in accordance with these views provided that no colonial clergyman should be eligible for employment in England unless ordained by a bishop who had been appointed by letters patent. The effect, therefore, of abolishing these letters patent was to disqualify all clergy ordained by colonial bishops thereafter appointed from holding preferment in England or Ireland. It was quite true that an indiscriminate admission of such ordinations as qualifications for English preferment might have poured on us a multitude of clergymen little fitted for English parishes, and the question arose (shortly after I became a member of the House of Lords) what security should be taken against this danger. The question was complicated by a confused state of the law, and embarrassed by a variety of prejudices and jealousies—so much so that nobody would take it up. And it was admitted on all hands that I (who had brought this confusion to a climax) was the proper person, if not the only person, to bring in a Bill for its settlement. Having the good-will of all parties, I succeeded in passing an Act, of which the principle is this, that any person who has received episcopal orders, and is willing to accept all the tests required from an English clergyman on receiving an ecclesiastical appointment, may be admitted to employment in the English Church, and the status of an English clergyman, by any diocesan bishop who is satisfied that his orders are valid, and that he himself is a person whose admission to such status and employment is advisable. The bishop's power of rejection is absolute.'

CHAPTER IX

Eighteen Years (1871-1889); Partly Parliamentary Life; but chiefly Life at Blachford

THE letters which follow were written after his retirement from office. About six months, in the autumn of 1871 and the following winter, were spent in travelling. On his way to Italy he received a letter from Mr. Gladstone offering him a peerage, which he accepted, after hesitating for some time for reasons which are given in one of his letters. A consequence of this acceptance was that he was obliged to be in London from time to time, when Parliament was sitting. He spoke sometimes on subjects of which he had special knowledge, but not very frequently. He said himself that he did not find it easy to begin parliamentary debate with any prospect of success or usefulness so late in life. On various parliamentary committees he did a good deal of hard and useful work up to the year 1884, when he considered himself entitled, at the age of seventy-three, to rest altogether from the public service; and he was the more anxious to do so because, dissenting very strongly from Mr. Gladstone's Irish policy, he was no longer able to support, and found it painful to oppose, his old friend and leader; hence nearly the whole of the last five years of his life, and the greater part of the last eighteen, were spent in the country. He did not find the difficulty which is often supposed to exist in a change of this kind from busy years of constant official work. He gave some of his newly-found leisure to literary work—to articles and reviews for the 'Guardian' and occasionally for other journals

or magazines. How readily he threw himself into country occupations and duties—building or improving schools and cottages and farms, planting or thinning woods—and how completely he found his enjoyment in them, is shown clearly enough in his letters.

To Miss E. Marindin [Mrs. Franks].

Hotel Bellevue, Lucerne : September 17, 1871.

My dear Eleanor,—I am aware that I owe you a letter, but hitherto I have had nothing to say that you would not see better in Murray. On Thursday, however, we saw a sight not in the guide-books which is worth telling you, and so I shall do in Georgie's handwriting as you see (at least for the most part), because I am rather on the sick list. What I have to tell is a day at Einsiedeln, which you may remember in 'Anne of Geierstein' connected with the image of our Lady of Einsiedeln, one of those repulsive black images of the Holy Virgin which seem to be credited with an exceptional amount of miracles and sanctity. I must begin with a little guide-bookism. The monastery (Benedictine) must, I should think, be about the oldest institution in Switzerland, having a few years ago celebrated not its centenary but its millenary. It is certainly older than the canton of Schwytz, which was the core of the Swiss Confederation. This is pretty certain, for the first that is heard in history of Schwytz is that the knowing monks of Einsiedeln contrived to get from the Emperor of Germany a grant of the land occupied by squatting right by *les hommes de Schwytz*, a set of sturdy savages of whom, till that time, nobody had ever heard. Of course, when in due time the monks began to assert their rights, the mountaineers resisted, the case was brought before the Emperor more than once, and decided in favour of the written documents of the Abbot against the squatting rights of the *hommes de Schwytz*. To this the Schwytzers paid no attention. They were accordingly put under the ban of the Empire ; to this also they paid no attention. They were then excommunicated by various ecclesiastical authorities in succession, and their churches shut ; this they so far respected as to build a little chapel, and compel their priests to celebrate Mass there, but the rights of Einsiedeln they continued positively to ignore. Under these circumstances the Convent, the Empire, and the bishops thought it best to give up the job as a bad one, and the Schwytzers were relieved from imperial bans and ecclesiastical interdicts, and allowed to hold their lands in peace. This little incident was characteristic of the Schwytzers—they never calculated odds, went at everything, and were either destroyed or victorious. When victorious (as far as I can see from a Swiss history I have bought) they seem to have celebrated their victory by plundering *le couvent des gentils hommes à Einsiedeln.* However, the Reformation seems to have changed all this: Schwytz was one of the cantons which held fast to Rome, and I believe now have as much reverence for Einsiedeln as the rest of their Catholic neighbours. Now then for the occasion of our sight. On September 14, rather more than 900 years ago, when the ecclesiastical authorities were preparing to consecrate the church of Einsiedeln, the Bishop of Constance was informed by a voice from Heaven that he might dispense with the form, as the church had already been consecrated in Heaven and by the presence of our Saviour, who, the legend adds, had drunk of one of fourteen fountains which existed on the spot. Ever since, that day has been a great day at Einsiedeln, and we went to see it. We started from a place called Brunnen on the Lake of Lucerne, and got to Einsiedeln or near it without seeing any signs of what was going on except one group of thirty or forty pilgrims trudging along manfully and womanfully with their priest at their head, from some village on the other side of the lake, *i.e.* beyond Brunnen, for a twenty miles' walk. At our halfway stop they caught us up, and as they came up I was amused at the way in which the waiters and other hotel authorities rushed forward to hustle us out of the way, crying ' Place, place, place,' in order that the pilgrims might walk in with due honours. About 12 o'clock we arrived at Einsiedeln. The Convent is a very large quadrangle, of which one side, comprising about 100 windows and the west façade of the Convent church, overhangs a triangular *Place* very much as our National Gallery overhangs Trafalgar Square. The *Place* we guessed to be about the size of Trafalgar Square, but considerably steeper. In the place of the terraces and Nelson column is an imposing *perron*—very spacious, with a broad, inclined plane running down the hill from the west front of the church—and on each side two handsome quarter circles of arcades. Between the Nelson column and King Charles's statue is a stone canopy with fountain jets of water, being the springs above mentioned, and lower down still was a temporary wooden construction with an altar (a *reposoir*, as they would call it in France) prepared for illumination. The annexed rude plan and elevation will give you some idea of it.

The monastery is surrounded by hills, one of which may be said to overhang it and the village to the right of my picture.

The village, when we got to it, was crowded with pilgrims —estimated by the waiter at ten or twelve thousand— from all parts of (Catholic) Switzerland and further—few sightseers, but lots of booths, of which four-fifths were full of rosaries, little images of the Madonna, books of devotion, and so on—the fifth being usually, as far as I could see, for the sale of cotton pocket-handkerchiefs, mostly bright red. The days of costume seem to have gone by, but a fair sprinkling from the different cantons were to be seen—men and women. The *objets de dévotion* were intended to be blessed after Vespers, with the distinction that all might be blessed, but only those which were of some solid material could have Indulgences attached to them. Little fly-leaves were also to be got cheap, one of which (bought by Sir James Paget, of whose party we were) contained a very beautiful prayer, with an intimation that any person who said it, or had it said to him, or kept it about his person, would be preserved from all accidents and (I think) sin, that poison would not injure him, that he would be miraculously informed of the day of his death, that in certain specified conjunctures the prayer would act the part of an experienced surgeon, with other advantages which I forget. Among the first things which met your eye was a ring of circulating pilgrims round the fountain. Every one desires to drink of the spring which our Saviour tasted, and as nobody knows which that was, everybody goes the round. In the church you are faced by a massive shrine containing the black image with lamps, &c., and before it a crowd of people silent on their knees. The rest of the church was filled (there was no service going on) with a crowd moving quietly about with a kind of serious curiosity, except that, when we first got in, there was a knot of some ten or twelve women (I suppose neighbours) going the round of the chapels and saying before each, aloud and together, some stated form of prayer. It was a curious sight to see the businesslike but serious way in which they knelt down to utter their hum before one chapel, and then got up and moved on to do the same thing at the next. Then at two o'clock came Vespers—an orchestral service, with a fine old choral hymn tune sung by voices only in the shrine of the black image among the lamps. The words were what is called *Salve Regina*. It was curious to see the travelled look of the people trudging or sitting about in or out of the church, with their basket of (evidently) the day's provisions. One old fellow struck me very much with his dusty and worn (not over-fatigued) look, as he trudged down the church aisle slowly with his alpenstock in his hand. He had evidently had a good stiff mountain walk that morning. After Vespers we went to the church again, and the first thing which struck me was that the hum of groups ' doing ' the shrine had become a positive chatter, which filled the church. Every chapel had its one or two groups, all going through their appointed work —the louder because there were so many of them, without regard (most properly) to anything but themselves. Then there was a rush out to see a fresh arrival—some 200 people arranged in two long single files, well apart so as to take up a broad strip of road : first about 100 women, then 100 men, then some thirty or forty priests moving up to the church, singing antiphonally some chant or litany (Gregorian), and then, when they got into church, uniting in one great volume of hymn. Then came a break for dinner, in preparation for the great event of the day— the procession and illuminations. The course of events I don't distinctly remember, except that either then or on

the arrival of the 250 pilgrims we heard a grand singing of
'Sun of my Soul' (not the words, but the tune) note for
note as we have it. I shall like it better hereafter, for I
always had a kind of modern association about it which is
now effectually disposed of. As it got dark the *Place* began
to light up—sharp little lines of fire moved about it, which
on investigation turned out to be trays of illumination
lamps carried to and fro on men's heads. The windows of
the Convent (100) and of the hotels and houses, the arcades,
the front of the church, the fountain (?) and the *reposoir*,
all began to light up, till the *Place* was all of a blaze,
and, what was very beautiful, a gigantic cross lighted itself
up on the side of the overhanging hill, so as to seem, when
the hill became invisible in darkness, like a cross in the sky.
Meantime the inside of the church began to be alive. Two
grand organs with choirs attached began to play, echoing
each other, one loud, one low, from the different ends of the
great church. The distance was great enough to give the
effect of distance. Then at last the candles collected about
the altar, and after more music and singing streamed down
the centre of the church—some 200 or 300 men with candles
—out at the centre door, and down the slope to the fountains
and *reposoir*, all singing antiphonally some grand old chant or
hymn—first with some, say, twenty or thirty strong voices,
then with the whole mass of voices they could muster, plus an
accompaniment, most effective, of serpents and trombones.
At the end of the procession was the baldachino, and under
it the 'Prince-Abbot' with the Sacrament in a splendid
monstrance. At each event which occurred—*i.e.* as the
Sacrament was taken from the altar, as the procession started,
as the head of it cleared out from the church, as the Sacrament cleared out, as the Abbot mounted the *reposoir*—cannon
fired from the overhanging hill, as I call it, or bells rang--or
both—sometimes also the clock took the opportunity to strike.
And I can hardly describe the effect upon us of the whole
scene—the two single files of candles winding down the
slope from the church to the *reposoir*, the alternate chanting,
the guns, the bells, the clock, the multitude of faces lighted
up by the blazing *reposoir*—and, as the Sacrament passed,

the kneeling of the vast crowd : all far more beautiful, I think, because it was at night (as, indeed, is naturally the case with illuminations—but an intelligent being will see what I mean). In the crowd the remarkable things were, first, the general quiet; secondly, the downright way in which the country women elbowed their way to the place they wanted. Three of them rushed on Georgie and myself and our neighbours like Homeric heroes rushing into battle, sweeping opposition aside right and left with their elbows blindly, as a warrior would with his two-handed sword. However, we yielded with sufficient promptitude to escape a catastrophe. When the abbot reached the *reposoir*, a number of singers were drafted off to a distance, when a hymn or musical service was sung, with the same effect of distant response ; then the multitude was blessed, the cannons fired, the bells rung, the procession mounted again to the church, and we went home, arriving at our *gîte* on the lake about half-past twelve or one o'clock in the morning. There—there is a good long story for you, and so good-bye.

Ever yours affectionately,

F. ROGERS.

To Right Hon. W. E. Gladstone.

Hotel Bellevue, Lucerne : September 24, 1871.

My dear Gladstone,—You will, I am sure, do me the justice to assume that I have only just received your letter of the 31st ult. I have just got it, and that, I may almost say, by accident. I can hardly say how it surprised and gratified me, but I think I must answer it by explanations. I do not for a moment suppose that you would offer me or any one else a peerage, except with the full expectation that its duties would be performed with entire independence. But neither can I suppose would you do so without some definite idea of the turn which that independence would probably take. And this is one point on which I wish to speak as clearly as I can. Partly perhaps from disposition, partly from the habits of a Permanent Under Secretary, I am singularly averse from party politics, and find myself almost equally unable to attach myself to any existing division of political parties. On some points I find myself radical, some would say revolutionary—a thing I detest. On the other hand I utterly dislike democracy, abhor demagogy, doubt whether any country can be for any long time safely and honourably governed in which an aristocracy more or less hereditary is not a leading element, and I apprehend evil for the country from the opposite tendencies of the day. This rather cross-cuts existing divisions of parties and, in default of party guidance, I should probably be guided by personal or temporary considerations to an extent which most men would denounce as impracticable and inconsistent. To take an actual illustration :—Two years ago I should, if engaged in political life, have been an earnest supporter of yours as to the Irish Church, while I should as vigorously have supported our Devonshire members, Lopes and Kekewich, against Lord Amberley. You would generally, I think, find me cordially with you in all that part of your policy which goes to benefit the poor or to purify the public service, military or civil. But I might find myself taking part decidedly against you on questions of yielding to what I should call the populace, or when it appeared to me that constitutional changes were precipitated from any party necessity. So much for politics—which, however, I say rather to relieve my own mind than because I expect you to attach much weight to it.

Next as to personal matters. I understand the offer of a peerage to be made to me, not as a mere decoration or an easy chair, but as an occasion for useful public work. It is on this point of view that your offer and my acceptance would be justified. Now I should have been much disappointed if you had not, as time went on, found some means of making me (of course gratuitously) useful to the public. It was part of my scheme of life. But first, in point of strength and health the public has had the best of me. For some months I have felt that I could not do again what I have done, or anything like it. I should fail, which would be an evil for the public ; or I should break down, an evil for myself, which no man is bound to incur for the sake of doing what can be sufficiently done by others. And next, I could not afford to do anything which required much expense. But for my pension I could not live in my own country house and meet what I consider imperative local claims, and with it I cannot add to that country life, which I consider a duty and a necessity, a regular London residence during the parliamentary session. What I can do in that way I hardly yet know. It would certainly be intermittent, and possibly very short of the expectations with which your offer is made.

All this being the case, what I now want to do, and very sincerely is to place you as far as possible in the position of not having made the offer, and to ask you to consider with the light this letter gives you whether you would make it afresh if it had not been made already. If you would not, I should then like to know whether you would wish me to consider the whole matter as *non avenu*, or whether I shall consider myself as having declined it on the ground of narrow income—*i.e.* on the ground, which if true in your judgment will be true in my mouth, that my income will not allow me to perform the duties of a peerage in the way in which they ought to be performed in order to justify your recommendation of me to the Queen. In either of these cases I shall retain the very great gratification of having received the offer in fact. If you adhere to your offer you can treat this letter as a most grateful acceptance of it.

As you send a message to my wife, I will say that she is delighted at the *offer*, and still more, if possible, at the terms in which it is made. But she is such a conservative (domestically I now mean, not politically) and so unadventurous that I am not sure she will be quite as much pleased at its taking effect. I cannot say how much I was pleased at your appointment of Church.

Ever yours sincerely,
F. ROGERS.

To Sir Henry Taylor.

Milan: October 13, 1871.

My dear Taylor,—If it had been possible to help it, I should not have let you learn from the newspapers my wise or unwise acceptance of a peerage. But the fact is that you knew it some days before I did. Gladstone had written me a very kind offer of it, and I had replied by explanations leaving him at liberty to treat the offer as *non avenu* or to treat my letter as an acceptance. And on the same day I learnt here by a letter from him (a long time on its road) and from the 'Times' that he had taken my acceptance, and that the Queen was pleased to approve me.

It is in many respects more than pleasant. As a recognition of my own services its only fault is that it is too much, and that others may think it so. The work and semi-political status are just what I should expect to like. But it will cut rather more deeply than I could have wished into our intended country life and into our income. To begin with, you will have us back in town for a more or less long period in February.

Have you any views as to the use of a peer? Mine are very vague, and I look to be enlightened by practice before I form any scheme of conducting myself. I look forward with some apprehension to the necessity of forming opinions that will hold water on a lot of questions which I have kept at bay while I could say to myself that I did my share of public duty in working at the Colonies. I don't know whether others ever feel the same, but I used to feel that the constant habit of taking decisions under responsibility tried the determining powers of the intellect, just as walking up hill fatigues a certain set of sinews; and my great rest was in refusing to form conclusions out of office hours. And now I shall have to set to work making up my mind *de rebus omnibus*, much to the dissatisfaction, I am afraid, of many friends and relations, who will think me unaccountable when I develop myself, if I have to do so.

We have spent a very pleasant month in Switzerland (Lucerne), which I think has been very useful to some of the family who had been a good deal shaken by the events of the year. I met Lord Carnarvon there, and, lounging with him and Lady Carnarvon to get *his* letters from the post office, I thought it just worth while to ask if there were any Poste Restantes for me, and got Gladstone's letter, which had been waiting three weeks, and would be waiting there still, I suppose, but for this chance (I had not expected Poste Restante letters, and most of them so addressed had been sent to me at the hotel). It was fortunate, as it was a satisfaction (which I could not resist) talking it over with him, but rather odd. Since that we crossed the Alps, glanced at Turin—a dry uninteresting place to my mind, I have no doubt practical to the highest degree. The people—all of them—go about as they do in London, as if they were going somewhere and had something to do, quite unlike the refreshing enjoyativeness of French and Italians (proper). Here, too (Milan), there is a good deal of modern thrivingness. But it is carried off by a few magnificent bequests of antiquity (Duomo and so on), and a cheerful stateliness which Turin wants. Then we have had a few days on Lago Maggiore, strolling in chestnut woods delightfully warm and delightfully cool, with pleasant reminders of home scenery in the way of ferns, mosses, rocks, and rivulets sprinkled among the enchanting Italian scenery proper. Now we are on the point of starting for Florence viâ Bologna. If you are good enough to send us a line it will find us till near the end of the month at the Hotel de l'Europe, Florence. Our very best love to you.

Ever yours,
F. R.

Florence: October 19, 1871.

My dear Taylor,—I confess the cacophony—though, strange to say, I had never remarked it—'Frederic Rogers Baron Blachford' contains an accumulation of bumping and creaking and crashing and rattling difficult to parallel in four words. The three first words, however, are unavoidable, and as to the last, I am inclined to place considerations of family and local feeling and semi-constitutional propriety rather higher than you do, particularly as my decoration is practically a life one, and concerns not a series of generations—for whose ears, no doubt, consideration would be due—but merely a knot of friends and relations who are more accessible to association than to euphony. Viewing the title as a reward of exploits, perhaps I ought to propose myself as Baron of Heligoland or Wagga-Wagga. But I am disposed to think that if a man happens to have in his hands that which in old times was the basis of a baronial title, *i.e.* a fragment of manorial jurisdiction, there is a kind of constitutional propriety in fixing upon that, and if so Blachford, Wisdome, and Blachworthy[1] (which has been scouted) are my only alternatives. Now let me thank you for your letter. I need not tell you what pleasure your pleasure gives me. My wife tells me that she has liked everybody's letters very much, and yours better than anybody's that has been written. However, I am writing for post, and must finish.

Ever yours,
F. ROGERS.

To the Rev. E. Rogers.

Florence : October 26, 1871.

Sight-seeing is sight-seeing at a place like this. We have had a pleasant drive to St. Miniato, a pleasant walk (aided by lifts) to Fiesole, a pleasant stroll in Boboli Gardens, all with charming views of Florence and its *contorni*; the quays along the Arno are bright and beautiful at certain times—sunset and moonlight—but for regular strolling, stony and dusty, without the charm of Paris quays, and gardens, and Boulevards. Purchasing is an attraction. I hope I have not been horribly bitten, but I think that, though I have doubtless paid plentifully too much (Florence is very dear, and Berne curiosities were very cheap), yet I am not out of conceit with what I have got, broken about as some of them are. The wealth of pictures is wonderful, but confusing. I am not sure now that I agree with those who like simply to carry away a clear recollection of the best things. I want to feel a little acquainted with schools and individual painters, which cannot be done without wading through a good deal. I think at present my admiration of Ghirlandajo, Masaccio, and suchlike late pre-Raffaelite Florentines increases. But I never have admired like other people, and am getting tired of Fra Angelico. Looking at his works is like reading the same story in different types.

Our American neighbours improve on acquaintance. The lady is rather proud of her pure English blood and descent

---

[1] Blachworthy was the old name of Blachford; Wisdome was another manor on the property.

from Royalists, who, however, seem to have adapted themselves to the new state of things, as her uncle married the daughter of the patriarch Adams, and went with him to England in his suite as Ambassador. He was a Colonel, and one day (as the parental relation was kept up in those days) my friend's grandmother, who seems to have been a Tartar, thought it her duty to take him to task, opening with 'Child, I am surprised,' &c. The Colonel meekly inquired, 'Madam, when will you cease to call me child?' To which she replied, 'When you cease to be my son. Leave the room.' On which he dutifully retired, and penned an apology promising not to object again. I think my friend would rather like to repeat the process.

To the Hon. Mrs. Legge.

Assisi: October 1871.

Our next perch (after Florence) was Perugia, which was thoroughly charming. It occupies the top of something half mountain, half ridge, and spreads itself about up and down, and sideways, and crossways, in such a way that you are always passing under arches, with houses on the top of them, and coming unexpectedly on beautiful views of the plains of Umbria and the Apennines, through holes and under arches, and down flights of steps, and off terraces. Then there are inside noble buildings in the Piazza, and hosts of Peruginos, *capi d'opera*. The days were perfect, and we had panoramas from the terraces of magnificent sunset, of early mists, and of clear forenoon. The old city walls run about in every possible direction and at every possible angle, with great Etruscan vases, Roman superstructure, and mediæval towers. It came upon me with all the pleasure of novelty. Indeed a thing which you have only seen for a few hours thirty years (pretty exactly) ago may well do so. But still Perugia was a case of '*vide* Murray.' To-day has been better. In the first place, this place is charming, the picturesqueness of Perugia without its splendid architecture, but with an element of wildness quite its own.

Every house and lane and corner is a study; there is the same profusion of outlook, and (what we have not seen yet) the same profusion of art, only of a still earlier age. But there is also the connexion of St. Francis, whose history I have just been reading, and this it is which we have come across to-day. He is one of those men whose conduct has a kind of mad brilliancy about it, but a madness founded at bottom on the most noble principles and the most attractive character, and producing such results (for a time at least) in the reformation of the world that if a tree is to be judged by its fruits you can hardly help believing him inspired. His celebrity was so rapid that before his death everything connected with him had become, so to say, a relic, and so there is no possibility of doubting the genuineness of what you see. The first sight which meets you is in the plain under Assisi a handsome cinquecento church, dome, transepts, and so on. When you enter it you see in all its rudeness a coarse stone construction, the walls of an old substantial hovel, inside which again is a rich altar with lamps burning, &c., and (when we saw it, on a fair-day) a stream of peasants entering, kneeling, and passing. This is the first small construction— made, in fact, by his own hands—in which St. Francis and his first two or three followers dwelt together. Then in the afternoon we rode off to his retreat in the mountains. The ride was charming, along the side of the mountains with the great plain at our feet, encircled by the Apennines, Assisi, with its walls, towns, citadel, and the rest on a spur behind us, and Perugia and other towns and villages on slopes or hills in the distance. Then we turned into a wild combe, very desolate except for one patch of some fifty or a hundred acres of wood, the 'bosco' of St. Francis, and almost at the head of the combe a group of rude buildings. The views through and across the wood (of oak and ilex) lovely.

The buildings were shown by an old Franciscan, who was evidently so taken by what he saw, and what I suspect our conductor had told him of our interest in the matter, that he unburthened himself very much of his legends. We had not the heart to show incredulity, and felt a little like traitors while he went on. It was a strange place, with doors, and passages, and descents through which one almost had to creep, with little grottos, of which we saw one which formed the oratories of the first companions, and St. Francis' bed (of the authenticity of which I should think there was no doubt)—a bit of hollowed rock, with a log where his head lay. Our conductor was very anxious we should walk on the bed, and lay a little card on the pillow (log) to take it away blessed, for which it is proper to take off your shoes. This I duly did, and G. was prepared to do the same; but she was excused, 'perchè non è per disprezzo' and she kept them on. Then came the stories. First there was a miraculous painting of our Saviour on the cross over the little altar. It had done many things, one of which was this. One of the brethren had come in after his day's work, hot and tired, and, resorting to the chapel to pray before this picture, had gone to sleep. He was awakened by a slight slap on the face 'non per far male,' and looking about him saw the arms of our Saviour extended so as to show that He had done it. Then the picture said: 'Figliuolo mio, questo è luogo per pregare, non per dormire; se volete dormire, andate in dormitorio.' Then there was an ilex (of which I have a sprig), on which the birds collected round St. Francis chattering when he was at prayer. On which he told them to be quiet, and hear him preach. And they were silent, and he preached to them, not about sin, 'perchè gli animali non hanno peccato.' But he said: 'There is a great God who made me, and you, and the sun and all things else. You should praise Him, and now you may praise Him with me.' And he then began singing and the birds all began singing with him. Then there was a stream at the bottom of the combe which disturbed him at his prayer, and he prayed that it might cease, and it ceased from that time, however violent the rain might be, except when some great 'gastigo,' war, or famine, or pestilence was imminent. In 1869 water ran, and an Austrian prelate, 'uomo santissimo,' was there to see it and said 'Ci sarà molto sangue,' and 'molto sangue' there has been (in the Prusso-French War). This year the water has run, and 'è da vedere' what calamity will happen.

Then on the edge of the precipice there is a flat flag-stone, with a hole through which you look to the bottom of the ravine as into a well. This is a hole through which

St. Francis cast the devil when he came to tempt him. Then there were other stories too long to tell about the devil, and intercession, and the gift of prophecy. But the strange thing was that the monk stood on this spot where things really as wonderful as miracles did go on, and where the stones remained as the first inhabitants had left them, telling us his stories one after the other with all the attitudes and gesticulations which you see in pictures, and all the conviction of the middle ages. Beside him was the wild-looking conductor (of the omnibus) sucking it all in; but, as he knew it all by heart already, every now and then throwing in a correction or amplification that the monk had forgotten, like a child who corrects you in telling him a story that he knows. I don't think I was ever so taken out of the nineteenth century before. Finally our guide told us (what was natural) that we should leave something for a mass to be said for the 'defunti' in whom we were interested. We gave something of course, but without the condition; but that would not satisfy our friend, who insisted before we left that the *frate* was to say a mass 'per l' intenzione del Signore'—that is to say, in favour of any object that I may choose to fix on. We had already told him that we were not Catholics in his sense of the word, and I did not think it necessary to trouble his mind or disturb the *frate* by any further protests. I am afraid he thought me unduly careless about the 'intermediate state' of my 'antenati' (predecessors), for whose benefit he desired us to exert ourselves, the altar being one at which any amount of plenary indulgences are obtainable. To-morrow we see the regular Assisi sights, and get to Rome, where I hope we shall find letters.

Love to all,
Ever yours,
F. R.

To Miss Rogers.

Hôtel de l'Angleterre, Rome: November 3, 1871.

Our second day at Assisi was quite as good as the first. The point was the convent and convent church of St. Francis. There were magnificent Giottos, Cimabues, &c., some of which we saw well and carefully, others not at all.

But the point was the general scene. It was a great day, All Saints' day, when at all the great altars there was a great musical service—great in respect to the place, but, as the poor *frate* lamentably told us, very slight in comparison with the grand doings before the suppression of monasteries in the palmy days of the convent. However, it was quite grand enough ; more grandeur would have been in the way. The church consists of a crypt—interesting as it contains St. Francis' remains, and splendid in point of brass work, marble, &c., and striking because seen only by candle light —but it was just what you might see anywhere in Rome, or Milan, or Paris. Above that was *the* church, a dark labyrinth of columns and altars, and aisles, and flights of steps, and *impasses*, half lighted by fine painted windows and absolutely covered by the richest old frescoes, low and spacious in comparison with its height, and with a constant movement (not amounting to a crowd) of Italian peasants, men and women, come to be there on the great day, and some kneeling, some simply wandering about. One of Cattermole's pictures or I think Roberts, of some of the Eastern shrines would give you the best notion of the general effect. This church serves as the foundation for an upper church, built upon it as one storey of a house is on another. This is a simple cruciform one-aisled church—covered with painting, not entered except once or twice a year for purposes of worship, and in which we could just study Giotto and Cimabue at our leisure. When we went down we got entangled, as it were, in the high mass which was celebrating at the high altar—or rather shrine, for it is not, like other high altars, a central point commanding the whole of the church, but in a kind of corner, with its back to the labyrinth of shafts and chapels. When we had listened for some time, a stream of bright Italian dresses swept suddenly along and threw themselves on their knees between us and the altar. You can scarcely imagine the beauty of the pictorial and scenic effect of this natural movement of people so dressed in such a scene under the double light of lamps and painted windows. It was as if Ravenna had come to life again.

Our guide was a *Papalino*—not a bad fellow, but pretty well crammed by the priests. His view was that Victor Emmanuel was King of Sardinia and might go to Sardinia. But King of Italy he was not till he was crowned; and of course, in the present state of things, crowned he could not be till the Pope chose. King elect or King designate he might be, but not King. One of our cabmen at Rome was in the same line. His view had the merit of simplicity. Bread was 15 centimes a pound under the Pope. It is 25 centimes under Victor Emmanuel. Therefore he was for the Pope and not for Victor Emmanuel. His view of the position of affairs was that in Rome at least there were plenty of Papists and plenty of Mazzinians, but a very small proportion of Victor Emmanuelites; and he promised that in the following summer, or rather in March or April, we should have a blow up—not yet, but presently. Severne (the consul) did not talk very cheerfully about the state of things. His view was that the Italians (as has been always the case) could not understand such a thing as equal rights. Their view was, what was the good of being uppermost if you were not to plunder, crush, and exterminate your opponents? So the Liberals are disposed to persecute the Papists, and have tried it. On the first occasion the troops put them down, but fresh occasions will arise. Unless the Pope comes to terms (which he will not), the Liberals in Severne's opinion will make what the Italians call a 'strada pulita'—or, as we should say, 'clean sweep'—of Pope, cardinals, Vatican, monks, Leonine city, and everything else: and if Victor Emmanuel tries to stop it by the soldiery the soldiery will not act. These are difficulties not greater than a great man could tackle. But then the Italians do not seem to have a great man, or anything like one, among them.

Tuesday we move to Naples (Hôtel de la Bretagne), where I hear Vesuvius is in eruption.

Ever yours affectionately,
F. R.

To Miss Rogers.

Naples: November 14, 1871.

My dear Kate,—The weather has been so bad that I think it not impossible that unless it mends we may turn tail and run back to Rome, leaving Baie and Amalfi undone. However, we have had one beautiful day at Pompeii, and beautiful patches of weather, including a most magnificent sunset seen from the Strada Victor Emmanuel, a kind of terraced road running behind the city along the side of the hill. This morning we have been greatly amused at watching the fishermen drawing the nets. The sea was swarming with boats, and at intervals along the shore under the Chiaja were the seines being hauled in. The way is this: several hundred yards out to sea is the net—buoyed so that you can see it—with a boat to look after it; at each end of the seine is a rope carried to the shore, and at the end of the rope some thirteen or fifteen men. One is stationary at the end of each rope, coiling it as it comes in; the rest are pulling away at the rope in a line; then, each has hold of the rope not with his hands, but with a little instrument attached to a broad belt diagonally round his body, a little rope and peg, so that if he keeps his own rope and peg gripping the net rope, he pulls by his belt with the whole weight of his body. As the man at the head of the line gets up to the coil he looses his peg, lets go the rope, and walks down to take hold at the tail of the line, so that there is a continual circulation of men pulling up to the head of the line and then leaving go and walking back to take their place at the tail. Their clothes are so tucked up that the whole leg, including the thigh, is naked; on their heads they have caps of various sorts, principally the old Phrygian, and their torsos are enveloped in every variety of rags. Their legs are of a fine Venetian brown and shaped like so many Greek statues, and there are about a lot of imps, active and impudent, begging, chattering, laughing, &c. Some groups are mending the nets as they come in, some lighting the fires to cook, as far as I could see, the small fish they could pick up. Five, during part of the time, were occupied in looking in the sand for a penny which I had imprudently thrown to one of them, and being called away to take their share of the work rushed back again to prosecute their search the moment the net was landed. From this you may see that the rate of profit was not high ; nor could it be, for as far as I could see the whole produce of this great exertion of some thirty men was some two or three hundred small fishes rather smaller than sprats. Meantime the urchins who had got hold of a few of these wretched little animals were shaking them in our faces and asking for money, indicating that for the smallest consideration they would do something the nature of which for a long time we could not make out, but which at length appeared to be the eating those creatures raw, or perhaps alive. Some of the creatures so to be eaten were small crabs. When I (for G., luckily for herself, was not by) was evidently unable to make out what was meant, a bystander pinched off the head of the wriggling little fish with his fingers, and then the holder, after exhibiting its convulsive movements, ate it at two bites—very nasty. Nastiness apart, the place was picturesque beyond measure, and Vesuvius (which formed the background) took occasion to throw out great jets of black smoke, one every three or four minutes, for the first time since we have been here. It was rather solemn ; a black column rose slowly and perpendicularly from the peak, and then fell asunder, as it were, into the shape of a tall elm tree. Then it ceased to issue ; the wind caught it and blew it into a thin cloud, in which shape it floated off to the north and, while it was still a floating patch of black, another discharge took place. Meanwhile as far as we could make out there was a constant gush of silvery smoke or vapour coming out to the south of the black smoke above the spot which I have marked O. But this may have been a mere cloud. At present everything is hidden behind thick rain. The fantastic picturesqueness and incongruity of everything in this place strikes one. In the Toledo you jostle dirty ragged little vagabonds that nowhere appear in the decent parts of every other Christian city ; you meet first a cart driven by a Capuchin (begging of course), then a cab loaded with people in rags, pleasuring ; then you turn aside up something between a lane and a flight of steps, get entangled in a drove of goats, are nearly run over by donkeys coming down ; then you find a lot of cabs on the landing-place. Returning to Toledo (the Regent Street) you fall upon a hay stack, and by diligent scrutiny discover the head and tail of a horse in the middle of it, which horse has been carrying it down the hill (a sharp incline paved with smooth flagstones), and of course has come as nearly over head and heels as the nature of his load admits. How the creatures keep their legs at all I cannot understand, but they do so. The place to-day after a slight drizzle was like an inclined plane of ice, and in going up and down the whole street I do not think we saw more than nine or ten tumbles. Our own cab horse did not tumble more than once, and picked himself up in a moment. It is wonderful the pace they go, even when paid by the hour.

To Miss Rogers.

Rome : November 1871.

We got here on Saturday evening. William Palmer and Sir A. Paget are both away, but I hope much from the Sermonetas (to whom the Stanleys introduced us). I first asked the *directeur* here whether he knew their address. His answer was : ' Palazzo Gaetani '—but I wish I could do justice to the tone and expression of face. The tone was what I think they call a ' slide ' on the violin—running to a very high note, expressive of the extremest of surprise and amusement, and being an Italian translation of what an Englishman would say in Windsor if you asked him whether he knew Queen Victoria's address : ' Why the Castle, to be sure ; where the devil do you suppose it would be ? ' However, I still had to find out where the Palazzo Gaetani was (he is the head of the family, and he and his son, the Principe Teano, have married English women), which we did, and left our cards and letter about 2 P.M. Before we sat down to dinner we got their cards in return, and the next day, yesterday, we found a card (which it was explained was left by the Duchess in person) with ' *Sta in casa ogni sera dopo le otto.*' I don't know how often we can go, but I imagine pretty constantly. We thought, however, that an instant appearance would be rather too much of a good thing, and so shall go this evening.

The company here is a decided improvement on what it was, the torrent of Americans seeming to have passed, and we have some intelligent people (as at Naples) coming home from India ; also a queer pair now gone that I should like to make out. The husband might have been a correspondent (in France, where they had lived a great deal) of some north country house of business. I was amused at one or two of his French stories about sugar (at cafés). He said he was having some coffee at the Rotunda in the Palais Royal (just in front of the Trois Frères Provençaux) with a French friend when somebody who had also had his coffee left without taking away his remnant of sugar. On this the French friend quietly put out his hand and pocketed the derelict sugar. 'You know I did not know where to look—I was ready to jump into my own pocket.' 'What are you doing there?' says I. 'Mais c'est payé,' says he. 'But you didn't pay for it,' says I. 'Mais qu'est que ça fait?' says he. On another occasion one of his friends, *habitué* at a certain café, left his sugar similarly behind him, and the next day asked for it in addition to his usual allowance—the claim was allowed, and the sugar duly given him. Judging from recollections of Chasseloup Laubat, I suppose it is their luncheon. It is a great comfort to be settled quietly for some time, and after the first brush I shall try to get a little regularity, having as a habit an hour or two of reading, writing, and such like in the morning. It is a place, I am inclined to think, where you are not easy till you have more or less cursorily swept over the ground, and are at liberty to please yourself in idling with or without friends or objects, without considering whether there is or is not something you *ought* to be doing.

To-day my little indisposition will prevent me from seeing some functions of the day ('Saint Cecilia') which, however, may come to nothing, as the ecclesiastical authorities are in a state of sulk and stop everything they can. Our Neapolitan marquis was of opinion that strangers would not go to Rome this year ; his view was that the *funzioni* being stopped, 'Il n'y a que les ruines, qui sont peu de chose,' and this was said so naturally that it was evident he believed in it.

To the Hon. Mrs. Legge.

Rome : November 30, 1871.

In spite of G.'s sprained ankle, we are likely to plunge into dissipation. We have been to see the illuminations (at least I did), we are to dine with the Sermonetas on Monday, and with certain Walpoles on Tuesday. He is a blind man, a brother of Lord Orford's, who is active in charities and one of a body of people of all nations who called on the Pope to express sympathy with him on the great illumination day, the opening by the king of the first Roman Parliament. I went to the Piazza Colonna to see the king pass. He was well received—that is to say, there was one of those shouts which seem to unite in one voice, and of which it is difficult to judge the amount. But what struck me was the more than grave look of the people. People say it is the way of the Romans to be grave. But I think it must be something more. I was so much struck by it that I stopped at a corner where the stream was passing after the sight to see whether I could see a cheerful face : and staying for some little time it was literally true that I could not see *one*, except two, or at most three, chattering women—not a single male ; and they had an air, not only grave, but somewhat anxious or unsatisfied, like people coming back from a lottery in which they have not won. The only excitement I saw was a lot of people pointing out to one another something in the sky or on the top of Antonine's Column, I could not see which. At last it appeared that the morning star was just visible up there, and the people settled that it was the ' Stella d' Italia ' appearing to them on Italian Unity, which they were the more pleased at because the Pope's Council, you may remember, was saluted by thunder, lightning, and rain of a portentous kind. The impression was that the whole thing went off well. I am hardly surprised to see how the intelligent people here distinguish between Napoleon and the French as their creditors for the freedom of Italy.

A particularly pleasing and intelligent Italian officer who sat next me at *table d'hôte* (the pleasantest neighbour I had) for one day said that the history of the treaty of Villa Franca was that the French army would not go on. They thought they had made enough sacrifices for Italy. Our first evening at the Sermonetas'[2] was rather a failure; they proclaimed themselves accessible 'dopo le otto,' so we went at half-past eight and found ourselves a good quarter of an hour too soon. The Duchess, who is our stand by, had gone off (evidently) to take an after-dinner nap, and had to be hunted up; the Duke is blind, and so was unhandy at helping us through; the servant could not pronounce nor the company understand our names, and we interrupted in the middle some quiet family after-dinner music. However, the Duchess got on very well (she is so kind and cordial that it is impossible it should be otherwise) with both of us, and she and I talked as old acquaintances and settled that we must have known each other in 1840-1. The Duke is very amiable and intelligent, but I find great difficulty in understanding his English and I doubt his understanding mine, and this is a difficulty to which blindness adds much. Consequently there was a want of *suite* in our conversation which prevented much progress. Last Tuesday I went again (leaving G. on the sofa) and got on more easily. I was not too soon, the room was not full but pleasantly filled with deputies and such like, and I was introduced to the Walpoles and to an *avocato* Vera, appararently an *habitué*, who felt it his duty to take some charge of the stranger and talked French. I wish it were fairly the practice to do so; as a matter of course, one does not know what to be at when one has a miserable choice between English, French, and Italian. As to lionising, we are obliged by G.'s ankle to go *tout doucement*, which to me personally is

---

[2] The Duke of Sermoneta, the father of the present Duke, was the 'Don Michelangelo Gaetani' (then Prince of Teano) with whom Sir Walter Scott made acquaintance in 1832. In Sir W. Gell's 'Memoranda of Scott's Visit to Rome' he is described as 'a person of the most amiable disposition, gentlemanly manners, and remarkable talents. Sir Walter, to whom he had paid every attention during his stay at Rome, had conceived a high opinion of him, and added to his agreeable qualities he had a wonderful and accurate knowledge of his own country during the darker days . . . . these historical qualities, added to the amenity of his manners, rendered him naturally a favourite with Sir Walter.' The Duchess (his second wife) was a Miss Knight, and was in Rome with her mother when Lord Blachford was there in 1840.

rather a relief. To-day we shall go to hear Vespers at St. Peter's (having bought a camp stool), and to-morrow the Vatican sculptures. I am making a few purchases in a small way, and am rather tempted by lace; there is a good deal of the old guipure and such like about, and it seems to me cheap. We bought two metres yesterday (about two yards eight inches, I believe) for thirty francs; that, however, was rather specially cheap. It is of a massive pattern, looking almost liked a pierced ribbon. There is also a good deal of what I think they call Spanish point, and a finer and broader sort of guipure at a higher price, some thirty or forty francs a yard, very handsome. All which I mention in case you would like us to pick up some for you if we have a chance. Antiquities are certainly dear. Everything at Florence seemed to be 200 francs; here everything worth looking at is 800 francs. However, I have got a very pretty little terra-cotta female figure, old Magna Graecia work and I should say unmistakably Greek in its character, for sixty francs (some people would call it dear at six); and I think a charming bit of old Roman mozaic, two goldfinches flying at each other within a wreath the size of a reasonable paper weight, for fifty francs; and meditate a little more terra cotta if I can, which has always been in my line. In architecture I am getting very much attracted by the old Imperial style of church: lines of columns with flat entablature, a flat, highly ornamental ceiling, smooth semi spherical apses, and lots of mosaic—the old basilica in fact—and proportionately tired of the St. Paul's and St. Peter's style, of which, however, one must of course acknowledge the imposingness.

A lot of people of all nations got up a deputation of sympathy to the Pope on the day of the opening of the Italian Parliament, and they say the poor old gentleman was so overcome that he could hardly thank them. Somebody told us that he was also very much overcome at a failure to perform a miracle. It seems authenticated that a Princess Odeschalchi being dangerously ill from an impossibility of swallowing, the Pope sent her something with a command to swallow it, which (under the excitement) she did, and got at once well. It is said that the other day he bade a lame man walk. The man, under the excitement again, sprang up, but at once sank back again; the Pope repeated his command twice but with no further effect, and had to drive on, throwing himself back in his carriage in an access of disappointment. If true, it must be a strange excited state of mind; however, I tell it 'under reserve.'

To Right Hon. W. E. Gladstone.

Hôtel d'Angleterre, Rome : December 7, 1871.

My dear Gladstone,—An ignorant man must always run the risk of being fussy or of being wrong. I am perfectly ignorant of the mode or modes in which I can make myself quietly useful to you and the public in the new capacity which you have been pleased to impose upon me, and equally so as to the formalities or proprieties which attend the taking my place in the House of Lords; so I will just report what as at present advised I propose to myself if I do not hear from you that there is any reason to the contrary. (I shall be here, *i.e.* at this address, till Christmas.)

I hope to be in London in the first fortnight in January. Probably neither you nor Lord Granville will be in town, but I shall call on the Chancellor to get *renseignements* and instructions. I suppose the Court will ensure his being forthcoming. I shall not make any plans which will prevent my being guided mainly by what I hear from him, or from you, or Lord Granville if either of you are accessible. In the absence of any reason to the contrary, I should (for the sake of a country summer) probably make a settled stay in town during the earlier part of the session and run backwards and forwards during the latter part. But if, as I am told, the latter part is really the working time, it would be better, I presume, to reverse the order. Of course I should place myself among your supporters, and should be glad to make myself useful, not only to the public, but to you as a Government, making the most of agreement and the least of any difference. Under the latter head I may say that Coleridge's University Bill is the matter which (unexamined) I least like the look of.

I write this by way of keeping myself *en rapport* with you, without troubling you to answer me. I should perhaps hardly have troubled you to read it, but that I am not absolutely sure whether a note which I wrote to Lord Granville reached him or not.

Yours most sincerely,
BLACHFORD.

To Miss S. Rogers.

Rome: December 12, 1871.

My dear Sophy,—I have been greatly idle in writing to the family, partly because I have had some other letters to write, partly on general grounds. I think I left you before our Sermoneta dinner. They were very friendly and fixed a day for our dining with them—a family party, with the usual evening gathering after it. We of course had the Duke and Duchess between us, and each got on very pleasantly with our neighbours. She is very cordial and amiable, and plainly so much enjoys her good English talk that it is always pleasant to be with her. I was introduced then and before to a succession of deputies; a Sicilian (rather heavy in his French, and I did not encourage Italian), two Milanese, both very nice fellows, who talked mightily about irrigation and Italian farming—which, though I did not carry away much, was pleasant to hear.... But the feature of the evening was a Madame Peruzzi. Signor Peruzzi I take to be about the ablest *homme d'état* that they have. He was 'Sindaco' of Florence (Lord Mayor plus Governor, I take it), and so administered the city that the Tuscans would be ready to make him (says her Grace) 'Ubaldino' the first—Grand Duke of Tuscany—if he would hold up his little finger. He is a very good speaker, and his wife evidently one of those people who always have been popular.

We were all sitting in a state of propriety round the tea table, when down she plumped in the middle of us, and without a moment's delay began talking aloud to everybody at once, as if she had said to herself: 'Oh, all this dignity will never do, I must set all this right '—and in five minutes we were in the middle of a battle royal about Italian pronunciation. The Duke of Sermoneta's she was kind enough to patronise, he had 'really no Roman accent at all'—on which some of the Romans remarked, 'so much the worse for him,' for 'lingua Toscana in bocca Romana'—but that she would not hear of: 'lingua Toscana in bocca Toscana' was the true thing. Nobody else pronounced words as they were written —as for the Romans, they doubled all their consonants. 'So,' it was replied, 'do you in *académia*, which you pronounce *accadémia*.' 'Well,' she said, 'we spell it with two c's'—an invention, I believe, made on the spot. I was a good deal struck by the fineness of their ears for enunciation; nobody seemed capable of confusing between *académia* and *accadémia* as pronounced by them, but my ear with difficulty detected the difference. Of course it is easy to make a difference by imagination and emphasis, but this was what they did not do. Since that time we have been there in the evening, and made, I will not say more acquaintances, but talked to more Italians. I got rather into a corner, but G. had a very pleasant evening in the thick of it with the Sermonetas and a pleasant Italian ex-Premier, Minghetti, through some of whom, by the way, we have got a general order of admittance to the diplomatic tribune in the Chamber of Deputies.

After the last evening G. was surprised by a message from below stairs from the 'Principessa di Caserta'[3] to know whether she received. I was out, but came up to the hotel staircase just in time to see the Duchess of Sermoneta depositing herself on a bit of web (don't you call it?) preparatory to being carried upstairs to our *troisième* by her grand footmen, and a facchino (she is a confirmed invalid), and a very cosy little talk we had over our wood fire. One got on so well asking her all sorts of questions about Italian politics and so on; it was evidently (I thought) such a pleasure to her to go on telling us.

Yesterday we made the first experiment of our ticket for the diplomatic tribune. Very comfortable, and we (coming an hour too soon) had the very best places. It is a great

---

[3] Caserta was a possession of the Dukes of Sermoneta till it was sold to one of the Kings of Naples. The Roman people still spoke of the Sermonetas as Casertas.

place, like a theatre ; the deputies are in the pit, in concentric circles round the centre, where the President is, each having his place numbered, with his little desk and inkstand and paper (like the French). Above in the 'dress circle' are the public ; above them a great semi-dome, with a circular skylight in the centre. G. says that our House of Commons looks much more businesslike—I admit it looks more like a field of battle—and from being much smaller (the gallery as well as the floor being appropriated to members) I think it does not show emptiness so dismally as this must. At present the attendance seems rather large—at least there seemed many more members present than would be in the House of Commons on so trifling an occasion as yesterday was. But the sittings are short. The debate, or rather the questions and answers, seemed prosy—but so to me is the House of Commons in a general way—and here we did not understand more than some thirty or forty words an hour.

Ever yours,

BLACHFORD.

To the Rev. E. Rogers.

Rome : December 31, 1871.

My dear Edward,—I think we owe you more of a letter than any one else. We have of course been doing the usual things. Yesterday we went to Frascati ; but the day clouded, and the distant mountains and sea were in fog. We got, however, some beautiful sights—particularly a wonderfully beautiful sunset effect on the plain (purples and reds) without any adequate sun to account for it. I am greatly struck by the Italian villas, both the grounds, which are charming beyond expression and perfectly enjoyable for their purpose, and the marble in the interiors—which, however, are almost oppressively magnificent. In order to rival them at Blachford, I have invested some 5*l*. in scraps of marble, which (unless the working them up is terribly costly) I think may be made to look pretty. Somewhere about 250 bits or so ; all sorts of fragmentary shapes ; but, if put into squares, varying, I suppose, from 2 to 12 inches square may come in well. . . . .

I met at dinner on Tuesday a Doctor Pantaleone, now

(and I think formerly) chief of the great hospital here—the Santo Spirito—and politician of, I suppose, the Cavour ideas and something more. He talked very interestingly. He was, while a leading physician here, employed by Cavour to negotiate something or other quietly with the Pope; but his negotiations were abruptly brought to a conclusion by an order transmitted to the then Secretary for the Police, a Monsignore or Cardinal Mattei, to leave Rome in a month. He represented that the health of the patients depending on him required him to remain at least three months, but, finding that Mattei was under orders, he employed the night in writing a letter to the Pope himself. The next morning Mattei wrote to him—('I was a very good friend to Mattei and the Cardinals—to some of them I gave physic, and to some I gave dinners')—and asked him what in the world he had written to the Pope which had made him give orders that he (Pantaleone) should leave Rome in twenty-four hours after service of the orders. Mattei added that he would keep it back as long as ever he could, but that '*en revanche*' P. must keep himself in readiness to be off at six hours' instead of 24 hours' notice. P. after a little delay told him he could not conveniently be off till a steamer which left Rome at 11 o'clock (say) on Wednesday, to which Mattei replied that that would do very well, as he should see the Pope at once and be able to tell him that he was gone. So Pantaleone took himself off and remained in exile for ten years, till he came back at the tail of the Italian army.

He declares that he was the emissary of the Italian Government at Paris at the breaking out of the Prussian war, that he saw in a moment how it would all be; that he went to Lord Lyons and prevailed on him to prevail on his Government to prevail on Austria to come to a common agreement with Italy and England that none would interfere unless all interfered; that this served his Government as an excuse for inaction to the Emperor; that he wanted the Italians to go at once to Rome, but was stopped by the unanswerable reply that they were pledged to the Emperor not to do so; that the moment the Emperor was down he went to Thiers and Favre and persuaded them that it was not a time for France to make enemies, and that if their troops went out of Rome they must not object to the Italians coming in; that therefore things took the course they had taken, &c., &c., &c., all along of Doctor Pantaleone. He, like all the Italian newspapers, plumes himself on the Italian plan of playing their cards, of securing what is for their interest and doing it, and rejects with scorn the notion that they are wild or *exaltés*. He says it is their character to be prudent. 'An Italian,' he says, 'you may observe, never makes an imprudent marriage.' He complained of the want of political intelligence of the nobles, excepting Sermoneta, whom he spoke of as a man of surpassing talent, but surprised me by saying that he failed once as Minister of the Interior because he made a joke of everything—a very good joke, because he was full of wit, but no more than a joke; my impression of him would be of a depressed, gentle person. Of course blindness (joined, I believe, to a painful disease in the arm) is subduing; but it is only now and then, when his face has lighted up for a moment, that I should have thought him capable of hilarity. *Now* I connect him with the Prince de Teano (which he then was) who called on Hope in P. Barberini, and kept us laughing by his satirical account of a Derby Day.

Pantaleone has his theory about the malaria; it is that it is the result of a minute 'cryptogamous' plant growing on the damp land, the infection of which is stopped or absorbed by trees. So he purposes to plant a few millions of trees round certain infected tracts, and then, he says, everything else would be healthy. He states that in South America and elsewhere to sleep on the infected side of a strip of wood is certain death—on the other side is perfect safety. The only letter I have got beginning 'My dear Blachford' is one from Gladstone. What a mess about Sir R. Collier![4]

Ever yours affectionately,
BLACHFORD.

---

[4] The Act required that the members of the new Court of Appeal should have been previously judges of the lower courts. The Attorney-General, Sir R. Collier, was made a judge and then immediately promoted to the higher court. Nobody denied his fitness for the post; but it was felt by many that the Government was 'getting round' the Act by this technical qualification.

To Miss Rogers.

Blachford : January 27, 1872.

My dear Kate,—I had to splash about a little in London on Wednesday and Thursday, but was none the worse for it.

Henry Vivian set the bells ringing—and very nice bells they are—and the men set up an arch of laurel on the gate at the lodge. Unluckily, nobody told us of it; we, being packed up in a brougham in the dark, did not see it. But we have been to look at it to-day, and said our compliments, and ordered a supper for all concerned.

Your house is charming.[5] It is now all roofed except the tower. The tower is rising, all the stones cut and on the spot, and the foreman (who, by the way, has a dreadful cold, caught, I suppose, in your service) says the stone arch will be all up in a few days.

I saw Lord Granville, who was of course civil. He plainly wished me to come up to vote on the question—which I must say, in my opinion, improves on acquaintance.[6]

But I should think with a hostile H. of Lords it was notwithstanding very likely to turn out the Chancellor [Lord Selborne], whom, by the way, Lord Westbury describes as 'a character unredeemed by a single vice.' I think the chances are that I shall have to be back about the 16th; then it is on the cards I may not be up again (to say 'up') till July. In and for July they will want me to stop in town; Lord G. implied that as to committee I would pretty much please myself, but hoped that before long I should be taking part in the debates.

To Sir Henry Taylor.

Blachford, Ivybridge : February 7, 1872.

My dear Taylor,—The statement that I have been twice at the Colonial Office ought, like other public rumours, to have been halved before being believed. I got there once, almost managed to see Lord Granville (who was a necessity), and dropped a card or two on the other bigwigs to whom

---

[5] A house was being built by his sister close to Blachford.

[6] The Opposition moved a vote of censure regarding the appointment of Sir R. Collier. Votes were important, since the motion was defeated by a majority of only two.

Z

they were urgently due. This in the way of work was about as much as I could manage. But I should have been delighted to see you at Rutland Gate if you would have taken the trouble to come up.

How I envy your friend King Stephen.[7] But there is no use in envying or wishing to imitate him. I have to pay 33*l.* for my robes, 80*l.* or so for a new coat which I have kept at bay this ten years, and am now reduced to get—then 50*l.* for *supporters*—I being represented by a roebuck, and my wife (this is not a joke, but fact) by a griffin with gold tongue and claws and a gold rosette in her or its buttonhole. And this besides 350*l.* for Letters Patent. Well, I am down here, launched in a way, but just at present without being able to touch my future life. I cannot get out to look at anything that has to be looked at, and my indoor time is taken up with ascertaining as a matter of *l. s. d.* where I stand and what I have to play with—so that I cannot set to work even at the paper preliminaries of what is to be done. The griffin with gold rosette meanwhile is trying to reduce to order an innumerable army of tables and chests of drawers —one house containing at the present moment the furniture of three, and being consequently so choked that there is hardly room to make things change places. Then there are piles of old carpets—fulfilling your idea of what is due to the peerage. At least, I think they must be of about the same quality as Stephen's breeches. However, the disorderly atoms are beginning to float into their places, and I hope we shall soon be in some degree at peace.

Remember that we expect all of you here—we shall be ready for you. When? I suppose I must be in town to vote on the Collier case (colliery explosion, I hear it is called), and I shall try somehow or other to catch you. As yet I hardly know where I shall be ; either Blackheath or with the Dean of St. Paul's.

As to my getting on—I should have said, three days ago,

---

[7] Sir H Taylor in a letter to Lord Blachford had quoted the lines :

'King Stephen was a worthy peer,
His breeches cost him half a crown.'
(*Autobiography of Henry Taylor*, ii. 286.)

that I was getting well in a gallop. But I have had a check which reminds me that I must be patient. I find it difficult to settle matters between the necessity of exercise and the evils of damp air. The latter has almost taken away my voice, which I thought I had recovered.

Kindest remembrances to all of you,
Ever yours,
BLACHFORD.

To Lady Blachford.

The Deanery, St. Paul's: June 6, 1872.

I had a prosperous silent journey to London, made my way here, and then to the House, after correcting proofs in Burleigh Street.

Lord Russell opened, of course,[8] but I could hardly hear a word he said. Lord Granville in reply was, I thought, very good and persuasive; then Lord Grey, acrid and not particularly good (as I thought). When he got up the House was crowded, but thereupon an outward current set in, and before he had spoken ten minutes it had half emptied itself. Whilst he was at it, Lord Granville came up to me to ask if I intended to speak. I said no, but as he was going away I mentioned a mistake of Lord Grey's. He, Lord Grey, had attacked Lord Granville for misstatement, the charge depending on the date of a letter printed in the 'Times' as of May 14 (in the correspondence which you looked out for me, and

---

[8] This debate in the House of Lords was on a motion made by Lord Russell against the 'Alabama' Arbitration (Lord Russell, as it happened, was Foreign Secretary in July 1862 when the 'Alabama,' through want of prompt action, slipped out of the Mersey). By the Treaty of Washington, in 1871, it was arranged to submit to arbitration the American claims for damage done by the 'Alabama' during the Civil War (besides the disputes about the San Juan boundary and the Canadian Fisheries). Most of the Conservative party, and perhaps some others, considered the English Commissioners to have failed alike in firmness and in adroitness; but there would have been little opposition to the treaty, of which the general principles were unquestionably fair, had not the American Government (owing, as it afterwards appeared, to the insistence of Mr. Sumner) chosen to include in their case for the arbitration court claims for 'indirect losses' —*i.e.* general loss of trade, prolongation of the war, &c., which they affected to trace to the cruises of the 'Alabama.' This was manifestly and absurdly unjust, and there is little doubt that the arbitration must have fallen through if the American Government had not withdrawn the indirect claims.

which I had been studying). I thought it odd, and, on looking, it appeared that the dates of the letters (in chronological order) were May 2, May 3, May 14, May 6, and so on. Of course it was evident (and ought to have been so to Lord Grey) that 14th was a misprint for 4th. Lord Granville left me, and, without resuming his seat, walked straight to the table, begged a moment to explain, and said that the date of the letter was not the 14th, but the 4th, and sat down. I was alarmed and rushed down to explain that it *was* the 14th in the 'Times.' 'Oh!' he said, 'all right—we have it here,' and in a moment Lord Ripon was up and shaking the 'New York Herald' with the *true* date in Lord Grey's face. The matter was nothing, but I was amused at the audacious promptitude with which Lord Granville acted on my suggestion (for it was hardly more) that the date was wrongly printed. It is just his way.

Well, then came Lord Denman, with still more violent ebb-tide among their lordships, and it became evident to me, as it had to them, that it was a convenient time for dinner. While I was thus usefully employed Lord Stratford spoke how, I know not—and Lord Derby began, and after my return went on without great effect. His line is not, I think, attack. If he is not sensible and considerate he appears to me not to be much, and in attack, sense and consideration are not the successful qualities.

Lord Kimberley was good. Lord Salisbury was very clever indeed, and very acrimonious. His sentences told, however, and I could hardly help myself cheering at his proposal that Lowe, or '*still better*' Ayrton, should have been sent out to deal with the Yankees instead of Lord Ripon. It was certainly brilliant, and people, some on our side of the house, evidently enjoyed the pokes at the Yankees, and did not like the want of spirit of ministers' policy. Also the Duke of Somerset and Lord Westbury have established a corner for themselves, just behind the ministerial bench; a kind of little, very little Adullam in the most effective place geographically for being 'nasty;' and they, it was evident, were not discoursing good to their friends, though I heard (could not help hearing) one say, as in a tone of consultation: 'We can't prevent a division!'

Then Lord Ripon—nil; Lord Malmesbury—nil; Lord, Westbury—spoke from a false position. Of course he was clear, flowing, and amusing now and then, but the amusement was principally from a sense of the absurd insolence with which he managed to convey his contempt for the ministers and all their helpers, and he was in this difficulty that he was desirous, or affected to be so, of preventing the adverse vote while he was equally desirous to intensify the feeling of dissatisfaction with ministers which justified (if anything could justify) the vote; hence he had so to distribute his arguments as to serve both purposes, and did not make a consistent whole.

Then a youthful maiden speech from Lord Rosebery, and the great speech of the evening—from Cairns. His speeches are very like one another, and very unpleasant for those against whom they are directed from their extreme excellence of arrangement and terrible lucidity. It seems as if you had never done with him. He makes a case against you—a clear, incisive case—and then when that is worked out, and you are thinking how to get out of the scrape, you begin to find that what you have as yet heard is not the scrape, but only the beginning of it; the foundation of a series of aggravations and misfortunes which sink you deeper in the mire and close all avenues of escape. Yet through all this there is a feeling that there is a fallacy here, and an exaggeration (not of language, but of thought) there, and that with time, and power, and liberty to write a book on the subject, a tolerably good book might be made of 'the dissector dissected.' You feel that it is a skilful accumulation of all that is bad and a skilful exclusion of all that is good, which really places the affair, as a whole, on the most utterly false footing. However, he is very unpleasant to his adversaries, and his *sentiment*, when he tries it, is neat bunkum.

He and Lord Westbury, as you will have seen, both echoed the claptrap about Bernard's 'less accurate.'[9]

---

[9] Mr. Mountague Bernard (then Professor of International Law at Oxford) had been one of the English Commissioners for the Treaty of Washington. The others were Lord Ripon (then Lord de Grey), Sir Stafford Northcote, and Sir Edward Thornton.

.... To-day I hunted up Lord Granville to ask whether he would like me to speak, and he said—Yes, very much, unless the Opposition were well enough drilled to keep silence ; in which case, as the Chancellor and the Duke of Argyll wanted to speak, a third speaker *on the same side* would be improper.

.... Going down to the House rather late (6 o'clock), as I knew the Chancellor was to be long, I was met by the news that Fish [1] had telegraphed that, subject to our agreement as to future proceedings, the United States Government considered the additional article as a withdrawal of the indirect claims.

Lord Ripon, who told me of this, told me that the news exploded like a shell among the hostile ranks. Of course it made it necessary to withdraw Lord Russell's motion, but Lord Russell was nowhere to be found to withdraw it. Lord Ripon wanted to propose that *Lady* Russell, then present, should withdraw it, as Lord Russell's deputy, from the gallery. But at last Lord Russell himself was, I suppose, found, and the whole affair is over for the present. And my beautiful speech, about which I felt an odd mixture of terror and amusement, is lost to the world.

.... Church gets credit with those from whom credit is compliment for his dealings with the Lord Mayor. People (some) thank him for his dignified rebuke. *Vide* correspondence printed by Lord Mayor.[2]

To Lady Blachford.

The Deanery, St. Paul's : June 8, 1872.

My dear Georgie,—Not much more to say, except that, as you see by the enclosed, I have not got off my 'endowed schools.'

Yesterday I had my second sitting at the Appellate Jurisdiction Committee. Sir Barnes Peacock examined, and gave us long accounts of the mode of administering justice in

---

[1] Mr. Fish was Secretary of State in the United States.

[2] The Lord Mayor had proposed to call a meeting of the subscribers to reconsider the arrangement made by the executive committee, that Mr. Burgess should be asked to submit plans for the completion of St. Paul's. The correspondence is printed in the *Times* of Jun , 1872.

India, without much reference to the consideration whether it was relevant to the appeal question.

We were rather amused, in the middle of a grave cross-examination, by the interposition of Lord Chelmsford (to the shorthand writer), 'I don't desire this to be taken down:' then: 'Sir Barnes, I am glad to find that you are able to give a positive denial to the statement made in Lord Brougham's autobiography that you died in India.'

We were all so completely taken in by the confidential exordium to the shorthand writer, and the gravity with which the question was delivered, that there was a regular burst of laughter when the shot went off.

. . . Then Sir H. Mayne was examined, and there was a discussion—carried on, I thought, very pleasantly—between the bigwigs—Cairns taking decidedly the lead; and I think the inquiry will not last so long as I had supposed. It seems to me that they are all pretty well agreed, in principle, except on the question whether the proposed court shall keep up a purely colourable connexion with the House of Lords.

Church says that there is in the city a considerable cry against the *Puseyite* chapter. But, though he is continually saying how much better it would be to make Lightfoot Dean I do not see that the cry is a trouble or scare to him. And I think he seems to feel himself a match for the Lord Mayor, Cavendish Bentinck & Co. If he talks about things, it is not in the tone of a man at all puzzled or at sea, or in want of opinions, but by way of letting off schemes. He catches at a hint if it is good, but he does not the least seem to want advice as a *stay*.

Bernard was here yesterday, and seemed in better spirits than I expected. He talked freely enough, and took all those rubbishy criticisms [3] for what they are worth. At least, so it seemed. Church rather invited or encouraged me after dinner to tell Bernard what I *should* have said in the House of Lords—at which he seemed pleased. I did it gladly because I thought he would be encouraged by the free, aggressive, thorough-going way in which I proposed to have said (in effect) that the main article of the Treaty was good and sufficient and

---

[3] See note on the previous letter.

well considered, and that, with all the general cry about its ambiguity, nobody who looked into the matter had yet dared to say that the arguments by which its meaning was established had any sort of flaw in them or were anything short of conclusive, except Lord Cairns; and that his only argument was such that it really was an admission that with all his efforts to say something he had nothing to say.

It is no doubt a triumph for the Government, but there are still difficulties to be got over; the main one being the difficulty of making that which is nothing take a colourable appearance of being something.

Meantime the adjournment, while it has (by letting in this incident) prevented a beating, has left the Opposition *oratorically* in possession of the field; their great speech (Cairns) remaining unanswered.

To Sir Henry Taylor.

Blachford: November 25, 1872.

My dear Taylor,—'Mea culpa, mea culpa, mea maxima culpa.' I *am* lazy, and not only that, but lazier every day. Rural life certainly tends to comatosity. But, moreover, a man in the country has nothing to say except just now that 'the rain it raineth every day;' and the more entertaining a letter you receive, the more ashamed you are to send in return—a yawn.

I will look up your letter, but I feel somewhat doubtful about finding it. I have been criminally careless about papers of all kinds (except Colonial Office proper) for the last ten years, and upon this looseness of custody has come the upheaving of a change of residence into a house filled with other people's property; so till my sisters and their belongings are gone, I do not know what I have or where I have it, or how to look for it. In a few days, I hope, I shall begin to investigate.

Your account of your London doings almost tempts me to come up to the Deanery to look at you. Meantime, about your autobiography. You asked me what I thought about printing *letters*—*i.e.* whether you should tell your story, or exhibit it by extracts. At first I thought I could say nothing but that you must judge for yourself on inspection of the letters. But I think I have something more to say, though not much. It seems to me that if an event or impression which deserves a place on its own historical merits in your autobiography is recorded in your correspondence, or if a certain correspondence is in itself a fact in your life, there is *prima facie* reason for exhibiting it by extracts from the correspondence; it is more authentically, and very likely more vividly, stated. But it appears to me that an autobiographer should be much on his guard against printing letters merely because, however rightly, he thinks them good. To publish correspondence on account of its intrinsic value is rather for a man's friends than for himself. And to do it is to come out of doors in undress, and seems to me to savour of self-exhibition, which I take to be the danger of autobiography. It is as if Sydney Smith had published a volume of his 'Table Talk.'

Therefore, though I think that extracts from your letters are likely to be among the very most interesting parts of your book, yet I should like them only where it was (or appeared to be) the case that they were only introduced for the purpose of telling what had to be, or could not better be, told. Have you looked at Stanley's Arnold? He is considered to have handled correspondence very successfully. But that is not *auto*-biography.

That poor old fellow to whom you gave some medicated wadding, and who would like to have given you a present, is dead, poor fellow. He did not leave you anything in his will; but was very anxious to explain to those whom he left behind the amount of his debts, which were, I think, two and sixpence for a shovel and two shillings for repairing some tools. He was, I think, the only link with the generation of my grandfather—whom he remembered swearing, as he did when he was angry, 'By my salvation.' It is creditable that the bad words (if these are to be called such) are reported never to have gone any further. My sister was told that the old man wandered very much, but had been quieter for some time '*after the Lord came to him.*' I was horrified to find that 'the Lord' meant me. I supposed it something quite different.

What a state the Continent is in—monarchy asserting itself in France, and nobility shattered in Germany. In one thing I have profound faith, the ascendency of snobs. . . . .

To Rev. E. Rogers.

London : February 15, 1873

My dear Edward,—As to Chronicle. The Queen's speech went off tamely enough. Those who desire to depreciate the Washington Treaty went on pecking at it, but I suppose the thing is at an end. Since that time attendance on the House of Lords has been simply formal and stupid, except on Thursday, when Palmer opened his scheme of Land Reform, going through the whole matter with great clearness and scrupulous desire to butter their lordships into acquiescence. And from Cairns's speech I should anticipate an easy passage for the whole. The difference between them reduces itself to a question on the Appellate Jurisdiction of the House of Lords, which is retained in respect of Scotland and Ireland, but extinguished as to England (where appeals to them are comparatively infrequent). Cairns proposes to leave the appeal to the House of Lords in those *English* cases in which the two courts through which the case must reach them disagree, abolishing it only when those two courts are unanimous—a faint difference which cannot greatly signify, I should think.

The Bishop of Salisbury[4] has been here all the time (leaving to-day), very pleasant and full of life. At Nobody's,[5] on Wednesday, I got between Harrison and Kenyon and spent a pleasant evening, only disturbed by the necessity of making a speech—bad, but short. On Thursday we had Oakeley of Balliol here, evidently most happy at going back with Moberley to old times, in which he seems very much to live, and about which, he says, he is continually dreaming (I mean literally). It was rather pathetic. However, I saw very little of him, having been kept till eight in the House, and then dining at the Club with or next to Coleridge, Bruce,

[4] Dr. Moberley.   [5] A dining club.

and Acland. Coleridge is sanguine about Gladstone's Irish University Bill. He seems to have started with the Cabinet against him and to have converted them all (their point being, I presume, to have something that would *pass*), especially Lowe, whom Coleridge describes as full of admiration for the *clearness* of the scheme. I don't understand it, but I imagine that it just gives or leaves to everybody enough to stop their mouths without infuriating their neighbours.

I have had one or two talks with (or rather from) Lord Kimberley, who hands the Colonial Church question over to the bishops and me, and I am accordingly to meet Selwyn, Moberley, Isambard Brunel (a canon-lawyer, and a friend of Froude's) at Lambeth on Tuesday, to feel our way. I had a few words with Lord Granville, and a long talk (not about much) with Lord Carnarvon, who wants me to yacht with him in the Mediterranean till Easter, which would not suit my book in any way.

To Rev. E. Rogers.

London : March 28, 1873.

My dear E.,—Well, the great event has gone off, and I hope satisfactorily.[6] (I may as well say that the 'Times' has simply made a speech out of the bill having no affectation of similarity with any part of what I said.)

Having fortified myself with cold beef, and, according to V.'s especial advice, with soda-water and sherry, I proceeded down with G. and deposited her in the gallery opposite me, and took my place, speculating on the quantity and quality of my audience, which appeared (ten minutes before the time) rather thin and disconsolate. I had previously, *i.e.* since the beef and soda-water, rehearsed my speech to myself in St. James's Park, so I felt I had no more to do or think about. The Bishops' bench of course filled. Canterbury, York, Winchester, Carlisle, Lichfield, Salisbury, and some others. Then the House filled fairly, and I was told that the Duke of Richmond would follow me. I had a pretty good notion that Cairns and Belmore would follow on the same side (*i.e.* on the

---

[6] The debate on the Colonial Church Bill, which Lord Blachford introduced (see above, p. 305).

Scotch and Irish points). Two or three formal things were disposed of when Lefevre solemnly proclaimed : ' Second reading of the Colonial Church Bill. Lord Blachford.' I did not feel the slightest nervousness, and began, as I thought, speaking very distinctly and with ease. They seemed to listen attentively, but as I approached the only little bit of liveliness in the speech, without the vestige of a cheer (which, indeed, would have been out of place), I felt how difficult it was before such an audience to lift oneself beyond the mere statements of fact and argument which were necessary. However, I went at it—and, the passage being obviously one which invited a cheer, I got one. Lord Granville, who had turned and looked attentively at me in a way which gives heart, had said ' Speak louder,' which I attended to for a moment, and then, I am afraid, forgot. I think he led off this cheer. Then I went on, still feeling as if I were attended to up to the end.

Then got up the Duke of Richmond, but, as they say, ' yielded to ' the Archbishop of Canterbury, who paid me some compliments (*vide* ' Times '), observing that my speech justified the sound judgment of the bishops in not bringing in the bill themselves, but asking me to do it. Then he went into some statistics to show the *size* of the Colonial Church, and therefore of the grievances. Then followed the Opposition : Duke of Richmond, Cairns, Belmore, Courtown, broken by Archbishop of York, Bishop of Winchester, and Lord Chancellor on what I may call my side. The argument was entirely on their side, nobody attempting really to meet them, and was directed not against the colonial part of the bill, which everybody accepted, but against the bearing of the bill on Scotch and Irish. I got a full share of compliment for knowledge of the subject. The complimenters were Duke of Richmond, Lord Cairns, Archbishop of Canterbury, and Lord Kimberley clenched them by saying that the subject (which all agreed had been clearly presented to them) was without any exception the most difficult to understand or explain that he had ever met with.

The Archbishop, with a kind of side hit, said that the Church had a claim on me to extricate them from the difficulty, as it had been my influence with successive Secretaries of

State that had got them into it. When it was over, Lord Granville came up to me and sat down and said, 'Well, I congratulate you on your great success. We have been agreeing that you said in twenty minutes what it would have taken Cairns an hour and a half to say.'

. . . I have little hope of its passing this session. But I am not sure that it may not stand a better chance on the whole by being hammered out in Select Committee, and passed in the House of Lords this session, and then re-introduced—fresh and approved, quite at the beginning of next session.

I almost think I shall make and send to the 'Guardian' a report of my speech. It is really wanted, as a brief for those who talk about it now or may have to talk about it in the House of Commons. I think, viewed as establishing my character, I have satisfied their lordships that I can state intelligibly a difficult case, that I shall not unnecessarily trouble them with words, and that though the subject was a dry one, I have the capacity (to some extent) of being otherwise than dry.

Lord Stanley of Alderley made the House laugh by speaking of the 'noble lord' (me) 'and the *other* Right Rev. Prelates.'

I must finish, both because I must be off, and because my eyes are shaking.[7]

To Lady Blachford.

London : July 8, 1873.

I got on pretty fairly with my committee yesterday, but was worried by Archbishops, who started various hares of their own, and a fresh hare is to be started by the Bishop of Winchester to-morrow.

Lord Shaftesbury got a baiting from Lord Salisbury and the Chancellor yesterday.[8] Lord S. made him appear

---

[7] It is well to note that the descriptions of this and some other debates in which Lord Blachford took part were written solely to give pleasure to his near relations. Some of the more personal parts of such letters are, however, inserted because it is thought that they are not without a general interest.

[8] Lord Shaftesbury introduced a bill to prevent frauds in charitable funds.

blundering, and the Chancellor made the whole House laugh at him, so that he fairly lost his temper, and told them that if he was so treated he would never be philanthropical again. Selborne pointed out that certain wives of Archbishops and even of Prime Ministers were concerned in 'charitable institutions,' and unless they kept their accounts correctly to the minutest particular and posted over the door 'at Lambeth or Carlton H. Gardens' in legible Roman characters the nature of their institution and the hours of the day at which their accounts would be open to the inspection of subscribers, they would be liable on the first offence to imprisonment with hard labour (without the alternative of a fine), and for the second to penal servitude.

Lord Salisbury had got up saying that 'with all respect,' &c., for his noble friend, there was nothing which he heard of with greater apprehension and horror than legislation by a distinguished philanthropist; then he proceeded to cut the bill to bits, ending by saying that as it was not to go beyond the second reading he would not oppose it, but hoped that in the recess it would be mended.

Then Selborne began by saying that he could not help thinking that his noble friend was taking a lenient view of the bill when he proposed to let it have a second reading; and then proceeded to expose it as a piece of laughable tyranny, in a way which the House thoroughly appreciated.

I suppose Shaftesbury will take it out of them by some special ferocity on Monday. I rather shiver to think what may happen.

To Hon. Mrs. Legge.

Blachford : August 25, 1873.

My dear Marian,—You will have heard about the Manœuvres. Cardwell's visit was on the whole successful, in spite of misadventures, which were certainly many. In the first place the weather and other things wholly put an end to the sham fights on which we had counted for Monday and Tuesday. The weather also destroyed (except as a matter of business) a party which Cardwell[9] had planned for the inspection of the fortifications in the Sound. Cardwell's luggage and servants missed trains at Plymouth. Storks[1] left his luggage in London. Edward and I both met with accidents which disabled us from riding. Northcote was thrown from his horse and also laid up for a day. Our carriage broke a spring on our way to the march past, and I and Bruno upset an intoxicated pedestrian coming home; so that to have sent everybody away pleased—as I really think we did—was rather creditable to all parties concerned.

The great point was that the 21st was beautiful. The site was not so good as Ringmoor, but very fine, and the day was absolutely perfect, cool and warm, with plenty of sun and flying clouds and clear distances.[2]

The sight was less picturesque and instructive, but more imposing of course, than anything we had had before, and our carriage—though late, owing to the broken spring—had the best possible place. After the show we had luncheon with Sir C. Staveley to meet the Prince. G. was opposite to him, and in the knot of conversation of which he was the centre. I was next General Smith, commanding the 1st division, who was strong in praises of his soldiers—no complaints even of incivility, all cheerful and in the best spirits in spite of the rain, and all, men and horses, in the best health. He had a strong view of the benefit of the soldiers' recreation rooms, and said that he had walked round one of them, while some fifty or sixty men were engaged in writing and reading, without any of them perceiving that he had come in and gone out. . . .

I walked yesterday to Anglepool, on the Erme. The bed was a raging mass of rush and foam, the whole of the rocks being absolutely covered. The same flood drowned poor Colonel Mackenzie. I have crossed the ford where he was drowned once or twice lately.

---

[9] Secretary of State for War at that time.
[1] Sir Henry Storks, see p. 265.

[2] These military manœuvres were on Dartmoor near Cadover Bridge, a few miles from Blachford.

To Sir Henry Taylor.

Blachford : October 23, 1873.

My dear Taylor,—We are just now recovering our breath, in solitude and torrents of rain, from a course of visitors, partly pleasure and partly duty.

This is the first year in which we have set to work to get through conscientiously what we 'ought' to do in that way. And the autumn manœuvres weighted us further with Cardwell, Storks, and others. We had the Dean, and wished for you and yours.

Have you ever seen military manœuvres on anything of a scale in anything of a country? They are exceedingly beautiful. The scampering of artillery and infantry to cover, the fighting from cover, the clustering for attack, the indications, and conjectures, and appearances of troops (in a sham fight) from expected or unexpected quarters—all give a great deal of flesh to one's imaginations of real battles, if (as was our case) you can get a good commanding situation where you are in the thick of what is going on on one side.

I cannot quite make out to my own satisfaction whether I am or am not doing anything besides entertaining visitors. I find myself keeping a lot of labourers at work about this and that, stirring them up, insisting, hunting up omissions, deciding on cottages and lines of fencing. And I think certain people, and certain grounds, and certain woods will be to a certain extent more comfortable and pretty and productive for what I do ; but it is so unlike what I have been accustomed to call work that I do not know whether it is so or not. There is a tremendous proportion of gossip and dawdling in it.

Do you keep your eye on Spain? I was rather amused at a young naval officer's account of Admiral Yelverton's proceedings, which furnished the explanation, which I have always thought the most probable one, of Lord Russell's preference for post captains as diplomatists. Admiral Yelverton had first required a delay of bombardment for four days, to which he added two more at the request of the French Commodore, and sent an English captain to communicate this extended prohibition to the 'Intransigente' commander.[3] The 'Intransigente' stormed and blustered, and said with many words that he should do as he liked. The Englishman, being a man economical of the Queen's English, merely said: 'You had better not. Good morning,' and stepped into his boat.

The next day the 'Numencia' took up a position of offence, on which the 'Lord Warden' (of which my young friend is, I think, first lieutenant) swept up to her side, close. The 'Numencia' asked what he or she meant, to which answer was given: 'To sink you if you fire a shot.' The diplomacy was completely effectual for its purpose. But then it was conducted under circumstances of advantage.

Certainly conservatism is strong in the 'Paullo post futurum.' Dizzy, Chambord, and Carlos. The Count of Chambord's position just now illustrates what I am in the habit of thinking, that in one sense 'nothing succeeds like (ill) success.'

If you want to be praised by opponents, acquire a habit of failing. Sir R. Inglis had the full benefit of this. And for a certain time he of Chambord had. Liberal papers were full of his power, and honesty, and logical consistency, and so on, so long as they considered that his impracticability was playing their game. But now that the poor man is showing something of a certain bewildered common-sense, and appears to have a kind of possibility of winning after a fashion, he becomes an impostor and traitor, and I do not know what else.[4]

Good-bye, and kindest regards to all of you from us.

Ever yours affectionately,
BLACHFORD.

---

[3] The 'Numencia' was one of the insurgent frigates from Cartagena, which was bombarding Alicante. Early in the following year, when Cartagena surrendered to the troops of the Madrid Government (Jan. 11, 1874), the 'Numencia' took off the insurgent Junta to Oran and surrendered to the French.

[4] It was reported in the papers of October 18, 1873, that the Comte de Chambord was prepared to make concessions; but in his letter to M. Chesneslong a few days later (Oct. 27) he absolutely refused to substitute the tricolor for the white flag, and whatever hopes of his success may have been entertained at once disappeared.

To Dean Church.

May 30, 1874.

My dear Church,—Thank you. I should have liked very much to have come up to meet Newman, and I have just got Coleridge's letter asking me to do so. But I have a houseful for Whitsun week, and, though I *could* steal a day or two, it would not be very gracious. So, after hesitating till Coleridge's letter forced me to say 'yes' or 'no,' I have decided to stay here.

My wife is in distress at the loss of one of her Guernsey cows—milk fever—after giving birth to a calf. I wish you could have seen the way in which our cowman received my suggestion that, as the poor creature could not survive, and was only suffering, she should be put out of her pain. He had 'niver heerd of a cow being killed that way.' I felt at once that I had to apologise, and said that it was to save the poor creature suffering, to which he said gravely that 'All living beings had to suffer when it came to the end.' I think he felt that ' He who killeth a cow was as if he slew a man.' So he stayed up all night with her till she died in the morning.

Ever yours affectionately,

BLACHFORD.

To Sir Henry Taylor.

The Deanery, St. Paul's : July 15, 1874.

My dear Taylor,—I have never answered your letter, nearly a month old (June 23), because I was in continual hopes of answering it by a telegram asking you to bed me the next day. But it is inconceivable how, with very little really to do, there is always something which is just enough to prevent you from being a free agent. . . . What a worry passing a bill is ! I do not wonder at what I used to think the cowardly indisposition of our chiefs to take one in hand. In my case there is an execrable clergyman who would seem to have given his whole mind to the Colonial Clergy Bill, except that I hear he contrives to be as great a bore to other persons on other subjects—one of those creatures of minute, patchy learning, who are always being led astray by some laboriously acquired shred of knowledge, which, if he understood more, he would understand to be nothing to the purpose, but which enables him to impose on M.P.s who know less than himself, and so to give honest men like myself an amount of trouble for which I can only forgive him in my capacity of Christian. —Well, ' Peace be with him '—which in Latin is *pereat male*, or at least *pereat*.

Gladstone's apparition is curious. I am sorry to say I cannot go with him on either of his points—indeed, I may almost say, on any. I see no reason why the Scotch Church should not have their way about patronage. I think the cry against the Public Worship Bill a scare, and I particularly object to the working and principle of the Endowed Schools Act.[5] However, everybody seems to agree that he made a great speech on the Public Worship Bill as a matter of oratory He does not seem to care much about what was his party, who, I suppose, are dead against him on two out of three of these points.

To Dean Church.

Blachford : July 21, 1874.

My dear Church,—My eyes are almost out of my head with writing. But I cannot help saying how very much I like that letter of yours to the ' Times.' It is in every respect excellent.[6] I see why you put in the sentence about swapping. And I think, what you could not expect, that I should have taken off a little of the edge of one or two expressions about

---

[5] Mr. Gladstone reappeared in Parliament on July 6 to oppose the Bill for the Abolition of Church Patronage (Scotland), having taken no part in debates since the first nights of the session (*i.e.* about four months before). He opposed Archbishop Tait's Act for the Regulation of Public Worship when it was introduced into the House of Commons on July 9. He also opposed the Bill for Amending the Endowed Schools Act of 1869. This Amending Bill transferred the powers of the Commission of Endowed Schools (under the 1869 Act) to the Charity Commissioners, and also made provision for retaining connection with the Church, if prescribed by the founder, in the case of schools founded since the Toleration Act of William and Mary. (In adopting this limit Mr. Forster's amending Act of 1873 was followed in preference to Lord Sandford's original draft).

[6] The letter of Dean Howson (on the subject of the ritual in the Eucharist), and Dean Church's reply, appeared in the *Times* of July 18 and 20.

the Ritualists. But these do not at all affect the impression produced by the letter, which seems to me excellent in every direction, as against Howson in particular, persecutors in general and ritualists, and as asserting the Anglican sacrificial doctrine, which, without understanding what it amounts to, I quite see ought to be asserted as you have asserted it.

Ever yours affectionately,
BLACHFORD.

To Dean Church.

Blachford : July 22, 1874.

My dear Church,—I return Newman's letter. I wish he had fiddled.

I dare say writing your letter was a fret to you. But you were evidently bursting with what you had to say before I left you. And I think it rather a godsend that Howson furnished the negative electricity necessary for an explosion. You would have died of suppressed Tractarianism if something had not occurred to determine it to the surface.

I shall be much disappointed if it does not do much good. It just arrests the tendency of well-enough-meaning men to take for granted that the doctrine of sacrifice is Popery. And I wish to point out that the fact of your being Dean, and the eminence which you have acquired as Dean, is what makes it possible for you thus to speak with effect *ex cathedrâ*.

It seems to me a thoroughly well-planted blow, and I suppose a *réponse sans réplique*.

Yours ever affectionately,
BLACHFORD.

To Sir Henry Taylor.

Blachford : November 27, 1874.

My dear Taylor,—What a curious series of publications Gladstone is pouring forth! Ritualism, Rome, and Bishop Patteson. . . . I think I am sorry that he has gone in at Rome. I have a strong belief, in spite of all appearances to the contrary, that, with patience and justice, even Irish Roman Catholicism can be mitigated into sense. But it requires all the power of such a man as Gladstone to control the ebullitions of our Protestantism while the process of taming is going on. And if he sets himself to widen the breach between the countries, as his pamphlet must do, I do not know who is to patch it up.

Have you observed a Canadian case, in which Christian burial is denied a man for belonging to a society which has in its library books prohibited by the Index? There is to my mind something singular and rather impressive in the daring which not only proclaims the doctrines of the Syllabus &c., but is beginning in remote parts of the world to give effect to them. It seems as if the Pope really supposed himself capable of effecting such a revolution as would turn the Roman Catholic body into a society floating separately about the face of the earth, like the Jews or Quakers of the last century, or the Three Children in Nebuchadnezzar's furnace. Either he must be rather foolish, or Roman Catholics must be a more docile body than I have ever supposed possible. Of course one always knew that there was such a thing as the 'Index,' but when you practically come across the idea that a Roman congregation really assumes to tell some 200 or 300 millions of people, adults, litterateurs, and all what they shall or shall not read, it seems like a dream.

To Sir Henry Taylor.

Blachford: December 30, 1874.

And now as to egotism—which is always a pleasant indulgence—if it did not bring to a head certain unpleasant thoughts which without such definite self-consideration would be mere floating vapours.

The unpleasant thought here is that I waste a great deal of time, partly from idleness, partly from want of method, partly from want of an interesting task to pick up my stray ends of time, partly from the real interruptions of country life on such a property as this, and partly because, when I get keen about anything requiring continuous use of eyes, I get pulled up short by them more easily than you would suppose from Colonial Office recollections. At this moment the letters are floating or rather quivering before me.

I have had a good many floating intentions on coming here—county business of a public kind, experiments on the poor, improvement of estate, literary work, society of neighbours and visitors, parish improvements moral and physical, and so on. On this came the very disturbing influence of Parliament. And I am only now beginning to find out into what form all these things are condensing.

In the first place county business has *not*, and county society has *hardly*, come near me. This is, I suppose, partly because I have not met society half-way, keeping aloof from the occasions when men do mostly congregate—balls, races, agricultural meetings, archery, platforms of all sorts and sizes —and this again is partly from taste, and partly because I have desired to see my way before plunging into anything like expense.

In the second place, *material* work, building, planting, draining, and so on, takes hold on me. Everybody has a kind of ambition which is by no means what he most approves, but which he feels congenial. Now I am defectively defective in intellectual, or social, or political, or philanthropical ambition. If I accomplish anything in these departments —as I know it is my duty to accomplish it—it is as a task, which only carries with it the pleasure—a great one—of accomplishing a task. The measuring yourself against a difficulty and overcoming it, whether weeding a grass lawn or solving a problem, is a pleasure when you have once made the effort of beginning. But as a matter of *ambition* I think my pet object would be changing the face of a country. To feel that fields, and woods, and cottages, and roads, and the faces of men, women, and children had changed their character since I had had the handling of a territory, would be *the* thing which I should really enjoy in the prospect, and in the progress, and in the result.

So this is taking hold of me. I dare say I waste more time and money than I ought on improvements that are luxuries, but I also say to myself that I should like, if possible, before I die or become past work, to be able to think that everybody on my property is, except for his or her own fault, as well lodged, with reference to his station in life, as I am with regard to mine. I am making the first advances to this, and in doing so I am beginning to enlarge the very pleasant relations which existed between Blachford and the labourers in my mother's time (charity proper I leave to my wife). Those who were mere labourers, and sometimes dull ones, are beginning to contract with me for work, and I think are in a way to rise in comfort and intelligence. And this is in some degree an excuse for spending perhaps more than I ought on beautifying my own house, grounds, and pretty places.

However, this, though it causes a good many interruptions, does not take up any great proportion of time, and ought not, and I hope will not take up hereafter the time it does now. Also I do not doubt that I *waste* a good deal of money —which is not only inconvenient in itself—but, so far as it is mismanagement, demoralising to my accomplices.

Then, as to literary work, I do not, or perhaps *I do*, know what you will say when I tell you that I am in the habit of writing for a weekly newspaper, a clerical paper called the 'Guardian,' in which I feel an interest, first because I had a hand—I may say was the principal hand—in setting it up in times of High Church distress ... I have once or twice tried my hand at thinking or writing on somewhat larger subjects. I began a parallel between the lives of John Mill and Bishop Patteson. But when I had got a certain distance with a view of Mill's personal history, I did not see what was to become of it when I had done it, and so stopped short. What I should have liked to have shown would have been the different growth of two characters, each intrinsically noble and thoroughgoing, but one having the advantage of a family and a God, and the other not having those advantages. If, when the occasion offered, I had any outlet for such a composition, I think I should have finished it.

Also I turn in my mind, in a half minute, half desultory way, fragments of thought intended to combine into a short *Religio Laici*—'What do I believe and why?' But when I look at a modern book I find that what has occurred to me has occurred to others before me, and that, as I cannot make myself learned, I shall not be able to open my mouth without exposing my ignorance.

In point of learning, my great difficulty is to find anything which, when read aloud to save my eyes, or indeed when read anyhow, will keep me awake. And this is really a more serious difficulty than you would suppose in the way of a person who would be glad to make himself capable of doing anything.

There is a still further difficulty, as to reading aloud, in finding what will keep *both my wife and* myself awake. The heaviest articles which answer these purposes are, I think, the lighter forms of history, and particularly French history, to which, after useless excursions in other territory, we are always recurring.

Well—you have asked for egotism, and now you have got it. I am sorry for you, but you should not have set the stone rolling.

Ever yours affectionately,
BLACHFORD.

To Dean Church.

Blachford: January 17, 1875.

So Gladstone goes: I am not sorry. His position was, I should imagine, an intolerable kind of position, and I own to a certain constant apprehension of what he would do next. Is his retirement a step from or towards his adoption of disestablishment?

I suppose for the present he is full of something or somethings or other. But will he not soon become *désœuvré* and take to prowling round the political pen, from which he has excluded himself and snuffing for an entrance? And when he begins to snuff it will not be long before he makes a rush —an ugly one—at the door.

I shall feel at liberty to feel malignant satisfaction if Lowe and Harcourt and Co. mess matters in the House of Commons. Hartington, Forster, Goschen, Harcourt, Low, —is there any one else who has the ghost of a pretension to lead?

To Dean Church.

Blachford : February 8, 1875.

My dear Church,—I enclose a letter from Newman which will interest you. I told him that I did not quite know what to make of his 'Schola Theologorum,' meaning in my heart that it seemed to me that the Church seemed to say one thing, 'Nulla salus extra ecclesiam ;' and when in the course of things this was found to be untenable, to invent a variety of modifications which constituted an unavowed abandonment of what had been decreed, as if theologians were now to undercut the Nicene Creed by a new definition of οὐσία.

I told S. to send you my article on Manning. If you object to anything, use your discretion. . . .

I wish you would come here. The foxhounds meet in front of the house on Tuesday week (the 16th), and if you will promise to wear your Dean's hat (I will spare the knee breeches and silks) I will mount you on a little pony that will jump nicely and scramble through the rocks like a cat. They draw up the valley through Combe Wood, so that with good luck and in fair weather it is the prettiest sight possible.

What a curiously Whig leadership![7] Is it a first attempt at a Middle party, a recovery of the old Liberal position demolished for the time, by John Mill, Gladstone, and Cobden ?

To Dean Church.

Blachford : April 5, 1875.

I have been engaged with Froude in a species of correspondence which has elicited from me a paper on Huxley's 'Automatism of Animals,' which again has led me to begin Carpenter on Mental Philosophy, which is about the most interesting book I ever read, and one reads with a certain repose as he is a distinct Theist. It is a satisfaction to have a really *thorough* treatise on the quasi-spiritual functions of the nerves, with a distinct religion and belief in free will at the bottom of it.

---

[7] Mr. Gladstone announced his retirement from the leadership of the Liberal party on January 13. Lord Hartington was chosen as leader of the party on February 3.

To Dean Church.

Blachford : April 24, 1875.

I remember discussing you with a select Committee, Gladstone, Manning, Hope, Rogers, as a contributor, with James Mozley, to William Palmer's quarterly (I forget its name) [8] in succession to the 'British Critic.' It was a dinner at Gladstone's, I think, brought together for the purpose of coming to some conclusions as to the then intended periodical, and I told him that I was sure Mozley would soon break away from Palmer. Manning represented the safe and plausible interest, rather afraid (if I remember right) of people going too far.

I wish I could live to see a fight between Church and State represented by Manning as Pope and Gladstone as English Prime Minister.

Ever yours affectionately,

B.

To Dean Church.

Blachford : May 27, 1875.

My dear Church,—I doubt whether I quite go along with you about the Irish business.

Nor do I quite agree about the 'compromise' of 1662.[9] I should have supposed it not so much a compromise as an imposition of terms by a victorious party. And I should say that the High Church movement was such an upset of the *status quo* (or what may be called practical compromise of the eighteenth century) that it hardly lay in our mouths to appeal to a pacification 200 years old, I mean as against the acts of a lawful authority, or in curtailment of the liberty of such an authority.

---

[8] Apparently, the *Christian Remembrancer*. In the autumn of 1844 it was started as a quarterly (having been a monthly magazine before) to take the place of the *British Critic*, which, under Mr. Ward's direction, was considered to be Romanising, or anti-Anglican, in tone (see Church's *Oxford Movement*, pp. 322, 348). James Mozley became the editor of the *Christian Remembrancer*.

[9] The Act of Uniformity, enforcing for all who held livings Episcopal ordination, acceptance of the Prayer Book, and abjuration of the Covenant ; upon which about 2,000 ministers resigned their livings.

My leading feeling is that our principal danger now is touchiness all round, and the great duty of such a paper as the 'Guardian' is to write it down if possible, more among those whom it can influence (of course) than among those whom it cannot ; and in the hope that reasonableness, like unreasonableness, may be catching.

To Sir Henry Taylor.

Blachford : June 19, 1875.

I think one great use of a newspaper is to abuse your readers. If they take you in, it is to read you, and because they rely on you. So you are in a favourable state to amend them—no doubt *primâ facie* at some loss of circulation—but with effect.

Also what I have set myself often to do as a press writer is to *stem manias.* It is an amusing process—from the first delicate suggestion of a doubt, founded skilfully on one occasion, when you can go, generally, with the stream, to the free denunciation on which you can venture when you think you have worked your readers up to it.

To Rev. J. H. Newman.

Blachford : October 28, 1875.

My dear Newman,—Nothing could, it appears to me, be possibly better than what you have written about Keble. Turn it how I will, it seems excellent in every way.[1] It brings out most admirably the picture of his excellences, parrying the depreciatory remarks that a certain class of people would be inclined to make. I can quite believe what you say as to the trouble which it cost you. It does not, however, show in the way of awkwardness or effort.

I think I shall send you my production, though it is really not worth sending. I should like to know what you

---

[1] A short preface to a volume of Keble's *Essays.* Cardinal Newman had on October 26 sent to Lord Blachford what he had written, asking him to say 'whether as a whole, and next in separate parts, it wil answe itspurpose —or whether I shall pluck it.

thought of it. Paget (Sir James), to whom I showed it in MS., says, ' I am afraid there is an answer.'

Ever yours affectionately,
BLACHFORD.

To Sir Henry Taylor.

Blachford : December 28, 1875.

My dear Taylor,—I think that all that you send me of your autobiography is excellent. And I do not know why you should tell me to ' make what I can of it.' . . . Certainly country life has a tendency to the vegetative. When I try to think of something to say, I cannot think of anything but that I am in the middle of building a greenhouse, and have succeeded (I hope), after struggles inexpressible, in buying a pair of carriage horses. Also I have (for the first time) attended a local board of magistrates, and ascertained that the stones of which our roads are made should pass through a ring of two and a half inches in diameter—also an agricultural dinner— very dull—about fat cattle—also a charity meeting—as bad as a debate in the House of Lords or Commons.

What do you know of, or think about, Lord Carnarvon's Cape of Good Hope agitation ? It seems to me (as to the Cape people) that the Froude mission was an error, both as to the thing and as to the man.[2]

I wonder Herbert, with his Australian experience, agreed to it. And Froude was not the kind of man (I should think) to make it go down—a man who would take up a view and work it, not with reference to truth or practical success, but with reference to scenic effect. No doubt he is a very clever fellow, and when he has got a truth he makes it tell. But I cannot imagine a more unpersuasive person—judging from his books and a long-ago recollection of his person.

Ever yours affectionately,
BLACHFORD.

---

[2] Lord Carnarvon (as Colonial Secretary) was trying to effect a Confederation of South Africa. Mr. J. A. Froude (the historian) was sent out to negotiate.

To Sir Henry Taylor.

London: December 9, 1875.

What a curious affair this Suez Canal business is![3] I like it (with the rest of the world), but I am rather horrified at the generality of our acquisitiveness just now. Here we have Suez with Egypt in the distance—Perak with Siam in the distance—Fiji with Oceania in the distance, and Ashanti with Central Africa in the distance. The defence of the whole to rest on the one or two hundred thousand men whom we can scratch together in this highly-paid country—or on foreign mercenaries.

To Dean Church.

Blachford: December 28, 1875.

My dear Church,—We are making up our London plans after a new fashion. . . . So we shall not—what shall I call it?—trespass on your hospitality. I shall from time to time regret my deanery quarters, but the arrangement somehow comes naturally. And it has the advantage of throwing my country time into the pleasantest part of the year; rhododendrons, strawberries, and all sorts of good things lend themselves to it. . . . Lord Carnarvon has, it seems to me, dropped into a scrape in South Africa. His Natal policy is (I am sure) essentially unsound, except as a transitional state. He meant it as a transition to Confederation. But Confederation is failing him. And he remains with an unworkable constitution on his hands, which he might have altered with a high hand a year ago, but now can only alter by Act of Parliament.

This reminds me to ask you to tell your servant (as he has done before) to pack up my parliamentary papers and to send them here to me. I ask it because it is on the cards that I might be expected to say something about colonial affairs early in the session, and at any rate ought not to be unable to talk about them.

[3] The shares in the Suez Canal held by the Khedive were purchased by England in November 1875.

What could the Duke of Cambridge mean by blurting out what was understood as a warning of possible war? Certainly the Turkish question is cropping up in earnest. How oddly the Pope and the Turk, Rome and Constantinople seem to run abreast! Both, in one sense, on their last legs, but yet Mahometanism and Roman Catholicism, one in Europe, the other in Africa, are showing great vitality independent of their centres, or at least of the present temporal condition of their centres.

I am delighted with Asa Gray (on Botany). It is exactly what I wanted. I shall soon have finished the outlines, and shall then fly at the growth and behaviour. I did not conceive that I could have read so much terminology by any effort of perseverance. But it is so lightened by rationales, and so absolutely devoid of ' padding,' and so clear in language and arrangement that I never feel *wearied*, only *tired* by it.

To Dean Church.

Killerton, Exeter: January 26, 1876.

My dear Church,—Your letter reached me yesterday morning just in time, for at dinner I met Cook [4] here (who, by the way, considers you the best English writer of the day), and I had a long talk with him.

I do not doubt that if I were you I should sign, because I do not doubt that you have ground for thinking and saying, what I take for granted, partly because I wish to do so, that the 'agreement' at Bonn about the word *filioque* was a 'happy' one.[5]

---

[4] Dr. Cook, Canon of Exeter, and editor of the *Speaker's Commentary on the Bible*.

[5] There were two Conferences at Bonn, in 1873 and 1874, arranged by the ' Old Catholics ' of Germany, whose leader was Dr. von Döllinger, in correspondence with some prominent members of the Anglican Church, chief among whom were Bishop Christopher Wordsworth and Bishop Harold Browne. At the second of these Conferences six articles of agreement were drawn up regarding the doctrine of the Procession of the Holy Ghost, that being one of the questions which had divided the Eastern and Western Churches. From the Eastern Church, Archbishop Lycurgus of Syros took an active part in the Conference. Bishop Wordsworth in Convocation commended to the sympathies of the Anglican Church the cause of intercommunion with Old Catholics and with the Eastern Church.

But I dislike the whole system of getting a number of signatures of mere well-wishers to manifestoes, or testimonials or projects, on which the 'signatories' are really not entitled to pronounce, on the notion that the number of the names or their general eminence are to supply the place of appropriate knowledge. So I am disposed still to hold aloof, as I do from most things. However, we shall soon be able to talk of that and other things.

I am, or rather was, staying a couple of days here with Acland (who is, of course, full of everything in particular), and shall then work our way *via* Odcombe and Bournemouth to the opening of Parliament (for which I have to recover my robes, as the Queen opens in person).

Ever yours affectionately,
BLACHFORD.

To Sir Henry Taylor.

London : February 19, 1876.

My dear Taylor,—If you 'do not know anything about it' without my speech, you are not likely to learn much from the 'Times,' and still less from any other report.[6] I endeavoured to show at length that the deadly nature of the climate, which made it impossible to send civil officers there except on the understanding that if they showed capacity they should be removed before they knew their business, and which made it impossible to send white soldiers or sailors there at all, rendered it impossible to perform our obligations to any subjects there, and therefore made the notion of extending our dominion absurd and disastrous. Hence it was desirable to consolidate by abandoning our outlying districts. Then follows the rest of the speech. The 'Times' did not report it exactly, but did not (as in the former part) make it the absolute reverse of what I said. Whether it was good or bad I do not know.

I have been spending pleasantly a day and the adjacent nights at Blackmoor—Selborne's—a handsome modern Gothic house that he has built the other side of Godalming on the

---

[6] The debate in the House of Lords was about certain territorial exchanges in West Africa, involving the cession of Gambia to France.

edge of Hampshire and Surrey, with farms behind him, and heaths and woods and blue distances before: a very attractive place, and becoming more so every year as his plantations grow up. In making his garden he has dug up some old vases containing some 30,000 Roman coins, of base metal, of the half-century preceding Constantine, which he is engaged in sorting very energetically. Many of them, as coins of British usurpers, are curious as showing the degree of art which the Romans had carried with them as far as Britain.

As to my 'place in the House of Lords,' that is visionary. I am too old to make it worth while to spend years in making a Parliamentary position, even if I am not too old to be able to do it. I do not see my way to do anything but a set speech—and most disagreeable it is to do that.

I find, partly I suppose from the habit of trying to write tersely, that if I cannot get the expression which I think best, I cannot get *any*; and that when I have got the expression which I think best I cannot get any other. And one consequence of this is that I cannot emphasise (by oratorical repetition) the joints or links or keys of the argument. And I should think that a hearer, from failing to have these critical points enforced, would sometimes feel that I was presenting him with premisses and leaving him to draw for himself the desired conclusions—a process which Bishop Butler recommended as a mode of compelling readers to think.

I am glad to have spoken because I certainly obtained some agreement; and among the speakers I stood alone in an outspoken advocacy of abandonment.

Ever yours affectionately,

BLACHFORD.

To Miss Rogers.

London: March 14, 1876.

I have established a place for myself in the House, in the centre of a group—(1) Lord Rosebery, with whom I have contracted something of an alliance, clever, amusing, but not thinking small beer of himself or great beer of others. I think I told you that he touched a suspicion in my mind, while C—— was speaking, by leaning over to me and saying contemplatively, ' I think that, with a little encouragement, C—— might become a bore.' I had talked with him about Heligoland, and of course a speech of whatever kind gave importance to his motion. . . .

Last night we had a very good debate, good down-right cut and thrust. Lord Halifax was long and rather tedious, but had a good deal to say. Then Lord Salisbury was good, and seemed to make out his case pretty well, not without letting drive at the enemy, and particularly Lord Halifax and the Duke of Argyll, who was reddening and chafing under it like an angry bantam. Perhaps the sight of this inspired one of Lord Salisbury's expressions. He was describing the position of a certain commission, which was being worried by the Indian Government on one side and the Duke of Argyll on the other, till at last 'they got tired of playing shuttlecock to these two ferocious battledores,' &c. &c. The application was so absurd that in our quarter we could call him (the Duke) nothing but 'the ferocious battledore' for the rest of the debate. And certainly he jumped up and justified his name. I have not often heard a *better* speech, but certainly never one so *aggressive*.

On the whole there was a great deal of rubbish talked, in the way of exaggeration of points of form and language. But the Duke of Argyll seemed to me to be unanswered on the *substance* of the matter, which amounted to this : ' Yes, Lord Salisbury, Secretary of State for India, stumped it in Lancashire and won golden opinions in Manchester by promising, without consultation with the Indian Government, to repeal an import duty on Manchester cottons. Then you find that the Indian Government think, and are right in thinking, that this repeal is not for the interests of India, and, instead of yielding, you try to force the repeal down their throats, and scold and bully them because, in the interests which you and they are bound to consult, they turn your flank.'

I think myself that if Lord S. had been right at bottom, the scolding was not more than the Indian manœuvres deserved. But a harsh scolding when you are at bottom *wrong* is a very different thing from such a scolding when you are in the *right*.

To Lady Blachford.

Blackheath: April 4, 1876.

The Monday's debate [on the Royal Titles Bill] was dull enough; the only *sparkle* was Lord Rosebery's, who fired off an amusing speech, which kept the House alive. He is evidently a great favourite, because everybody knows that he will amuse them. One of his jokes went off at half-cock. The great point, as you know, is that 'Empress' is to be used in India but not in England. He talked of it as for 'external application,' and then said it reminded him of the rows of chemists' bottles which are labelled to be applied externally but are poison if taken within. But the House caught at once the words 'external application' and so spoilt the effect of his sentence by cheering and laughing too soon. Selborne was effective, and so was Cairns, but the rest were dull exceedingly. The Opposition were on the whole, I think, well pleased with their minority (91) and cheered as lustily as Government.

To Dean Church.

Blachford: May 12, 1876.

How would an article compounded of your letter and mine on the Burial question do for the 'Guardian' next week?

I personally think that your argument is an *imaginative* one. Logically my answer would be that *instalments of justice* are no doubt frequently inefficacious—Corn Laws, Irish Disestablishment, Slavery, and so on. But I think that you are more likely to keep your hold on rights which are on all grounds defensible, if you give up what, though your due in point of technical justice, cannot be defended on its own moral merits.

As a matter of impression it seems to me that the argument from dissenting disorderliness is one of those which in practice will not be found to have a substantial existence. This was rather 'borne in' upon me in thinking over what I had myself written the other way. However, this kind of impression goes for little, and, to those who have it not, for nothing.

Setting imagination against imagination I say this: suppose that Lord Granville, commanding the present assent of the Liberal party, is now speaking to Selborne thus. I will try first to lay down a basis of settlement on the principle of security. If I can combine upon that basis you and your friends, and all but the extravagant dissenters, well and good. But if I fail with my combination, we must go in next time for the pure article, with all the force, whatever it may be, of the Liberal party.

Is it not generally held that Reform might have been staved off (for good or evil) for years and years if the Duke of Wellington would have given up East Retford and Old Sarum?

To Dean Church.

Blachford: May 15, 1876.

As to 'imaginary,' I do not think I did justice to my meaning. Practical considerations are logical or they are impressional. The latter are perhaps the most valuable. In the dissenters' case, I imagine the case of the dissenters making themselves disagreeable, and I also imagine the case of their not doing so. And I set one against the other; and, I do not know why, one or the other at length strikes me as being the real thing, and the other not. I can give no reason: I can only say that *to me* one has got to feel more real than the other.

And I have so no answer to the counter case except to call it 'imaginary.' When I said that your objection *seemed to me 'imaginary,'* I did not mean that that settled the question; but rather to express my state of mind. On the contrary, to call it 'imaginary' only says that I have no logical answer to it, only an adverse impression. Good-bye.

Ever yours affectionately,

BLACHFORD.

To Dean Church.

Blachford : June 8, 1876.

I am glad the flowers arrived safe. I think I can hardly have been here before exactly at this season, the hedge flowers seem to me so beautiful. Sometimes it is quite a tricolor of stitchwort, bluebells, and campion, sometimes a blaze of one or the other. Now and then a whole hedge side is covered with Geranium lucidum or Herb Robert: and on the moor (or as I am sorry to say in some fields) we have a regular extensive carpet of Pedicularis; orchises only occasional.

By the bye, are you coming to me for the Church Congress? Moberly, as you know, half accepts, so far that he will be a shabby dog if he fails me without a good excuse. (At his age really not liking it is one.) Keep him stirred up if you can. If he comes here on plea of going to Congress, he is still not bound to attend unless he likes.

If there is a *chance* of you, I shall keep places for as many as you like to bring, and that will best please me. But if there is no chance of you (early in October)—that is, if you prefer another time (for I take the visit for granted)—then I should look about elsewhere.

I am (as I think I told you) at work on Mill, and very hard work I find it. The subject works into ' The fundamental blot of Benthamism illustrated by the mental history of J. S. Mill.' I am afraid it is getting too long, and I am rather in distress for a judgment on it. I am afraid I shall have to trouble you with it.

I am writing in a tumult, the deer almost jumping in at the window to get beans (of which I think a sack must have been consumed in the last week), and a small pug-nosed spaniel with his legs a-kimbo, very like (excuse me) Canon ——, barking at them.

Ever yours affectionately,

BLACHFORD.

To Lady Blachford.

London : July 5, 1876.

Last evening there was rather an amusing 'episode,' as people call it, about the Domesday Book. Lord Belmore wanted the Irish part corrected ; then up got Selborne and said that in his neighbourhood the mistakes were absurd ; then Lord Granville to say that he was misrepresented ; then Lord Salisbury said so was he ; then I put in my oar and said so was I. I wish I had thought of proposing that the Lord Chancellor should put it from the woolsack that ' Those who are properly reported in the Domesday Book should say " Aye," and those who are improperly reported should say " No," adding that it seemed that the " Noes " have it.'

To Dean Church.

I had heard of Hope Scott's dangerous, or I suppose hopeless, state, also of John Mozley's death. They are among the things which make one feel one's own time short. Till you are about 60, the deaths of your contemporaries seem premature and exceptional ; now they have a *hodie mihi* character.

We have had the Walters here for a series of stormy days borne by us all with a cheerfulness almost heroic. He was like old times, almost divesting himself of Jupiter, which really does not suit him. And she is most singularly pleasant ; I never was so much struck before at the way in which a country house brings a person out. I had always liked her rather particularly ; but, living in the same house, one finds a bright, apprehensive, inquiring, and very well informed mind, which makes the old outside quite like a shell. Love to all your belongings.

Ever yours affectionately,
BLACHFORD.

To Dean Church.

December 16, 1876.

Certainly there is an inconceivable amount of Turkish feeling abroad. W. Froude professes himself a Pall-Mallite.

I suspect that whatever the blockheads or mere partisans may do or think, the men who furnish brains for both parties are gravitating towards real autonomy. What is being written *must* have its effect. The great facts of the case clear out, and men of real thought learn to neglect what is irrelevant.

It is only gradually that we are getting to know our own

case. Till lately it has been mainly instinct. But with Denton and Campbell, and Barkley and Evans, we are getting able to *préciser* our ground, which I take to be the poisonous incapacity for good government, not of Mahommedans in the abstract, nor of Turkish races in the abstract, but of the Constantinopolitan government, and of those of whom any Constantinopolitan government must be composed.

I believe it to be a case of *magna est veritas*.

Ever yours affectionately,

BLACHFORD.

To Dean Church.

Blachford : January 1, 1877.

Can Dizzy pull us into a war? I hope not. But I feel towards them as I used to feel towards colonial authorities who, being in contact with natives, could manipulate the relations so as to compel the natives to compel the home authorities to fight. My real fear is just now that the Russians will look after their own interests in Armenia and the Bosphorus and then give a mere illusory protection to the Bulgarians.

To Right Hon. W. E. Gladstone.

Blachford, Ivybridge : January 11, 1877.

My dear Gladstone,—I do not like troubling you with divergences actual or possible when you have so much on your mind, and, in regard to the great question which presses, are doing such splendid services to this and all other Christian countries.

But I think, all things considered, I ought to tell you that I feel these Birmingham meetings as a shake to my politics. Of course it often happens that what looks formidable blows over, and my feeling of something like alarm at the great organisation of which Birmingham and Mr. Chamberlain are the centre may be dissipated by events. But I feel more strongly the opposite possibility that this rising power may take a place in politics which may force me to reconsider a good deal; and, feeling this, I think myself bound to tell you so. Meantime do not trouble yourself to answer this letter, which is only the expression of an indefinite apprehension, to which no answer is required, or indeed possible.

Yours very sincerely,
BLACHFORD.

To Dean Church.

January 12, 1877.

My dear Church,—I think I agree with your letter entirely.[7] I think it an *immense* difficulty to say what the Church *is* to accept. And I wish wise men would think it over and give us some guiding principles. At present my prevailing feeling is that this question should not be settled in a passion by a set of second-rate people who are really fighting the battle of (as it seems to me) their own perversities.

Moreover I am anxious that the Anti-Establishment party should not be allowed to play off the errors of the Ritualists for purposes of disruption. I cannot help feeling that that is *our side* of the present movement.

The possibility of such tactics is immensely increased by the multitude of small incumbencies not state paid, occupied by men who hang loose on the existing state of things, and, not having a great deal to gain or lose, 'like their play (like somebody's geese) better than their food.' They are an element, as the case may be, of strength or confusion.

Turning to a very different matter, I am beginning to set to work on my Roman scraps of marble and shall soon plunge, I hope, into combinations of colours. I wish we could experimentalise together. But the time for that is not yet come.

To Dean Church.

January , 1877.

My dear Church,—So the Conference is over.[8] It seems to me more and more like the end of the Turks. I cannot

---

[7] The letter is printed in Dean Church's *Life and Letters*, p. 252. It related to the prosecution of Mr. Tooth, and to the action of the Law Courts in ritualistic cases.

[8] The Conference at Constantinople opened on December 23, 1875, and closed on January 20, 1876, with the rejection by the Turkish Government of the reforms proposed by the European Powers, which had been gradually reduced to two demands, an International Commission, but without executive powers, and the appointment of Valis approved by the European Powers.

see now how Europe can interfere to save them, or how they can save themselves from Russia. However, the whole thing is so strange in its later stages that I expect something unexpected.

What sets me speculating is Ignatieff's moderation. I cannot imagine that he would have so completely or so nearly caved in, if he had not been confident that Turkey would accept nothing. I could quite imagine that Russia had set afloat the rumour about their own unpreparedness in order to lure the Turks on to their ruin. I dare say they will fight, but I can scarcely fancy them permanently holding their own.

How are they to feed and pay their troops? You see Midhat tells them that they must get their ammunition from America. Has this anything to do with the Russian squadrons going there? or is it merely to get out of the way of Hobart?

To Sir Henry Taylor.

Odcombe Rectory: February 5, 1877.

My dear Taylor,—Perhaps you have seen an elaborate article of J. A. Froude's in the 'Quarterly' on S. African policy.

It is an attempt, attractively written, to show that our policy to the Boers has been one from the beginning of 'neglect and disdain' and blundering, culminating in the basest breach of faith on the part of Lords Granville and Kimberley.

Reeve has written to me to ask me to answer it in the 'Edinburgh,' which I consider myself bound to do.[9]

With regard to the climax (regarding the annexation of Basutoland and the diamond fields), I know where to go for information: and if I cannot take care of myself and the C. O., I can blame no one but myself.

But it is not so with the early history. I do not at all know either what the facts are or where to find them. I shall probably have to deal lightly with that part of the subject. But it occurs to me that you must have had at times

---

[9] The article (still worth reading), 'On Native Policy in South Africa,' appeared in the April number of the *Edinburgh*, 1877 (vol. cxlv. p. 447).

something to say about it, and that you may be able to help me without much trouble to yourself—first by directing me to some *points* or considerations which qualify or overthrow Froude more or less signally, and secondly by referring me to books or Parliamentary papers, in which I can get at the truth without more labour than I have time for.

I am on my way to the opening of Parliament. I expect a good deal of interest. This Turkish question is the first in which I have felt a real interest for years. All the chief political movements are to me either matters on which we are all agreed in principle, and on which the details will just work themselves into shape, in the hands of those who handle them ; or else changes which are called for by the growth of the world, and which sweep away things to which I am personally more or less attached, though I see that they have to be got out of the way with as little as possible of distress and inconvenience. This Turkey question is one on which I feel a clear faith and strong interest on the merits.

I have been a good deal interested by a certain Mr. Wallace's account of the Russian *communes*, and ask myself whether the time will come when the world will look on inequality of fortune (then extinct) with the same undoubting reprobation with которым we now look on slavery.

Ever yours affectionately,
B.

To Sir Henry Taylor.

Blachford : April 2, 1877.

I did not, as you see, speak in the House of Lords on the Eastern question, partly because, being occupied with my own composition, I had not time to get it up in the way in which a speaker should have done—*i.e.* to read the big Blue Books. You will say that the Eastern question was greater than the South African. True : but the one could be done best, and had to be done, *by me* ; and the other could be done far better by lots of other people. I had nothing to say that others had not.

There was some answer of the Duke of Wellington's to

somebody who recommended him to take up some philanthropic object—that 'F. M. &c. was one of the small number of persons who minded their own business.'

A dilemma which occurs to me continually on subjects on which I have no special qualification is this : Either I agree with (other ?) people of eminence, in which case they will say what I have to say ; or I do not, in which case I am probably wrong. However, the question is one on which, from time to time, I idly imagine myself speaking.

And the South African question is also a *big* one. It is capable of working up into the worst cluster of native wars that we have yet had.

. . . Do you see the 'Nineteenth Century'—a secession from the 'Contemporary'—(the old case of the foreman setting up shop against his master) ? There is a curious new invention in it called the 'Modern Symposium,' a succession of small papers on the same subject (the effect on morality of a decline in religious belief) in the way of discussion. I read it and was much struck by the weakness in *thought* of the representatives of unbelief (Frederic Harrison, Comtist, and Clifford, materialist). They seem to me to think that a few flippant or turgid words will do, instead of firm grasp of mind. There is so much that is solid to be said against everything, and among other things against Christianity, that they seem to me quite *unnecessarily* loose and shallow.

To Sir Henry Taylor.

Blachford : April 13, 1877.

My dear Taylor,—I have read your Autobiography, Vol. 2, with even more interest than when I read it first disjointedly. What strikes me still more than at first, when I see it all together, is the *variety* of its interest: anecdote, character, thought, sentiment, and idiosyncrasy—the last, as it ought to be in an autobiography, by no means the least. There is something, excuse me for continuing to say, highly amusing, not only in the thing revealed, but in the revelation, in the composed manner in which you turn yourself upside down and inside out, to your own, and therefore to your readers', satisfaction, with occasional illuminations by flashes of side-light from Lady Taylor and other of your friends.

. . . I think I said how much I was struck and interested by the letters from your mother-in-law, Miss Fenwick, and Lady Taylor; but there is no flagging in the worldly and political matters from which they are absent, and I feel about these as I remember an Oxford hairdresser saying to a friend of mine about a lecture which, I think, Edward Denison (afterwards of Salisbury) gave to the bourgeoisie about the French Revolution. (No! I beg his pardon. It was an impudent fellow called ——, candidate for the representation of Oxford town.) 'And then, sir, that was very pleasant, sir, for those of us who had read about it, sir, because we liked to be reminded, and it was very pleasant, sir, to those who had not read about it, sir, because we liked to be told.' And so it is very pleasant, sir, to be reminded of James Stephen, and told about Lord Melbourne.

I do not feel satisfied with what I said to you about myself. It is a great pleasure to me that you should form a high estimate of me; but I feel a touch of unmeant irony in the amount of it, and I should feel the pleasure more if the evidences of kind partiality were a little less overpowering.

So war is upon us—I mean on Europe. It is of course a terrible thing, perhaps unusually terrible. But it comes, as it seems to me, like a necessary surgical operation, only avoidable under conditions which (thanks, I fear, to this country) cannot be fulfilled, or with enduring consequences worse than war itself. All I hope now, though I am afraid that it is hardly to be hoped, is that it may be so short, sharp, and decisive as to give the Turks little time for exterminating the Christians of Bulgaria. I never have been able to persuade myself that there was any real alternative between foreign occupation and *carte blanche* for the Turks. And so the sooner Russia is in possession of Bulgaria, and Austria of Bosnia, the better I shall be pleased.

Ever yours affectionately,
BLACHFORD.

To Sir Henry Taylor.

Blachford : May 28, 1877.

I do not know what to think about Carnarvon's annexation.[1] My own impression would have been to have allowed the Boers to drink rather more deeply of the cup which they have mixed for themselves, strengthening the Natal garrison to meet any native attack on Englishmen, but keeping back till we were almost physically forced into interference for the preservation of Englishmen.

I think I would have told the Dutch that if they would not become English subjects we would not defend them; and I would have told the English in Dutch territory—gold-diggers and others—that England was in no degree responsible for their safety while they remained outside our frontier. And then I would have strengthened myself and waited. But this is mere guesswork, and I dare say Carnarvon may be able to show good reasons for what Shepstone has done, and what, I assume, he will approve.

I think it very likely that our resolute indisposition to annex up to 1871 was incapable of being maintained, and that we had run up a kind of arrear of necessity in that way. But I still look with a certain distrust on our accessions of responsibility in West Africa, Fiji, the Straits, and South Africa.

I am deep in mud just now. We are clearing out some feet of sand, dead leaves, and other dirt from the bottom of our pond, and constructing an island, to be hereafter covered, I think, with rhododendrons, hydrangeas, azaleas, and such like things.

Ever yours affectionately,
BLACHFORD.

---

[1] The annexation of the Transvaal Republic, then in financial difficulties and seriously threatened by hostile native tribes, was proclaimed on April 12, 1877, by Sir T. Shepstone, who had at that time satisfied himself that the Boers wished to belong to the British Empire.

To Dean Church.

Blachford : May 6, 1877.

My dear Church,—I have told Sharp to send you a proof of a review of 'Darwiniana' [by Dr. Asa Gray]. It is a difficult book to review, being so much of it review itself—in one case a review of a review. I should like to have brought out some of the scientific part, particularly the essay on the Sequoia, which is, I understand, original and very interesting and curious indeed. But you pointed my attention to the Natural Theology, and I found I had enough to do with that, especially now that the 'Guardian' seems pretty well crowded. Dr. Gray is very difficult to *quote*. Thoughts and phrases, which are just and telling, are bound up with passages which cannot be taken in without scientific knowledge or a clear recollection of what has gone before, and so cannot be quoted effectively without explanations which would altogether dilute the effect. However, you will see what I have done. To me the book is hard reading from my want of familiarity with the lines of scientific theory.

I get more and more astonished at the absence of reasoning power which some of these scientific atheists display, and also somewhat satisfied.

To Sir Henry Taylor.

Blachford : October 26, 1877.

My dear Taylor,—Thank you for your praise: which I need hardly say is very grateful. I think that the notion of Empire is really gaining ground, and that as political people like Lord Kimberley do not like to take up a ground against it which is unpopular, and gives opponents an advantage at the hustings, it is likely to establish itself in John Bull's mind as a principle of policy, unless somebody or other can get a hearing on the other side. And it appeared to me that an old official who had nothing to hope or fear was the kind of animal that might be expected to bray aloud on the subject.

I have had one or two notices from friends on what I have written ; and it strikes me rather painfully that while they compliment me on my clearness, they make some observation or other which shows that I have totally failed to make them grasp what I suppose to be my argument. I console myself by supposing that I serve them in the same way when they write, and recollect Bishop Butler's sentence—'By this means' (idle way of reading) 'time even in solitude is happily got rid of without the pain of attention; neither is any part of it more put down to idleness—one can scarce forbear saying, is spent with less thought—than great part of that which is spent in reading.'

I enclose an effort at historical writing which may amuse you, and which may be read without labour (this runs as if I intended to charge *you* with inattentive reading, which was the last thing in my mind). I have sent it to the 'Guardian.'

I wish you would have come here for the beautiful weather we have just parted with. My rheumatic sprain, which still confines me to easy walking on tolerably level ground, would have made us appropriate company for each other, so that we could have buzzed up and down our mile of flat road like two old bluebottles in the sun, and, when we went in, dozed in front of the fire to our respective benefits.

Our autumn is not a very fine specimen of its kind. The beech-leaves fall and wither, a dead brown instead of the beautiful scarlet of which they are capable; and the hurricane of last week bruised and knocked off the glory of the trees on the side which it hit, besides mangling them and tearing their heads off.

I am dawdling through Lady Minto's 'Sir Gilbert Elliot;' it is an extremely pleasant lifelike picture of himself and his friends. It is curious to be brought into such intimate contact with the relations of political *men*, with so little contact with political or historical *events*. Of course it is no defect in a book that it does what it does, and does not do what it does not pretend to do. But it produces an odd effect on the reader's mind (unless he is very well instructed) like being shortsighted, and only seeing six feet from your nose.

To Sir Henry Taylor.

Blachford : November 7, 1877.

I will send you my 'Edinburgh.' But as it is the only copy I have of my production I should like to have it back again.

What pleasant work the writing of history must be—not the 'indefatigable research' which is called conscientious, but the knitting together the characteristic and telling parts of what the hewers of wood and drawers of water have edited, or what forms the cream of personal memoirs. I never knew the amusement of it till I tried my hand on these sketches. I am now putting together a short sketch of the Florentine aristocracy from the second book of Machiavelli, which is very interesting to me. His cold balanced satire is almost as amusing as de Retz's buoyant fun. But I think it is rather demoralising to go on reading books in which you have nobody and nothing to admire.

I agree with you in caring about individual fellow creatures more than evolution of forces. But then the creatures or their doings must be worth caring about. I do not know whether or not to envy the power (which I do not possess) of what people call 'caring about little things'— memoranda of dinner parties, genealogies, and such like. My wife is waiting for me, so good-bye.

Ever yours affectionately,
B.

To Sir Henry Taylor.

Blachford : November 19, 1877.

My dear Taylor,—Thank you very much for Leti, which has arrived. I have his 'Cardinalismo della Santa Chiesa,' which lets you see the man, a vagrant littérateur, who is a kind of unattached hanger about between Catholic and Protestant, and collector of stories about Cardinals and such like things—if scandalous, so much the better—but certainly, as you say, lifelike and amusing beyond measure.

He seems to have been born some forty years after Sixtus' death, and must (unless he is a liar of singular genius) have got hold of some personal memoirs of the Conclave. But then the translator professes to have recast his work, which introduces a fresh element of doubt. I hear that Ranke ('History of Popes') mentions and gives a value for him. I want to find out (and shall) what that value is, and if it is enough to justify me, I shall certainly compile an account of his election.

It is a wonderfully good myth at any rate. One sees and hears the men, and there is such an exuberance of characteristic stories.[2]

Ever yours affectionately,
BLACHFORD.

To Sir Henry Taylor.

Blachford : November 21, 1877.

I am disappointed about Leti. I had adjusted in my head a kind of historical sketch, which would have been, I think, highly amusing and characteristic. In fact, all that is necessary for such a sketch is a pair of scissors. But I found from the Dean that Ranke had given an estimate of Leti's authority in his 'History of the Popes,' and I asked my brother, who has the book, to see what Ranke said.

I enclose his account of the matter, and you will see that after such a judgment by such a man I cannot very well present his history as anything but a romance, in the matters which are most racy and relevant. However, it is most amusing reading, and I am very glad to have seen it—viewed as Roman gossip.

---

[2] Leti in 1669 published a *Life of Sixtus V.* The current anecdotes about that Pope, some of them mythical, are derived from this Life. Ranke's criticism is given in Appendix xlviii. to the *History of the Popes.* He shows by several instances that Leti's biography was not original, but a garbled copy of an Italian MS., itself full of apocryphal stories. In particular, the famous story of Sixtus throwing away his crutches after his election is discredited. Leti is paraphrasing a 'conclave' written at the time of the election, yet he interpolates the passage about the pretended bodily weakness of which the original says nothing; indeed, it speaks of Cardinal Montalto as full of life and health. As regards Leti's dealings with the MS. life which he copied, he sums up : 'Leti has not only omitted to examine his MS. and to correct the errors in it, but to the best of his ability has rendered it still more mendacious. Nevertheless his book went through edition after edition, and was often translated.'

From the 'Cardinalismo,' written by him (Leti), he seems to have been an inquisitive gentleman—going everywhere, to Protestant meetings, Jewish synagogues, and Turkish mosques —always asking questions and chattering with everybody he met, subject to the apprehension that they may have been spies, which however he soon forgot. Once or twice his omni-voracity for small inquiry reminded me of Arthur Stanley.

To Miss Rogers.

Killerton : December 6, 1877.

My dear Kate,—Our proceedings here have been very pleasant. Lord Portsmouth is genial and country-gentleman-like, very clear-headed and shrewd, bearing in mind the duty of having his eldest son returned sooner or later for the county, and from that point of view snubbing Acland for his farming politics—economical talk of putting down deer. 'No, no, don't do that. I find nothing so pacific as venison. He is evidently immensely popular, and the cheering for him, with a whole chorus of ' view holloas ' was almost like that for Northcote. He only stayed one night and did not come back after the banquet.

. . . . The dinner went off exceedingly well.[3] Nothing at all jarring or unpleasant. Everybody here was plainly on tenterhooks as to what Acland would say. Lord Portsmouth was beseeching his wife, and his wife was beseeching Lord P. to keep him prudent, and Lady Susan Fortescue was offering to bet him that he would not keep his speech under ten minutes, and he had, you will say, the good sense to rehearse his speech to me as we were driving together to Exeter, omitting, with great docility, various objectionable topics. So the result was that he was quite a success, though plainly less popular, as well he might be at a Conservative banquet, than the other members. Northcote's speech was very good. The first part particularly so. But before long he got to bunkum about the city of Exeter, and Acland kept up grumbling to me, hardly *sotto voce*, ' Ah, now he's getting like himself;'

---

[3] The occasion of the dinner was the presentation of a portrait to Sir S. Northcote. Members of both political parties had joined in the subscription.

till at last a reporter, who was doing his shorthand opposite to us quite irrespective of party, burst out, 'I do wish you'd hold your tongue, Sir Thomas.' Which he obediently did for the rest of the speech.

To Sir Henry Taylor.

Killerton : December 7, 1877.

My dear Taylor,—Thank you for all the enclosed. The reviews have a great deal that is very good in them. I should not have applied the epithet 'cold' to ' Philip van Artevelde' as a composition ; and it seems to me that the man who does so has *not* some perception that I *have*. Stately and self-controlled, if you like, and highly economical of gush. Sir G. Clerk's praise is pleasing and his criticism of the French amusing.

I read and was much affected by the Dean's sermon. One's feeling towards such a composition wants an English word to express it—something that is not merely admiring nor merely taking home, but a warm compound of the two.

I should think that Mackonochie was spoiling his own game. I imagine that, though he is a very zealous man, he is not a very wise one, and is open to the temptations of a man not quite strong enough for a prominent position.

To Lord Selborne.

Blachford : February 7, 1878.

My dear Selborne,—Thank you for taking the trouble to keep me *au courant*. I had an uneasy feeling that the vote of 6,000,000*l*. might be meant as a pledge to Austria that we were ready to join her, to the extent of war if necessary, in controlling Russia.[4] But I was reassured by the vehemence with which Cross & Co. denounced as calumnious the charge of a war policy, and the way in which Lord Salisbury threw over the old 'independence and integrity' τόπος of Lord Beaconsfield which seemed like capitulation on Lord B.'s part. For myself, it does not appear to me that Russia should be

---

[4] The Government had, on Jan. 24, asked for a supplemental estimate of 6,000,000*l*. to increase the naval and military strength of the country.

allowed to get the mouths of the Danube (which she wants), or Constantinople (which she does not want) or the *exclusive* passage of the Dardanelles, which is a barbarous kind of arrangement. The more she takes in Armenia (to my mind) the better. And the more Turkish provinces in Europe are practically made independent the better.

I would go this length with Austria, that, subject to the decision of a European Congress, I would oppose the transfer of Roumanian Bessarabia with her, if she would with us oppose the *exclusive* passage of the Dardanelles by Russia, and I would in general sacrifice something of the *completeness* of provincial independence in Europe, in order to extend its area to Thessaly and the islands (with substantial guarantees of course) only taking care that the whole was placed on a footing (as to physical force) which would develop forwards to freedom, and not backwards to tyranny.

What is just now hideous to me is the general apprehension that everybody wants to fight everybody if only they can get a convenient occasion. There is not a Power, except ourselves, who does not appear to have a kind of growling desire to be at somebody else.

This feeling of mine may be derived from reading the 'Pall Mall Gazette,' which is always preaching that we ought to go mad because Europe is becoming a military Bedlam.

I, on the other hand, hold fast by our two great advantages, our seas and our *sang-froid*.

I am sometimes very indignant at the injustice which is done to the Russians. A great deal that is said of their past, and perhaps of their present, general conduct may be true, but looking not to suspicions, but at proved facts, there is nothing to show that this war is not on the whole an enormous sacrifice for a noble object, and it is quite plain that they have done their best to conduct it in a civilised way, under the most tremendous provocations to savagery.

After all this, one hardly likes to pass to poor Coleridge's loss. What a terrible blow! and, I suppose, quite unexpected.

Ever yours sincerely,
BLACHFORD.

To Dean Church.

Blachford : May 28, 1878.

My dear Church,—It is some time since we heard of each other, so I vent on you a certain sense of relief which comes of having sent off the last corrected copy of my article.⁵ The less a man has to do, the more he thinks of the little which he has. Reeve cut the historical part to shivers! observing that I had sent him two articles instead of one, and that the least interesting of the two must be got rid of, or, as he put it, that the review was in the case of a nursery in which twins had made their appearance when preparations had only been made for one baby.

Of course all this was done with great propriety (*avec des égards—avec des égards*), of which the result only was, that, instead of drowning my baby at once, I had to tear it to pieces with my own hands, and throw it away bit by bit. Now he says that it is 'highly satisfactory, after all the trouble you have had,' to find that it is quite what it ought to be 'in length and matter'—a two-edged kind of consolation. However, it is done with. . . . . . .

How tiresome all these reports about the [Berlin] Congress are! It seems to me that to attach importance to the miserable distinction between *submitting* the Treaty to the Congress and *communicating* it is the most absurd thing that we have yet seen ; remembering that, on the one hand, any Power may raise in Congress any question relating to the Congress (so that the *submission* gives no advantage to England), and that no member of the Congress is bound by the majority (so that the submission imposes no disadvantage on Russia).

To G. E. Marindin, Esq.

Blachford : May 15, 1878.

My dear Eden,—Thank you for your letter.⁶ I did not intend to have given you the trouble of more than an acknow-

---

⁵ A review of May's *Democracy* in the *Edinburgh Review*.

⁶ The letter in question referred to an article on Turkish affairs of which Lord Blachford had sent a reprint.

ledgment—still less ought I to trouble you with reading an answer. But sometimes one's fingers itch a little.

1. I dare say you are right in saying that there is a large section which upholds war against the Turks as 'a crusade'—the 'Pall Mall' is always saying so. But I never myself happened to see any person in the flesh who advocated it—or to read any printed or written paper in which it was avowed or could be inferred.

2. I dare say that the feelings of Russians are partly crusading, partly Panslavist—just as my feelings might be partly sportsmanlike and partly domestic, if I shot a wolf which was tearing to pieces my brother—but the basis of my action would be the desire to save a human being from a savage brute. The English who felt strongly about Bulgarian atrocities were neither Slav nor 'Orthodox.'

3. As you allow of a war for 'suffering humanity' you of course do not agree with the passage of Mackintosh which you quote (unless you explain it away)—neither do I.[7] It seems to me transparently rhetorical. It is plainly much more wicked to attack on insufficient grounds a prosperous and virtuous government than a corrupt and desolating one. In one you injure the people, in the other only the rulers and their armies, with (supposed) benefit to the people. It is also plainly a subject of regret that a *good* government should be destroyed, while it may be a subject of just and stern rejoicing that, by whatever agency, a *bad* one should be destroyed, and its subjects transferred to those by whom they will be better used.

4. Of the past history of Russia I know next to nothing. I only see with my eyes on maps the respective annexations of England and Russia during the last century and a quarter, and am astounded at the fact that England should assume the position of accuser in this respect.

---

[7] The passage is in Mackintosh's *Essay on the Partition of Poland*: 'There is no political doctrine more false or more pernicious than that which represents vices in its internal government as an extenuation of unjust aggressions against a country, and a consolation to mankind for the destruction of its independence. As no government is without great faults, such a doctrine multiplies the grounds of war, gives an unbounded scope to ambition, and furnishes benevolent pretexts for every sort of rapine.'

5. I am disposed to look leniently on our Minister's omission to notice the hint about Bessarabia. So long as independent Roumania lies between Turkey and Russia I cannot see why 50 or 60 miles more or less of sea coast should signify. Russia's crime (which is very disgusting) is in taking it *against the will of her ally*, which did not appear till the Treaty of S. Stefano (and perhaps does not now much concern *us*; unless we want a quarrel).

6. I agree with you in not confining the delinquencies of England to a single act (the Berlin Memo.). I begin by hating with my whole soul, what may be called our traditional policy (avowed by Palmerston and Beaconsfield) of bolstering up, for our own purposes, such a desolating and loathsome oppression (I conceive these words to be chosen with accuracy) as Turkey. Then I think it was our bounden duty to retrieve the tremendous error of guaranteeing the 'independence and integrity' of such an oppressor as soon as the Seraglio put itself in the wrong by not giving effect to the provisions of the Hatti Humayun of the Treaty of Paris. This duty arose probably very soon after the Treaty, but may be said (by an apologist) to have escaped notice, in so far as it merely appeared in reports and official documents. It was allowed to slip out of sight.

But three years ago this duty *forced* itself upon our notice by the Herzegovinian revolt, and the English Ministry adopted a course of action by which they did not merely *neglect*, but *deliberately repudiated* it, taking 'independence and integrity' as the key of their policy, not in one case or another, but time after time. The Constantinopolitan conference was an exceptional incident, almost avowedly forced on the Government by the Bulgarian agitation—made abortive by parallel communications with Turkey—and at the close of which the Government (by the appointment of Layard and other matters) have come back to what I should call 'their vomit,' that is to say a course of obstructive special pleading, hiding the reconstruction of what is intolerable, under the phrase (which I see you adopt) 'the faith of treaties.' I say this because it is too evident to be denied that our present proceedings are such as to enable Turkey to prepare for a fresh struggle, that in case of such a struggle we have her as an ally, and that in case of such an alliance we must necessarily repay the Sultan and his Ministers by replacing them more or less in possession of the authority of which Russia threatens to deprive them.

On the main point, I think the great difference between us is that I am thoroughly impressed by the belief that Turkey is incorrigible, while Russia is in process of improvement. These things—both of them—come to my mind with the clearness of the sun. And the suggestion of allowing Turkey a year for improvement appears to me like allowing a notoriously bankrupt debtor a month's respite, during which he will remove his goods, and at the end of which the creditor (Russia) will have to recommence an expensive litigation which, when the dilatory plea was urged, was on the point of being brought to a hearing, sure to end in a success. I should be very sorry to stand godfather to the motives of Russian statesmen. I dare say they are as selfish as our own profess to be. But they have this advantage that their interests (so far as the liberation of the Turkish provinces go) coincide with the interests of humanity with which our own (alleged) interests conflict. And the result is that their present position, as viewed in future history, is on the road to grandeur—ours on the road to meanness.

Of course all this would change if we became the liberators and Russia the conqueror. But this does not yet appear.

Meantime I collect the difference between Turkish and Russian misgovernments *in esse* and *in posse* to be such that the most extensive transfer of Armenia from Turkey to Russia would (except to the Kurdish robbers) be an enormous blessing. And I think Russia has a clear right to expect 'compensation' (not 'extensive,' but such as she is now proposing) from a vanquished enemy who cannot pay in coin.

Surely you are wrong in supposing that the acquisition of Bessarabia will give Russia access to Bulgaria. All Wallachia lies between.

If the Russians had patronised the Thessalians should not we have made it a fresh charge against them? I think they may fairly say that, with England watching every step which they took, they had quite enough on their hands.

Ever yours affectionately,
BLACHFORD.

To Miss Rogers.

London : December 1878.

My dear Kate,—As letters amuse you I enclose one from Lord Portsmouth and one from H. Taylor. I think I told you that Lord Fortescue's defection from the Liberals was a matter of great speculation at Eggesford. The Duke of Somerset, as you may see by the papers, made a sharp speech against the amendment but did not vote. . . . We have had a long debate, seven hours on Monday, and eleven on Tuesday, but on Tuesday I took Spohr's 'Last Judgment' in a parenthesis at St. Paul's. It was most beautiful, but I found that the parts which we used to sing came out like jewels among the rest, which seemed, and perhaps were, much inferior. The arrangement which made a kind of service of it (I enclose the paper) was very good and gave a really devotional character to the whole. The people who were admitted without tickets (all comers, as on an ordinary service) were about 7,000 and thoroughly well behaved.

The debates [on the Afghan War] were not generally brilliant, but interesting and characteristic. Cranbrook spirited and loud, but the bunkum rather overdone, Lord Halifax (to me) inaudible, and I should think to the last degree prosy. Lord Lawrence I thought interesting and instructive, but his very bad hesitating manner, his (not unnecessary) egotism, and his aged look (he is not so old as I am) gave an appearance of weakness, and the matter itself was sometimes weighty, sometimes not. Lord Derby cold and balancing, but often hitting the nail on the head, the Duke of Somerset very amusing. The next day Lord Grey (I should say) statesmanlike (them's my sentiments), Lord Northbrook able, full of matter, but too detailed in self-justification. . . . Dizzy was to me, for the first time, thoroughly amusing. I have hitherto found him dull. But this time he did some light chaff in a manner which was as good as a stage play. It gave me the idea of a man who had a thorough contempt for human nature in general and his audience in particular, but still thought that some of them might be worthy of the strain of amused and amusing irony with which he addressed them. It is impossible to appreciate it without hearing it. On paper it appears (in parts at least) dry and unmeaning, particularly perhaps his solemn enumeration of the various Treaties of Rectification of Frontier which have been contracted of late, but when you heard his tone of mock solemnity which seemed to say 'I really believe the lot of you are fools enough to take all this in earnest,' with a kind of stony twinkle in his marble face, one could hardly believe that one was not at a comedy. I was next to Lord Sydney and almost at the same moment we ejaculated, I 'What a fellow it is!' he 'What a buffoon!' But there was a kind of divine impudence about it, particularly his treatment of an interruption by Lord Grey, 'You are impetuous,' and a sustained ironical chaff of Lord Derby which really almost inclined me to vote for him *coûte que coûte*. But at the end of the speech he thought it necessary to go off in bunkum, and that cured me completely.

To Sir Henry Taylor.

Blachford : February 26, 1879.[a]

My expression about being at war 'with everybody everywhere' was a rough and unjust one, as is sometimes the case when one thing leads you to give vent to a pent-up impatience about another.

What was in my mind was this : In Natal, in Afghanistan, in Turkey we are always assuming—at least there are a quantity of people who assume that, because this or that state or potentate is an inconvenience to us, making us keep more troops or ships than we like, or unsettling trade, or threatening the balance of power, *that* is at bottom a sufficient reason for trying to disable them, and the only question is one of waiting for a pretext. This I take it was the old

[a] News of the disaster at Isandlwana in the Zulu War reached London on February 11, 1879.

theory of foreign policy, which I, for one, flattered myself was exploded or nearly so, and it is one which, if carried out to its full extent, *would* keep us engaged in disabling everybody, the U.S. because they will evidently one day threaten our naval supremacy, Prussia, Russia, France, with their great armies and ambitious objects; Italy and Greece with their prospects with regard to Mediterranean trade, and so on.

And the revival of this kind of Chauvinism, jingoism, or whatever you choose to call it, which is and always has been the great enemy to the peace of the world, keeps me, I confess, in that state of disgust which one feels at a thing which you find to your surprise is not too stupid to be formidable, like what I suppose Cobdenites feel towards the resuscitation of protection.

But of course I must admit that the question is one of degree, and that there is a point at which you *must* take measures to clip the wings of a neighbour who is at once powerful and ill-intentioned.

To Sir Henry Taylor.

Blachford: March 8, 1879.

My dear Taylor,—As to Frere—you told me once that I was possessed of an 'impetuous surefootedness'— I suppose I have bestowed my impetuosity on you, and my sobriety on the 'Nineteenth Century.'

I *am* angry with Frere and have been (before this affair) since I read his memo. which is at the root of the Afghan war. It seemed to me then, on contrasting his paper with that of Lord Lawrence, that he was one of those over-confident men, who make and ruin joint-stock companies in private life, and destroy the princes and nations who trust them in public. This prepossession may colour my views on this Zulu matter.

. . . I do not think Indian administrators understand the conditions under which Colonial Government has to be carried on. And I confess I think Frere takes this ignorance for superior knowledge and does not hesitate to overrule and force the hand of his superiors.

To Sir Henry Taylor.

Odcombe Rectory: March 30, 1879.

My notion about the recall is this. I agree with you that if Frere's presence in South Africa was good for the public, it might not be wise to sacrifice the Colony to departmental discipline. But I think that he is a mischief, and that his recall is in itself a good. Nothing, I conceive—or rather infer—will make him carry into effect with reasonable loyalty a policy that is not his own. And he has the power, so long as he is there, of forcing the hand of Government to any extent. If he does not choose to make peace it will not be made. If he chooses to go on massacring those unlucky savages, on the plea that if we do not kill them, they will kill us, the Government which upholds him must send as many troops as he asks for. And if another disaster should occur, and if the Cape natives whom we are trying to disarm should rise behind us, and the Boers declare themselves independent in front of us, we shall have a pretty job on our hands.

The announcement of an intention to disarm even friendly natives I have heard long ago spoken of by South Africans as wildly imprudent.

To Cardinal Newman.

The Deanery, St. Paul's: December 23, 1879.

My dear Cardinal,—Church tells me that this is the right and allowable way of beginning a letter to you, to ask whether you have any commands for Rome. Without his instruction I do not think I should have got beyond the first two words.

If, which is most unlikely, we can take or do anything for you, we shall of course be delighted, but we are off on Friday.

If any friend occurs to you to whom it seems natural to you to give us a letter of introduction, we shall be very grateful. But I do not write with that object, or want you to trouble yourself about the matter.

. . . All sorts of good Christmas wishes to you. My wife is not by me, or she would send hers most heartily.

Ever yours affectionately,

BLACHFORD.

To Cardinal Newman.

Mentone : January 2, 1880.

My dear Cardinal,—Thank you very much for writing to tell me of the death of your sister Jemima [Mrs. John Mozley] —her release, I suppose I may say. I often think of those old Iffley days in which she added so much to the pleasure of all about her, and certainly—I was going to say not least— to mine. What a long time back it is, and how pleasant to remember! Before Germany or Italy or a Reformed Parliament, and when so many other things were so little what they are, and Froude used to say, 'When will anything happen to disturb this stagnancy?' It seems such a time of repose that the world seems since that time to have been driven out of (a fool's) paradise.

To Sir Henry Taylor.

Rome : February 19, 1880.

From Pisa where you heard of us, we came straight to Rome. . . . It is a curiously changed place since I was first here. Then by the side of the Papal Court, lay and clerical *y compris*, the old Italo-Papal nobility, there was a comfortable little English colony with an aristocracy of old residents and artists, which touched the Italian society at its edges, and lived with a quiet sociability which enabled every one to spend his evenings (if he liked) with some friend or other, and to organise archæological or picturesque or ecclesiastical gaieties in an easy inexpensive kind of way. Everything was very dirty out of the best hotels, and every corner was full of character—*contadini* and processions and cardinals' carriages met you in the streets, and altogether the place had an atmosphere of its own. But now the Embassies have revolutionised society. 'The thing' is to be asked to the Embassy and meet the kind of people whom people aspire to meet in London. The monks are shut up, the Pope and Cardinals sulk, the artists are put into a corner, the archæologists are turning the picturesque old ruins into deserts, or museums, or quarries, or tea gardens, and the public places are occupied by

Cook's tourists. 'A different class of people,' grumbled an old resident with bitter scorn. 'People you never see at a banker's, but who go and change a five-pound note at a moneychanger's.' Of course, churches and ruins and museums remain, and most wonderful they are, more so as you know more of them, but the pleasant dilettante side of Rome is gone. I must say, however, it remains otherwise remarkable. Judging by the enormous amount of what women call 'wash' which you see hanging on long ropes in all sorts of impossible and magnificent places, and by the floods of Indulgenze Plenarie which are advertised on church doors as to be had dogcheap, I should say that there can hardly be a place in the world where there was so much moral and physical washing, not many places perhaps in which there still is more dirt.

Then (during the carnival) the *contadini* in their wonderful dresses, getting up dances to the sound of the tambourine on the public places, and on the grand steps of the Pincian— really as if they were doing it from *gaieté de cœur*—a kind of polka, I suppose (waltz without rotatory motion), in which the figure seemed to be in the various movements of the arms. Also certain itinerant sellers of things are charming. Last Sunday we saw a crowd being harangued, and found the orator to be a seller of brass watch-chains. The oratory was an energetic, unbroken current, coming out unceasingly from his mouth as from an instrument of music—of the most beautifully pronounced and (as far as I could see) perfectly grammatical Italian—all about the watch-chains. They were sent to Francia, Inghilterra, and Allemagna—nothing was charged for the labour of making them, for it was 'lavoro forzato'—'dei poveri disgraziati che sono in carcere.' A manufacturer would give a 'regalo di cinque cento lire to the man who could make them: and now he was selling them for what? non è di cento lire; non è di cinquanta lire; non è di venti lire; non è di dieci lire; non è di una lira; non è di novanta centesimi; non è di ottanta centesimi; non è di settanta centesimi; non è di sessanta centesimi; ma è di cinquanta centesimi ciascuno.' The figure of oratory with this immense and deliberate descent from a hundred francs to fifty centimes was too much for me, and I put forward my cinquanta, which he took, and gave me the chain without a second's disturbance of his eloquence ; and I was glad to see that I had induced one or more bystanders to do likewise.

Then the beggars, the old and maimed, are certainly very repulsive, and I, for one, prefer giving to some kind of almoner ; there is a half-savage, half-whining professionalism about them which is unpleasant. The boys are some of them obnoxious, as when they affect to sell things. 'Msoo, Msoo, vaar chip, vaar chip,' 'one franc, vaar chip, vaar chip.' Also when they hustle and crowd you, still more when they pelt you with mud, as they did me when I was trying to sketch S. Giorgio in Velabro, the church which gives a title to Cardinal Newman. (I shall send him a complaint of his parishioners.) Also very bad when they stop playing to whine. 'Muoio di fame : madre ammalata.' But I am rather overcome by the handsome little vagabonds who look up laughing at you and cry for a soldo, trusting to nothing but their beauty, their manners, and their impudence. ' No, no, non c' è—andate via ' (with a deprecating movement of the palm of the hand, which is supposed to be a specific). ' Sì, sì, c' è, c' è,' from a little bright varlet who keeps trotting round you ; or again, ' No, no, non c' è ; e poi—se vi do qualche cosa, verranno tutti gli altri a rubarmi.' ' No, no, non lo dirò a nessuno, che m' avete dato qualche cosa.' That little rascal got a penny for being so bright and handsome and quick. Very immoral.

To Sir Henry Taylor.

Blachford : May 4, 1880.

My dear Taylor,—Well ! What do you say to it all ?[9] Lord Ripon seems rather weak for India, Lord Cowper rather shy for Ireland. Chamberlain tolerably well muzzled by the Board of Trade. Forster an odd master for the Irishmen. Dilke prudently harnessed with Granville, and the rest not very originally but effectively and promisingly placed. I wonder to myself much what the effect of truth and justice in the fleshly shape of Forster will have on the *perfervidum in-*

---

[9] Lord Beaconsfield resigned, after the general election, in April 1880, and Mr. Gladstone became Prime Minister.

genium. I never quite know whether Irishmen will think truth and justice divine or ridiculous, either being on the cards. Forster is neither one nor the other nor a compromise between the two. I expect that his grim uncouthness will impress them with an amiable sense of funniness, and that they will be rather puzzled at first to decide whether his truthfulness is folly or wisdom, but will end by determining on the last. What will be the effect of his aversion for jobbing (unless he leaves it in Yorkshire) on the public opinion across the Channel I am unable even to conjecture. I think I shall run up to town for a day or two (at the Deanery) when Parliament meets in earnest, which I suppose to be about the 20th.

Ever yours affectionately,
BLACHFORD.

To Lady Blachford.

London : May 28, 1880.

I went last night to see the 'Merchant of Venice' and 'Iolanthe'—Irving and Miss Terry. She is quite charming. In the casket scene (I am bound to confess) I fairly cried. The admirable scenery and grouping helped the effect, but it was produced *in spite of* a Bassanio who was a butcherly stick. The judgment scene was admirable, in that difficult speech of Portia's about mercy there was a pretty feminine earnestness, without a shadow of declamation, which was quite beautiful, every word *coulait de source*, seemed to be suggested by the abundance of the heart as it rose to the mouth, the earnestness rising to the throne of heaven as its natural climax. Irving was often very good, but the facial contortion was terrific, and the occasional rant abominable (although, they say, much retrenched). The speech 'Hath not a Jew eyes? &c.,' which seems to me one of concentrated wrath and scorn, and sense of injustice, burning at heart, but under the steady guidance of logical intellect, was bellowed as it might have been in Billingsgate, only bass instead of treble. 'Iolanthe,' the one-scene afterpiece, was a piece of poetry acted. The story—so to call it—is absurd beyond ordinary absurdity. A beautiful princess, blind from her birth, but betrothed to a neighbouring prince who does not know her or her defect, is kept by her father in a garden of delights with nobody in her reach but a nurse, or servant, the father from time to time, and a physician who is to cure her, without being instructed as to the nature of sight, or told that anybody has more senses than herself. For her cure (which must be effected at a particular moment if at all) it is necessary that she should be told of her blindness, which her father has not the heart to do. But the gallant knight her betrothed (who has never seen and knows nothing on earth about her) penetrates the garden by chance, falls in love of course, and finds out only gradually that she is blind, and explains it to her. This bit is really very beautiful. Her movements, which tell the spectator that she is blind, but yet leave it possible that her chance visitors may not find it out, the gradual way in which the knight discovers and tests it, the tenderness of his explanation, and her curious surprised half comprehension, probably owe a great deal of their effect to the fine delicacy of her acting, but seemed to me as if they would read very beautifully as poetry. Of course the cure is successful; while the knight, writing instantly to reject his betrothed, and invading the valley to carry off his mistress (who, of course, has avowed her own position with the utmost promptitude and innocence), finds that he has only troubled himself ' enfoncer une porte ouverte.' The perplexities of untutored sight are well written and well acted. She is impressed by the sky, and asks with awe (as I understood) ' Is it God ? '

I went to see Lear's drawings with Church, and if I had not spent so much on ourselves, should have been grievously tempted by one of *Nemi*, showing quite clearly the zigzag road by which we descended from the town to the lake.

To Sir Henry Taylor.

Blachford : October 13, 1880.

My dear Taylor,—I confess to a share in debauching the Dean. That is to say, I persuaded him to stay here till the last moment at which he was obliged to go to London. My engine of persuasion was a certain marble manufacture, in which I am engaged, and of which he became enamoured.

Eight or nine years ago I brought home from Rome a few pounds' worth of fragments of various old marbles, and now I have set to work (after giving the matter some study last winter in Italy) in trying what can be made of them, experimentalising in contrasts and harmonies on a very small scale. Every morning after breakfast the Dean (who of course has great schemes of decoration of St. Paul's floating about him) started off with me to the 'shop,' and I believe would have spent the day there fidgeting and watching, to the neglect of all other duties, if I would have let him, and towards the end of September we were approaching a climax (not yet reached), and so he stayed on and on. Engagements are certainly his weak point, so when I have got him I keep him. When he went away he was meditating a visit to Bournemouth, and now he is complaining that London makes him ill. So I expect you will hear or will have heard from him. Lord Monteagle's outburst against the House of Peers (as an institution) took me altogether by surprise.[1] It seems to me that a very real use of that House is to prevent a *Ministry* from stealing a march on the *nation* by means of a majority among the *representatives*. And this the House of Lords did in the case of the Irish Land Bill.

The country is lovely just now, and I think with horror of having to go to town. How lazy one gets!

Ever yours affectionately,
BLACHFORD.

To Dean Church.

Blachford: October 17, 1880.

What a muff European concert is, unless one or more powers are prepared and allowed to act constable! The Sultan is something between a farce and a bad dream, in which the same ridiculous or disgusting dilemma is always turning up, in the midst of all your struggles to avoid it. The eternal promise and the eternal breach, and the eternal surprise at being eternally taken in exactly the same way, and the eternal objections to the only mode of breaking through the eternal dilemma, are enough to choke one.

---
[1] See below, letter of October 18.

To Sir Henry Taylor.

Blachford : October 18, 1880.

No doubt 'the sword of justice' (though sometimes unwittingly the sword of injustice) is a noble thing, so is it a safe thing to 'judge not that we be not judged.' And one has to pick and choose between them. In the course of my newspaper life I certainly feel that I have rather exceeded propriety as a swordsman, and feel the temptation grievously still. One feels that he who smites to the point is a public benefactor, but it is sometimes at the expense of his own credit and conscience.

I cannot find Monteagle's speech, but this is the less matter, as he writes to say that it is incorrectly reported. I should doubtless have said, like you (only with less knowledge), that there were few men of whom a pleasing modesty was more characteristic than of him. But modesty is after all a local disease, extending to a man's manner but not his speech, or to his speech but not his writings, and I thought with some surprise that he might be of those who are carried out of themselves when 'on his legs.' What I take to be the case is that he was *reported* as saying that the House of Lords would be well out of the way, when he really said or meant to say that he for himself would rather be eligible for the Commons than have a seat in the Peers, which of course any man may say. It was pluckily done of him, to take his chance with a set of Land Leaguers.

What a set of messes are afloat!—Turks, Afghans, Basutos, and Irishmen, and floating in the clouds a possible European war.

Ever yours affectionately,
BLACHFORD.

To Dean Church.

Blachford : October 28, 1880.

Forster's fate in being nicknamed 'Buckshot' is amusing. I remember in old days at Blackheath an old lady who supported at her own expense a school of 50 girls whom she indulged alarmingly, and whom, when they were naughty, from sheer dislike of giving them pain, she caused to lie down in a long rather coffin-like box. What she got for her humanity was, that she got mobbed in the streets as the old woman who buried children alive—so much for venturing on unusual punishments or modes of self-defence.

To Sir Henry Taylor.

Totnes : December 11, 1880.

My dear Taylor,—You will have seen by the papers the death of James Colvile.[2] You know what a loss it must be to his wife ; but you have hardly seen enough of the family to know what he was to them. An eldest brother and distinguished head of a family is always an idol, more or less, to his sisters ; and he was so exceedingly kind and attentive, that he was an unusually great part of their happiness, particularly to his bedridden sister. It is, I need hardly say, a great grief to my wife. I am at this moment staying here with her and two of her sisters. Two of them are gone with Lady Colvile to the funeral in Scotland at Craigflower, where he will lie by his boy.

I suppose I ought to be in town at the opening of Parliament, though there will probably be little of interest in the Lords. To say the honest truth I am getting more and more doubtful whether the Liberal Party, as at present constituted, can govern the country—such as Ireland makes it—without involving us in some great calamities.

Ever yours affectionately,
BLACHFORD.

To Sir Henry Taylor.

Blachford : January 27, 1881.

My dear Taylor,—How have you got on with old father Winter ? We have got off very well, and I really think have had more amusement than inconvenience from the weather.

---

[2] Lady Blachford's brother, Right Hon. Sir James Colvile, at one time Chief Justice of Bengal ; afterwards a Privy Councillor and Judge of the Court of Appeal.

There has been little or no distress in the neighbourhood to wring our hearts. But for a day or two we had a curious sense of isolation—no butcher, no baker, no postman, no doctor, of course no letters or newspapers, and everywhere a great mass of white, filling the lanes, and sometimes with drifts 10 or 12 feet high. As our weather was bright and sunny (between the storms) the earth and sky were very pretty to look at, which made the inside of the house cheerful. Charming sunsets over the white snow, and purple branches of trees and grey distance : then a pretty scene of the men and horses and punt getting out of the pond a doe who had tumbled in through the ice : then the gradual establishment of communications with the outer world, principally the village and the railway station : then the news of the wearing or cutting of paths, the reappearance of joints of meat and loaves of bread in the village, news of the sheep which had been lost in the snow and found again. In one case six sheep were dug out, because the vigilant farmer had observed that a fox had been trying to scratch his way into a snow drift ; and wisely judged that it was not for nothing ; so, pursuing the fox's unfinished work, he recovered his animals. Now the thaw is making way fast, and we see almost as much green as white from the windows.

What a set those Irish are ! And what a very good speech Forster's was. I wonder whether ever before in the history of the world a set of individuals, in the face of an established government, succeeded in establishing themselves and their nominees as a machine for deciding how much of his property every proprietor should be allowed to keep, and in enforcing their decrees by carding, houghing, ear-cropping, bludgeoning, and shooting, with the universal acquiescence of the population, and the certainty that no jury would convict any of their ministers. I thought there was something very pathetic in Forster's cry that if he could have foreseen all this he would never have been Irish Secretary, or indeed a politician, which means that his theory of government, resting on the notion that the multitude is reasonable, has been wrecked upon Ireland.

To Sir Henry Taylor.

Blachford: March 9, 1881.

We are just back from London, where I have been on the Cathedral Commission and kept by the Afghan debate. Lord Derby's was, I thought, the speech of the debate, which was, I imagine, a creditable one to their Lordships' House. I arrived here last night in wind and rain, leaving behind me our brougham upset (not with me in it), our enormous coachman pitched into a hedge, and our horse half-stunned, wholly numbed, and chipped all over. However, it might have been worse. The big coachman is only bruised, the carriage will be set right, and the horse is to be available again.

This Transvaal business seems to be getting worse and worse. I only hope they will not adopt the Protectorate scheme, which according to the old precedent will disable us from controlling the Boers and compel us to protect them from the consequence of their misdoings. 'Felix opportunitate mortis' is the phrase which recurs to my mind when I think of Colley's death.[3] It would have required some resolution in him to survive this third disaster. What terrible mischief these attractive, plausible, self-confident people are capable of doing! People seem to get sick of that school, and yet I believe they will scarcely tolerate a really calm and just and considerate policy.

Ever yours affectionately,
BLACHFORD.

To Sir Henry Taylor.

Moorcross[1]: June 8, 1881.

My dear Taylor,—I have just come into possession of the 'Nineteenth Century,' and read your article on Carlyle. I like it very much indeed, in every way. It is very interesting and I am not disposed to quarrel with it, if it is a little on the friendly side of just. The evil qualities which the reading of his remini-

---

[3] At Majuba Hill, in February 1881.
[4] His sister's home, near Blachford.

scences suggests are envy and egotism ; and your paper leaves on the mind the impression that, after all, there was a great deal in Carlyle's circumstances and disposition which would account for *an appearance* of these things far in excess of the reality. Also it is very just to remind us that we are misled, by the solid, deliberate appearance of a printed book, into forgetting the passing character of Carlyle's disagreeable thoughts. Let him that knows of no internal contemptiblenesses in himself cast the first stone. All this, of course, weights the condemnation of Froude, which I myself feel to be righteous. Here I read your article a second time, by way of parenthesis. It is very good indeed. How you can write a thing of such force and richness on the wrong side of eighty, I do not understand. But I have just had an argument about 'sulphuretted hydrogen.' I think you unjust (for once) to Carlyle ; others otherwise. The saying seems to me not a mere 'knocking over of another man's pageantry.' But, in form of causticity, a sad reflection on the difference between outward appearance and underlying truth.[5] But no doubt the person who hears a thing said is the true interpreter.

I am, as you see, in the country, to lay the first stone of a new church. How charming it is ! We are in a blaze of rhododendrons, cows up to their knees in grass, hay growing as fast as it can lay legs to the ground, martins, thrushes, blackbirds, chaffinches all whisking about in the sun, making me feel as if I would never go to London again, which notwithstanding I must on the 13th for particularly disagreeable business.

Ever yours affectionately,
BLACHFORD.

---

[5] In Sir Henry Taylor's review (*Nineteenth Century* for 1881) of Carlyle's *Reminiscences* the passage occurs : ' He [Carlyle] delights in knocking over any pageantry of another man's setting up. One evening at the Grange a party of gentlemen returning from a walk in the dusk had seen a magnificent meteor. . . . they described what they had seen in glowing colours and with much enthusiasm. Carlyle, having heard them in silence, gave his view of the phenomenon : " Aye, some sulphuretted hydrogen, I suppose, or some rubbish of that kind."'

Note of a conversation with Cardinal Newman,[6] *June* 30, 1881.

Newman began by talking about his portrait—Millais only has his sitters for one hour at a time ; he so often paints children that he has got a knack of catching expressions with great rapidity, so that he can get what he wants in an hour, even though for part of the time his subject flags, or goes to sleep, in which case he has to stop. After an hour the sitter flags. For Newman he only requires six sittings.

Then he talked of his journey to Rome and his stay there : how he went with a strong presentiment that he should be ill ; he caught cold going to mass at Turin, and he wrote a letter to Rome to have a physician to receive him. There they just patched him up for the four days of ceremony, and then he fell at once into the chill of fever. They told him it would come back after 24 hours ; it did not, but it seemed to make rushes at him ' like a mosquito ' and then to be checked. Another very sharp attack came at Leghorn. He saw nothing of the buildings at Rome as he had wished, and his friends only for some moments, each like a bewildering pageant. I asked if he had known the Pope before he was Pope, and he said ' no,' and ' did not know how he could have heard of *him* (J. H. N.), nor did he understand how the Pope could ever have been elected by Cardinals all or nearly all nominated by Pius IX. and belonging to the other of the ' two parties ' in the Church. He had lived entirely at Perugia and was not of the Ultramontane party at all. The Pope desired to build up, not pull down, *i.e.* make peace with sovereigns : he had failed in Germany, Newman did not know how he stood in Italy. He spoke of the election solemnly, as if it were a marvel—' God's will.' I asked if the Pope had a charm of manner ; Cardinal Newman said very great to him, and that he did not think he was entirely prejudiced, as the Warden of Keble said the same thing. He added that he was still ' very kind ' to him, inquiring after him, sending messages &c., and in one case speaking very warmly of him in the presence of several persons to friends whom Cardinal

---

[6] Cardinal Newman had breakfasted with Lord and Lady Blachford at their house in London. Notes of the conversation were afterwards written down.

Newman had recommended to him. I asked if there were any prospect of the Church and State drawing together in Italy. He answered doubtfully; but said there was shortly to be a Jubilee, and that among the subjects put forth to be prayed for, besides the usual peace among princes &c., was the *private intention* of the Pope, which might relate to his dealings with the State. The Jubilee was in its nature not 'jubilant' but a solemn supplication under such circumstances as now exist—a great uprising of infidelity, especially in the matter of education. Then there came some talk about there being really a closer union between religious men at bottom than appeared to be on the surface of things. He spoke of the interest which men of all sects showed in himself, Dissenters, Unitarians, Free Kirk, and the good that there was in their publications, which he recognised. He said he hoped there might be a levelling up going on—a growing up of external conformity from internal assimilation, like lava bursting out hot, cooling down on the surface—then giving rise to lichens, then mould, then herbage, and then depth of rich soil, rich with trees, vines, and all that nature produces.

After that we got on the sadder subject of unbelief, beginning with the School Board question, and the difficulty of keeping up the Roman Catholic schools, where there were high school board rates to pay, and the hardships to poor Roman Catholics of having to pay for both. He spoke of the grandeur of the schools built by the school boards; one in particular was made to 'look like a church' with its well-planted entourage mimicking a graveyard (he seemed to have a notion of Anti-Christ about it). He made a grievance (I think a little needlessly) of being obliged to give the religious instruction (rooms are provided with good intention, which he acknowledged, for the purpose in this grand building 'into which our boys and girls are decanted') either at the beginning of the school time when the children do not come perhaps till the lesson is half over, or at the end when they are tired. He said some Protestants send their children to a Roman Catholic school because they say they wish their children to be taught religion of some kind; some are converted, others not.

From this we got to the more general question of scepticism. He spoke of the great intellectual unbelieving movement—'It was so easy to be an atheist.' I tried to make him talk on the question whether in a sense a man may not believe because he wishes it, in spite of a logical argument to the contrary. He recurred to the familiar topic that instinct, which is unanalysed argument, is often truer than what is logically cogent. I observed that there seemed a question beyond this—whether a man may not sometimes rightly be unfair to himself, determining *e.g.* to take a charitable judgment or to think what will keep up his own and other people's spirits for a great effort (say, in a shipwreck). He gave a kind of assent, but said it was a subject to be written about.

To Sir Henry Taylor.

Hollyhedge House : December 10, 1881.

My dear Taylor,—I must confess I have been this time unpardonably negligent in writing. As a half excuse I have been unusually busy for the last three weeks attending almost every day one of the Royal Commissions, in which I have contrived to be. I am a good deal amused (amid a ponderous amount of dull detail of which 'Cathedrals' have at least their share) at the internal politics and contrivances of a Commission of master minds, managing men, and modest men. Canterbury is the master, Carlisle the managing man, and your humble servant, Mr. Walter James and Mr. Dalrymple, Conservative M.P. for Bute, the modest men. To whom may be added Lord Cranbrook, the man of the political world. The master and manager pull the coach. The man of the world oils the wheels, and the modest men make suggestions, of which some are snubbed, some are accepted, and one or two which upset a pet form of managerial progress are outflanked. This outflanking is not unamusing. The old idea which was supposed to be shot down bobs up with nothing but a few feathers shot away, and somehow or other, without one's exactly knowing how, and without any special move which gives occasion to opposition, replaces itself in the scheme. Then it is amusing to see how the idea of 'Divide et impera,' dealing with the Cathedrals one by one, and so subduing them in detail, is opposed by a novel combination of Deans and Chapters who cry 'shoulder to shoulder,' so that each Dean and Chapter meets the solid weight of the Royal Commission before him by the solid weight of the Capitulate (will that do for a word?) behind him. However, our differences are few, and, if we are wise, will be accommodated.

What are you saying or thinking about Ireland? I have always thought the Government are playing a most doubtful game in allowing Chamberlain and Co. to dictate the policy of coquetry. And now, of course, it seems likely that we must do more in the way of civil war than what might have been sufficient a year ago. However, it is a question whether any one else could have done any better.

Ever yours affectionately,
BLACHFORD.

To Sir Henry Taylor.

Blachford: April 25, 1882.

My dear Taylor,—I have been most sincerely grieved at seeing in the papers the death of Lady Minto.[7] What a loss to every one who knows her! There was a kind of gracious brightness about her which must have been charming to everybody who came near her. The relinquishment of that and all that it signified must make a sad blank in her home and to you. I thought when I saw Lord Minto lately in London that he spoke sadly and seriously about her state, but I had no idea that it was so immediately anxious.

I have just finished the first draft of a long, perhaps lengthy, report on Fever and Smallpox Hospitals which has filled my mind for the last three months, and shall have to spend most of the first fortnight in May in London to try to finish it with corrections, excisions, and so on. I am glad to do it, for I feel I am of some use to the Government, and I am getting less and less disposed to be of use to them (if I could be so) in domestic politics. So I am glad to do some

---

[7] Wife of the third Lord Minto, and the authoress of the *Memoirs of Hugh Elliott*. She had been living for some time near the Taylors at Bournemouth.

non-political work which may be my excuse for sitting still while political turmoils are going on. I do not know how far it is epicurean to feel that the world is going its own way, which is not mine, and that I have shot my bolts for good or evil, am not likely to launch any more effective ones, and may arrange myself quietly for adding what I can to the comforts of those within my arm's length, during the few next years, leaving to the rising politicians who 'would outwit God' to turn their sails to the winds and storms that they are rousing. I think, however, I shall hardly be put to bed before we have some very vigorous outburst of English commonsense or English insanity. And I only hope Gladstone may not go in for insanity.

Ever yours affectionately,
BLACHFORD.

To Lady Blachford.

Hollyhedge House : May 8, 1882.

It [the murder in Phœnix Park] is certainly in all its horrors the most dreadful thing of our days. . . . What is terrible is that we have no right to be surprised at it. The 'Irish World' and the 'United Irishmen' and demagogues of all sorts have been threatening it, and I suppose we all feel that if the murderers were caught and hanged they would be martyrs in the eyes of the Irish people, like the Clerkenwell murderers. This it is which the Government ought to feel, and what some of them, I suppose, do feel. . . . R. told me that he had gone into a shop on Sunday to buy an 'Observer.' The woman of the shop said they were all gone, but 'it is all true.' She added that she had not been able to read it for crying. My experience was different. We heard it before breakfast through a servant and the 'Weekly Dispatch.' But we thought it might be a *canard*, and I went to the railway station to seek some other paper. The stall was closed, but I went up to a seedy old man who was creeping out to the railway, reading a paper. 'From a man round the corner,' he said, and added 'It's true,' as if nobody could be thinking of anything else. To the shop I went, and bought an

'Observer' from a decent, respectable young woman, much occupied in seeing that her boy handed out the newspapers. Her observation was, 'Those Irish seem to be at it. Is it the President they have killed?' Strange ignorance, and indifference to anything but the sale of the news!

To Sir Henry Taylor.

Blachford : May 29, 1882.

My dear Taylor,—These are terrible times. *Inter alia* Jerry ⁸—late Olaf—is no more. The poor fellow had a bad toothache (it is said), became unable to eat, fell off, was sent into Plymouth to undergo dentistry at the hands of the veterinary in most esteem there, was dosed (it is dimly suspected) too much, and died. The gardener who looked after him could not for a week speak or hear of him without tears in his eyes, a compliment which he altogether failed to pay to his own mother-in-law who died at the same time in his house. My sisters are inconsolable (at least whenever they think about ponies), and a general feeling of attachment and respect has developed itself, which none of us suspected in one another. A gipsy offered them (my sisters) another pony, probably stolen, this morning. When they asked him where he lived, he almost laughed in their faces, and answered, 'Why, about.' 'They were so jolly green!' However, they did not buy the pony.

What do you hear of Ireland? I feel almost hopeless, particularly because Gladstone seems incapable of really taking in the idea that the Parnells and the Dillons and the Anna Parnells have to be treated as irreconcilable enemies. In all his proceedings there seems to me a kind of undercurrent of 'Do-ee, now,' which is incompatible with an inflexible 'you shall,' and this even among his biggest words. It always seems to me that it is certain ruin to have to trust a bitter enemy, not because you think him honest, or have any fair ground for thinking him repentant, but because you suppose him to be the only man who can rein in his own adherents. Even if you can buy him outright, which you probably can't do, '*uno avulso non deficit alter*,' ten to one he 'leaves

⁸ A Norwegian pony.

his tail behind him.' And you have weakened your position for nothing.

I think I shall vote myself out of politics altogether. I am old enough to hold myself thoroughly shelved. I will not oppose Gladstone and Granville. I shall soon find myself unable to support them (here in England), and so I shall grow strawberries and go to sleep. I have always felt that as everybody—by the side of the duties which come to his hand—has some work which he would take up with true natural gusto, the regeneration of mankind, philosophy, advancement of art, and so on, so I in particular should like to succeed in changing the face of a country, so that the hills and valleys and people and cattle and houses and roads looked cheerful and well cared for, and pleased with one another (if one may say such a thing of hills and valleys), and I should like well enough to crawl about for my last few years mending holes and picking up loose stitches in that direction.

I forget whether you ever met at our house an old American friend of ours, whose death appears in the newspapers—Colonel Chester, a curiously simple-hearted genealogist, who always reminded me of the Jesuit saying which Pascal bitterly attacks, that (with an application to the good works of men) 'God had graciously given to the poor frog the same delight in his croaking as the nightingale took in her song.' He (Col. C.) devoted his life to genealogy, and thought it well spent in ferreting out the minutest particulars of the minutest families with a kind of enthusiastic devotion which enabled him to say that at least he had done one thing as no man had done it before him, or (I add) will probably do after him. But, with all this, a keeper of the two great Commandments, and as pure, affectionate, and simple-hearted a man as I ever knew. One of the many 'good-byes for the present,' which one has now to say, at least which one desires to be able to say.[9]

All kind things from both of us to all of you.

Ever yours affectionately,
BLACHFORD.

[9] Colonel Chester came over from America partly because he had a commission to trace the pedigrees of several American families who claimed descent

To Miss C. Colvile.

October 1882.

My dear Charlotte,—I have been reading chapters here and there of Mr. George,[1] selecting some of which he appeared to be most proud. He is a kind of man who provokes me beyond measure, because I know him so well, without the power of exactly formulating him. He has a certain amount of knowledge and reading, and, when he clearly understands what he is writing about, a highly respectable power of clear statement and illustration. Consequently passages in which he states a course of familiar phenomena, or sticks closely to a beaten track which has been worn for him by wise men, he is readable, though unnecessarily diffuse.

But he is totally without the power of sound original thought, and totally without consciousness of his deficiencies. Consequently, he is always trying to set wise men right, and in consequence floundering in a sea of blunders which he vainly attempts to disguise by a profusion of sentences. In short, he is a voluble, shallow quack.

No inconsiderable part of my life (at the Emigration Office) was spent in reporting upon the projects of such pretenders, so that I have acquired a kind of feverish sensibility in respect of such persons, a kind of wrath at feeling that there are a lot of people who will think them fine, and that it will take more labour than their whole generation is worth to clear out the tangle in which they have enveloped themselves, and to expose them to the unlearned.

If you want to see a specimen of fluent floundering, read the chapter on 'Wages not drawn from Capital but produced by Labour' (at least if you can). It is an evidently pretentious and unmitigatedly shallow attempt to disprove

---

from John Rogers, the first of the Protestant martyrs in the reign of Mary. He proved to his satisfaction that none of them could possibly be descended from John Rogers (which, he said, would almost prevent his returning to his own country); but he thought it probable that the Rogers of Blachford were descendants. This, however, seems to have been rather because he could not disprove it than because he could establish the pedigree.

[1] *Progress and Poverty*, by Henry George.

what is self-evident in itself and utterly untouched by his argument.

A and B are thrown on a desert island, with food to sustain them till their next crop. A sows and reaps provisions for two years. B sows and reaps nothing. A having thus a superfluity of food (which is capital), and B having none, A agrees with B to feed him for twelve months if during that time B will build him a wall round his field to keep off goats (who eat his crop) and will so double his crop. It is a plain matter of fact that B's wages were paid out of A's first crop. George spends two or three pages to show that they were paid out of the third crop, and this even though a ship were to touch at the island and carry them all off before that third crop is reaped.

Really this is not an exaggeration of the man's folly, and all done with the air of an oracle. *Anathema esto.*

Ever yours affectionately,
BLACHFORD.

To Lady Blachford.

Athenæum Club : December 12, 1882.

The change in Oxford as a city is certainly wonderful. There was no walking about or seeing anything in the cold fog (on Sunday), but the mere walking from Rickards's [2] to Oriel and back led one through a suburb of villas, inhabited by widows (of whom nine called on Rickards in his first six weeks), professors, tutors, generals, retired India officers (civil and military), and what was cornfield has become a large University Park.

The number of undergraduates has increased 80 per cent. ; there are two ladies' colleges ; the University and College buildings are increasing every day (the University running into debt), and altogether it is a 'Great Babylon.'

At Oriel I was much pleased to find myself and Church made much of as patriarchs. We went to chapel there at half-past five P.M. on Sunday, dinner immediately after in

---

[2] The late Sir George Rickards, who had just resigned his office of Counsel to the Speaker and was living at Oxford, where several years before he had been Professor of Political Economy. He was a contemporary of Lord Blachford's at Eton but a little junior to him.

hall; the common room as in old times. They collect prints of their old Fellows, and wanted to know whether I could give them one of me. They picked up one of Beau Brummel, who, it seems, was at Oriel, and (I suppose) not a footman there. And on the whole I went home much gratified.

I think I told you that I had considerable talk with Jowett, who thinks that Latin and Greek are gone off in the University.

On Monday Church declined Birmingham,[3] so I went alone at 11.45, with much fear lest I should be blocked up by fog or snow. I got there half an hour late, about 2, and was shown up to the Cardinal in a dormitory (not his) where a bed was prepared for me, if I chose to stay and sleep.

We talked about many things—old times, I think, largely. While we were talking he was told that Mr. —— would be with him at four o'clock. I told him not to mind me, when he said, *au contraire*, Mr. —— was for me, and that two others with him (the music teacher) were to give me a trio of Beethoven's (I must find out which it was, I knew it very well), which came to pass, and I listened from four o'clock or so till it was time to wash for a quarter before six dinner. The dinner was in a large bare room, with panelled sides, say eight feet high, and a line of dusky pictures above, I should think portraits of the Heads or Saints of the Order. Round the room were small square tables, about half as big again as a card table. The Cardinal had one to himself (he did not, however, seem to eat), I another next to him, then two of the fathers at each of the others; one mounted a pulpit in the corner of the room, and two carved the victuals at a table in the centre, and handed it about as waiters—fathers, not lay brethren. The father in the pulpit read first some ten or twenty verses of one of the Gospels (from the Vulgate), then in English a short anecdote of St. Philip. He was a confessor to a rich lady, and her relations were afraid that she would give him her money. So they ordered St. Philip to give her up, he went on. Then they ordered the servants to keep him out, he

[3] To visit Cardinal Newman who was at this time head of the Roman Catholic College at Birmingham.

went on. Then they threatened his life, and his friends begged him not to run the risk. He said that he had a soul to save, and that if he was killed for saving it, it would be the happiest end a man could have. There ended the story. There was a letter from St. Philip, whether playful or serious I could not well make out, to a man who had somehow deserted him. After this the reader and waiters moved into their places to eat their own dinners, and one of the fathers put two questions: one was the old one of lying to save a man's life, giving a story as an instance; then two or three fathers gave their views. Newman had already told me that he was too deaf now to hear what the fathers said on such occasions, and so did not perform his part of summing up, but left it to the interrogator, who gave us St. Augustine's views and his own, nothing very new about either. Then soon we got up and went away to the common room, very plain and ascetic, but spacious, where we sat round the fire and talked till my cab came to fetch me for the 7.20 train.

Of course it was late in such weather, and I did not get to the Deanery till 12 o'clock, and sat up talking with them till near one

To Cardinal Newman.

Blachford : December 22, 1882.

My dear Cardinal,—Will you tell me or cause me to be told what was the trio you gave me at the Oratory? I know it very well, but unless you give me its designation I shall not be able to distinguish it hereafter from other old friends. I want to 'ear-mark' it.

So Church has refused to sit in the seat of Anselm, or in what we hold to be such. How strange it seems! But there is no doubt, though he himself was doggedly silent on the subject, that he had the offer.[4] The work would have been plainly too much for him.

Ever yours affectionately,
BLACHFORD.

I cannot say what a pleasure it is to me to have had the afternoon at the Oratory.

[4] Of the Archbishopric of Canterbury on the death of Archbishop Tait.

To Sir Henry Taylor.

Blachford : May 28, 1883.

My dear Taylor,—I find it a little difficult to answer your question shortly about Aubrey de Vere's article,[5] viz. how far it and others in the same strain are likely to be useful in affecting religious and irreligious convictions.

In the first place it is very interesting, attractive, and elevating in its treatment of a side of moral theology. Many a religious man will find that it gives flesh and colour and development to thought which he had inchoate or undeveloped, or not at all. There is a clear usefulness of a high character.

But what he is principally thinking of, I imagine, is not its didactic, but its controversial use.

And on this it is that I find it rather difficult to see clearly. Somebody has said (perhaps Coleridge) that every one is born either an Aristotelian or a Platonist.[6] Of course, every one who is worth a farthing is in some measure both. A man must be something of a goose who has *nothing* of the cogency and hard-headedness of (say) Bentham, and something of a block who has *nothing* of the transcendental imagination of (say) Coleridge. Of course, also sentiment, moral sentiment, lies at the root of all that is good or great in faith. But some men are irresistibly governed by cogent reasoning, and some by captivating ideas. And those who are peculiarly sensitive to one are not quite sound judges of writers who appeal to the other. Now, I think that I am Aristotelian and Aubrey de Vere Platonist, and I feel a great difficulty in seeing how far considerations which would not touch *me* if I were an adverse disputant *would* touch persons of the (shall I say?) opposite and more transcendental cast of mind.

A. de Vere says to his reader, 'Throw yourself into a state of faith; it is the noblest, wisest, happiest state—just look at it and see.'

---

[5] An article by Mr. Aubrey de Vere in the *Nineteenth Century* for May 1883, 'On Subjective Difficulties in Religion,' written in defence of Christian Faith, chiefly against Agnosticism, and certain views of Evolutionists.

[6] It is in Coleridge's *Table Talk* under July 2, 1830.

'No doubt,' the man replies, 'if I could get there. But I find difficulties.'

'Yes, but a hundred difficulties need not make one doubt.'

'True again ; " but," says the doubter, " there are difficulties and difficulties, and *my* difficulties are of a class which *do* make doubts, and, worse than doubts, disbeliefs. I find it impossible to reconcile the existence of evil with the belief in a good and all-powerful God, to accept eternal punishment, to get over the philosophical argument from necessity, &c."'

If these do not present themselves to a man's mind as solid grounds of doubt, he need not, *me judice*, go out of his way to worry himself about them. But *if they did* to *my* mind I should require something more than a general argument for distrusting difficulties. I should require something to show me why I was at liberty to dismiss this difficulty and not that, and that I was at liberty to dismiss the difficulties of, or rather objections to, Christianity, while I was not at liberty to insist on the objections to atheism. If I am to shut my right eye, why the right ? If my left, why the left ?

The answers to these questions may be in the article. But if so, they do not march up in battle array. The considerations in which they are involved form an inspiring sight, but they will not storm a fort held by Aristotelians of the hard-headed kind.

But perhaps it is intended to teach (and this seems to be involved in the title) that Christianity, by its mere exhibition of itself, proves itself to a certain class of minds, and that for those to whom it does not so prove itself, independently of obstacles to belief or insufficiency of what is generally called evidence, there is no help.

Probably of the mass of mankind this is true. But in the 'Nineteenth Century' we deal, or try to deal, with men of mind.

With men of this class, who have a strong conviction that our reasoning powers were given us to be something like sovereign guides in sifting religious and moral truth the article would not, it appears to me, produce much effect. Nor, I think, would it convince that class of persons that they were not intended to take reason as something like a sovereign guide.

But I quite understand that to those persons who have more power of overbearing the reasoning power when they have a firm grasp of a vivid idea, A. de V.'s picture of faith (for this is what it comes to) might be an assistance to believe what they desire to believe, or even an inducement to believe what they were disposed to consider indefensible by reason. This, of course, would be a sphere of usefulness independent of the merely didactic effect of preaching *aux convertis.*

Ever yours affectionately,
BLACHFORD.

To Sir Henry Taylor.
September 7, 1883.

My dear Taylor,—One of the growing evils of old age is having nothing to say. Another is not knowing that you have nothing to say. From the second I am happily preserved. But to the first I am more and more a prey, and one result is that for I do not know how many weeks I have been asking myself what I have said to *you,* and have been answering 'Nothing,' *et sic de aliis.* And now I only write in a desperate way, for shame ; and because I shall get more, I know, than I deserve in answer.

We have had here the Dean, his daughter Mary, and his married daughter Helen, with her husband, F. Paget, son of Sir James, and Rector of Bromsgrove.[7]

The visit is a kind of appendix to their honeymoon. And this has been an occasion for making the father and son-in-law really know one another (for which there is nothing like a country house), taking good long *tête-à-tête* walks, which, as they are sympathetic souls, pleases everybody. He (the Dean) is, I think, getting a little worn out by the air and the duties of London.

I am glad to receive this morning the report on 'Ecclesiastical Courts.' There is always a satisfaction in feeling that you have really done with a thing, even though you may be but fifteenth fiddle in it. It may lay some dust. Especially it includes what I suppose will be a standard account of the growth of ecclesiastical jurisdiction, by Dr.

---

[7] Now Dean of Christ Church.

Stubbs, the great historical *indagator* of the day in such subjects, which will render certain sorts of loose talking almost impossible. But I can hardly hope for any such agreement between political and ecclesiastical parties as will make remedial legislation possible. The existence of Gladstone is the only thing which gives it a chance. And as the report and evidence comprise little short of a thousand folio pages, mostly of small print, the subject may have a charm for him. I wish you were here. It would do you good, I am sure, in the (rare) intervals of sunshine, to look out on the trees and grass and water and wild ducks and deer, not to say, on Wednesday last, some two hundred and fifty school children eating and drinking and trundling hoops and swinging from the branches of the trees.

What an insanity of objectless greed seems to possess those Frenchmen, unless indeed they seriously desire to overrun China, which could hardly be called objectless.[1]

Ever yours affectionately,
BLACHFORD.

To Cardinal Newman.

Athenæum Club : February 11, 1884.

My dear Cardinal,—I have not had time to look up much in the *curiosity* line ; and what I have done makes me think that I cannot improve on your suggestion of a book. One of the best things I have seen for your purpose [a present to a friend] was a pretty and genuine-looking old cabinet of ebony and ivory (20*l*.). But at Sotheran's (whither Beresford Hope sent me) I have seen one thing which seemed to me excellent. I enclose a few leaves from his catalogue, marking a few articles which are about your price. The best was Lacroix (p. 41), to be bound in 9 vols. morocco, cost from 16*l*. 10*s*. to 18*l*. (rather trifling). But the two best things I saw were :

1. A large folio (2 vols.) of the ' Roman Catacombs,' with careful engravings, but not coloured (15*l*. in morocco), and what I should recommend.

2. 'La Renaissance' (price 16*l*. 16*s*. in morocco), 2 folio

---
[1] The French annexed the Tonquin province in 1883.

volumes, large margin, magnificent print, altogether 'de luxe' and plenty of excellent etchings of buildings—a beautiful book, in *art* far superior to the 'Catacombs,' whatever the latter may be in point of interest.

Sotheran seems to be in constant communication with the Oratory, and would readily send you a volume for inspection. If you like it you can settle a binding (why cannot you put outside one of those splendid coats of arms surmounted by a Cardinal's hat which one sees on some old books?).

If not, I shall be in town again for the levée of the 22nd (to thank the Queen for making me a G.C.M.G.), and will try my hand again. I suspect, however, that it will require some idling about in curiosity shops to find anything better than the 'Renaissance.' The price of antiquities, china, &c., I am told, has multiplied itself by ten in the last thirty years. Some measure of the growth of great fortunes.

Ever yours affectionately,
BLACHFORD.

To Cardinal Newman.

Athenæum Club : February 21, 1884.

My dear Cardinal,—First, all good wishes to you on your birthday. You will not receive them, but I write them, on that day.

Next, I have just ordered 'The Renaissance,' which is, as you suppose, a book of which the value consists in its etchings of ecclesiastic and other Renaissance architecture. Sotheran says it shall be bound up in three weeks, meaning, I suppose, six. I have told him when it is finished to write to you for directions.

I was half tempted to put it in an ecclesiastical livery, but I could not see any purple leather that pleased me, and so ordered a smooth polished brown morocco, with no gilding except the lettering on the back and (more ornately) on the side, fit for a book that lies on a table.

Ever yours affectionately,
BLACHFORD.

To Cardinal Newman.

Blachford : January 16, 1885.

My dear Cardinal,—I have been reading Boswell's 'Life of Johnson' actually for the first time. What do you say to the following?—' Sir, your disquiet is a foolish affair. Why, sir, if my wife bade me give you her love she would never, to be sure, tell you to say nothing about it. No, sir. If the Pope, who I am informed is a man of sense, intended to afford you a gratification, he would never have imposed a condition to destroy half its value. Mr. Warton used to say at Trinity College, " Quod tacitum velis nemini dixeris," and if the Pope had been ashamed of his affection for you, why, sir, he would have said nothing about it.'[9]

As somebody says, 'Them's my sentiments.'

Ever yours affectionately,

BLACHFORD.

To Sir Henry Taylor.

Blachford : January 20, 1885.

My dear Taylor,—I send you, in case you should not be in the way to see it, cuttings from a 'Pall Mall Gazette,' containing a letter from me on a proposed Federative Council, also the editorial comment. The editor wrote to me, pointing out his and Lord Grey's suggestions, and asking me either to allow myself to be interviewed on the subject or to give them my opinion in publishable shape.

I am rather glad of this, as I totally disbelieve in the possibility of Federation, into which the world is running with its eyes shut, and really think that the question ought not to go 'by default.' The cat wants belling.

I hope my letter will compel people to think out the question seriously. And if nobody agrees with me I must suppose myself wrong.

I am ordering the 'Edinburgh' with Aubrey de Vere's review of Spenser. I shall expect a great deal from it, and

---

[9] This is an answer in the Johnsonian manner, to a letter in which Cardinal Newman wrote that he had scruples about repeating to others some kind and complimentary sayings of the Pope.

shall be curious to see what he makes of Duessa and Archimago, which must be offences to him.[1]

I see the 'Pall Mall' is attacking the *Peer Ministers* (Granville, Derby, Northbrook). I have long thought that the number of these in every Ministry was an indication of something skin deep in democracy. And I am not surprised at the Radicals making a grievance of it.

What is our next Parliament to be? Has any one whatever any guess?

Ever yours affectionately,
BLACHFORD.

The Objections to the Colonial Board of Advice.

You invite me to give an opinion on a proposal contained in your leading article of the 9th inst., and founded on a suggestion of Lord Grey's, for the establishment of a Council to advise the Colonial Office. I do not desire to discuss Lord Grey's proposal, which is that this Council should be a Committee of her Majesty's Privy Council—not necessarily, I suppose, of ministerial politics. I will only say that I have not personally a great faith in councils of advice, which seem to me calculated to embarrass strong administrators, and perhaps still more to embarrass weak ones. I believe that departmental business is most effectively performed by one officer, to whom his subordinates are responsible, and who is himself responsible to some further superior or to the public, without the shelter of colleagues or Council. In the case of a Board, which has somewhat of the nature of a Council, I feel confident, from many years' experience, that unprofitable discussion, with its consequent friction, delay, and indecision, is best avoided by doing as much individually and as little collectively as possible. When higher matters are concerned, it seems to me that if a Minister, and not least a Secretary of State for the Colonies, should want advice, he should take it from the Cabinet, or from a Committee of the Cabinet, to which he belongs, and to whose judgment his policy must conform itself. If he wants information he should be at liberty to seek it where it is to be found without any official

---

[1] Mr. de Vere had joined the Church of Rome.

restriction on his choice of informants. Nor, I would submit, should he be hampered by the necessity of communicating with any but those whose interests give them a right to be heard, and that to the extent only which in his opinion the public interests permit. If a man is not fit to be trusted with this discretion he is not fit to be Secretary of State. In discussing your own proposal I am afraid I must write more of a treatise than either of us would wish.

In the first place you will at once see that I approach the question from a departmental point of view, and if I seem to ignore the broader considerations with which it is supposed to be connected it is because I hold them to be delusive. For I am bound to avow myself one of that apparently small minority who look upon Federation as an unattainable phantom, on grounds which I ought at least generally to indicate. Even in the matter of foreign policy, about which alone the question could arise, I cannot conceive the possibility of our having continued to conduct the Government of the United States of America and the United Kingdom of Great Britain by one sovereign authority, localised either in London or in Washington, or with one foot in one place and one in the other. And what would, in any contingency, have become impossible by this time in the case of the United States, must, as it appears to me, become impossible, as time goes on, in the case of all great and distant Anglo-Saxon colonies. If so, the question is not whether the useful and interesting tie which at present connects us can last for ever —or even for very long—but whether that transitional relation will be longest and most beneficially preserved by tightening or relaxing it. Hitherto we have proceeded on the principle of relaxation, and by so doing we are admitted, I believe, to have gained more in mutual contentment than we have lost in authority. I admit, however, that the question has changed its aspect. Formerly it was found that we endangered the connexion by claiming to interfere with the local affairs of the colonists. The doubt now is whether we shall not endanger it and ourselves by allowing them to interfere with our Imperial policy. My own strong impression is that we shall. The notion of a great Anglo-Saxon alliance, not formed with a specific object, as to arrest the supremacy of some overgrown power or immoral principle, but on a general understanding (as I conclude) that all shall join in furthering the wishes and interests of each, seems to me likely, if, *per impossibile*, it should last long enough, to degenerate into a successful or unsuccessful contrivance for bullying the rest of the world. To contend for such an alliance on the ground that Anglo-Saxons—the great exterminators of aborigines in the temperate zone—would, when confederated, set a new and exceptional example of justice and humanity, seems to me a somewhat transcendental expectation.

Having said so much, I proceed, subject to the prejudice which I have raised against myself, to the specific proposal made in your paper. Like Lord Grey, you propose a Council of Assistance for the Colonial Office, but one which is to consist, not of Privy Councillors, but, with possible and immaterial additions, of the High Commissioner of Canada and the Agents-General of the other colonies having responsible Governments. It is with this, the backbone of the matter, that I now desire to deal. I first point out that all these officers are servants, not of the Queen of England, but of the Queen of Canada, Victoria, New South Wales, and the rest. I mean this: Queen Victoria is Sovereign of the British Empire, and through the British Parliament exercises, within certain constitutional limits, legislative authority over that empire. She is also Queen of the United Kingdom, and conducts its government through Ministers designated by the people of the United Kingdom—and not otherwise. She is also Queen of Canada, and a Governor appointed by her conducts the government of that Dominion through Ministers designated by the Canadians—and not otherwise. The High Commissioner is not the servant of the Queen of England, responsible through the English Ministers to the people of England, but of the Queen of Canada, responsible through Canadian Ministers to the people of Canada. You may quarrel with my language, but the facts which it is intended to exhibit are indisputable and inevitable. To illustrate their relations we may imagine, what is quite imaginable, that Ministers of Canada or Victoria or the Cape of Good Hope, to whom the support of the Irish party had become indispensable, might appoint Irish Agents-General, with special instructions to ally themselves with the National party in embarrassing the existing English Government. To execute those instructions would be their duty, and we see that much might easily be done in that way. The supposition is not, I trust, likely to be realised, but it illustrates the duties of a Colonial Office as they are and as they would remain.

And now what is the actual and what the proposed position of these officers in relation to the Minister of the Queen of England? Their actual position is one which, originally viewed with some jealousy in Downing-street, has been of late cordially accepted and studiously raised in dignity and influence. Everything seems to be done and to be doing by the Imperial Government to give Agents-General, relatively to the Colonial Minister, a status analogous to that which is held by the representatives of foreign States of equal importance in relation to the Minister for Foreign Affairs. They are held, I apprehend, to be within their proper sphere when they ask from the Colonial Office any information which they need, and present any remonstrance or representation which they think is in place. This they are able to do with the full weight of their position, individually, or in groups, or as a whole. And for this purpose they are at liberty to consult together, and by mutual consent to combine into an organisation as coherent legally as that of the British Cabinet. What is proposed is this—that the association of those colonial servants shall not be left to voluntary agreement, but, as a matter of form, shall be established by an act of the Imperial Sovereign, and, as a matter of substance, shall have a certain Imperial standing and authority over against the English Minister—a *locus standi* not only outside the walls of Downing-street but within it—'a footing inside the office,' with the 'right to demand information,' and a 'responsibility for the advice' which (asked or unasked?) they are to give. What this responsibility is to be, beyond that which they are now under to those whom they represent, I do not understand. What it would soon come to, I suspect, would be this: not that they would be responsible for giving the advice, but that the Secretary of State would be increasingly responsible for neglecting it.

And now let me consider the working of the scheme. It is certain that in at least nine colonial cases out of ten no association would be of the slightest use. The questions with which the Colonial Office is concerned arise between the English Government and this or that colony, and would only be confused by extraneous meddling. Where there is community of interest there is no difficulty in bringing about common consultation.

In the case of intended and united pressure on the Imperial Minister, the Colonial Agents might possibly be a little strengthened (if that is an advantage) by their Imperial position. But, on the other hand, when I consider what common interests Canada has either with Australia or the Cape Colony, I cannot help thinking that the combined Council would in reality have no appreciable work to do; and when I consider further that they might think it due to their dignified position to do something or other, and that there is somebody who is always finding mischief for idle hands, I cannot help fearing that occasions might be embraced for inopportune ventilation of embarrassing principles, or for what our Transatlantic relations call 'log-rolling.' 'I will roll your log if you will roll mine. If you (Queensland) will help me (Newfoundland) to induce John Bull to risk a quarrel with France for the sake of my fisheries, I will help you to induce him to risk a quarrel with Germany about the occupation of New Guinea.' It seems to me desirable from an English point of view not to give momentum and authority to this kind of pressure, which tends to make many suffer for a few. Still less should I think it advantageous that a body of the Queen's colonial servants should have a footing inside the office of her English Minister. Communications between them appear to me to stand best as they are—matters of discretion and courtesy. Friendly as the relations should always remain between the colonial representatives and the English Minister, there may always be matters which it would be imprudent or premature for either to disclose to the other. And if so, the limits of disclosure must of necessity be discretionary, according to the nature of the subject, and, I add, the character of the person to whom the communications are made.

But you may think that my own reasonable limits as a correspondent have long been over-passed. I can only apologise by saying that you have set me writing, and that if a writer belonging to a small minority does not say what he has to say for himself nobody else will say it for him.

BLACHFORD.

To Sir Henry Taylor.

Blachford : March 26, 1885.

My dear Taylor,—No, I am not gone to what you call the bad—meaning I suppose Acheron or Phlegethon or worse, only getting a little like the 'dull fat weed that rots itself at ease' in that neighbourhood. I have been up to town to give a vote about Egypt, and to finish off that very Lethean process, the Cathedral Commission. And now I am back again to my cabbages.

I have not yet got your revised Autobiography. But I have read the 'Times' article, which is in a satisfactory tone and will I suppose make the book at once an object of curiosity. I shall be disappointed if it does not take hold of people. I did not think that the review caught very well the characteristics of the book, or rather I thought that it did not exhibit them in good perspective. . . .

I have been exerting myself to give a lecture to the 'Cornwood Recreation and Improvement Society' (I need not say this name was composed by the schoolmaster) on Egypt, and was much gratified by the great guffaws of laughter which were produced by some of the stories which the Egyptian priests told Herodotus. There is an odd sense of mixture between the venerable and the frivolous in a series of jokes 3,000 years old, coming out as compact and genuine as mummies, and very like ours. . . . The Dean I wish were better ; he was very ill in the winter, and recovers his strength slowly. I want him to come here, which always does him good. But he has to enthrone his new Bishop and to keep the peace between irreconcilable Canons, and generally, like other tender-conscienced people, thinks himself more necessary than he is, not recognising the virtue of 'wholesome neglect' (I have often thanked thee, Jew, for teaching me that word). And I am afraid he will not slip cable till he slips off to the South.

Ever yours affectionately,

BLACHFORD.

To Sir Henry Taylor.

Blachford : June 22, 1885.

My dear Taylor,—I have been constantly thinking of a letter to you, but am always repelled by the sense that in the solitude of Blachford I have nothing to say, minding my own affairs and scarcely reading more than an epitome of the newspapers. It seems almost a waste of nervous power to excite yourself about events which you cannot influence and which you have not long to endure.

However, I am deep in stone and mortar, planning, or rather now building a village clubroom, a village schoolmistresses' cottage, dormitories for single men (labourers) attached to the clubhouse, and arranging for the settlement of some labourers in cottages with some cows attached. All which, however, is settled when it is settled, and, when the work begins, is only a pleasant occasion for idling. . . .

I have been a good deal amused at reading (or rather hearing read, for I have greatly to spare my eyes) a set of biographies or letters—Mountstuart Elphinstone, the Indian statesman, Disraeli, and Gordon. It makes one curiously alive to the differences of which our species is capable, in the single 'variety' of English public men.

Elphinstone is a type of character which I admire greatly except as compared with a Christian ideal. A great but not overpowering desire for distinction, absolute devotion to the public good, courage, intellect, cultivation, no jealousy or desire to surpass others—in short, a man wholly noble, and, what is getting rare among Indian statesmen, possessed with the idea that, at bottom, India is to be governed with a view to what is good for the Indians and not for the present or prospective interests of England, except so far as the two may fairly be considered as bound up together. A perfect character of its kind, but without the warmth of religious enthusiasm, and so with something of the cold beauty of a Greek statue, though with powers of friendship and beneficence which fascinated those within reach of him.

Dizzy's letters (a thin duodecimo) [2] make one like his sincere affection for his family, but exhibit shamelessly on his part, and I suppose unconsciously on the part of his editor, an appetite for low notoriety, even that of a buffoon, which is really beneath contempt, and is only elevated by his undisguised contempt for the people whom he labours to impose upon. There is a sparkling enjoyment of his own impudence and the stupidity of his neighbours which is really attractive; but one thinks, 'That this man should have been a belauded Prime Minister, and (of all countries in the world) of England, to whom on "Primrose Day" Conservative cultus is paid as to a political saint!' And this is the effect, on a reader, of letters written by himself and edited by an admirer.

Gordon makes up the triad. It is impossible to imagine a man living more completely in the presence of God, or more absolutely careless of his own distinction, comfort, wealth, or life, a man unreservedly devoted to the cause of the oppressed. One bows down before him as before a man of a superior order of being to one's own. But he is almost as 'odd' now and then as Sir Francis Head. And though he is constantly engaged in keeping down vanity, there is a degree of self-gratulation which jars on you.

Our country is beautiful just now; we live among seas of rhododendrons, the beauty of which follows on that of spring. But we are immersed in misty rain, and only see what there is to see in short bursts of fine weather.

Well, so Lord Salisbury seems in the saddle. What is to be done with a party who cannot trust English finance in the

---

[2] ['Home Letters, written in 1830, 1831.']

hands of the only man of them (Northcote) who understands the subject, and who place India under the dominancy of Lord Randolph Churchill?

Ever yours affectionately,
BLACHFORD.

To Lady Taylor.

Blachford : August 17, 1885.

My dear Lady Taylor,—I am really vexed at not complying with any wish of your husband's, but in some things a man must act according to his own nature ('can but stand on his own legs' some people say) whether that nature is abstractedly the best or not.[3]

Now, *in limine* (beg pardon for Latin) I have perhaps a morbid repugnance to those monster petitions which derive their weight from *numbers* of signatures, given in a great measure because they are asked for, without any real guarantee that the signatories care or know much about the matter. I have been asked to sign many such but have pretty steadily refused.

Next, allow me to observe that it seems a *Roman Catholic* petition. It addresses the Pope as head of the *Catholic* Church, and begs him to issue his advice to the bishops of 'the Church,' silently unchurching all others than those of his communion.

But I am not a Roman Catholic, or *quasi* Roman Catholic. Again, on the one hand, I am not inclined to address a 'humble petition' to a prelate who is always anathematising me (at least once a year, I believe); on the other, I do not feel that I could properly come forward to teach him his duties.

May I say that I am inclined to think that the old Italian would feel an amusement not altogether respectful at the sight of the presenting Cardinal followed by four flunkies staggering under what Mr. Colam describes as the 'immense' package of orthodox and heterodox signatures

---

[3] This letter was in answer to a request that Lord Blachford should sign a petition to the Pope begging him to use his authority for the prevention of cruelty to animals.

procured by 500 registered 'unsectarian' societies? It would be an odd sight.

Finally, I cannot honestly say that I believe that the example of his Holiness (in issuing a pastoral on the subject) 'will be followed by all sects and nations in the world' and cruelty to animals 'checked if not banished from the face of the earth.'

On the whole, I hope you appreciate my difficulties of principle and detail, and will accept the answer which I got some fifty-three years ago when I invaded the rooms of an undergraduate to get him to sign an Anti-Reform petition: 'Thank you, I should be very happy, only I had rather not.'

Yours affectionately,
BLACHFORD.

To Sir Henry Taylor.

Blachford: Sept 24, 1885.

My dear Taylor,—Turning over some old letters lately I have found various complaints of my being 'irresponsive, unacknowledging,' &c., which naturally turned my mind to you who are always saying that I owe you a principal debt of letters with large interest in the way of contrition. But what have I to say? Life, I hope not very blamably, gets taken up with matters which interest no one but one's self, what Lord Granville scornfully calls 'growing cabbages,' but which includes not only propagation of shrubs, trees, wild duck, deer, pheasants, and so on, but also the building of cottages, clubhouse, schoolhouse, which change my level of occupation, for better or worse, from yours to Lady Taylor's.

In the matter of cruelty to animals, I am really sorry to show you a cold shoulder. I think, however, that, if I do not join a multitude to worry the poor old Pope, I furnish a happy existence while it lasts to a large number of eatable birds and beasts, wild and tame, and a comfortable subsistence to a stable of horses, in all say about 250 or 260 living beings, all being more or less petted, the pheasants for the first half of their lives, the ducks, deer, chickens, horses, cows, and pigs, after their respective scales of enjoyment, for the whole of it, and none being exposed, so far as can be prevented, to the discomforts of a deserted old age, such as I am liable to if (*quod absit*) I were to survive her who has promised to look after me.

Is not all this indeed a proof of having nothing to say? I have had the Dean with me for a short visit, looking, I think, better than he has for some time, in spite of an August of work in London. But I think London winters tell on his constitution, and (as is natural after seventy) his physical strength is not what it was. I am told by my doctor that I must expect one year between seventy and eighty to do as much execution on me as four between sixty and seventy.

So the Eastern question is showing signs of life. What a humbug (I venture to think) the Palmerston-Disraeli policy about Russia seems to be, except that it may bring in Austria as a counter-claimant against Russia for Constantinople.

Do you remember that at the Berlin Conference, after all was settled, the Ambassadors were chaffing each other about their feastings, and Dizzy accused (I think) the Russian of having overdrunk himself, to which the Russian replied, 'Ah, but you have seen double too. When you left the Conference you thought you saw two Bulgarias'?

What do you think of Gladstone's manifesto? For myself I agree with what I see written, in thinking it a public affair. Of course that is from the necessities of a divided party, but so it is. It sounds as if he desired now to leave the party to itself as soon as he could honourably disengage himself from leadership;[4] and his position as connecting link between Whig and Radical seems pretty much played out. The key-note seems to be: 'Just keep the peace till I am out of your way.' With regard to Ireland it seems to me that there is

---

[4] Mr. Gladstone's address to the Electors of Midlothian on September 18, 1885, which formed the New Liberal Manifesto, putting aside as not ripe for discussion the question of Disestablishment, and answering Mr. Parnell's demands by saying 'that to maintain the supremacy of the Crown, the unity of the Empire, and all autho-rity of Parliament necessary for the conservation of that unity, is the first duty of every representative of the people;' but he considered that, 'subject to this principle,' a grant of enlarged powers to parts of the country to manage their own affairs was a source of strength and a benefit.

no leader or party that dares to say 'such and such things are necessary to restore the authority of law in Ireland, and I will do them if you will let me.' A pitiful attempt to humour the Irish leaders seems all that anybody now runs to, as if you could out-blarney an Irishman. It is carrying coals to Newcastle with a witness. Poor Lord Carnarvon has certainly got his blarney thrown back in his face.

With what satisfaction after discharging oneself upon such matters does one's mind recoil upon cabbages, which for a few years it is given to us in Devonshire to enjoy in peace!

Ever yours affectionately,
BLACHFORD.

To Sir Henry Taylor.

Blachford : March 15, 1886.

My dear Taylor,—How are you? You ought to be better during the last few sunny days, if, as my gardener assures me, plants under glass can endure any amount of cold outside, but pine for sunshine. However, I believe this has reference to putting out blossoms, which is not, I take it, your present occupation.

I have been engaged in my first prosecution of a poacher. I have been in the habit of keeping a keeper, with the view of conforming to the usages of the country, but with a distinct intimation that I did not 'preserve,' and would not prosecute. This limitation of the keeper's powers, of course, got wind, and enabled the great and notorious poacher of the parish, a celebrated drunkard and blasphemer, but a very sharp fellow even when half drunk, to be continually jeering at the lanky stupid keeper for his inefficiency, without the risk of receiving the only possible answer, before the bench of magistrates, of which, however, one of my labourers says, 'That 'ere Jarge, he's been so often before the magistrates, that he had as lief be there as anywhere else.'

Of all this triumphant jeering I used to hear continual complaints, to which I turned a deaf ear, till it appeared that the labourers, now some of them out of work, were encouraged by his notorious and jubilant impunity to follow his example along the road to ruin : so I thought it time to favour one of the unemployed with work, and 'George' with a prosecution, which, as he has the faculty of making the Justices laugh, is always a kind of ovation for him, but cost him on this occasion thirty shillings—say three or four days' rabbiting. After keeping the audience well amused for some time, his parting shot at the Board and its subordinates was delivered while he was fumbling for the amount of his fine and costs, which he always has forthcoming. The clerk squeaked out, 'Your worships, the man has got the money in his pocket,' on which George turned with severe dignity and said, 'Young man, you seem to know what is in my pocket much better than I know what is in yours, or wish to know what is in any man's pocket but my own.'

And so he went off, virtuous all over.

When my wife, who does not half like meeting him drunk, was remonstrating with him, with a courage which does her credit, for not sending his son 'Bobby' to school, he stopped her with dignity, 'Madam, his name is Robert.'

I give you a full-length portrait of this man, as an unimpeachable candidate for admission to your proposed paradise of incorrigibles. . . . .

What weather it is! The pleasant feature here is the flocks of peewits which it brings upon us. I must have seen forty or fifty the other day between Blachford and Moorcross, and it is pleasant to see them strutting and flapping about under the drawing-room windows, and hardly taking the trouble to rise and wheel round me as I walk about. It is curiously pretty.

Ever yours affectionately,
BLACHFORD.

To the Earl of Selborne.

Blachford : April 24, 1886.

My dear Selborne,—Let me thank you for your admirable letter to the 'Times.' I have been longing for such an exposition, which brings out the Anti-Repeal argument, not as an Imperialist one, but as affecting peace and righteousness *in Ireland* itself.[5]

---
[5] Mr. Gladstone's Irish Home Rule Bill was introduced on April 8.

Matters, to my mind, are come to such a strait that I should not be much indisposed to absolute separation from Ireland, if only we could conscientiously consent to it. But the United Kingdom finds itself commissioned to protect innocent people, in Ireland and elsewhere, against pillage, murder, and so on, even though this involves the employment of violence against pillagers and murderers, and I do not see that it is otherwise than a disgraceful abandonment of duty to transfer this duty to those who are on the side of the pillagers.

If and when it is shown that we *cannot*, or even that the governing classes in England *will* not, do this, I think, as at present advised, I should go in for separation with all its evident evils. I am afraid, in that case, I might be very hard-hearted in leaving the Irish people to take the consequences. 'Tu l'as voulu, George Dandin.'

Does Chamberlain wish to keep the Irish Members in Parliament as a resource to the Radical party there, as the Scotch, in a different way, were to the Puritans in Charles I.'s time?

Yours ever,
BLACHFORD.

To Cardinal Newman.

Blachford: June 11, 1888.

My dear Cardinal,—Yes. Doyle has been my intimate friend for sixty-one years, a year longer than we have known each other.[6] I have not seen much of him lately, but what I have seen of him has been very pleasant. He had so much heart. It is, no doubt, sad to see our contemporaries (and juniors) pass away, not one by one, but rather by twos and threes. There are not many left, though (as I count them up) more than I should have thought at first sight.

I received from Church, and passed on to my sister Marian, a letter telling me that you thought of calling on her; she, and my eldest sister Katherine, who is staying with her, were much excited, and in an incoherent, feminine kind of way, stayed in a whole afternoon for fear of missing you, though it

[6] See page 4.

was patent that you would have left town before she got the notice of your having been there.

However, if at any time hereafter you should again think of calling, please to give her notice. It would be very provoking to her to miss you.

It is not so very long ago since she was writing about your playing of Beethoven, and saying of one particular passage in one of the Salieri duets, that, after hearing many big people, she had never heard it played as you played it. I almost think I remember it—a few piercing notes.

There, now I think you owe her a visit.

Ever yours affectionately,
BLACHFORD.

I was very glad to hear so good an account of your strength and spirits from Church. He seems to be in the way of trouble about the St. Paul's reredos, which is very fine, but certainly not 'Ultra-Protestant.'

To Lady Taylor.

Blachford : February 23, 1889.

My dear Lady Taylor,—The packet of letters has arrived —many thanks. I have not yet opened it ; but I remember that you desired to possess some of the letters. And I shall look through them, in order to send you back all except those (if any) which have no interest greater than that of autographs, or which have special interest for myself. They will have a greater and more lasting value for your children (to say nothing of yourself) than for those into whose hands they may fall after my death, now not a very remote period.[7]

I am surprised that the success of the volumes is only 'moderate.' But 'quiet and wisdom' are not the characteristics which attract just now, or seem likely to become more attractive in the immediate future.

For myself I feel the attraction (of what *is* quiet and to my mind wise) more and more. I remember Greig saying in

---

[7] This refers to letters which Lord Blachford had returned to Sir Henry Taylor to be used in his 'Autobiography,' published in 1885. Sir Henry Taylor died in 1886.

a kind of essay on possible Immortality that in his experience what old people longed for was *repose*. I certainly for myself agree with him, and am almost forgetting that my juniors (like your young people) are of a different mind and like London. I am thinking of turning Buddhist for the sake of Nirwâna—a dormouse for the sake of hibernation.

My sister-in-law's death was scarcely unexpected, and, of course, as people approach, or pass, their threescore and ten, such passings away among those dear to them must be accepted as only natural. But I am not sure that, though the keenness of the blow is less, the deprivation is not greater among the old than among the young. Gaps cannot be filled up, and every death makes you feel more alone. But perhaps this is not so with those who have children and grandchildren.

This smells, does it not, of the octogenarian rather than the septuagenarian. But somehow we seem to have been surrounded for some time by death or threatening of it.

Our love to your party.

Yours affectionately,
BLACHFORD.

To Right Hon. W. E. Gladstone.

Blachford : May 21, 1889.

My dear Gladstone,—I see by our local paper that you purpose spending your Whitsun holiday in or about Devonshire. If you can pardon political defection, is there any chance that you would be able to make a perch at Blachford? If you would, and could, I cannot say how much pleasure it would give us. And though we have nothing to offer in the way of company or sumptuous entertainment, we really have some beautiful country to show.

A Devonshire river, as you possibly know, (1) rises in a sponge, (2) cuts its way through peat and boulders to the slope of the moor, (3) then plunges down through rocks, woods, and what may be called in England waterfalls, to (4) undulations of wood and meadow, till it finds salt water (5) in a generally picturesque estuary.

Blachford is an old-fashioned country house of the last

century, imperfectly but respectably supplied with modern appliances, on the river Yealm, with No. 3 behind and No. 4 before it, and moor in various forms and directions a couple of miles from the house.

I do not know what your party is, but we can put up a fair number of uncritical people.

I wish I could hope that we were likely to see you, were it even for a day, though so scanty a visit would be rather a slight to the scenery, of which we are not a little proud.

Ever yours sincerely,
BLACHFORD.

To Right Hon. W. E. Gladstone.

Blachford : October 16, 1889.

My dear Gladstone,—Church has sent me your kind letter of inquiry. At the door, the answer would be 'Much the same,' but that does not tell much to a friend at a distance.

My disorder the doctors speak of confidently as 'incurable,' very slow in its progress, but, apart from accident, painless, I understand free from *severe* pain, except as to the pains of weakness and the annoyance of a long struggle with approaching death. Just at this moment I may perhaps be making a step downwards.

I am capable of little or no mental or bodily effort, reading, writing, or still less conversation, as the disorder fastens on my vocal chord, and I cannot *listen* long without exhaustion; so that, *humanly speaking*, I am incapable of echoing your kindly wish for a 'prolonged life.'

From the other point of view, my own personal correction, the matter is in other hands; I know, most merciful ones.

With kindest regards to your family,
Believe me,
Yours ever sincerely,
BLACHFORD.

Early in 1889 an illness began, from which Lord Blachford never recovered, though he was not entirely confined to the house until the autumn of that year.

Dean Church came down to see him at Blachford in September when his illness had taken a turn which left little real hope; and shortly afterwards, when the doctors had announced that his life could not be prolonged many weeks, he wrote his last letters, one of which is printed above, to his three oldest friends, with whom his intimacy had begun, at Eton or at Oxford, sixty years before—to Mr. Gladstone, to Cardinal Newman, and to Dean Church. He died on November 21, followed in less than a year by Cardinal Newman, and a few months later by Dean Church.

There was a touching record of the old friendship in Newman's last illness a very few days before his death. In bequeathing a present which Lord Blachford had brought to him from Italy in 1880, he dictated a message to be sent with it, saying whose gift it had been, how much the donor had been to him, and how constant his regret that his friend had not joined the same Church with himself: 'that of all his friends Lord Blachford was the most gifted, the most talented and of the most wonderful grasp of mind,' and that of all the intimacies which he had formed in his Oxford life, close though some of them were, 'none had approached his intimacy with Lord Blachford.'

INDEX

ABDUL

ABDUL AZIZ, the Sultan, 270
Abeken, Dr., 88
Aberdeen, Lord, 143
Abraham, Bishop, 137
Acland, Sir Henry, 59
Acland, Sir Thomas, 37, 42, 47, 59, 151, 347, 367, 385
Adam, Lady, 91
Adderley, Right Hon. C. (Lord Norton) 230, 243
Adelaide, Queen, at Oxford, 25
Afghan War, debates on, 392
Africa, South, affairs of, 299, 364, 365, 376, 378, 380, 395, 405
Airey, Professor, 109
'Alabama' Arbitration, debate in the House of Lords, 339
Albano, 84, 93
Allen, Mr., 139
Amalfi, 94
American Provinces, the North, Act for the Confederation passed, 270 *note*; discussions on the confederation of, 253, 300
Anderdon, Mr., 59, 93, 102
Angelo, Miss, 2
Angoulême, Duchess of, 98
Apennines, 318
'Apologia,' extract from Newman's, 35 *note*
Argyll, Duke of, 342, 369
Arnim, Baron von, 291
Arnold, Dr., 28, 41
Artois, Comte de, 204
Assisi, St. Francis of, 319; legends, 319-321; Church, 319, 322
Auckland, Lord, Bishop of Sodor and Man, 137
Australia, legislative independence of, 157; growth of, 297; gold found in, 145, 146
Autemarre, Colonel, in the Crimea, 161
Avellino, Bishop of, 94
Ayrton, Mr., 240, 276

BLACHFORD

BADELEY, Mr., 108, 135
Baggs, Monsignore, 74, 78
Bagot, Bishop, 105, 110
Baillie, Mr., 204, 220
Baines, Bishop, 73, 80, 88
Barkley, Mr., 374
Barnard, Mr. Edward, 139
Bathurst, Mr. William, 241
Beaconsfield, Lord, 353, 374, 392, 431 resignation, 398 *note*; (see also Disraeli, Mr.)
Belling, M., 192
Belmore, Lord, 348, 372
Benedetti, M., 193, 195, 203
Berlin Congress, 388
Bernard, Mr. Mountague, 118, 125, 165, 257, 272, 341, 343
'Bertrams, the,' 222
Bethell, Sir R. (Lord Westbury) 229, 230
Bills, Ecclesiastical Titles, 141; New Zealand, 229; Church (Irish), 278 *note*; Colonial Church, 305, 347; Abolition of Church Patronage (Scotland), 354; Endowed Schools Act of 1869, amending the, 354; Public Worship, 354; Royal Titles, 370
Binsted Wyck, 283
Birmingham, 246, 416
Biron, Princess, 93
Bismarck, Prince, 283, 286
Blachford, Lady, letters to, 339, 342, 349, 370, 372, 399, 411, 415.
Blachford, Lord, 1; birth, 1; at Worplesdon, 1; Eton, 2; fondness of swimming, 3; at Oxford, 5; pupil of Newman, 6; at Iffley, 6; examination, 8; secures a double first, 10; Fellow of Oriel, 14, 18; friendship with Newman, 14; Vinerian Scholar, 20; on the measure for freeing undergraduates from subscription, 21, 23; on Dr. Hampden's Convocation, 28; at Hursley, 31; interviews with French priests, 53,

BLACHFORD

61; account of the flood at Lyons, 64; at Milan, 67; visits to Manzoni, 68; at Genoa, 70; Rome, 72, 326, 396; present at the institution of two Cardinals, 74; on the Roman Catholic ceremonies, 78; Carthusians, 78, 81; the election of the Pope, 82; the system of *retraites*, 83, 95; on Cardinal Micara, 89, 91; leaves Rome, 92; tours round about Naples, 94; at Venice, 97; on Tintoret's style, 99; at Innspruck, 101; on the two systems of education in France, 101; the Capuchins and Jesuits, 102; the Redemptorists, 102; on the election of Williams and Garbett, 107; in London, 112; account of his work of writing articles for the 'Times,' 112–116; appointed to the post of Registrar of Joint Stock Companies, 116; Assistant Under-Secretary to the Colonial Office, and Emigration Commissioner, 117; resigns his Fellowship, 117; starts the 'Guardian,' 118; marriage, 120; tour in Brittany, 120; at Landerneau, 120; account of a 'pardon,' 121, 126; at Guingamp, 124; at Quimper, 128; at the Colonial Office, 130; offered the appointment of Secretary of Governor at Malta, 131; special constable for the Chartist riots, 135; his opinion of Lord Stanley, 143; of Mr. Gladstone, 150; the Kingsbridge election, 151; criticism of Newman's letters on Universities, 163; of 'Callista' and 'Fabiola,' 164; at Chambéry, 166; his first view of Mont Blanc, 167; mission to Paris on the Coolie question, 170, 220; interviews with M. de Persigny, 173, 177, 178; on the Ionian Commission of Enquiry, 183; at the Château de Chantilly, 185; interviews with Prince Napoleon, 191, 193; dines with him, 195, 197, 199; meets the Comte de Bruce, 204; M. Mohl, 207; ball at the Hôtel de Ville, 212; interview with Lord John Russell, 215; with Chasseloup Laubat, 216–219; appointed Under-Secretary for the Colonies, 225; opinion of the Duke of Newcastle, 225, 227; of Mr. Cardwell, 226; interview with Lord Palmerston, 229; letter to the Bishop of Oxford, 234; on the famous Giotto frescoes, 236; letter to Sir George Grey, 237; to Dr. Low on

BLACKHEATH

Wirima Repa, 238, 242; at Clumber, 239; his New Zealand despatch, 243; criticism of Kinglake's 'Crimea,' 244; his visit to Cardinal Newman, 246, 416; on Mr. Ward's account of Newman, 249; letter to Miss Nightingale, 251; views on the method of writing despatches, 253; on the rebellion in Jamaica, 255; on the author of 'Ecce Homo,' 259–261; visits to Highclere, 265, 266; description of Stowe, 268; letter to Lord Monck, 270; his presentation to the Sultan, 270; committee on military matters, 273; on the Red River insurrection, 278, 281; at Walmer Castle, 280, 285; at Binsted Wyck, 283; on the war of 1870, 284; on Père Hyacinthe, 290; his resignation, 295; his account of the development of Colonial self-government, 295–303; on the emancipation of the Churches, 303–305; account of a day at Einsiedeln, 307–312; offer of a peerage, 312; at Florence, 317; on St. Francis of Assisi, 318–321; at Naples, 324; visits to the Sermonetas, 329, 332; meets Dr. Pantaleone, 335; on the debate in the House of Lords on the 'Alabama' Arbitration, 339; on Sir Henry Taylor's 'Autobiography,' 344, 364, 378; his speech on his Colonial Church Bill, 347, 348; on the military manœuvres, 350, 352; on his life at Blachford, 357–360; literary work, 359, 361, 372, 376, 381, 382, 383, 388; at Killerton, 366, 385; on the cession of Gambia, 367; at Blackmoor, 367; on debates in the House of Lords, 369, 370, 392; his article 'On Native Policy in South Africa,' 376; on the annexation of the Transvaal Republic, 380; on the war between Russia and Turkey, 387, 389; on Sir Bartle Frere's recall, 395; on Carlyle, 405; note of a conversation with Cardinal Newman, 407–409; account of a Royal Commission, 409; his report on Fever and Small-pox Hospitals, 410; on the Phœnix Park murder, 411; on Mr. George's 'Progress and Poverty,' 414; at Oxford, 415; on Aubrey de Vere's article, 418–420; his objections to the Colonial Board of Advice, 424–429; illness, 440; death 441

Blackheath, 22

INDEX 445

BLACKMOOR

Blackmoor, 367
Blakesley, Mr., 60
Blanc, Mont, 167
Blanshard, Major, 27
Bloxam, Mr., 109
Boboli Gardens, 317
Boers, the, 376, 380, 405
Bolgrad, negotiations about, 174
Bonn, conferences at, 366 *note*
Borghese, Princess, 78
Borrett, Mr., 10
Bossons, Glacier des, 167
Bouillé, Marquis de, 206
Bouverie, Bartholomew, 4
Bowden, Mr., 30, 83
Bowring, Sir J., 162
Bradfield, 22
Bradford, Lord, 271
Brand, Mr. (Lord Hampden), 250
Bransgore, 33, 38
Brest, 121
Bretons, costumes of the, 121
Brewer, Mr. J. S., 10
Brieuc, St., 125
Bright, Right Hon. John, 197, 278
'British Critic,' 19, 48, 50, 61 *note*, 106, 362
'British Magazine,' 34
Brome, Adam de, 27
Brougham, Lord, 147
Browne, Bishop Harold, 366 *note*
Brownrigg, Colonel, 161
Bruce, Hon. J. (Lord Elgin), 12
Bruce, Mr. (Lord Aberdare), 276, 346
Bruce, Comte de, 204
Bruce, Lady Augusta, 203, 204, 207, 214
Bruce, Lady Frances, 204
Brühl, Count, 91
Brunel, Mr. Isambard, 347
Brunnow, Baron, 287
Bruno, Father, 78
Buckingham, Duke of, 264, 270, 302
Buckinghamshire, Lady, 146
Budget of 1853, 150
Buller, Sir John, 152
Burdett-Coutts, Lady, 304
Burgon, Dean, 119
Burial Question, the, 379
Buxton, Mr. Charles, 255
Byron, Lord, 100

CADEILLE, Comte de, 120, 123
Cairns, Lord, 348, 370; style of his speeches, 341
Cambridge, Duke of, 273, 274, 366
Canada, 232, 253, 270, 296, 300, 301

CHURCHES

Canning, Lord, 289
Canrobert, Marshal, 156
Capri, 94
Capuchins, the, 77, 102
Cardinals, institution of, 74
Cardwell, Lord, 250, 252, 263, 265, 301, 350; characteristics in office, 226
Carlisle, Lord, 147
Carlos, Don, 353
Carnarvon, Lord, 182, 214, 221, 265, 301, 315, 347; his policy in Natal, and in the Transvaal, 364, 365, 380; characteristics in office, 263
Carrara, Francesca II. da, 100
Carthusians, rules of the, 78, 81
Cartier, Sir G., 301
Caserta, Principessa di (Duchess of Sermoneta), 333
Cathcart, Sir G., 160
Cathedral Commission, 405, 409, 429
Cawdor, Lord, 250
Cecil, Lord Robert, 230 (see Lord Salisbury)
Chamberlain, Mr., 375, 398
Chambéry, 166
Chambord, Comte de, 353
Chamonix, 167
Chantilly, 185; Château, 186
Chapman, Bishop, 2
Chartist Riots, 135
Chateaulin, 121, 122, 128
Chelmsford, Lord, 343
Chelsea, Lord, 185
Chester, Colonel, 413
Childers, Right Hon. H., 276
China, war with, 163
'Christian Remembrancer,' 362
'Christian Year,' 41
Christie, Mr., 59
Church, Dean, 55, 57, 63, 105, 109, 118, 122, 256, 342, 417, 420, 429, 434, 438, 441; on the friendship between Cardinal Newman and Lord Blachford, 16; 'Life and Letters of,' 83, 101, 375 *notes*; his reply to Dean Howson's letter, 355; 'Oxford Movement,' 362 *note*; his refusal of the Archbishopric, 417
 Letters to, 124, 133, 136, 149, 150, 152, 156, 157, 160, 162, 165, 168, 176, 180, 195, 199, 215, 217, 259, 260, 262, 272, 293, 355, 356, 360, 361, 362, 365, 366, 370, 371, 372, 373, 374, 375, 381, 388, 401, 402
Churches, emancipation of the Colonial, 303-305, 347

CHURCHILL

Churchill, Lord Randolph, 432
Cisterna, 93
Civita Vecchia, 72
Clarendon, Lord, 147, 170, 172
Claughton, Bishop, 107
Clementine, Princess, 134
Clerk, Sir G., 80, 386
Clifford, Mr., 378
Clotilde, Princess, 204
Clumber, 240
Cobbett, Mr., 17
Cockburn, Lord Chief Justice, on Martial Law, 272
Colam, Mr., 432
Coleridge, Sir John, 48
Coleridge, Lord, 119, 346
Coleridge's 'Table Talk,' 418 *note*
Colley, Sir G., death of, at Majuba Hill, 405
Collier, Sir R., 336; vote of censure on his appointment, 337 *note*
Cologne, Archbishop of, 62
Colombo, Bishop of, 2
Colonial Board of Advice, objections to the, 424–429
Colonial Church Bill, 305, 347
Colonial Governor, extract from a letter to a, 253
Colonies, development of the self-governing, 296–303, 426, 427; emancipation of the Churches, 303–305
Colvile, Lady, 403
Colvile, Sir James, 1, 120; death, 403
Colvile, Mr. Andrew, 120
Colvile, Hon. Mrs., 1
Colvile, Mrs. Eden, 282
Colvile, Miss C., letter to, 414
Colvile, Mr. Eden, Governor of the Red River Settlement, 282 *note*
Colyar, Mr., 88
Compiègne, 185
Constantinople, Conference at, 374
Cook, Dr., 366
Coolie emigration question, 170
Courtney, Mr., 49
Courtown, Lord, 348
Cousin, M., 222
Cowley, Lady, 185
Cowley, Lord, 185, 188, 214, 287
Cowper, Lord, 398
Cranbrook, Lord, 257 *note*, 392, 409
Crimean War, 151, 156, 218; stories of the, 158, 160, 161
Croix, Sainte, 126
Crozon, 128
Cullen, Archbishop, 249

EVANS

'DAILY NEWS,' 119
Dalgairns, Mr., 250
Dalhousie, Lord, 117
Dalrymple, Sir C., 409
Daman, Professor, 48, 105
Dante and Giotto, 236
Davenport, Mr., 49
Davy, Lady, 76
Deare, Colonel, 1
Delhi, siege of, 168
Denison, Archdeacon, 35, 165
Denison, Bishop, 47
Denison, Mr. Henry, 6, 56
Denison, Mr. J. E. (Lord Ossington), 239
Denman, Lord, 340
Denton, Mr. 374
Derby, Lord (the 14th), 241, 263, 271
Derby, Lord (the 15th), 340, 392, 405, (see also Stanley, Lord)
Despatches, suggestions for writing, 253
Dilke, Sir C., 398
Disraeli, Mr., 162, 266; his 'Home Letters,' 431 (see also Beaconsfield, Lord)
Disraeli, Mrs., 267
Dodsworth, Mr., 43, 139, 141
Döllinger, Dr. von, 104, 366 *note*
Domesday Book, mistakes in the, 372
Donkin, Professor, 109
Dornford, Mr., 27
'Dorothy,' 160
Doyle, Sir Francis, 4, 10, 26, 275, 289, 437
Duelling, 115
Dunkellin, Lord, 263
Durant, Mr., 151

'ECCE HOMO,' 259, 260, 261
'Ecclesiastical Courts,' report on, 420
'Ecclesiastical Titles Bill,' 141 *note*
Egerton, Mr., 276
Einsiedeln, ceremony at, 307–312
Elgin, Lady, 199, 205, 214
Elgin, Lord, 204
Ellenborough, Lord, 289
Elliot, Sir Thomas, 131, 134, 226
Elphinstone, Sir Mountstuart, 430
Elvey, Sir George, 59
Emigrants, Irish workhouse girls, 136
Emigration Office, 117
Encombe, Lord, 30
Eton, 2, 138
Eton and Harrow cricket match, 251
'Eton Miscellany,' 4
Evans, Mr A. J., 374

INDEX

EXHIBITION
Exhibition of 1851, buildings, 142; opening, 145
Eyre, Mr., Governor of Jamaica, 255, 258

FABER, Mr., 250
Favre, M., 283, 292
Fiesole, 317
'Fire Annihilator Company,' demonstration, 140
Fish, Mr. Secretary, 342
Fitzroy, Sir C., 145
Florence, 317
Follett, Mr., 61
Forster, Right Hon. W. E., 258, 276, 398, 402, 404
Fort Garry, 282 *note*
Fortescue, Lord, 392
Fortescue, Mr. Chichester (Lord Carlingford), his interview with Lord Palmerston, 229
France, the two systems of education in, 101
Franks, Mrs., letter to, 307
Franzoni, Cardinal, 81
Frascati, 334
Frazer River, 282 *note*
Frere, Sir Bartle, 394
Freshwater, 32, 35
Fresne, M. de, 220
Froude, Mr. Hurrell, 5, 15, 16, 24, 25, 26; his 'Remains,' 43, 48
Froude, Mr. J. A., 48, 364; his article on South African policy, 376
Froude, Mr. William, 144, 293, 373
Fuad Pasha, the Grand Vizier, 270
Fulford, Primate of Canada, 304
Fullerton, Lady Georgina, 285
Fullerton, Mr., 285

GAISFORD, Dean, 25
Gallipoli, 155
Gambetta, M., 289
Gambia, cession of, 367 *note*
Garbett, Archdeacon, 107
Genoa, 70
George, Mr. Henry, 'Progress and Poverty,' 414
Gifford, Lord, 93
Gilbert, Dr., 107
Giotto, the frescoes of, 236
Giustiniani, Cardinal, 95
Gladstone, Rt. Hon. W. E., 4, 17, 22, 108, 110, 117, 133, 158, 257, 412; 'Church and State,' 50; his Budget of 1853, 150; mission to the Ionian Islands, 182; Prime Minister, 275,

HARRISON
398 *note*; his Irish University Bill, 347; opposition to various Bills, 354; retirement, 361 *note*; his manifesto of 1885, 434
Letters to, 159, 259, 261, 276, 312, 375, 439, 440
Glover, Mr., 28
Goldsmid, Mr. Nathaniel, 52
Gordon, General, 431
Gorham, Mr., 138 *note*
Goulburn, Dr., 134, 249
Graham, Sir J., 143, 266, 267
Grammont, Duc de, 286
Grant, Sir Hope, 273
Granville, Lady, 280
Granville, Lord, 153, 275, 278, 280, 282, 286, 287, 331, 337, 348, 373, 398; on the 'Alabama' Arbitration, 339; characteristics in office, 264
Gray, Dr. Asa, 366; 'Darwiniana,' 381
Gray, Bishop, 304
Gregory XVI., Pope, 74, 96
Gregory, Colonel and Mrs. Sherwin, 239
Greville, Mr. Charles, 241
Grey, Lord, 134, 183, 297, 392, 424; his offer to appoint Lord Blachford Secretary of Governor at Malta, 131; on the 'Alabama' Arbitration, 339
Grey, Sir George, 156; letter to, 237
Grossi, author of 'Visconti,' 69, 71
'Guardian,' extract from the, 16; the work of starting the, 118, 359, 363
Guingamp, 124
Guisot, M., 136
Gulden, Mdlle., 285
Gully, Mr., 17

HADDAN, Mr. Thomas, 118
Halifax, Lord, 112, 369, 392
Hallam, Arthur, 3
Hamilton, Bishop, 57
Hampden, Dr., 21 *note*; appointed Regius Professor of Divinity, 28 *note*; Bishop of Hereford, 133 *note*
Hanmer, Lord, 4
Hansard and Stockdale case, 61
Hansell, Mr., 152
Harding, Mr., 24
Harding, Sir J. Dorney, 163
Hardinge, Lord, 156
Hardy, Mr. Gathorne (Lord Cranbrook), 257
Harrison, Mr. B., 26
Harrison, Sir E., 346

HARRISON

Harrison, Mr. Frederic, 378
Harrow and Eton cricket match, 251
Harrowby, Lord, 12
Hartington, Lord, leader of the Liberal party, 361 *note*
Hassan, Prince, 289
Haussonville, Count de, 288
Havelock, General, 168
Hawtrey, Dr., 20 *note*
Head, Sir E., 228, 232
Heathcote, Sir William, 34, 35, 257 *note*
Heaviside, Anthony, 4
Helps' 'Conquest of America,' 166
Henri V., 98 (see Chambord, Comte de)
Herbert, Hon. Auberon, 265, 267
Herbert, Mr. Edward, 266, 267, 364
Highclere, 265, 266
Hoare, Archdeacon, 41, 46
Hodgson, Provost, 20 *note*
Hohentahl, Count and Countess, 93
Holland, Sir Henry (Lord Knutsford), 264
Holwegg, M. Bethmann, 90
Hooker, Sir Joseph, 268 *note*
Hope, Mr. G., 221
Hope Scott, Mr. James, 42, 57, 63, 68; illness, 373
Howe, Lord, 25
Howe, Mr., and Nova Scotia, 300, 301
Howick, Lord, 233
Howson, Dean, 355 *note*
Huelgoat, 126
Hursley, 32, 38
Hurstpierpoint School, 243
Huyse, Dr., 88
Hyacinthe, Père, 290

IFFLEY, 6
Ignatieff, 374
Imhausen, M., 231
Imola diocese, 95
Inglis, Sir R., 41, 47, 50, 353
Inglis, Colonel, 168
Ionian Islands, 182
Ireland, 362, 404, 410, 411, 412, 435, 437
Irving, Sir Henry, 399
Isandlwana, disaster at, 393 *note*
Itri, 94

JAMAICA, rebellion in, 255, 256, 258, 260
James, Sir Walter (Lord Northbourne), 281

LIBRARY

James, Mr. Walter, 409
Jelf, Mr., 108
Jenner, Sir H., 138
Jermyn, Frais, 4
Jesuits, the, 77, 102
John, St., Lateran Church, relics in, 76
Johnson, Dean of Wells, 11, 56

KEATE, Dr., 3
Keble, Rev. J., 19, 26, 32, 34, 36, 41, 63, 109, 137, 141, 158, 165; his 'Life of Dr. Thomas Wilson,' 137 *note*; 'Essays,' 363
Keble, Mrs., 36, 37, 58
Kennaway, Sir John, 151
Kennington Common, Chartist meeting at, 135
Kerr, Lord Henry, 247
Killerton, 366, 385
Kimberley, Lord, 299, 340, 347
King, Mr. Bryan, 223
Kinglake, his 'Crimea,' 244
Kingsbridge election, 151
Knight, Miss, 329 *note*
Knutsford, Lord, 264 *note*
Kuserow, Count, 285, 287

LA FORÊT, 120
Lablache, 35
Labouchere, Mr. (Lord Taunton) 172, 177
Lake, Dean, 149
Landerneau, 120
Landevenue, 128
Lansdowne, Lord, 144
Latrobe, Governor of Victoria, 146
Laubat, M. de Chasseloup, 172, 215; interview with Lord Blachford, 217-219
Lawrence, Lord, 392, 394
Layard, Sir Henry, 158
Le Boeuf, Marshal, 286
Le Faou, 126
Lear, Mr., 100
Lefevre, Sir John Shaw, 117, 124
Legge, Hon. and Rev. Henry, 43
Legge, Hon. Mrs. Henry, letters to, 126, 197, 236, 318, 328, 350
Leghorn, 72
Leinster, Duke of, 147
Leti, 383; 'Life of Sixtus V,' 384 *note*
Lewis, Sir G. C., 223
'Library of Fathers, translated by members of the English Church,' 41 *note*

INDEX   449

Liddell, Dean, 26
Liddon, Canon, 289
Lindsay, Colonel Loyd (Lord Wanstead), 288
Littlemore, consecration of the Church at, 38
London, Bishop of, 57
Lord Mayor, 342
Lords, House of, its value, 313, 401, 402; debates in, 143, 339, 342, 347, 349, 367, 370, 372, 392, 405
Louis Napoleon, Emperor, 175, 196, 198, 216, 218; his letter to Prince Napoleon, 184
Louis Philippe, 134
Low, Dr., letters to, 238, 242
Lowder, Rev. Charles, 224
Lowe, Right Hon. R., 347
Lucknow, 168
Lyndhurst, Lord, 147
Lyons, Lord, 283
Lyons, floods at, 64
'Lyra Apostolica,' 18, 31
Lysons, Colonel, 232
Lyttelton, Lord, 147
Lytton, Sir Edward Bulwer, 182, 184, 201, 213

MACARTHY, Sir Charles, 222
Macdonald, Sir John, 253, 300
Macdonald, Mr., Reginald Somerled, 278
Mackarness, 119
Mackenzie, Colonel, 351
Magee, Bishop, 277
Maggiore, Lago, 316
Majuba Hill, battle of, 405
Malais, Abbé, 124
Malakhoff, Duke of, 268
Malmesbury, Lord, 184, 185, 196, 202, 341
Malo, St., 124
Man, Isle of, 47
Manning, Cardinal, 42, 46, 141, 250, 362
Manœuvres, military, 350, 352
Mansel, Dean, 265
Manzoni, visits to, 67
Maories, their reception at Osborne, 246
Marie Antoinette, 205
Marindin, Miss E., letter to, 307
Marindin, Mr. G. E., letter to, 388
Marriott, Mr., 17, 18
Martial Law, 272
Mason, Mr., 232
Mattei, Cardinal, 335

Maudslay's engineering works, 145
Maurice, Mr. F. D., 42
Maynard, M., 126
Mayne, Sir H., 343
Mayotta Island, 172
Mayow, Colonel George, 160
McMahon, Marshal, 195
Melbourne, Lord, anecdote of, 233
Melville, Mr. Leslie, 85
Mer de Glace, 167
Merivale, Mr. Herman, 202, 225, 279
Mérode, Count, 51
Mezzofanti, Cardinal 82, 91
Micara, Cardinal Bishop of Frascati, 77, 81, 89, 91
Milan, 67, 236
Milnes, Monckton (Lord Houghton), 48
Minghetti, Signor, 333
Miniato, St., 317
Minto, Lady, 382, 410
Minto, Lord, 410
Mitchell, Sir John, 282
Moberly, Bishop, 26, 165, 346, 372
Mohl, M., 207; his anecdotes, 208–211
Mola di Gaeta, 94
Monck, Lord, letter to, 270
Monsell, Mr., 278, 283
Montagu, Philip, 4
Montalembert, Comte de, 189
Monteagle, Lord, 401, 402
Moorcross, 405
Morpeth, Lord, 50
Morris, Rev. J., 109
Moulins, 64
Mozley, Mr James, 50 *note*, 63, 109, 118, 138, 141, 149, 252; Regius Professor of Divinity, 292; editor of the 'Christian Remembrancer,' 362; letter to, 134
Mozley, Mr. John, 373
Mozley, Mr. Thomas, 26
Mozley, Mrs. John, 396
Murdoch, Mr., 117, 131

NAPLES, 94, 324
Napoleon, Prince, 188, 191, 193, 197, 198; receives Sir F. Rogers, 190, 193; his marriage, 200, 214
Napoleon I., 196
Napoleon III., 175, 184, 196, 198, 216, 218
Nemours, Duc of, 134
New Brunswick, 300
New South Wales, gold in, 145; population, 297

G G

NEW

New Zealand, 156, 223, 227, 229, 243, 297, 298; church in, 303
Newcastle, Duke of, 147, 215, 227, 304; characteristics in office, 225
Newman, Cardinal, 5; his characteristics, 14; 'Letters and Correspondence of,' 18, 31, 43, 45, 50, 52, 55, 56, 87 *notes*; 'Apologia,' 46 *note*; extracts from letters to Keble, 47; to James Mozley, 50 *notes*; joins the Church of Rome, 118; his letters on Universities, 163; 'Fabiola,' 164; visits from Lord Blachford, 246, 416; his 'Faith and Reason,' 250; preface to Keble's 'Essays,' 363; note of a conversation with Lord Blachford, 407-409
Letters to, 17, 18, 22, 26, 30, 33, 34, 39, 40, 42, 43, 45, 46, 48, 49, 50, 51, 53, 55, 60, 61, 83, 87, 94, 101, 106, 110, 275, 363, 395, 396, 417, 421, 422, 423, 437
Nightingale, Miss Florence, letter to, 251
'Nineteenth Century,' 378
Northbrook, Lord, 392
Northcote, Sir Stafford, 119, 142, 341 *note*, 351, 385; at Kingsbridge, 151
Nossibé island, 172
Nova Scotia, 300
'Numencia' the insurgent frigate, 353

O'CONNOR, Feargus, 135
O'F., Mr. 147
Oakeley, Sir H., 57, 63, 109, 346
Oliphant, Laurence, 282
Omar Pasha, 156
Orford, Lord, 328
Oriel College, pictures at, 416
Orioli, Cardinal, 103
Orsini, 179 *note*
Overbeck, 75
Oxford, 5; undergraduates, question of releasing candidates for matriculation from subscription to the thirty-nine articles, 21, 23 *notes* (see Universities)
Oxford, Bishop of, letter to, 234
'Oxford Movement,' The, 16, 21, 23, 28 *notes*

PADUA, frescoes at, 236
Paestum, 94
Paget, Sir A., 326

RANKE

Paget, Sir James, 309, 364
Paget, Dean, 420
Pakington, Sir J., 230, 274
Palmer, Mr. William, 57, 108, 326, 362
Palmer, Sir Roundell, 284, 304, (see also Selborne, Lord)
Palmerston, Lord, 163 *note*, 165, 170, 181, 229, 250; his 'Conspiracy to Murder Bill,' 179, 201 *notes*
Pantaleone, Dr., 334
'Pardon,' account of a, 121, 126
Paris, the Bourse, 200; Hôtel de Ville, 212
Patrizzi, Cardinal, 81
Patteson, Bishop, 243
Paul, Mrs., 160 *note*
Pavia, 70
Peacock, Sir Barnes, 342
Peel, Sir Robert, 47, 61, 113; resignation, 131 *note*
Peel, General, 264
Pélissier, General, 158
Pentini, 83, 95
Persigny, M. de, 171; his interviews with Sir F. Rogers, 173, 177, 178, 191
Perugia, 318
Peruzzi, Signor, 332
Pfyffer, Mr., 77, 81
Phillimore, Sir R., 304
Phillpotts, Bishop, 137 *note*
Phœnix Park, murders in, 411
Pickering, Mr., 138
Pinturicchio, 73
Pisani, M. Ferri, 190, 192
Polehampton, Mr., 1
Pomarets, Mdlle. des, 220
Pompeii, 94, 324
Pont Charlan, 64
Pope, the, 140 *note*; election of the, 82, 407; his miracles, 330
Portsmouth, Lord, 385, 392
Potemkin, Madame, 76, 87
Prevost, Sir G., 63
Price, Professor Bonamy, 165
Prussia, King of, 283
Pusey, Dr. E. B., 22 *note*, 42, 63, 106
Pusey, Mr. P., 17, 22

QUIMPER, 128

RAGLAN, Lord, 153, 155
Ranke's 'History of the Popes,' 384

Rawlinson, Mr., 149
Red River Settlement, insurrection in, 278
'Redemptorists' order, 102
Reeve, Mr. Henry, 239, 241, 376, 388
Reform Bill, 12 *note*
Registration of Joint Stock Companies, 116
Retraites, system of, 83, 95
Reumont, M., 91
Réunion, a delegate from, 231
Rhone, rising of the, 65
Rice, David ap, 4
Richmond, Duke of, 347
Richmond, Mr. George, 72, 85, 221
Rickards, Sir George, 284, 415
Riel, Louis, 281
Ripon, Lord, 340, 341, 398
Ritualism, 224, 335, 336, 375, 376
Rivington, Mr., 31 *note*, 48
Robinson, Mr. Crabbe, 115
Rogers, Rev. Edward, 1, 14, 49; 'The Life and Opinions of a Fifth Monarchy Man,' &c., 256; letters to, 19, 64, 137, 147, 212, 229, 242, 255, 256, 317, 334, 346, 347
Rogers, Miss Emily, letter to, 38
Rogers, Frederic, 1 (see Blachford)
Rogers, Sir Frederick Leman, resigns his post in the Audit Office, 120; letters to, 12, 92
Rogers, Colonel Henry, 58, 162
Rogers, Sir John, 1; death, 120
Rogers, John, 'The Life and Opinions of,' 256 *note*
Rogers, Miss Kate, letters to, 20, 23, 24, 48, 63, 76, 90, 130, 139, 140, 143, 144, 145, 146, 154, 164, 182, 184, 185, 190, 204, 213, 222, 226, 232, 243, 247, 250, 252, 258, 268, 280, 281, 283, 292, 294, 321, 324, 326, 337, 368, 385, 392.
Rogers, Miss Marian, letters to, 6, 28, 31, 56, 80 (see Legge, Mrs. H.)
Rogers, Miss S., letters to, 35, 58, 70, 105, 106, 108, 120, 173, 196, 207, 275, 332
Rogers, General, 169
Rogers, Mrs. (Lady Rogers), letters to, 8, 10, 11, 37, 72, 85, 97, 124, 131, 133, 135, 151, 158, 166, 172, 178, 179, 183, 185, 187, 189, 192, 201, 203, 220, 221, 227, 228, 229, 231, 233, 239, 240, 245, 246, 252, 257, 265, 266, 269, 270, 273, 277, 278, 283, 284, 285, 289, 290
Rohan, Cardinal de, arrest of, 206

'Romanism and Popular Protestantism,' 41 *note*
Rome, 72, 326; changes at, 396; Roman Catholic services in, 78; the diplomatic tribune, 333
Rose, Archdeacon, 41
Rosebery, Lord, 341, 368, 370
Rosmini, 70
Ross, Sir Hew, 155, 156
Rothschild, 153
Rouen, 53
Round, Mr., 133
Ruskin, Mr., 73, 98
Russell, Lord John (Lord Russell), 131 *note*, 143, 263; appoints Dr. Hampden to the See of Hereford, 133 *note*; on the Papal usurpation, 141 *note*; his Reform Bill, 153; interview with Lord Blachford, 215; on the 'Alabama' Arbitration, 339
Russia, war with Turkey, 387, 389
Russia, Czar of, 155, 156, 162
Ryder, Mr., 24, 109

SADOWA, battle of, 265 *note*
Salerno, 94
Salisbury, Lord, 264, 268, 278, 340, 369, 373, 431; on Lord Shaftesbury's Bill, 350
Sallenches, 167
Sandford, Lord, 276
Saône, rising of the, 65
Sargent, Mr., 18
Sargent Mrs., 33
Schleswig-Holstein, Prince of, 195
Schwytz, canton of, 307
Scott, Sir Walter, 329 *note*
Scott, murder of, by Riel, 281
Seaton, Lord, 153, 183
Seeley, Sir John, 'Ecce Homo,' 261 *note*
Selborne, Lord, 57 *note*, 337, 370, 373; his schemes of Land Reform, 346; on Lord Shaftesbury's Bill, 350
Letters to, 386, 436
Sellon, Miss, 137
Selwyn, Bishop of New Zealand, 3, 157, 303
Sermoneta, Duke and Duchess of, 326, 329, 332
Serpents, Isle of, 174 *note*
Severne, Mr., 323
Seward, Mr., 232
Sewell, Professor, 83
Seymour, Sir H., 153, 155
Shadwell, Mr., 53

SHAFTESBURY

Shaftesbury, Lord, 165 ; his bill to prevent frauds in charitable funds, 349
Sharp, Mr. Martin, 119, 156, 381
Shepstone, Sir T., 380 *note*
Sibthorpe, Mr., 109
Siga, Bishop of, 73
Skinner, Major, 265
Slidell, Mr., 232
Smith, General, 351
Somerset, Duke of, 340, 392
Somerville, Mrs., 91
Southey, 41
Spedding, Dr. James, 60
Stanley, Dean, 96, 204 *note*, 290, 385
Stanley, Lord, 143, 199, 201 (see also Derby, Lord)
Stanley, Lord, of Alderley, 349
Stansfeld, Right Hon. J., 276
Staveley, Sir C., 351
Stephen, Sir James, 51, 130
Stockdale, Mr., 61 *note*
Storks, Sir Henry, 265, 269, 273, 351
Stowe, 268
Straits Settlements garrison, committee on, 273
Stratford de Redcliffe, Lord, 171
Strossmayer, Bishop, 291
Stubbs, Dr. (Bishop of Oxford), 421
Suez Canal shares, 365
Sumner, Mr., 339 *note*
Sydney, Lord, 393
Symonds, Mr., 124

TADDEI, Rosa, 103
Tait, Archbishop, 279, 348, 409
Talbot, Dr. (Bishop of Rochester), 289, 407
Tarracina, 93
Taunton, Lord, 173 *note*
Taylor, Lady, letters to, 432, 438
Taylor, Sir Henry, 130 *note*, 233 ; his autobiography, 344, 364, 378 ; article on Carlyle, 405 ; death, 438 *note*
 Letters to, 271, 314, 316, 337, 344, 352, 354, 356, 357, 363, 364, 365, 367, 376, 377, 378, 380, 381, 383, 384, 386, 393, 394, 395, 396, 398, 400, 402, 403, 405, 409, 410, 412, 418, 420, 423, 429, 430, 433, 435
Terry, Miss, 399
Thesiger, Sir F. (Lord Chelmsford), 168
Thévenot, M., 97
Thiers, M., 222
Thomas, Mr. Vaughan, 29
Thompson, Archbishop, 348

WARBURTON

Thornton, Sir E., 341 *note*
Thornton, Mr., 41
'Times,' the work of writing articles for the, 112-116
Tintoret, 99
Tooth, Mr., prosecution of, 375 *note*
Torrens, General, 160
Townsend, Mr., 41
Tract XC. 63, 96 *note*, 103, 105
Transvaal Republic, annexation of, 380 ; affairs of, 376, 405
Tremlett, Captain, 237
Trench, Archbishop, 48
Trevor, Mr., 30
Trieux, 125
Trochu, General, 283, 292
Turin, 316
Turkey, war with Russia, 387, 389 ;
Turkish Question, the, and Turkish misgovernment, 366, 373, 374, 377, 379, 387, 391, 401, 434
Twisleton, Mr., 35, 42
Tyrolese, the, 102

UGINE, 166
Umbria, plains of, 318
Uniformity, Act of, of 1662, 362
United States, 228
Universities and the Church, 21, 22, 23, 28, 44, 107, 155, 158, 272
University of Oxford election in 1865, 257
Utterton, Mr., 48

VANCOUVER Island, 282 *note*
Vaughan, Mr., 26, 42
Venables, Mr., 239, 241
Venice, 97, 236
Vera, Signor, 329
Verdon, Sir George, 266, 267
Vere, Mr. Aubrey de, 141 ; his article on 'Subjective Difficulties in Religion,' 418
Verona, 102
Vesuvius, eruption of, 325
Victor Emmanuel, 323
Vitali, Ambrogio, 67
Vyvyan, Sir R., 17

WALEWSKI, 188, 189
Wallace's 'Russia,' 377
Walmer Castle, 280
Walter, Mr. John, 22 *note*, 112, 120, 373
Warburton, Dr., 50

INDEX

Ward, Mr., 44, 63, 109; his account of Newman, 249
Washington, Treaty of, 339, 341 *notes*, 346
Waterton, Mr., 85, 96
Watson, Mr., 72
Weedall, Dr., 103
Wellington, Duke of, 12, 21, 25, 135
Wendischmann, Dr., 104
Westbury, Lord, 337, 341
Westmacott, Mr., 50
Wetherall, Mr., 285
Wharncliffe, Lord, 12
Wickham, Mr., 283
Wight, Isle of, 39
Wilberforce, Mr. H., 18, 24, 32, 33 *note*, 38, 53, 139
Wilberforce, Mr. Robert, 5, 32, 33
Wilberforce, Bishop Samuel, 26, 32, 36, 41, 42
Wilberforce, Mrs., 37
Wilkes, Captain, 232 *note*
Williams, Mr. Isaac, 28, 39; opposition to his election to the Professorship of Poetry, 107
Wilson, Bishop, 137
Wilson, Mr., 18, 24, 27, 32, 37, 48, 54, 57

Winchester, Bishop of, 109, 348
Windham, Colonel, in the Crimea, 160
Wirima Repa, 237; illness, 242, 248; his visit to Osborne, 245; death, 248 *note*
Wiseman, Cardinal, 45, 56 *note*, 141, 250; his 'Callista,' 164
Wodehouse, Sir P., 299
Wolfe, 221
Wolseley, Lord, 281 *note*
Wood, Colonel, 160
Wood, Mr. A., 131, 134, 154, 158
Wood, Mr. Page (Lord Hatherley) 276
Wood, Mr. S., 30, 42, 43, 45, 49, 50, 112; his account of 'Endowments,' 60
Wootton, Dr., 9
Wordsworth, Bishop Christopher, 26, 366
Worplesdon, 1
Wraxall, Sir Nathaniel, 115
Wynne, Mr., 141

YALPUK River, 174 *note*
Yelverton, Admiral, 352
Young, Sir J., 282

0

MR. MURRAY'S LIST

OF WORKS OF

BIOGRAPHY AND MEMOIRS.

ALICE (Princess, Grand-Duchess of Hesse.) LETTERS TO H.M. THE QUEEN. With a Memoir by H.R.H. PRINCESS CHRISTIAN. Portrait. Crown 8vo. 7s. 6d.

BROOKE (Sir Victor, Bart.), SPORTSMAN AND NATURALIST: HIS DIARIES AND CORRESPONDENCE. With a Chapter on his researches in Natural History, by Sir WILLIAM H. FLOWER, K.C.B., Director of the Natural History Branch of the British Museum. Edited, with a Memoir of his Life, by O. LESLIE STEPHEN. With Portrait and Illustrations. Crown 8vo. 12s.

BROWNE (Edward Harold, D.D., Bishop of Ely and subsequently of Winchester.) A MEMOIR, by the Very Rev. GEORGE WILLIAM KITCHIN, D.D., Dean of Durham. With Portraits. 8vo. 18s.

BUCKLAND (William, D.D., F.R.S., sometime Dean of Westminster, twice President of the Geological Society, and President of the British Association at Oxford in 1832.) LIFE AND CORRESPONDENCE, by his Daughter, Mrs. GORDON. With Portraits and Illustrations. Crown 8vo. 12s.

BURGHERSH'S (Lady) LETTERS FROM GERMANY AND FRANCE DURING THE CAMPAIGN of 1813-14. Edited by her Daughter, Lady ROSE WEIGALL. Portraits. Crown 8vo. 6s.

BUXTON (Sir T. Fowell). MEMOIRS. By CHARLES BUXTON. Portrait. 8vo. 16s.; or post 8vo. 5s.

CLARENCE (H.R.H. the late Duke of). A MEMOIR, written with the sanction of H.R.H. the Prince of Wales. By JAMES EDWARD VINCENT. With Portraits and Illustrations. Crown 8vo. 9s.

CROWE (Sir Joseph A., K.C.M.G., C.B.) REMINISCENCES OF THIRTY-FIVE YEARS OF MY LIFE. With Plans. 8vo. 16s.

DARWIN'S (Charles) LIFE AND LETTERS, with an AUTOBIOGRAPHICAL CHAPTER. Edited by his Son, FRANCIS DARWIN, F.R.S. Portraits. 3 vols. 8vo. 36s.
Or Popular Edition, condensed in 1 vol. Crown 8vo. 7s. 6d.

MR. MURRAY'S LIST—continued.

DE ROS (Georgiana, Lady). A SKETCH OF HER LIFE: with some Reminiscences of her Family and Friends, including the Duke of Wellington. By her Daughter, the Hon. Mrs. SWINTON. With Portraits and Illustrations. Crown 8vo. 7s. 6d.

EASTLAKE (Lady). JOURNALS AND CORRESPONDENCE. Edited by her Nephew, CHARLES EASTLAKE SMITH. With Facsimiles of her Drawings and a Portrait. 2 vols. Crown 8vo. 21s.

FRANKLIN (Admiral Sir John). THE LIFE: based on private and hitherto unpublished documents. By H. D. TRAILL. With Maps and Portraits. 8vo. 16s.

FRERE (Sir Bartle, Bart.) THE LIFE AND CORRESPONDENCE: derived from hitherto unpublished documents. By JOHN MARTINEAU. With Portraits, Illustrations, and Maps. 2 vols. 8vo. 32s.

GOODWIN (Harvey, D.D., Bishop of Carlisle.) THE BIOGRAPHY. By H. D. RAWNSLEY, Hon. Canon of Carlisle. With Portrait and Illustrations. 8vo. 16s.

GREGORY (Sir William, K.C.M.G., formerly M.P., and sometime Governor of Ceylon). An AUTOBIOGRAPHY. Edited by Lady GREGORY. With Portrait. 8vo. 16s.

HEBER (Bishop): POET AND CHIEF MISSIONARY TO THE EAST, 1783-1826. By GEORGE SMITH, C.I.E. With Portrait, Maps, and Illustrations. Crown 8vo. 10s. 6d.

LIND (Jenny), THE ARTIST, 1820-51. Her Early Art Life and Dramatic Career. From original Documents, Letters, Diaries, &c., in the possession of Mr. GOLDSCHMIDT. By Canon H. SCOTT HOLLAND, M.A., and W. S. ROCKSTRO. *Popular Edition.* With Portraits and Illustrations. Crown 8vo. 9s.

LYSONS (General Sir D.) EARLY REMINISCENCES. By Sir DANIEL LYSONS, G.C.B., Constable of the Tower. With Illustrations. Crown 8vo. 9s.

OWEN (Professor Richard). THE LIFE, based on his Correspondence, his Diaries, and those of his Wife. By his Grandson, the Rev. RICHARD OWEN. With a Chapter by the Right Hon. T. H. HUXLEY. With Portraits and Illustrations. 2 vols. Crown 8vo. 24s.

STANLEY (Arthur P.) LIFE AND CORRESPONDENCE OF ARTHUR PENRHYN STANLEY, late Dean of Westminster. By R. E. PROTHERO. With Portraits and Illustrations. 2 vols. 8vo. 32s.

JOHN MURRAY, ALBEMARLE STREET.

www.ingramcontent.com/pod-product-compliance
Lightning Source LLC
Chambersburg PA
CBHW022115300426
44117CB00007B/713